# HANDBOOK OF SOCIAL MEDIA USE ONLINE RELATIONSHIPS, SECURITY, PRIVACY, AND SOCIETY, VOLUME 2

# HANDBOOK OF SOCIAL MEDIA USE ONLINE RELATIONSHIPS, SECURITY, PRIVACY, AND SOCIETY, VOLUME 2

Editor-in-Chief

## VLADLENA BENSON

*Aston Business School, Aston University, Birmingham, United Kingdom*

Associate Editor

## JOHN MCALANEY

*Faculty of Science and Technology, Bournemouth University, Poole, United Kingdom*

Section Editors

### JACQUI TAYLOR

*Faculty of Science and Technology, Bournemouth University, Poole, United Kingdom*

### REYNALDO GACHO SEGUMPAN

*City Graduate School, City University, Malaysia, Malaysia*

**ACADEMIC PRESS**

An imprint of Elsevier

ELSEVIER

Academic Press is an imprint of Elsevier
125 London Wall, London EC2Y 5AS, United Kingdom
525 B Street, Suite 1650, San Diego, CA 92101, United States
50 Hampshire Street, 5th Floor, Cambridge, MA 02139, United States

**Notices**
Knowledge and best practice in this field are constantly changing. As new research and experience broaden our understanding, changes in research methods, professional practices, or medical treatment may become necessary.

Practitioners and researchers must always rely on their own experience and knowledge in evaluating and using any information, methods, compounds, or experiments described herein. In using such information or methods they should be mindful of their own safety and the safety of others, including parties for whom they have a professional responsibility.

To the fullest extent of the law, neither the Publisher nor the authors, contributors, or editors, assume any liability for any injury and/or damage to persons or property as a matter of products liability, negligence or otherwise, or from any use or operation of any methods, products, instructions, or ideas contained in the material herein.

ISBN: 978-0-443-28804-3

For Information on all Academic Press publications
visit our website at https://www.elsevier.com/books-and-journals

Publisher: Nikki P. Levy
Acquisitions Editor: Joslyn T. Chaiprasert-Paguio
Editorial Project Manager: Tracy Tufaga
Production Project Manager: Swapna Srinivasan
Cover Designer: Vicky Pearson Esser

Typeset by MPS Limited, Chennai, India

Working together
to grow libraries in
developing countries

www.elsevier.com • www.bookaid.org

# Contents

## Section 1  Cyberbullying and online toxicity

# Section 2  Politics and influence

## Section 3  Relationships and the self

# List of contributors

**Loren Abell**
Department of Psychology, Nottingham Trent University, Nottingham, United Kingdom

**Lucy R. Betts**
Department of Psychology, Nottingham Trent University, Nottingham, United Kingdom

**Sarah L. Buglass**
Department of Psychology, Nottingham Trent University, Nottingham, United Kingdom

**Nimrod L. Delante**
School of Humanities, Nanyang Technological University, Singapore

**Tommy Dunne**
Department of Psychology, Bournemouth University, Bournemouth, United Kingdom

**Philip A. Fine**
School of Psychology, University of Buckingham, Buckingham, United Kingdom

**Anna Ruby P. Gapasin**
Office of the Vice President for Research, Extension, Planning and Development, Polytechnic University of the Philippines, Manila, Philippines

**Sally-Ann Hicken**
School of Psychology, University of Buckingham, Buckingham, United Kingdom

**Debora Jeske**
Department of Psychology, University College Cork, California State University, San Bernardino, CA, United States

**Jeremy Lay**
School of Psychology, Western Sydney University, Sydney, NSW, Australia

**Peter J.R. Macaulay**
School of Psychology, University of Derby, Derby, United Kingdom

**Mark McCormack**
University of Roehampton, London, United Kingdom

**Deborah A. Olson**
Department of Psychology, University College Cork, California State University, San Bernardino, CA, United States

**Maša Popovac**
School of Psychology, University of Buckingham, Buckingham, United Kingdom

**Andy Pulman**
Faculty of Health and Social Sciences, Bournemouth University, Bournemouth, BH, United Kingdom

**Jean A. Saludadez**
University of the Philippines Open University, Los Baños, Laguna, Philippines

**Lenis Aislinn C. Separa**
Office of the Vice President for Research, Extension, Planning and Development, Polytechnic University of the Philippines, Manila, Philippines; School of Communication, Journalism and Marketing, Massey University, Wellington, New Zealand

**Inyoung Shin**
Department of Computer Science, Yale University, New Haven, CT, United States

**Kenneth S. Shultz**
Department of Psychology, University College Cork, California State University, San Bernardino, CA, United States

**Oonagh L. Steer**
Department of Psychology, Nottingham Trent University, Nottingham, United Kingdom

**Jea Agnes Taduran-Buera**
University of the Philippines Los Bañ, Los Baños, Laguna, Philippines

**Catherine V. Talbot**
Department of Psychology, Bournemouth University, Bournemouth, United Kingdom

**Jacqui Taylor**
Faculty of Science and Technology, Bournemouth University, Poole, United Kingdom; Department of Psychology, Bournemouth University, Poole, Dorset, United Kingdom

**Olivia Tickle**
HM Prison & Probation Service, United Kingdom

**Seda Gökçe Turan**
Department of Educational Sciences, Bahçeşehir University, Turkey; Department of Cyberpsychology, Bournemouth University, Poole, United Kingdom

**Charity T. Turano**
University of San Carlos, Philippines

**Liam Wignall**
University of Brighton, Sussex, United Kingdom

# Foreword

Why does the world need yet another book on social media? And if it does, why this one?

Over the last three decades, social media has changed the world. Some of the changes have been beneficial; others, less so. The roots of today's social media platforms can be traced back to niche community websites with specialized appeal. Over time, these evolved into the massive businesses we see today—Facebook, Instagram, WeChat, and the like. It is estimated that over half the world's population is now active on these platforms, and they impact almost every area of our lives in one way or another. In addition to creating an electronically mediated "virtual world," social media permeates our offline lives as well. Older literature on the topic often refers to a dichotomy between "online" and "the real world." That no longer pertains. Through the ubiquity of high-powered portable devices and communications infrastructure, online is "the real world" just as much as the physical landscapes we live in. Therefore this is clearly an area that requires study. Furthermore, social media—and society's adoption, adaptation, and reaction to it—has changed over time and will continue to evolve. Research that was cutting edge 10 years ago is often now outdated; such is the speed of change. Therefore books such as this one are required and will continue to be required in the future.

Of course, social media is not some monolithic entity or "thing" that can be studied in isolation. Rather, it is a complex set of technologies, uses, and users, with multiple dimensions that are worthy of consideration.

Some research takes social media itself as the object of study. Social media platforms are designed as two-way streets, where people create and interact with "content" as well as simply consuming it. So, how do people communicate with each other and interact with published material online? What characteristics of individuals, systems, or the material itself influence our behavior? Research in this vein might include ethnographic or network analysis-based investigations of how peer-to-peer communities of social network users develop and operate or studies of the language used in social media communication. Approaches to exploring this might range from work leveraging "big data" techniques to fine-grained qualitative case studies.

A second area of research considers the application of social media to various tasks or problems. Individuals and organizations may try to leverage social media to achieve various ends. For example, social media platforms are very often used for political communication of various sorts, ranging from reminding people to complete their tax returns to outright propaganda and political influence operations. Educational institutions use social media platforms for delivery of course materials or attempt to develop communities among off-campus students. Businesses, for example, advertising firms, media publishers, and adult entertainment businesses, have a large social media presence. How effective are these approaches? What effects do they have on society?

Finally, perhaps most importantly, we need to consider how social media affects and changes us as individuals. What are the positive and negative effects of social media platforms, and everything they enable, on our thoughts, feelings, and behavior? There is a dominant, though not uncontested, narrative that social media has harmed individuals and society—particularly in terms of the effects of social media use on mental health. Bullying and harassment on social media are real problems. Social media—enabled crime, for example, online fraud of various sorts, is a real problem. However, social media can also have many positive outcomes—fostering community building and social cohesion and facilitating social activism that can have beneficial outcomes and perhaps effect real change in the world.

Given the importance of such issues, it is clear that we do need books on social media. So, why this one? Simply put, it provides an authoritative and wide-ranging snapshot of key topics in the study of social media. The editors are long-standing experts in the field, and they have brought together an excellent collection of authors and chapter topics. The chapters address a range of substantive questions from the three broad areas I have outlined previously, and beyond. Overall, this book considers a range of important issues, with an international focus and a range of disciplinary perspectives. Books on social media are clearly needed, and this one provides a valuable and illuminating resource.

**Tom Buchanan**

*Professor of Psychology, School of Science,*
*University of Westminster, London*

# Preface

## Introduction

How we perceive ourselves as humans is heavily influenced by our interactions with those around us. The rise of online technologies has fundamentally changed how we communicate. In the past, our social world was often restricted by physical constraints; before the invention of telecommunications, discussions took place in person or via postal mail. These imposed limitations on how and when we could express ourselves, for example, in the past, an argument with a friend may need to be paused until the following day when both parties saw each other again, by which point they may have calmed down. Now, however, it is often possible for people to communicate with each other immediately, 24 hours a day, regardless of where they are physically located. This may lead to acts of impulsivity and the escalation of conflicts that would not have otherwise happened. Social media and other digital technologies also greatly enhance the ability of individuals to shape how they are seen by the world. Again, this act of impression management is something that long predates the invention of Internet technologies, but these technologies enable individuals to engage with this behavior to a scale that is unprecedented. While this greater power to control public image and to connect with others has benefits, it also has risks, the full extent of which are not yet fully understood by researchers, or the public who use these technologies.

The aim of this book is to present and evaluate the research literature on the role of social media in relationships, security, privacy, and society. Arguments on how social media can influence interpersonal relationships, including how it may foster and enable toxic behaviors such as cyberbullying. The use of social media as a tool for expressing opinions and exerting power—for good or for ill—is also discussed. Finally, the impact of social media on the self is considered, along with thoughts on how we should seek to steer the evolution of social media, so that it is beneficial for those who use and are impacted by it. The goal of this book is to enable individuals, technology developers, policy makers, and other stakeholders to better understand both the opportunities and the challenges that social media presents society with.

## Book roadmap

This book is organized into three sections: (1) Cyberbullying and Online Toxicity, (2) Politics and Influence, and (3) Relationships and the Self. Each section contains several chapters supporting the section theme, presenting research, practical applications, consequences, and guidelines regarding the use of social media across varied settings.

### *Section 1: Cyberbullying and Online Toxicity*

The functionalities provided by the Internet and digital devices allow people to communicate with greater speed and ease than has ever before been the case. While this has many benefits, it also exacerbates the risks and harms associated with antisocial behaviors. This includes bullying and expressions of aggressive and discriminatory language. Online disinhibition and the, at times, perceived anonymity afforded by the Internet may make individuals feel that they can say things online that they would not say in an offline context. However, the same technologies that facilitate malicious online communications also have the potential to identify, prevent, and mitigate harms. The chapters in this section explore these opportunities and challenges that the Internet brings to communication in society, with a focus on the online behaviors that cause distress and suffering both online and offline.

Chapter 1 highlights what is known about children and adolescents' cyberaggression and cyberbullying experiences on social media. It also considers the impact of cyberbullying and cyberaggression on psychological and emotional well-being. The authors discuss the factors that may increase or decrease the risk of these harms and in turn identify the opportunities for developing and evaluating prevention and intervention strategies. Recommendations are put forward for working with all of the stakeholders in this space, including children and young people, parents and schools, social media providers, and legislators and policy makers. The authors note the importance of offline factors such as home and family-related factors in having a holistic understanding of the experience of cyberbullying and cyberaggression. They conclude by arguing that any effective solutions to this problem require an equally holistic approach that involves all relevant stakeholders.

· Next, Chapter 2 provides a narrative review of the research literature on cyberbullying. In doing so, it documents the strong association between cyberbullying and other online offline behaviors, including other types of digital harassment such as revenge pornography. It also observes the overlap between cyberbullying and Internet addiction. The author argues that it is important that young people learn from an early age how to navigate the digital environments. Doing so may empower young people to identify when they are being targeted by cyberbullying or other forms of digital harassment and to take appropriate action to prevent and mitigate these harms. This approach acknowledges that online technologies are deeply embedded in society and that they bring many benefits to people. Rather than calling for a cessation of the use of online technologies, the author puts forward a case for ensuring that young people learn how to manage risks online, in the same way that they learn to survive the offline world.

Following this, Chapter 3 explores high school students' involvement in cyberbullying. The authors apply the Semiotic Tradition of Communication Theory. The results of interviews with school students are reported, with comparisons made between those who do and those who do not participate in cyberbullying. The participants of the study saw cyberspace as a place for community building and freedom of expression, including the freedom to express grievances toward and criticisms of others. These results highlight the wider debate around the rights people have to express themselves online, and how we decide where the boundaries are between legitimate expression of opinion and inappropriate communications that are cyberbullying. The authors also note the role of intentionality, and how both intentional and unintentional online acts can result in deception, harassment, and reputational damage. The authors argue for the importance in promoting responsible and ethical social media use in schools and other human organizations.

Chapter 4 looks at the role of those who witness cyberbullying on social media. This draws upon the long history of bystander intervention research in social psychology, much of which has been based in offline settings. The authors note the social dilemma that young people may experience with cyberbullying, where they can either respond positively by supporting the victim, or negatively by supporting the perpetrator. The decision the bystander makes can have implications for their social status, something which can be of high importance to people within that younger adult age group. The chapter provides recommendations such as building empathy in young adults through activities such as role play activities and reflections. The authors also note creating a culture in schools of bystanders intervening when they witness bullying in any form, although they highlight that bystander processes may operate differently in online settings compared to offline settings. They conclude that further research is needed to understand the mechanisms that facilitate prosocial bystander actions to cyberbullying on social media.

Finally, Chapter 5 discusses the challenges of unpacking online communications that could be interpreted in different ways. This follows on from the previous chapters on cyberbullying, and the refrain from the perpetrators of cyberbullying acts that their comments were "just a joke." As the authors note the term "banter" is used downplay behaviors that would otherwise be identified as cyberbullying. This chapter conveys the harms that can be caused by the misinterpretation of ambiguous communication, including social anxiety, self-reported peer victimization, and avoidance behaviors. It also highlights that banter is not restricted to young adults in education settings. It exists in many organizational cultures, including in high pressure work environments, where how an individual responds to banter is used as a test of how that person will fit into that organization. The authors finish the chapter by recommending different strategies to frame and interpret communications to ameliorate the harmful impacts of ambiguous communications.

### Section 2: Politics and influence

The Internet allows for the sharing of information on a scale and at a speed that is unprecedented in human history. It has also shifted the balance in power in who can create and disseminate content. Mainstream outlets no longer have complete control over the media that is produced in society. Influencers on social media platforms can have millions of followers, with some individuals receiving most of their media content through social media sources. Content creation by such individuals takes place outside of the agendas, structures, and commercial drivers that underpin mainstream media, although of course this does not mean that social media influencers are free of their own agendas and motivations. Government bodies and other organizations can also make use of social media platforms for their own goals, both for the benefit of themselves or for the determinant of others, including governments and their citizens with whom a conflict exists. The chapters in this explore how social media can be used to attempt to influence others and share information, ideas, and beliefs, either intentionally or unintentionally, and both for the good or ill of society.

Chapter 6 discusses the case of YouTube creators, noting change in YouTube from a digital video repository to a broadcast platform. The authors report a study in which a netnography of vegan YouTube vlogs was conducted. Advocacy was evident in the analysis of the results, through interaction, inclusion, and influence. This work demonstrates how advocacy involves a multidirectional and continual relationship between the vlogger and their audience. This underlines the differences between social media and traditional forms of broadcast media, which are primarily unidirectional and do not typically include the facility for the broadcaster to respond quickly to audience feedback. This chapter also demonstrates netnography as a methodological approach to understanding vlogging through social media platforms.

Next, Chapter 7 explores the use of social media to influence the public through the use of trolling and misinformation. Through a thematic analysis of news articles, the authors identify and discuss the phenomenon of fake news and the impact this has on those targeted. The chapter argues that many of the fundamental techniques used to create and spread fake news can also be adopted by those who seek to challenge fake news, such as through the power story telling. Further, the authors call for other strategies, including media literacy citizenship activism to combat the harms caused by fake news and trolling.

Finally, Chapter 8 takes a deep look at the sociolinguistic aspects of language of social media posts, as expressed by young adults. As they note, social media platforms provide a new way for people to creatively express themselves in a way best represents how they think and feel. This includes the use of symbolism, acronyms, and jargon that emerges online and can often influence communication in the offline world.

### Section 3: Relationships and the self

Our sense of self is influenced by those around us. Online technologies have fundamentally changed how we interact with other people, providing opportunities for connections to occur outside of the constraints of geographical location. It is also substantially easier for us to find and interact with others who have shared values and beliefs as ourselves. This has positive benefits, allowing for example people who may feel marginalized in online society to develop a social support network. The potential benefits of online technologies in making and maintaining social and workplace connections came to the forefront during the COVID-19 pandemic and arguably demonstrated that a lot of activities previously considered to be offline ones could be done online. However, as has been shown to be the case in the chapters throughout this handbook, online technologies can also create harms, both intentional and unintentional. The ubiquity of online connectivity and the increasing integration of online technologies into everyday life means that it can be difficult for individuals to escape these influences. This chapters in this section explore how we as individuals navigate our complex social worlds, both offline and online, and the opportunities and challenges that we may encounter.

First, Chapter 9 discusses the role of social media in the development of connections relevant to the workplace. As the authors note, the COVID-19 pandemic accelerated the use of social media for professional purposes. As many people may have experienced, the use of social media of professional settings can be risky and involve blurring of the boundaries between work life and home life. This raises interesting questions around how we manage our sense of our self, if indeed there really is such a thing as a single self that we consistently express in different contexts. This chapter considers how to best use social media to support relationship building, networking, and career development. Practical recommendations are given for managing social media in a way that will be beneficial for career development.

Second, Chapter 10 reviews research into the relationship between social media use and loneliness, and whether there is a difference between online and offline loneliness. This experience of loneliness in a world where social media is everywhere may feel somewhat counterintuitive; however, as the authors discuss, the relationship between social media use and loneliness is not as they may be expected. Instead, other factors such as personality and social comparisons may need to be considered to understand the relationship between social media, social relationships, and the experience of loneliness. The authors recommend further research into the potential differences between offline and online loneliness, with an observation that the COVID-19 pandemic both highlighted the issue of loneliness and also provided an opportunity better understanding of how social media influences how people experience loneliness.

Following on from this, Chapter 11 discusses how social media may be used to help address some of the social challenges experienced by people who have dementia. The authors provide a narrative review on the evidence around social media use by people with dementia, along with a reflexive account by one of the authors on their own experience. The challenges that people with dementia may experience when using social media are also considered. The authors note that there are active online communities of people with dementia and that these communities provide a valuable sense of connection and identity, along with opportunities for self-expression. Nevertheless, there are also risks and challenges that people may encounter, including online stigma and issues with digital literacy, which the developers and designers of social media platforms should take into account to ensure that all users of the platform are able to have their voices heard.

The availability of social media means that we have easy access to the information we want to see. However, the cost of this is that we are also presented with information that we may not wish to see, despite the best efforts of the algorithms used by social media platforms. Chapter 12 discusses how the disclosure of life events is a common activity on social media. Such disclosures have of course long been part of human interactions; however, social media means that we are exposed to these disclosures far more frequently than would otherwise be the case. In this chapter, the authors present an analysis of interviews with Facebook users on why they experience negative emotions when viewing life experience disclosures on the platform. Several psychological factors are identified, including a sense of vulnerability, cost of caring, upward social comparisons, and norms violations. This work highlights a topic that is increasingly recognized as an important societal issue—the impact of social media on the mental health of individuals.

Next, Chapter 13 looks at the case of malicious and deliberate deception online, though the phenomena of catfishing and Munchausen by Internet. The authors report and discuss examples of these cases, along with their own study into the experiences and attitudes of respondents to an online survey. The report that perceptions of these behaviors vary by how much exposure the individual has had to them, with the view that onus should be on the social media platforms themselves to prevent such incidents. The authors also note that cases of catfishing and Munchausen by Internet appear to be underreported and will continue to rise globally unless steps are taking to prevent and mitigate such incidents.

Finally, Chapter 14 examines psychological approaches to understanding the intersection between pornography, social media, and sexuality. The authors put forward a methodological and theoretical critique of traditional research on pornography. It also evaluates current policy interventions and raises questions around the overlap between sexuality and the Internet when consent is not present. In doing so, it highlights the challenges that come from providing consenting adults with the ability to express themselves as they wish online, while still protecting those who are at risk. This chapter concludes by discussing the value of criminal justice interventions and the use of education-based interventions.

## Conclusion

There are recurrent themes that are evident throughout the chapters. The potential for social media to empower people to cause harm to others is given in several examples, including cyberbullying and the case of online banter. Challenging questions are raised around intentionality, and how much the perpetrators of such actions understand and should take responsibility for. These discussions reflect one of the underlying questions about the interaction between the individual and the internet—do we become a different person online, or do internet technologies just permit us to express aspects of ourselves that we normally try to hide from those around us in the offline world? This is further complicated by instances where an individual deliberately seeks to deceive others, such as in the case of catfishing. As online technologies become more ubiquitous and pervasive, the line between the online and offline world is becoming increasingly blurred. It is important that research continues to explore both the intended and unintended consequences of social media technologies.

More positive aspects of social media are also identified and discussed in the chapters, such as the potential to encourage bystander intervention in cases where online harassment or persecution occurs. This draws on the same potential of immediacy and visibility that can be used to cause harm online and demonstrates that as with any technology, social media is not inherently good or bad. Rather, it is how we use it and what as a society we deem to be appropriate behavior. Social media gives people new and nuanced ways in which to express themselves and to advocate their views which, if done carefully, can be beneficial for both the individual and society. Nevertheless, we should be attuned to the challenges that people may experience when using social media. For instance, it should not be assumed that an extensive online network means that an individual is free from any risk of experiencing loneliness. As was brought into sharp focus during the COVID-19 pandemic, not all forms of communication are equal. As social media technology continues to develop and world continues to change, there is an ongoing need for research into how best to ensure the well-being of the users of these technologies are protected and promoted.

**Vladlena Benson**
**John McAlaney**

# Cyberbullying and online toxicity

CHAPTER ONE

# Children and adolescents' experiences of cyberaggression and cyberbullying on social media and priorities for intervention and prevention efforts

**Maša Popovac, Philip A. Fine and Sally-Ann Hicken**
School of Psychology, University of Buckingham, Buckingham, United Kingdom

## Contents

*Handbook of Social Media Use Online Relationships, Security, Privacy, and Society, Volume 2*
DOI: https://doi.org/10.1016/B978-0-443-28804-3.00008-9

## Introduction: technology use and young people

Technology use has become nearly ubiquitous, particularly among young people. In the United States, 95% of adolescents either own a smartphone or have access to one, and 45% of adolescents report that they are almost constantly connected to the Internet (Anderson & Jiang, 2018). Similarly, in the United Kingdom, 97% of adolescents reported having access to the Internet (Popovac, 2017), and our research found that approximately 95% of adolescents in the United Kingdom and South Africa owned their own mobile phone that enables Internet access. Based on parental reports of younger children in the United States, 59% of 5—8 year olds and 67% of 9—11 year olds had access to a smartphone and 81% of 5—8 year olds had access to a tablet (Auxier, Anderson, Perrin, & Turner, 2020). Recent studies during COVID-19 reflect an increased use of technology overall, and social media in particular, for both adolescents and adults (Drouin, McDaniel, Pater, & Toscos, 2020). In fact, a recent Ofcom report (2021) indicated that nearly all 5—15 year olds in the United Kingdom went online in some capacity.

Young people engage in a wide variety of online activities, including accessing social media such as social networking sites (SNSs). Popular SNSs among 13—17 year olds include Instagram (72%), Snapchat (69%), and Facebook (51%) (Anderson & Jiang, 2018), coupled with increasing popularity of new platforms such as TikTok and Twitch (Ofcom, 2019). Although most SNSs have an age restriction of 13, studies have shown that considerably younger children are active on such platforms. For example, a study among middle school children found that 17% started using social media at age 9 or younger (Martin, Wang, Petty, Wang, & Wilkins, 2018). The recent report by Ofcom showed that 87% of 12—15 year olds, 44% of 8—11 year olds, and 30% of 5—7 year olds use social media sites, with an overall 42% of children using social media below the minimum age requirement (Ofcom, 2021). Our recent investigation among 253 children aged 8—11 in the United Kingdom provides support for this, as most reported owning their own mobile phone (63%) and tablet (76%) and 74% reportedly use social media, with half of these having their own profile. Most popular sites included WhatsApp (39%), TikTok (37%), and SnapChat (21%), and 40% accessed these platforms daily. However, online gaming was the most popular activity reported by this age group, with 92% of 8−11 year olds engaging with global platforms such as Fortnite and Roblox which allow players to interact. These statistics reflect the avid use of social media and the broad range of activities across multiple platforms among both children and adolescents.

Access to technology and use of social media can have a range of benefits for young people, including making positive social connections, accessing social support, entertainment, offering opportunities for positive identity exploration, engagement in social issues, and educational benefits (Best, Manktelow, & Taylor, 2014; Livingstone, Haddon, Görzig, & Ólafsson, 2011; Livingstone, Haddon, & Görzig, 2012; Mesch & Talmud, 2010; Patahuddin, Rokhmah, & Lowrie, 2020; Wood, Bukowski, & Lis, 2016). However, engagement in online spaces also presents a range of risks and potential harmful effects such as social isolation and ostracism (Allen, Ryan, Gray, McInereney, & Waters, 2014; Best et al., 2014; Martin et al., 2018), negative impacts on physical activity or sleep (Buda, Lukoševičiūtė, Šalčiūnaitė, & Šmigelskas, 2020), as well as depression, lower self-esteem, and poorer body image (Kelly, Zilanawala, Booker, & Sacker, 2018). Social media use also presents concerns around exposure to harm such as via inappropriate content (Hawdon, Oksanen, & Räsänen, 2017; Livingstone, Kirwil, Ponte, & Staksrud, 2014), contact risks via engaging with strangers (Livingstone et al., 2017; Schulz, Bergen, Schuhmann, Hoyer, & Santtila, 2016), and conduct-related risks that pose a risk either to privacy and security (Kite, Gable, & Filippelli, 2013), or to being involved in cyberaggression or cyberbullying (Hamm et al., 2015; Livingstone et al., 2017). The latter is of particular concern in the current chapter.

This chapter presents an overview of children and adolescents' cyberaggression and cyberbullying experiences on social media and their effects on wellbeing. We also explore key risk and protective factors that are particularly pertinent to younger social media users, focusing on individual-level and developmental factors, home and school factors, and social media laws and policies to determine how these may exacerbate or ameliorate the potential negative effects of such experiences. Finally, we outline key opportunities for developing and evaluating intervention and prevention efforts with young people, including recommendations for working with children and adolescents, parents, and schools, as well as in relation to social media providers, laws, and policies as part of a multilevel approach to online safety.

## Understanding cyberaggression and cyberbullying in the context of social media

Cyberaggression is a broad construct that refers to intentional acts of harm committed via electronic communication toward individuals or groups and is experienced as offensive, derogatory, harmful, or unwanted (Grigg, 2010). This includes a range of subtypes of aggression, including cyberbullying. Cyberbullying is an "aggressive, intentional act carried out by a group or individual, using electronic forms of contact, repeatedly and over time, against a victim who cannot easily defend him or herself" (Smith et al., 2008, p. 376). Similar to traditional bullying, cyberbullying involves repeated exposure to negative acts, which creates an ongoing pattern of abuse and includes intentionality and power imbalance as part of its definition. Thus, while cyberbullying is considered a form of cyberaggression, not all acts of cyberaggression constitute cyberbullying as, in addition to intentionality, cyberbullying also entails repetition and a power imbalance between the victim and perpetrator.

Although the core definitional criteria for cyberbullying are largely accepted by researchers, there are some unique features of online environments that result in these experiences being quite different online. For example, intentionality may be difficult to ascertain due to a lack of verbal or physical cues in online communication, and a single act of cyberaggression can lead to repeated victimization for the victim such as via the possibility to reread hurtful comments (Menesini et al., 2012) or where a single post can be distributed by a large audience (Patchin & Hinduja, 2015). The ease of accessibility and distribution of content, together with the potential for a larger audience online, plays a role in perpetration of this behavior (Chan, Cheung, & Lee, 2021). The online environment also influences power dynamics, with power imbalances playing out differently than in the offline world (Bauman, Toomey, & Walker, 2013). For example, perpetrators can be anonymous and the victim may feel a lack of control and an inability to escape the situation. Anonymity contributes to a sense of disinhibition for perpetrators, allowing them to behave more harshly and without consequence (Barlett, Gentile, & Chew, 2016; Chan et al., 2021; Suler, 2004; Wachs, Wright, & Vazsonyi, 2019; Wright & Wachs, 2021). Moreover, invisibility within online environments and the absence of social cues can reduce feelings of empathy (Suler, 2004), as perpetrators do not have to be personally confronted with the impact of their behaviors on others.

Cyberaggression and cyberbullying encompass a range of acts such as abuse via written or verbal communication, visual acts such as posting compromising images or videos, and exclusion (Patchin & Hinduja, 2006; Willard, 2007). While this can occur via any Information and Communication Technologies, social media provides ample opportunity for the abovementioned behaviors. SNSs in particular include digital profiles, relational ties, and dynamic interactions, as well as large potential for content sharing that can be used to perpetrate cyberaggression and cyberbullying. For example, it is easy to disseminate content widely and quickly via features of SNSs, such as use of hashtags, and to "like" and "share" content in a way that prolongs the bullying encounter (Chan et al., 2021). It is also possible to create fake accounts or to form online groups or pages to humiliate, threaten, or abuse others. Images and videos can readily be shared via both personal profiles and groups, allowing these behaviors to quickly escalate. Numerous studies indicate that social media facilitates cyberbullying and is often the most common venue for such experiences (Aizenkot, 2020; Cohen-Almagor, 2018; Craig et al., 2020; Kowalski, Dillon, Macbeth, Franchi, & Bush, 2020). Clearly, accessibility and popularity of social media has garnered new opportunities for cyberaggression and cyberbullying and, considering the pervasive use of social media among young people, it is important to examine the experiences, effects, and potential risk and protective factors in order to inform effective intervention and prevention strategies.

## How prevalent is cyberaggression and cyberbullying among young people?

An older meta-analysis indicated that the global prevalence rate of cyberbullying among young people was estimated at 20%—40% (Tokunaga, 2010), and a meta-analysis in 2014 showed a prevalence rate of 15% among adolescents (Modecki, Minchin, Harbaugh, Guerra, & Runions, 2014). Research conducted in Europe found that 21% of 14—17 year olds had been cyberbullied in the past year (Tsitsika et al., 2015). Similarly, in the United Kingdom, one in four 13—18 year olds had experienced cyberbullying in the past year, while 43% reported ever having been cyberbullied (Popovac, 2017). More recently, similar rates were found in Spain and Ecuador (Calmaestra, Rodríguez-Hidalgo,

Mero-Delgado, & Solera, 2020). Our research also showed that a third of adolescents (34%) in South Africa experienced cyberbullying (Popovac & Fine, 2016). When taking broader experiences of cyberaggression into account, we found that most adolescents in both the United Kingdom (69%) and South Africa (79%) had experienced at least one form of aggression online.

From the abovementioned figures, it is clear that cyberaggression and cyberbullying is a global concern. Prevalence rates do vary across contexts and between studies, however. For example, a systematic review of 63 studies showed a victimization rate of 13.9%–57.5% and a perpetration rate of 6.0%–46.3% for cyberbullying among children and adolescents (Zhu, Huang, Evans, & Zhang, 2021). Variations within countries were also large, with prevalence rates ranging between 1.9% and 65.0% across studies in Canada and between 11.0% and 56.8% in China (Brochado, Soares, & Fraga, 2017). These variations were also shown in a recent systematic review of longitudinal studies, with prevalence rates ranging between 1.9% and 84.0% for victimization and 5.3% and 66.2% for perpetration in ages 10–15 (Camerini, Marciano, Carrara, & Schulz, 2020). Prevalence rates may vary for a variety of reasons including economic, social, cultural, or policy differences, but may also stem from differences in conceptualization and measurement across studies. Additionally, meta-analyses and reviews include studies published over more than a decade and it is likely that underlying prevalence has changed over time. For example, SNSs have become increasingly important in the post-COVID world (Auxier & Anderson, 2021), potentially enabling an increase in cyberaggression and cyberbullying. Indeed, cyberbullying on Twitter increased in the second quarter of 2020 (when most of the world went into lockdown) (Karmakar & Das, 2021) and recent work in the United States showed that school bullying decreased while cyberbullying rates increased during COVID-19 school closures (Patchin, 2021). This should be borne in mind when comparing prevalence rates in contemporary articles with those published in 2010, for instance. Although these challenges make it difficult to form a complete or accurate picture of this phenomenon, it is nevertheless clear that cyberaggression and cyberbullying is a global issue.

Research in this area has also demonstrated the complex, multifaceted roles within these behaviors where there is often a link between victimization and perpetration (Bauman et al., 2013; Modecki et al., 2014). In fact, some research reports that the cyberbully-victim is more common than a cyberbullying victim (Betts & Spenser, 2017; Kowalski, Giumetti,

Schroeder, & Lattanner, 2014). In our own research, we found that 44.7% of adolescents in the United Kingdom and 63.5% in South Africa were both a victim and perpetrator of cyberbullying. Moreover, 3 in 4 adolescents in our study had witnessed cyberbullying while online and the same proportion also knew someone (such as a friend or sibling) who had been cyberbullied, indicating that this issue affects young people beyond just being a victim (Popovac & Fine, 2016, 2018; Popovac, 2017). This is important when considering appropriate strategies for tackling this issue.

Far less research is available on younger children, but studies looking specifically at 5—12 year olds do support the notion that cyberaggression and cyberbullying has emerged as a real online risk, and not just for adolescents (Arslan, Savaser, Hallett, & Balci, 2012; DePaolis & Williford, 2015; Ey, Taddeo, & Spears, 2015; Holfeld & Leadbeater, 2015; Monks, Mahdavi, & Rix, 2016). In fact, research involving seven European countries found that cyberbullying rates among 9—10 year olds trebled between 2010 and 2014 (O'Neill & Dinh, 2015), and others argue that cybervictimization is more prevalent in primary schools than secondary schools (Aizenkot, 2020). A United Kingdom study reported that 21% of 7—11 year olds were cyberbullying victims and 5% admitted to perpetration (Monks, Robinson, & Worlidge, 2012). This study specifically recommended further exploring young children's behavior and experiences on SNSs and gaming sites. A more recent study in Spain reported that 20% of 9—13 year olds had been cyberbullied, 6% had cyberbullied others, and 29% had witnessed cyberbullying (Machimbarrena & Garaigordobil, 2018). Considering the prevalence rates reported in both children and adolescents, this is an important area to investigate further given the potentially severe negative effects.

## What are the effects of cyberaggression and cyberbullying on young people?

The effects of cyberbullying are similar to those of traditional bullying and encompass a wide range of psychological, emotional, behavioral, and social problems, which will be highlighted in this section. Importantly, the effects are similar for both victims and perpetrators (Beckman, Hagquist, & Hellström, 2012; Gámez Guadix et al., 2013; Marciano, Schulz, & Camerini, 2020), and witnessing cyberbullying was also linked to depressive symptoms and social anxiety among 8—12 year olds (Doumas & Midgett, 2021), underscoring the importance of addressing this issue from multiple perspectives. Cyberbullying has been linked to general psychological distress and poor psychosocial adjustment in young people, including lower life satisfaction (Pillay, 2012) and quality of life (González-Cabrera et al., 2018). It also emerged as a significant predictor of emotional and behavioral problems in adolescents, with emotional problems being more strongly linked to females while behavioral problems were more strongly linked to males (Kim, Colwell, Kata, Boyle, & Georgiades, 2018). Links have also been made to substance abuse and delinquency (Hinduja & Patchin, 2007; Kim, Kimber, Boyle, & Georgiades, 2019), depression (Bauman et al., 2013; Gámez-Guadix, Orue, Smith, & Calvete, 2013; Rose & Tynes, 2015), anxiety (Mitra & Rath, 2017; Rose & Tynes, 2015), self-harm (Popovac, 2017), and suicidal ideation (Chang, Xing, Ho, & Yip, 2019; Iranzo, Buelga, Cava, & Ortega-Barón, 2019; Kim et al., 2019; Litwiller & Brausch, 2013; Van Geel, Vedder, & Tanilon, 2014). Emotional effects include frustration, fear, and anger (Hinduja & Patchin, 2009; Juvonen & Gross, 2008). Our research indicated that two in five adolescents in both the United Kingdom and South Africa reported feeling hurt or sad due to cybervictimization and nearly a third reported feeling scared or worried (Popovac & Fine, 2018; Popovac, 2017). In qualitative reports associated with this research, participants described feeling "worthless," "empty," and "not normal," and profound feelings of rejection and social isolation were expressed, highlighting the gravity of the emotional and psychological distress.

Cyberbullying can also manifest in psychosomatic ways through experiencing headaches and abdominal pain due to chronic stress, and it can lead to sleep problems (Albdour, Hong, Lewin, & Yarandi, 2019; Li, Sidibe, Shen, & Hesketh, 2019; Mitra & Rath, 2017). It can also lead to problems with attention and concentration (Mitra & Rath, 2017), school dropout and absenteeism (Lee, Chun, Kim, & Lee, 2020), low school commitment, and lower academic performance as well as school violence (Bauman, 2007; Farhangpour, Mutshaeni, & Cynthia, 2019). Our research among adolescents aged 13—18 years indicated that 28% in the United Kingdom (Popovac, 2017) and 22% in South Africa (Popovac & Fine, 2018) reportedly did not want to go to school on some days due to victimization experienced online. Thus, these experiences also have significant effects on educational outcomes and the school social climate.

Taken together, the literature broadly indicates that the central effects of cyberbullying include internalizing effects (e.g., depression), externalizing effects (e.g., substance abuse), and impacts on education (e.g., low school commitment). Thus, if not addressed, experiences of cyberbullying can have long-term effects on wellbeing and educational success. Considering that many cyberbullying experiences go unreported to adults, with only 22% telling a parent and 16% telling nobody (not even a friend) (Popovac, 2017), these behaviors can continue for extended periods of time with no support or intervention, which inevitably exacerbates the negative impacts on young people. Given the high prevalence rates reported and the worrying consequences, it is unsurprising that some have characterized this issue as a serious societal-level health concern (De Pasquale et al., 2021; Tokunaga, 2010).

## Risk and protective factors

Addressing cyberaggression and cyberbullying is a central concern among researchers, practitioners, policy makers, and those working with young people. However, an important consideration is to examine the potential risk and protective factors, that is, factors that can exacerbate or ameliorate both the risks of involvement in such behaviors as well as the potential effects. This section explores relevant demographic and developmental aspects as part of individual-level factors as well as contextual factors linked to the home and school, and the role of social media providers and policy. Consideration of these factors can help to pinpoint areas of focus for intervention and prevention efforts.

### Demographic factors

Studies have explored demographic differences in cyberbullying prevalence. For example, gender findings are mixed. Some research indicates that females are at higher risk of victimization (Arnarsson et al., 2020; Beckman, Hagquist, & Hellström, 2013) or both victimization and perpetration (Barlett & Coyne, 2014), while others indicate that males are more likely to be victims (Sincek, 2014) or perpetrators (Bae, 2021; Fanti, Demetriou, & Hawa, 2012), particularly when they had previously been cyberbullied (Zsila, Urbán, Griffiths, & Demetrovics, 2019). Others found no gender differences (DeSmet et al., 2018) and, in our investigation of 8—11 year olds in the United Kingdom, we also found no gender differences in cyberbullying rates with 19% of girls and 20% of boys experiencing cyberbullying on six or more occasions in the past 6 months. However, examining the cyberbullying context may highlight specific gender differences. For example, boys aged 8−10 experienced cyberbullying via gaming platforms (DePaolis & Williford, 2015), which is unsurprising as this is a favored activity among males (McInroy & Mishna, 2017). Interesting differences also emerge when examining specific cyberbullying acts. For example, while no gender differences exist among United Kingdom adolescents, we found that females were significantly more likely to have had an embarrassing picture posted online (Popovac, 2017). Thus, examining specific contexts and behaviors may highlight further nuances of cyberbullying.

Interesting findings also emerge for age. A meta-analysis showed that age moderated the gender differences, namely, females were more likely to be perpetrators at early and middle adolescence while males tended to be perpetrators at late adolescence (Barlett & Coyne, 2014). Similarly, De Pasquale et al. (2021) found that older age and male gender were linked to greater instances of both perpetration and victimization, whereas others note that adolescent perpetration of cyberbullying decreases with age in general (Bae, 2021). Some studies demonstrate an increase across age (Calmaestra et al., 2020) or a peak at mid-adolescence (Arnarsson et al., 2020; Popovac, 2017). However, when it comes to younger children and their cyberbullying experiences, there is a paucity of information concerning age and most studies generally focus on secondary school children. Some studies do include children aged 10−12 years (e.g., Menesini, 2012; Shakir et al., 2019); however, even here, the sample is often referred to as *en masse* as adolescents. The data is often aggregated, with studies rarely differentiating between the cohorts. Thus, findings are based on samples which are mainly comprised of adolescent experiences and do not provide specific insights into younger children (Mishna, Cook, Gadalla, Daciuk, & Solomon, 2010).

In our investigation of 8−11 year olds, the age differences in cyberbullying were surprising. When asked about frequency of cyberbullying in the last 6 months, children aged 9 and 10 reported the most incidents, which supported the research by O'Neill and Dinh (2015). However, having ever experienced cyberbullying increased across ages 8 (40%), 9 (44%), and 10 (47%), but 11-year-olds reported the lowest prevalence rates (24%). One potential explanation for this is that younger children may conflate acts of aggression and bullying, whereas older children have a better understanding of the behaviors and can distinguish between them more easily, which was shown to be the case for traditional forms of bullying (Monks & Smith, 2006), and this warrants further investigation. It is clear that cyberaggression and cyberbullying is a concern among younger cohorts. Children aged under 13 are developmentally, physically, intellectually, and emotionally at a very different phase from adolescents. These differences should not be overlooked especially when investigating how online risks are encountered and dealt with. Young children may be susceptible to similar online risks as adolescents (Monks et al., 2012) but do not possess the experience, knowledge, emotional understanding, and resilience to manage these difficult and potentially harmful situations (Englander, 2013). A greater understanding of their experiences and what younger children are exposed to would enable appropriate advice and support be given to them, their parents, and teachers in order to protect them from online risks such as cyberbullying.

Other individual-level factors may be more crucial in understanding risk and protective factors for cyberbullying. For example, studies have shown that nonheterosexual youth are more likely to be cyberbullied (Abreu & Kenny, 2018; Elipe, Muñoz, de la, & Rey, 2018), and that this can intersect with other aspects such as gender identity (Navarro, 2016), age, and race (Angoff & Barnhart, 2021). Moreover, studies have shown that aspects of identity such as one's race or religion can also predispose young people to cyberbullying (Ortiz-Marcos, Tomé-Fernández, & Fernández-Leyva, 2021), with negative peer attitudes predicting ethnic-based cyberbullying (Ergin, Akgül, & Karaman, 2021). The abovementioned examples demonstrate that individual differences and the intersectionality of a variety of demographic variables impact cyberbullying perpetration and victimization.

Minority groups can also be more likely to become cyberbullies (DeSmet et al., 2018; Ortiz-Marcos et al., 2021), potentially to account for the strain experienced from victimization. This has been found in studies more broadly where, for example, females who experienced traditional bullying were more likely to become perpetrators of cyberbullying while higher anger rumination in males increased risk of perpetration (Zsila et al., 2019). In this way, cyberbullying can occur in retaliation as a result of personal experiences of victimization both online and offline. This form of cyber-displaced aggression can alleviate anger and frustration in victims (Wright & Li, 2012) and aligns with General Strain Theory (see: Agnew & White, 1992; Agnew, 1999, 2017).

## Other individual-level and developmental factors

Outside of demographic factors, individual characteristics are also important. Cyberbullying victims tend to be individuals who are generally isolated or misunderstood in their social groups (Wells & Mitchell, 2008) or display higher neuroticism (Corcoran, Connolly, & O'Moore, 2012), agreeableness, and openness (Alonso & Romero, 2017). Perpetrators had lower overall social and emotional competencies (Zych, Beltrán-Catalán, Ortega-Ruiz, & Llorent, 2018) and displayed callous, unemotional traits (Fang et al., 2020; Fanti et al., 2012) and lower empathy (Ang, Li, & Seah, 2017; Zych, Baldry, Farrington, & Llorent, 2019). In online environments, the absence of emotional and social cues, coupled with a greater likelihood of anonymity and lower empathy on the part of perpetrators in general, allows cyberbullying to escalate. The lack of cues and inability to relate to the victim also reduce feelings of guilt (Perren & Gutzwiller-Helfenfinger, 2012). This highlights the effect of empathy on aggressive behavior as well as the aspects of the online environment which can further drive cyberbullying, and this too is an important consideration when looking at intervention and prevention strategies (Casas, Del Rey, & Ortega-Ruiz, 2013).

Use of technology in general and engagement in specific online activities can also be a risk factor for cyberbullying. As noted at the start of this chapter, use of social media posed a risk (Craig et al., 2020). Larger social networks and the process of adding unknown contacts to one's friends or followers on social media can enhance risk further due to higher interactions with strangers, indicating that certain patterns of communication influence cyberbullying risk (Festl & Quandt, 2016). Moreover, willingness to provide information about oneself online (Aizenkot, 2020; Twyman, Saylor, Taylor, & Comeaux, 2010) and behaviors surrounding control of personal data (Casas et al., 2013) such as via privacy settings also influence exposure. This may account for why cyberbullying has also been linked to other online risks including sexting and online grooming (Gámez-Guadix & Mateos-Pérez, 2019; Machimbarrena et al., 2018). During adolescence, peer relationships become central and studies have demonstrated the influence of subjective norms on behavior (Knoll, Magis-Weinberg, Speekenbrink, & Blakemore, 2015), including accepting strangers as friends on SNSs (Heirman et al., 2016).

Although a number of the abovementioned risk factors may also be applicable to adult users, specific developmental factors may present heightened risks to younger people. In addition to the importance of peer norms, adolescence has been identified as the developmental stage most likely to be characterized by general thrill seeking, impulsivity, and differential cognitive processing that influences decision making and planning, and this has been linked to cyberbullying (Cohen-Almagor, 2018). In fact, sensation-seeking was more influential as a predictor of cyberbullying than of traditional bullying (Graf et al., 2019). Literature generally shows that adolescents take more risks compared to children and adults, particularly when with peers, and they also display lower risk perception (Albert et al., 2013; Benthin et al., 1993; Gardner & Steinberg, 2005; Paulsen et al., 2011). These developmental factors are linked to brain development and social cognition (Blakemore, 2012; Steinberg, 2010) and have been demonstrated cross-culturally (Steinberg et al., 2018). Thus, similar processes may be accounting for online risk behaviors.

Other aspects of development include egocentrism, which significantly predicted general online risk taking among adolescents (Popovac & Hadlington, 2020). In this study egocentrism encompasses the constructs of imaginary audience and personal fable (Elkind, 1967) that reflect the amplified perceived presence of an audience constantly observing one's behaviors as well as feelings of uniqueness and invincibility. This aligns to social media as audiences (and their feedback) are inherent parts of the experience. In fact, more vivid imaginary audience strongly predicted online risk taking (Popovac & Hadlington, 2020). Coupled with lower perceived risk during this developmental stage and the social influence effect on risk taking, this highlights the importance of examining developmental factors in more depth to better inform online safety strategies.

Fear of missing out (FoMO), as a socially driven concept, is also of interest, as it has implications for the use and experiences of social media. Defined as a "pervasive apprehension that others might be having rewarding experiences from which one is absent" (Przybylski, Murayama, DeHaan, & Gladwell, 2013, p.1841), those with higher FoMO demonstrate a desire to stay continually connected with what others are doing for fear of being left out (Reagle, 2015). Higher levels of FoMO link to greater activity on a larger number of SNSs (Fuster et al., 2017) so as not to miss out on the experiences of others. FoMO is also associated with behaviors such as online self-promotion (Dredge et al., 2014) and could lead to some of the technologically related risks mentioned previously such as oversharing of personal information and adding strangers to social networks: both of these have been linked to increased risk of online victimization (Davidson & Martellozzo, 2013; Kite et al., 2013). Moreover, FoMO significantly predicted general online risk taking in adolescents (Popovac & Hadlington, 2020). For these reasons, there is a need to further understand factors that influence engagement in social media and potential behavioral and wellbeing effects (Tandon et al., 2021), including whether constructs like FoMO may influence cyberaggression and cyberbullying.

As noted earlier, younger children are also regularly using social media, but the motivation behind their desire to do so is not well understood. It is certainly feasible that some factors that govern adolescent online activities are also relevant to younger children, and FoMo could be a plausible motivation for social media use even in younger children. Being excluded from any social event, such as the birthday party of a classmate, could trigger FoMO. In fact, 35% of 8−11 year olds in our study indicated that it bothers them a lot when they miss out on a planned get-together with friends. Such links between FoMO and offline behaviors have been evidenced in adult samples (Hayran, Anik, & Gürhan-Canli, 2020; Przybylski et al., 2013). Although this is an offline example, this could also occur if a child is excluded from a group chat on Instant Messaging or group play in an online game. The desire to be online could be driven in part by siblings or peers being online and not wanting to feel left out. Given that FoMO in social media has been researched for almost a decade (Przybylski et al., 2013), it is somewhat surprising that studies have not focused on this relationship in younger children. One possible exception is a recent article investigating FoMO in young people in Bosnia (Tomczyk & Selmanagic-Lizde, 2018), which reported a sample with a mean and median age of 13. The age range in this study is not stated, but a proportion of the sample were potentially under 11. The results do suggest an association between FoMO and social media use, but any developmental effects will have been obscured by the inclusion of older children in the sample. Our preliminary data with children aged 8−11 shows that FoMO may be influential in online activities for some children, and this raises the question of whether FoMO also influences experiences of cyberaggression and cyberbullying.

## Home- and school-level factors

Home factors such as parental knowledge and supervision and school factors such as policy and overall school social climate are also crucial to consider as risk and protective factors for cyberaggression and cyberbullying. These aspects can contribute to more positive outcomes when supportive and functioning effectively, or they further exacerbate the negative effects on children and adolescents' wellbeing when absent or inconsistent.

When considering home-level factors, studies have indicated that parental knowledge of young people's online activities and experiences may be limited. For example, half of adolescents stated that their parents have no information about or access to the online activities they engage in (Baldry et al., 2019), and most parents in our study (85% in South Africa and 69% in the United Kingdom) believed that in general, adults do not know what adolescents are doing online. Our research also revealed that 4 in 5 young people believed they have better technological knowledge than their parents and roughly two-thirds (61% in South Africa and 66% in the United Kingdom) stated that they can do whatever they want online without anyone checking up on them. This is in stark contrast to their parents' reports, where only 38% of parents in South Africa and 43% in the United Kingdom admitted that their child could do anything they want online. As such, it is also unsurprising that parents underestimated their children's cyberaggression and cyberbullying reports and the emotional effects of these experiences (Popovac & Fine, 2016).

Aspects within the home and the parent—child relationship are important to consider in this regard. Earlier literature in this area showed that lower social support and guidance at home, higher conflict with parents, and overall poorer parental attachments were associated with higher vulnerability to online risks (Wells & Mitchell, 2008). More recently, these same factors were shown to be influential in the context of cyberbullying. For example, family activities acted as a protective factor for cyberbullying perpetration (Li et al., 2021), while poorer relationships with parents was a risk factor for both victimization and perpetration of cyberbullying (Fanti et al., 2012; Kowalski et al., 2014; Li et al., 2019). Moreover, young people in the cyberbully-victim group were more likely to report lower family support (Hellfeldt et al., 2020). In fact, in this study, perceived social support at home and at school mediated the relationship between cyberbullying and wellbeing such that depression and anxiety symptoms were lower for those with higher perceived support (Hellfeldt et al., 2020). This highlights the important buffering effect of positive home- and school-level relationships.

In addition to positive parent—child relationships and other broader home-level factors such as the composition of the family (Arnarsson et al.,

2020), the school social climate is also important (Safaria & Suyono, 2020). A positive school social climate and social support from peers was negatively related to cyberbullying behavior (Wang, Zhao, Yang, & Lei, 2019; Yang, Sharkey, Reed, & Dowdy, 2020), indicating that improving the school social climate can reduce cyberaggression and cyberbullying (Casas et al., 2013). Other aspects within the school such as the existence of rules and policies about cyberbullying also reduce perpetration (Bae, 2021). In our research, we found that schools had more mediation strategies and rules about technology use than homes, with 80% of adolescents in the United Kingdom and 65% in South Africa reporting stricter rules at school. This shows that children's proximal environments play an important role in reducing cyberbullying when they are supportive. Moreover, supervision and appropriate mediation strategies at home and school as well as educating young people about cyberbullying and its effects can be useful in preventing cyberbullying (Bae, 2021; Popovac & Fine, 2018). With the potential discrepancies in approaches across these two environments, efforts to bridge the gaps between homes and schools may provide a more consolidated approach to online safety for young people.

## Social media platforms and policy

We previously noted some of the technological risk factors in terms of online activities and usage patterns which can predispose individuals to cyberaggression and cyberbullying. In this section, we explore the broader-level technological risk factors, namely, the roles and responsibilities of social media platforms and the laws and policies in this regard. Social media providers can play a significant role in altering social norms of online behaviors and setting expectations for users by responding to toxic behaviors on their platforms. Moreover, their early intervention in such behaviors can reduce the longer-term effects on mental health and wellbeing for victims. It has taken a considerable amount of time to ensure more accountability from social media providers and there are many opportunities to enhance online safety in this regard.

When examining age restrictions, most social media platforms do not allow users below the age of 13 to use their services. This includes Facebook, Instagram, Snapchat, Twitter, and TikTok. WhatsApp has recently increased its age limit from 13 to 16 for users in Europe and, although there are no age restrictions on watching YouTube videos in general, users can only open an account from the age of 13 (Internet

Matters, n.d.; UK Safer Internet Centre, 2018). YouTube restricts some content to over 18s; however, a quick Google search easily comes up with hacks about how to bypass such settings. Considering that 68% of children aged 8−11 in our recent UK study report watching YouTube (with many having their own account) and half had their own profile in many popular SNSs (including Snapchat, TikTok, WhatsApp, and Instagram), it is possible that parents are supervising some of these accounts. However, age restrictions can easily be bypassed and users of all ages can sign up to these platforms on their own.

In addition to age restrictions, social media providers have terms of service. A number of these relate to cyberaggression and cyberbullying. For example, WhatsApp outlines its policies and values in relation to safety, security, and integrity and commits to dealing with abusive users by terminating their use or contacting law enforcement (WhatsApp, 2021). Facebook and Instagram both outline community standards or guidelines as part of their terms of service, which includes respect for other users within the community and a committed intolerance toward threats, degradation, shaming, and hate speech (Facebook, 2021a; Instagram, 2018). As part of their online safety initiative, Facebook has developed a Bullying Prevention Hub, with information and tips written for both adolescent and adult audiences (Facebook, 2021b). While this is encouraging, much of this action is relatively recent and it is important to note that this information does not target younger children who are also active on these platforms.

Examining legislation and policies in relation to online safety globally is beyond the scope of this chapter; however, we briefly take the example of the United Kingdom to illustrate some recent actions taken to boost the accountability of social media companies in online safety efforts. Section 103 of the Digital Economy Act (2017) outlines a code of practice for social media users. Key principles include the need for social media platforms to (1) have clear and accessible reporting mechanisms for harmful behaviors, (2) appropriately deal with such reports, (3) have easily accessible and clear information about reporting harmful behavior, and (4) communicate to the public the actions taken against such behavior. Further guidelines as to how social media providers should best align themselves with the principles are also included. The UK White Paper on Online Harms (2019) further set out government priorities and made companies more responsible for users' online safety, particularly children, due to the recognition that previous initiatives had not gone far enough or were inconsistent across platforms. The White Paper recognized a range of online harms including bullying and harassment and proposed the establishment of new legislation.

Most recently, the UK Online Safety Act was passed in 2023 (Online Safety Act, 2023). It covers a range of content (e.g., revenge porn, hate speech, bullying, and pornography), and social media sites and online search providers are required to act on harmful content. The Act outlines clear duties of care and codes of service to protect both adults' and children's online safety. Focusing particularly on children, social media providers must examine the likelihood of children accessing their platforms and mitigate and manage risks of harm and the impact of harm at different ages. Specific processes for reporting and redress are mandated. Broadly, the goal is to develop transparency and accountability, including publishing of regular reports submitted to an independent regulatory body. Such steps are important to ensure a multilevel approach to online safety efforts. These actions are an important first step; however, it will be important to monitor how this functions in practice and to continue to refine and consult. If successful, such legislation can have long-term effects on reducing incidences of cyberaggression and cyberbullying and promoting positive online social norms.

A key challenge for practical implementation will be in relation to fairness to ensure equal and nondiscriminatory experiences (Hoffmann, 2019; Jhaver et al., 2019). The process of content moderation is continuously improving but is subject to error, resulting in some harmful behaviors evading detection and some users being unfairly sanctioned due to false positives (Hosseini et al., 2017), which impacts user trust (Jhaver et al., 2019). Other questions that remain are whether removal of content and banning of users actually reduces the cyberaggression and cyberbullying behaviors and whether actions can extend to the care and wellbeing of the victim. Removal of content and sanctioning of offenders is argued to "write the targets of online harassment out of the justice-seeking process" and there is little opportunity for reparation (Schoenebeck, Haimson, et al., 2021; Schoenebeck, Scott, et al., 2021, p. 4). These authors argue for alternative approaches either in combination with or in place of existing punitive approaches, including potential for using restorative justice ideals such as compensation or apologies to victims (Schoenebeck, Haimson, et al., 2021; Schoenebeck, Scott, et al., 2021). Their research among 14–24 year olds indicated that 62% would welcome an apology from an offender. Moreover, young people showed low overall trust in social media providers to achieve a fair resolution following cyberbullying reports, with most believing that outcomes were not severe enough and were not adequately communicated to the victim (Schoenebeck, Scott, et al., 2021). Restorative justice approaches are an interesting notion, although it may be difficult to see how social media platforms could implement this in practice. However, considering the severe effects of cyberaggression and cyberbullying reported earlier in this chapter, this research indicates the importance of working to increase user trust and opportunities for investigating and building on approaches in future.

## Intervention and prevention: challenges and opportunities

Considering the prevalence, effects, and multidimensional risk and protective factors relevant to cyberaggression and cyberbullying, tackling this issue among children and adolescents is of the utmost importance and requires a multilevel approach that engages all relevant stakeholders. This includes working with young people at the individual level but also engaging with other aspects of their immediate environments (e.g., home and school) as well as the broader context to create a more comprehensive strategy for online safety efforts. We draw on Bronfenbrenner's (1994) Bio-Ecological Systems theory in this regard, which emphasizes the person—context relationship and posits that an individual is placed within a system of relationships that occur at multiple levels of the environment (see: Bronfenbrenner & Ceci, 1994; Bronfenbrenner, 1979, 2005). This is illustrated as concentric circles of influence (see Fig. 1.1), with bidirectional influences occurring across the different systems. Such ecological approaches have also been applied to cyberbullying (e.g., Cross et al., 2015; Popovac, 2017).

Using this theory as a foundation, we discuss recommendations aimed at the different "layers" of influence to young people's online safety, including both intervention and prevention efforts. Such a multilevel, holistic approach should involve the following: (1) working with young people (individual level); (2) targeting the home and school environments individually (microsystem level); (3) fostering collaboration and consistent approaches between the home and school (mesosystem level); (4) working with organizations, charities, and external support services (exosystem level); and (5) enacting laws, policies, and educational media campaigns

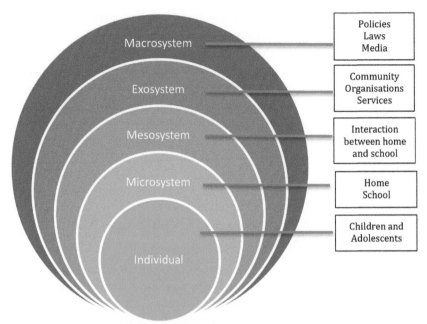

**Figure 1.1** Ecological multilevel approach to online safety. *Source: Adapted from Popovac, M. (2017). Beyond the School Gates: Experiences of Cyberaggression and Cyberbullying Among Adolescents in the UK. Technical Report. University of Buckingham, Buckingham; Bronfenbrenner, U. & Ceci, S. J. (1994). Nature-nuture reconceptualized in developmental perspective: A bioecological model. Psychological Review, 101(4), 568.*

(macrosystem level). Strategies that engage multiple levels ensure a more comprehensive approach to online safety efforts. Such efforts are particularly crucial given the constantly evolving technological landscape (Bond & Rawlings, 2018).

## Working with young people (individual level): digital literacy, skills, and peer leadership

It has been argued that much of the focus around online safety policy has been on preventative measures, which focus on controlling access to certain risks rather than equipping young people to manage risks (Phippen & Street, 2022b). It is important to focus on building digital literacy in young people to develop skills and confidence that will allow them to navigate online spaces more effectively and safely, to preempt the risks that they may encounter, and to generally develop good media choices. This should include practical skills such as managing privacy and security settings, being aware of blocking and reporting mechanisms on different platforms and considering their information-sharing practices and contacts (audiences) that are added to their accounts. These skills can help to equip young people to take ownership of their online safety at the appropriate developmental stages. Further to this, we have a responsibility to socialize young people into responsible digital citizens by emphasizing basic values of empathy and respect in online interactions, discussing the potential consequences of behaviors on others, and promoting prosocial conflict resolution. Open and reflective discussions about technology use and risks are key and can also serve to develop trust between children and adults so that they feel comfortable reporting when they have experienced cyberaggression or cyberbullying. This can lead to earlier detection and support, thereby reducing the potentially serious long-term effects on wellbeing. Young people often do not confide in adults about online risks, as they fear that adults will overreact or fail to understand their experience; therefore, it is also important to include young people's perspectives as part of solutions and to move away from adult-centered approaches to online safety (Phippen & Street, 2022a; Popovac, 2017). Finally, developing peer leadership capabilities in young people can lead to more positive peer norms and further support as young people can be encouraged to become upstanders to cyberaggression and cyberbullying for others, thus providing enhanced opportunity for victims to receive help and support. Importantly, these efforts should be continuous and consistent and start at an early age, with information, motivation, and skills tailored toward different developmental stages, which has been shown to be effective (Popovac & Fine, 2018).

## Working with parents (microsystem): open and positive parent−child communication

A central way for parents to increase online safety is to become more aware of the social media platforms, services, and online activities that their children are engaging in. Showing an interest in these activities allows the conversation to progress to discussing the potential risks surrounding such activities and ways of avoiding them. It also provides opportunities to instill positive values in how to engage with other users and handle online conflict. Direct and consistent engagement around these issues is important for developing trust in children when discussing negative online experiences with parents. Appropriate parental mediation strategies also need to be considered in relation to the developmental stage of the child (Livingstone &

Helsper, 2008). While control-based strategies are appropriate for younger children, they can reduce learning opportunities to develop digital literacy to navigate online environments safely. Thus, active, discussion-based strategies become more important as children get older.

## Working with schools (microsystem): promoting school policy, reporting, and support

Schools should have clear policies, reporting channels, and disciplinary measures in relation to cyberaggression and cyberbullying, and all staff should be aware of the processes and their roles and responsibilities. Policies need to be applied consistently, and these should be communicated clearly to the whole-school community (including parents), so that processes are defined and there is trust that action will be taken. Schools have the opportunity to openly discuss issues of online safety with young people and elicit positive antibullying-oriented social norms, with messages built into class discussions. Early education around online safety, beginning at primary school and extending into adolescence as online activities become more complex, can foster more confidence and skill in young people, and build positive social norms and values about online behavior and expectations. Schools are also an optimal means of putting peer leadership and mentorship programs into place to create peer support. Training sessions for all staff are required as part of this, so that all teachers feel confident in implementing policies and lesson plans around online safety. Training may also assist in early detection of issues and enhanced support to victims.

## Connecting parents and schools on online safety concerns (mesosystem)

Proactive approaches by parents and schools that include consistent messaging and promotion of similar key values of empathy and respect in online environments is important in consolidating the two most immediate environments in young people's lives. More collaborative engagement and a shared responsibility between homes and schools is fundamental in this process. Parents have the responsibility to become familiar with school policies on technology use and online risks and to discuss these with their children to ensure consistent messaging between the home and school contexts. Clear communication and information sharing between these two contexts is key to ensuring that the topic of online safety remains at the forefront of discussion.

## Working with organizations, charities, and support services (exosystem): drawing on resources

Many organizations, charities, and support services actively work to address cyberaggression and cyberbullying, including working with young people, parents, and schools. Thus, there are sources of support and resources available to draw on. Engaging with these resources and services is pivotal to training teachers, advising parents, and providing mental health support for victims and perpetrators as part of referrals, which can be beneficial for developing holistic approaches to online safety. Building relationships with organizations and charities can go a long way in consolidating and supporting strategies across the different layers as well as staying informed about new developments, new concerns, and new technologies, which allows policies and strategies to be amended more quickly. Apart from networking with such organizations, opportunities may arise to network with other schools as part of training, research, or events, allowing for sharing of knowledge to build on intervention and prevention efforts.

## Working with government (macrosystem): laws, policies, and defining roles and responsibilities of social media providers

Considering the serious impacts of cyberaggression and cyberbullying and its effects on both the school social climate and academic outcomes, efforts to address this issue need to be prioritized at the macrolevel and more work needs to be done to increase public awareness as part of educational media campaigns to promote online safety. Laws and policies also hold the key to prioritizing actions and strategies, including defining the roles of social media providers in online safety efforts so that all stakeholders understand where their responsibility and accountability begins and ends. Good strides have been made recently in this regard, such as the introduction of the UK Draft Online Safety Bill published in May 2021, but it will be important to monitor the implementation of the new laws aimed at social media providers and to continue to refine and update policies in line with stakeholder consultation so that actions remain relevant to ever-evolving technologies and needs. Moreover, work toward integrating online safety into the curriculum and supporting early education on this topic is key going forward, along with working with organizations, charities, and external support services to help bridge the gap across the different layers of influence. Further promotion of online safety strategies, training provision, and oversight can ultimately elicit more targeted and effective efforts.

## Conclusions and future directions

Social media is central in children and adolescents' online activities, and, while there are many positive effects linked to use of social media, this can be a key venue for cyberaggression and cyberbullying. Prevalence rates globally indicate that cyberaggression and cyberbullying in young people is a serious concern, carrying significant negative consequences related to mental health and wellbeing as well as educational outcomes. Risk and protective factors highlight the role of individual-level characteristics and the intersectionality of identity-related factors and stress the importance of further research into developmental and social influences. Further research with younger children is particularly important given the large developmental differences between children and adolescents, and this can inform more targeted, age-appropriate intervention and prevention strategies and priorities.

The chapter also highlights important home and family-related factors, particularly the importance of open communication and positive relationships within the home, as these present a buffering effect for risk experiences. Moreover, school-level factors further reflect the importance of engaging with the two most immediate environments in young people's lives to promote positive online engagement and safety. While progress has recently been made in relation to laws and policies and in defining the roles and responsibilities of social media providers, further work as part of a multilevel approach to online safety efforts is needed.

## References

Abreu, R. L., & Kenny, M. C. (2018). Cyberbullying and LGBTQ youth: A systematic literature review and recommendations for prevention and intervention. *Journal of Child & Adolescent Trauma, 11*(1), 81–97. Available from https://doi.org/10.1007/s40653-017-0175-7.

Agnew, R. (1999). A general strain theory of community differences in crime rates. *Journal of Research in Crime and Delinquency, 36*(2), 123–155.

Agnew, R. (2017). *General strain theory: Current status and directions for further research. Taking stock* (pp. 101–123). Routledge, In.

Agnew, R., & White, H. R. (1992). An empirical test of general strain theory. *Criminology, 30*(4), 475–500.

Aizenkot, D. (2020). Social networking and online self-disclosure as predictors of cyberbullying victimization among children and youth. *Children and Youth Services Review, 119*, 105695. Available from https://doi.org/10.1016/j.childyouth.2020.105695.

Albdour, M., Hong, J. S., Lewin, L., & Yarandi, H. (2019). The impact of cyberbullying on physical and psychological health of Arab American Adolescents. *Journal of Immigrant and Minority Health, 21*(4), 706–715. Available from https://doi.org/10.1007/s10903-018-00850-w.

Albert, D., Chein, J., & Steinberg, L. (2013). The teenage brain peer influences on adolescent decision making. *Current Directions in Psychological Science*, *22*(2), 114−120.

Allen, K.-A., Ryan, T., Gray, D., McInereney, D., & Waters, L. (2014). Social media use and social connectedness in adolescents: The positives and the potential pitfalls. *Australian Journal of Educational and Developmental Psychology*, *31*, 18−31. Available from https://doi.org/10.1017/edp.2014.2.

Alonso, C., & Romero, E. (2017). Aggressors and victims in bullying and cyberbullying: A study of personality profiles using the five-factor model. *The Spanish Journal of Psychology*, 20. Available from https://doi.org/10.1017/sjp.2017.73.

Anderson, M., & Jiang, J. (2018). Teens, Social Media & Technology 2018. *Pew Research Center: Internet, Science & Tech.* https://www.pewresearch.org/internet/2018/05/31/teens-social-media-technology-2018/.

Ang, R. P., Li, X., & Seah, S. L. (2017). The role of normative beliefs about aggression in the relationship between empathy and cyberbullying. *Journal of Cross-Cultural Psychology*, *48*(8), 1138−1152. Available from https://doi.org/10.1177/0022022116678928.

Angoff, H. D., & Barnhart, W. R. (2021). Bullying and cyberbullying among LGBQ and heterosexual youth from an intersectional perspective: Findings from the 2017 National Youth Risk Behavior Survey. *Journal of School Violence*, 20, 274−286. Available from https://doi.org/10.1080/15388220.2021.1879099.

Arnarsson, A., Nygren, J., Nyholm, M., Torsheim, T., Augustine, L., Bjereld, Y., Markkanen, I., Schnohr, C. W., Rasmussen, M., Nielsen, L., & Bendtsen, P. (2020). Cyberbullying and traditional bullying among Nordic adolescents and their impact on life satisfaction. *Scandinavian Journal of Public Health*, *48*(5), 502−510. Available from https://doi.org/10.1177/1403494818817411.

Arslan, S., Savaser, S., Hallett, V., & Balci, S. (2012). Cyberbullying among primary school students in Turkey: Self-reported prevalence and associations with home and school life. *Cyberpsychology, Behavior, and Social Networking*, *15*(10), 527−533.

Auxier, B., & Anderson, M. (2021). Social media use in 2021. *Pew Research Center.*

Auxier, B., Anderson, M., Perrin, A., & Turner, E. (2020). Children's engagement with digital devices, screen time. *Pew Research Center: Internet, Science & Tech.* Available from https://www.pewresearch.org/internet/2020/07/28/childrens-engagement-with-digital-devices-screen-time/.

Bae, S.-M. (2021). The relationship between exposure to risky online content, cyber victimization, perception of cyberbullying, and cyberbullying offending in Korean adolescents. *Children and Youth Services Review*, *123*, 105946. Available from https://doi.org/10.1016/j.childyouth.2021.105946.

Baldry, A. C., Sorrentino, A., & Farrington, D. P. (2019). Cyberbullying and cybervictimization versus parental supervision, monitoring and control of adolescents' online activities. *Children and Youth Services Review*, *96*, 302−307.

Barlett, C., & Coyne, S. M. (2014). A meta-analysis of sex differences in cyber-bullying behavior: The moderating role of age. *Aggressive Behavior*, *40*(5), 474−488.

Barlett, C. P., Gentile, D. A., & Chew, C. (2016). Predicting cyberbullying from anonymity. *Psychology of Popular Media Culture*, *5*(2), 171−180. Available from https://doi.org/10.1037/ppm0000055.

Bauman, S. (2007). *Cyberbullying: A virtual menace.* Paper presented at the National Coalition Against Bullying National Conference, 2−4 November 2007. Melbourne, Australia. Available from http://www.ncab.org.au/Assets/Files/Bauman,%20S.%20Cyberbullying.pdf.

Bauman, S., Toomey, R. B., & Walker, J. L. (2013). Associations among bullying, cyberbullying, and suicide in high school students. *Journal of Adolescence*, *36*(2), 341−350.

Beckman, L., Hagquist, C., & Hellström, L. (2012). Does the association with psychosomatic health problems differ between cyberbullying and traditional bullying. *Emotional and Behavioural Difficulties*, *17*(3–4), 421–434. Available from https://doi.org/10.1080/13632752.2012.704228.

Beckman, L., Hagquist, C., & Hellström, L. (2013). Discrepant gender patterns for cyberbullying and traditional bullying—An analysis of Swedish adolescent data. *Computers in Human Behavior*, *29*(5), 1896–1903.

Benthin, A., Slovic, P., & Severson, H. (1993). A psychometric study of adolescent risk perception. *Journal of Adolescence*, *16*(2), 153–168.

Best, P., Manktelow, R., & Taylor, B. (2014). Online communication, social media and adolescent wellbeing: A systematic narrative review. *Children and Youth Services Review*, *41*. Available from https://doi.org/10.1016/j.childyouth.2014.03.001.

Betts, L. R., & Spenser, K. A. (2017). "People think it'sa harmless joke": Young people's understanding of the impact of technology, digital vulnerability and cyberbullying in the United Kingdom. *Journal of Children and Media*, *11*(1), 20–35.

Blakemore, S. J. (2012). Development of the social brain in adolescence. *Journal of the Royal Society of Medicine*, *105*(3), 111–116.

Bond, E., & Rawlings, V. (2018). Virtual vulnerability: Safeguarding children in digital environments. In M. Dastbaz, H. Arabnia, & B. Akhgar (Eds.), *Technology for smart futures* (pp. 251–269). Springer International Publishing. Available from https://doi.org/10.1007/978-3-319-60137-3_12.

Brochado, S., Soares, S., & Fraga, S. (2017). A scoping review on studies of cyberbullying prevalence among adolescents. *Trauma, Violence, & Abuse*, *18*(5), 523–531.

Bronfenbrenner, U. (1979). *The ecology of human development*. Harvard University Press.

Bronfenbrenner, U. (2005). *Making human beings human: Bioecological perspectives on human development*. Sage.

Bronfenbrenner, U., & Ceci, S. J. (1994). Nature-nuture reconceptualized in developmental perspective: A bioecological model. *Psychological Review*, *101*(4), 568.

Buda, G., Lukoševičiūtė, J., Šalčiūnaitė, L., & Šmigelskas, K. (2020). Possible effects of social media use on adolescent health behaviors and perceptions. *Psychological Reports*, *124*(3), 1031–1048. Available from https://doi.org/10.1177/0033294120922481.

Calmaestra, J., Rodríguez-Hidalgo, A. J., Mero-Delgado, O., & Solera, E. (2020). Cyberbullying in adolescents from Ecuador and Spain: Prevalence and differences in gender, school year and ethnic-cultural background. *Sustainability*, *12*(11), 4597.

Camerini, A.-L., Marciano, L., Carrara, A., & Schulz, P. J. (2020). Cyberbullying perpetration and victimization among children and adolescents: A systematic review of longitudinal studies. *Telematics and Informatics*, *49*, 101362. Available from https://doi.org/10.1016/j.tele.2020.101362.

Casas, J. A., Del Rey, R., & Ortega-Ruiz, R. (2013). Bullying and cyberbullying: Convergent and divergent predictor variables. *Computers in Human Behavior*, *29*(3), 580–587.

Chan, T. K. H., Cheung, C. M. K., & Lee, Z. W. Y. (2021). Cyberbullying on social networking sites: A literature review and future research directions. *Information & Management*, *58*(2), 103411. Available from https://doi.org/10.1016/j.im.2020.103411.

Chang, Q., Xing, J., Ho, R. T. H., & Yip, P. S. F. (2019). Cyberbullying and suicide ideation among Hong Kong adolescents: The mitigating effects of life satisfaction with family, classmates and academic results. *Psychiatry Research*, *274*, 269–273. Available from https://doi.org/10.1016/j.psychres.2019.02.054.

Cohen-Almagor, R. (2018). Social responsibility on the internet: Addressing the challenge of cyberbullying. *Aggression and Violent Behavior*, *39*, 42–52. Available from https://doi.org/10.1016/j.avb.2018.01.001.

Corcoran, L., Connolly, I., & O'Moore, M. (2012). Cyberbullying in Irish schools: An investigation of personality and self-concept. *The Irish Journal of Psychology*, *33*(4), 153–165. Available from https://doi.org/10.1080/03033910.2012.677995.

Craig, W., Boniel-Nissim, M., King, N., Walsh, S. D., Boer, M., Donnelly, P. D., Harel-Fisch, Y., Malinowska-Cieślik, M., Gaspar de Matos, M., Cosma, A., Van den Eijnden, R., Vieno, A., Elgar, F. J., Molcho, M., Bjereld, Y., & Pickett, W. (2020). Social media use and cyber-bullying: A cross-national analysis of young people in 42 countries. *Journal of Adolescent Health, 66(6, Supplement)*, S100–S108. Available from https://doi.org/10.1016/j.jadohealth.2020.03.006.

Cross, D., Barnes, A., Papageorgiou, A., Hadwen, K., Hearn, L., & Lester, L. (2015). A social–ecological framework for understanding and reducing cyberbullying behaviours. *Aggression and Violent Behavior*, *23*, 109–117. Available from https://doi.org/10.1016/j.avb.2015.05.016.

Davidson, J., & Martellozzo, E. (2013). Exploring young people's use of social networking sites and digital media in the internet safety context: A comparison of the UK and Bahrain. *Information, Communication & Society*, *16*(9), 1456–1476.

De Pasquale, C., Martinelli, V., Sciacca, F., Mazzone, M., Chiappedi, M., Dinaro, C., & Hichy, Z. (2021). The role of mood states in cyberbullying and cybervictimization behaviors in adolescents. *Psychiatry Research*, *300*, 113908. Available from https://doi.org/10.1016/j.psychres.2021.113908.

DePaolis, K., & Williford, A. (2015). The nature and prevalence of cyber victimization among elementary school children. *Child & Youth Care Forum (Chicago, Ill.)*, *44*(3), 377–393.

DeSmet, A., Rodelli, M., Walrave, M., Soenens, B., Cardon, G., & De Bourdeaudhuij, I. (2018). Cyberbullying and traditional bullying involvement among heterosexual and non-heterosexual adolescents, and their associations with age and gender. *Computers in Human Behavior*, *83*, 254–261. Available from https://doi.org/10.1016/j.chb.2018.02.010.

Digital Economy Act 2017, §103 (2017). https://www.legislation.gov.uk/ukpga/2017/30/section/103/enacted. (Accessed 21 June 2021).

Doumas, D. M., & Midgett, A. (2021). The association between witnessing cyberbullying and depressive symptoms and social anxiety among elementary school students. *Psychology in the Schools*, *58*(3), 622–637.

Dredge, R., Gleeson, J., & De la Piedad Garcia, X. (2014). Presentation on Facebook and risk of cyberbullyingvictimisation. *Computers in Human Behavior*, *40*, 16–22.

Drouin, M., McDaniel, B. T., Pater, J., & Toscos, T. (2020). How parents and their children used social media and technology at the beginning of the COVID-19 pandemic and associations with anxiety. *Cyberpsychology, Behavior, and Social Networking*, *23*(11), 727–736. Available from https://doi.org/10.1089/cyber.2020.0284.

Elipe, P., Muñoz, M., de la, O., & Rey, R. D. (2018). Homophobic bullying and cyber-bullying: Study of a silenced problem. *Journal of Homosexuality*, *65*(5), 672–686. Available from https://doi.org/10.1080/00918369.2017.1333809.

Elkind, D. (1967). Egocentrism in adolescence. *Child Development*, *38*, 1025–1034.

Englander, E. K. (2013). Bullying and cyberbullying: What every educator needs to know. Harvard Education Press.

Ergin, D. A., Akgül, G., & Karaman, N. G. (2021). Ethnic-based cyberbullying: The role of adolescents' and their peers' attitudes towards immigrants. *Turkish Journal of Education*, *10*(2), 139–156. Available from https://doi.org/10.19128/turje.879347.

Ey, L.-A., Taddeo, C., & Spears, B. (2015). Cyberbullying and primary-school aged children: The psychological literature and the challenge for sociology. *Societies*, *5*(2), 492–514.

Facebook. (2021a). *Community Standards | Facebook*. Available from https://en-gb.facebook.com/communitystandards/.

Facebook. (2021b). Safety Center. Safety Center. Available from https://www.facebook.com/safetyv2?locale = en_GB.

Fang, J., Wang, X., Yuan, K.-H., Wen, Z., Yu, X., & Zhang, G. (2020). Callous-Unemotional traits and cyberbullying perpetration: The mediating role of moral disengagement and the moderating role of empathy. *Personality and Individual Differences*, *157*, 109829. Available from https://doi.org/10.1016/j.paid.2020.109829.

Fanti, K. A., Demetriou, A. G., & Hawa, V. V. (2012). A longitudinal study of cyberbullying: Examining riskand protective factors. *European Journal of Developmental Psychology*, *9*(2), 168−181. Available from https://doi.org/10.1080/17405629.2011.643169.

Farhangpour, P., Mutshaeni, H. N., & Cynthia, M. (2019). Emotional and academic effects of cyberbullying on students in a rural high school in the Limpopo province, South Africa. *South African Journal of Information Management*, *21*(1), 1−8. Available from https://doi.org/10.4102/sajim.v21i1.925.

Festl, R., & Quandt, T. (2016). The role of online communication in long-term cyberbullying involvement among girls and boys. *Journal of Youth and Adolescence*, *45*(9), 1931−1945.

Fuster, H., Chamarro, A., & Oberst, U. (2017). Fear of missing out, online social networking and mobile phone addiction: A latent profile approach. *Aloma: Revista De Psicologia, Ciències De l'Educació I De l'Esport*, *35*(1), 25−30.

Gámez-Guadix, M., & Mateos-Pérez, E. (2019). Longitudinal and reciprocal relationships between sexting, online sexual solicitations, and cyberbullying among minors. *Computers in Human Behavior*, *94*, 70−76.

Gámez-Guadix, M., Orue, I., Smith, P. K., & Calvete, E. (2013). Longitudinal and reciprocal relations of cyberbullying with depression, substance use, and problematic internet use among adolescents. *Journal of Adolescent Health*, *53*(4), 446−452.

Gardner, M., & Steinberg, L. (2005). Peer influence on risk taking, risk preference, and risky decision making in adolescence and adulthood: an experimental study. *Developmental Psychology*, *41*(4), 625−635.

González-Cabrera, J., León-Mejía, A., Beranuy, M., Gutiérrez-Ortega, M., Álvarez-Bardón, A., & Machimbarrena, J. M. (2018). Relationship between cyberbullying and health-related quality of life in a sample of children and adolescents. *Quality of Life Research*, *27*(10), 2609−2618.

Graf, D., Yanagida, T., & Spiel, C. (2019). Sensation seeking's differential role in face-to-face and cyberbullying: Taking perceived contextual properties into account. *Frontiers in psychology*, *10*, 1572.

Grigg, D. W. (2010). Cyber-aggression: Definition and concept of cyberbullying. *Australian Journal of Guidance and Counselling*, *20*(2), 143.

Hamm, M., Newton, A., Chisholm, A., Shulhan, J., Milne, A., Sundar, P., Ennis, H., Scott, S., & Hartling, L. (2015). Prevalence and effect of cyberbullying on children and young people: A scoping review of social media studies. *JAMA Pediatrics*, *169*. Available from https://doi.org/10.1001/jamapediatrics.2015.0944.

Hawdon, J., Oksanen, A., & Räsänen, P. (2017). Exposure to online hate in four nations: A cross-national consideration. *Deviant Behavior*, *38*(3), 254−266. Available from https://doi.org/10.1080/01639625.2016.1196985.

Hayran, C., Anik, L., & Gürhan-Canli, Z. (2020). A threat to loyalty: Fear of missing out (FOMO) leads to reluctance to repeat current experiences. *PLoS One*, *15*(4), e0232318.

Heirman, W., Walrave, M., Vermeulen, A., Ponnet, K., Vandebosch, H., & Hardies, K. (2016). Applying the theory of planned behavior to adolescents' acceptance of online friendship requests sent by strangers. *Telematics and Informatics*. Available from. Available from http://www.sciencedirect.com/science/article/pii/S0736585316300247.

Hinduja, S., & Patchin, J. W. (2007). Offline consequences of online victimization: School violence and delinquency. *Journal of School Violence, 6*(3), 89—112.

Hinduja, S., & Patchin, J. W. (2009). *Cyberbullying research summary: Emotional and psychological consequences.* Cyberbullying Research Center. Available from http://cyberbullying.org/cyberbullying_emotional_consequences.pdf.

Hoffmann, A. L. (2019). Where fairness fails: data, algorithms, and the limits of antidiscrimination discourse. *Information, Communication & Society, 22*(7), 900—915.

Holfeld, B., & Leadbeater, B. J. (2015). The nature and frequency of cyber bullying behaviors and victimization experiences in young Canadian children. *Canadian Journal of School Psychology, 30*(2), 116—135.

Hosseini, H., Kannan, S., Zhang, B., & Poovendran, R. (2017). Deceiving google's perspective api built for detecting toxic comments. *arXiv preprint arXiv:1702.08138.*

Instagram. (2018). *Instagram Community Guidelines FAQs.* Available from https://about.instagram.com/blog/announcements/instagram-community-guidelines-faqs.

Internet Matters. (n.d.). What age can my child start social networking? *Internet Matters.* Retrieved June 29, 2021, Available from https://www.internetmatters.org/resources/what-age-can-my-child-start-social-networking/.

Iranzo, B., Buelga, S., Cava, M.-J., & Ortega-Barón, J. (2019). Cyberbullying, psychosocial adjustment, and suicidal ideation in adolescence. *Psychosocial Intervention, 28*(2), 75—81. Available from https://doi.org/10.5093/pi2019a5.

Jhaver, S., Bruckman, A., & Gilbert, E. (2019). Does transparency in moderation really matter? User behavior after content removal explanations on reddit. *Proceedings of the ACM on Human-Computer Interaction, 3*(CSCW), 1-27.

Juvonen, J., & Gross, E. F. (2008). Extending the school grounds?—Bullying experiences in cyberspace. *Journal of School Health, 78*(9), 496—505.

Karmakar, S., & Das, S. (2021). *Understanding the Rise of Twitter-Based Cyberbullying Due to COVID-19 through Comprehensive Statistical Evaluation* (SSRN Scholarly Paper ID 3768839). Social Science Research Network. https://doi.org/10.2139/ssrn.3768839.

Kelly, Y., Zilanawala, A., Booker, C., & Sacker, A. (2018). Social Media Use and Adolescent Mental Health: Findings From the UK Millennium Cohort Study. *Elsevier Enhanced Reader.* https://doi.org/10.1016/j.eclinm.2018.12.005.

Kim, S., Colwell, S. R., Kata, A., Boyle, M. H., & Georgiades, K. (2018). Cyberbullying victimization and adolescent mental health: Evidence of differential effects by sex and mental health problem type. *Journal of Youth and Adolescence, 47*(3), 661—672. Available from https://doi.org/10.1007/s10964-017-0678-4.

Kim, S., Kimber, M., Boyle, M. H., & Georgiades, K. (2019). Sex differences in the association between cyberbullying victimization and mental health, substance use, and suicidal ideation in adolescents. *The Canadian Journal of Psychiatry, 64*(2), 126—135. Available from https://doi.org/10.1177/0706743718777397.

Kite, S. L., Gable, R. K., & Filippelli, L. P. (2013). Cyber threats: A study of what middle and high school student know about threatening behaviours and internet safety. *International Journal of Social Media and Interactive Learning Environments, 1*(3), 240—254.

Knoll, L. J., Magis-Weinberg, L., Speekenbrink, M., & Blakemore, S.-J. (2015). Social influence on risk perception during adolescence. *Psychological Science, 26*(5), 583—592.

Kowalski, R. M., Dillon, E., Macbeth, J., Franchi, M., & Bush, M. (2020). Racial differences in cyberbullying from the perspective of victims and perpetrators. *American Journal of Orthopsychiatry, 90*(5), 644—652. Available from https://doi.org/10.1037/ort0000492.

Kowalski, R. M., Giumetti, G. W., Schroeder, A. N., & Lattanner, M. R. (2014). Bullying in the digital age: A critical review and meta-analysis of cyberbullying research among youth. *Psychological Bulletin, 140*(4), 1073.

Lee, J., Chun, J., Kim, J., & Lee, J. (2020). Cyberbullying victimisation and school dropout intention among South Korean adolescents: The moderating role of peer/teacher support. *Asia Pacific Journal of Social Work and Development*, *30*(3), 195–211. Available from https://doi.org/10.1080/02185385.2020.1774409.

Li, Q., Luo, Y., Hao, Z., Smith, B., Guo, Y., & Tyrone, C. (2021). Risk factors of cyberbullying perpetration among school-aged children across 41 countries: A perspective of routine activity theory. *International journal of bullying prevention*, *3*, 168–180.

Li, J., Sidibe, A. M., Shen, X., & Hesketh, T. (2019). Incidence, risk factors and psychosomatic symptoms for traditional bullying and cyberbullying in Chinese adolescents. *Children and Youth Services Review*, *107*, 104511. Available from https://doi.org/10.1016/j.childyouth.2019.104511.

Litwiller, B. J., & Brausch, A. M. (2013). Cyber bullying and physical bullying in adolescent suicide: The role of violent behavior and substance use. *Journal of Youth and Adolescence*, *42*(5), 675–684.

Livingstone, S., Davidson, J., Bryce, J., Batool, S., Haughton, C., & Nandi, A. (2017). *Children's online activities, risks and safety: A literature review by the UKCCIS evidence group*.

Livingstone, S., Haddon, L., Görzig, A., & Ólafsson, K. (2011). *Risks and safety on the internet: The perspective of European children: Full findings and policy implications from the EU Kids Online survey of 9–16 year olds and their parents in 25 countries*.

Livingstone, S., & Helsper, E. J. (2008). Parental mediation of children's internet use. *Journal of Broadcasting & Electronic Media*, *52*(4), 581–599.

Livingstone, S., Kirwil, L., Ponte, C., & Staksrud, E. (2014). In their own words: What bothers children online? *European Journal of Communication*, *29*(3), 271–288.

Livingstone, S. M., Haddon, L., & Görzig, A. (2012). *Children, Risk and Safety on the Internet: Research and Policy Challenges in Comparative Perspective*. The Policy Press.

Machimbarrena, J., Calvete, E., Fernández-González, L., Álvarez-Bardón, A., Álvarez-Fernández, L., & González-Cabrera, J. (2018). Internet risks: An overview of victimization in cyberbullying, cyber dating abuse, sexting, online grooming and problematic internet use. *International Journal of Environmental Research and Public Health*, *15*(11), 2471.

Machimbarrena, J. M., & Garaigordobil, M. (2018). Prevalence of bullying and cyberbullying in the last stage of primary education in the Basque Country. *The Spanish Journal of Psychology*, *21*.

Marciano, L., Schulz, P., & Camerini, A.-L. (2020). Cyberbullying perpetration and victimization in youth: A meta-analysis of longitudinal studies. *Journal of Computer-Mediated Communication*, *25*. Available from https://doi.org/10.1093/jcmc/zmz031.

Martin, F., Wang, C., Petty, T., Wang, W., & Wilkins, P. (2018). Middle School Students' social media use. *Journal of Educational Technology & Society*, *21*(1), 213–224.

McInroy, L. B., & Mishna, F. (2017). Cyberbullying on online gaming platforms for children and youth. *Child and Adolescent Social Work Journal*, *34*(6), 597–607.

Menesini, E. (2012). Cyberbullying: The right value of the phenomenon. Comments on the paper "Cyberbullying: An overrated phenomenon?". *European Journal of Developmental Psychology*, *9*(5), 544–552.

Menesini, E., Nocentini, A., Palladino, B. E., Frisén, A., Berne, S., Ortega-Ruiz, R., Calmaestra, J., Scheithauer, H., Schultze-Krumbholz, A., Luik, P., Naruskov, K., Blaya, C., Berthaud, J., & Smith, P. K. (2012). Cyberbullying definition among adolescents: A comparison across six European countries. *Cyberpsychology, Behavior and Social Networking*, *15*(9), 455–463. Available from https://doi.org/10.1089/cyber.2012.0040.

Mesch, G. S., & Talmud, I. (2010). *Wired youth: The social world of adolescence in the information age*. Routledge.

Mishna, F., Cook, C., Gadalla, T., Daciuk, J., & Solomon, S. (2010). Cyber bullying behaviors among middle and high school students. *American Journal of Orthopsychiatry*, *80*(3), 362–374. Available from https://doi.org/10.1111/j.1939-0025.2010.01040.x.

Mitra, M., & Rath, P. (2017). Effect of internet on the psychosomatic health of adolescent school children in Rourkela—A cross-sectional study. *Indian Journal of Child Health*, *4* (3), 289–293. Available from https://doi.org/10.32677/IJCH.2017.v04.i03.003.

Modecki, K. L., Minchin, J., Harbaugh, A. G., Guerra, N. G., & Runions, K. C. (2014). Bullying prevalence across contexts: A meta-analysis measuring cyber and traditional bullying. *Journal of Adolescent Health*, *55*(5), 602–611.

Monks, C. P., Mahdavi, J., & Rix, K. (2016). The emergence of cyberbullying in childhood: Parent and teacher perspectives. *Psicología Educativa*, *22*(1), 39–48.

Monks, C. P., Robinson, S., & Worlidge, P. (2012). The emergence of cyberbullying: A survey of primary school pupils' perceptions and experiences. *School Psychology International*, *33*(5), 477–491.

Monks, C. P., & Smith, P. K. (2006). Definitions of bullying: Age differences in understanding of the term, and the role of experience. *British Journal of Developmental Psychology*, *24* (4), 801–821. Available from https://doi.org/10.1348/026151005X82352.

Navarro, R. (2016). *Gender issues and cyberbullying in children and adolescents: From gender differences to gender identity measures. Cyberbullying across the globe* (pp. 35–61). Springer.

Ofcom. (2019). *Children and parents: Media use and attitudes report 2019*. 36.

Ofcom. (2021). *Children and parents: Media use and attitudes report 2020/21*. 52.

O'Neill, B., & Dinh, T. (2015). Mobile technologies and the incidence of cyberbullying in seven European countries: Findings from Net Children Go Mobile. *Societies*, *5*(2), 384–398.

Online Safety Act (2023). UK Public General Acts c50. Available: www.legislation.gov.uk/ukpga/2023/50/contents/enacted. (Accessed: 15 November 2023).

Ortiz-Marcos, J. M., Tomé-Fernández, M., & Fernández-Leyva, C. (2021). Cyberbullying analysis in intercultural educational environments using binary logistic regressions. *Future Internet*, *13*(1), 15. Available from https://doi.org/10.3390/fi13010015.

Patahuddin, S. M., Rokhmah, S., & Lowrie, T. (2020). Indonesian Mathematics Teachers' and Educators' perspectives on social media platforms: The case of educational facebook groups. *The Asia-Pacific Education Researcher*, 1–10.

Patchin, J.W. (2021). Bullying During the COVID-19 Pandemic. *Cyberbullying Research Center*. Available from https://cyberbullying.org/bullying-during-the-covid-19-pandemic.

Patchin, J. W., & Hinduja, S. (2006). Bullies move beyond the schoolyard: A preliminary look at cyberbullying. *Youth Violence and Juvenile Justice*, *4*(2), 148–169.

Patchin, J. W., & Hinduja, S. (2015). Measuring cyberbullying: Implications for research. *Aggression and Violent Behavior*. Available from. Available from http://www.sciencedirect.com/science/article/pii/S1359178915000750.

Paulsen, D. J., Platt, M. L., Huettel, S. A., & Brannon, E. M. (2011). Decision-Making Under Risk in Children, Adolescents, and Young Adults. *Frontiers in Psychology*, 2.

Perren, S., & Gutzwiller-Helfenfinger, E. (2012). Cyberbullying and traditional bullying in adolescence: Differential roles of moral disengagement, moral emotions, and moral values. *European Journal of Developmental Psychology*, *9*(2), 195–209. Available from https://doi.org/10.1080/17405629.2011.643168.

Phippen, A., & Street, L. (2022a). Listening to Young People's Concerns. In A. Phippen, & L. Street (Eds.), *Online resilience and wellbeing in young people: Representing the youth voice* (pp. 43–63). Springer International Publishing. Available from https://doi.org/10.1007/978-3-030-88634-9_4.

Phippen, A., & Street, L. (2022b). *The online safeguarding landscape. Online resilience and welslbeing in young people: Representing the youth voice* (pp. 9–21). Springer International

Publishing In A. Phippen & L. Street (Eds.). Available from https://doi.org/10.1007/978-3-030-88634-9_2.

Pillay, C. L. (2012). *Behavioural and psychosocial factors associated with cyberbullying* [University of Zululand]. Available from http://196.21.83.35/handle/10530/1225.

Popovac, M. (2017). *Beyond the School Gates: Experiences of Cyberaggression and Cyberbullying Among Adolescents in the UK.* Technical Report. University of Buckingham, Buckingham.

Popovac, M., & Fine, P. (2016). Cyberbullying, online risks and parental mediation: A comparison between adolescent reports and parent perceptions in the United Kingdom and South Africa. *Poster Presented at Cyberbullying: A Challenge for Researchers and Practitioners—Prevention and Intervention, Gothenburg.*

Popovac, M., & Fine, P. (2018). *An intervention using the information-motivation-behavioral skills model: Tackling cyberaggression and cyberbullying in South African adolescents. Reducing cyberbullying in schools* (pp. 225—244). Elsevier.

Popovac, M., & Hadlington, L. (2020). Exploring the role of egocentrism and fear of missing out on online risk behaviours among adolescents in South Africa. *International Journal of Adolescence and Youth,* 25(1), 276—291.

Przybylski, A. K., Murayama, K., DeHaan, C. R., & Gladwell, V. (2013). Motivational, emotional, and behavioral correlates of fear of missing out. *Computers in Human Behavior,* 29(4), 1841—1848. Available from https://doi.org/10.1016/j.chb.2013.02.014.

Reagle, J. (2015). Following the Joneses: FOMO and conspicuous sociality. *First Monday,* 20, 10.

Rose, C. A., & Tynes, B. M. (2015). Longitudinal associations between cybervictimization and mental health among US adolescents. *Journal of Adolescent Health,* 57(3), 305—312.

Safaria, T., & Suyono, H. (2020). The role of parent-child relationship, school climate, happiness, and empathy to predict cyberbullying behavior. *International Journal of Evaluation and Research in Education,* 9(3), 548—557.

Schoenebeck, S., Scott, C. F., Hurley, E. G., Chang, T., & Selkie, E. (2021). Youth trust in social media companies and expectations of justice: Accountability and repair after online harassment. *Proceedings of the ACM on Human-Computer Interaction,* 5(CSCW1), 1-18.

Schoenebeck, S., Haimson, O. L., & Nakamura, L. (2021). Drawing from justice theories to support targets of online harassment. *New Media & Society,* 23(5), 1278—1300.

Schulz, A., Bergen, E., Schuhmann, P., Hoyer, J., & Santtila, P. (2016). Online sexual solicitation of minors: How often and between whom does it occur? *Journal of Research in Crime and Delinquency,* 53(2), 165—188.

Shakir, T., Bhandari, N., Andrews, A., Zmitrovich, A., McCracken, C., Gadomski, J., Morris, C. R., & Jain, S. (2019). Do our adolescents know they are cyberbullying victims? *Journal of Infant, Child, and Adolescent Psychotherapy (Chicago, Ill.),* 18(1), 93—101.

Steinberg, L. (2010). A dual systems model of adolescent risk-taking. Developmental Psychobiology, 52(3), 216—224.

Sincek, D. (2014). *Gender Differences In Cyber-Bullying.* Available from https://doi.org/10.5593/sgemsocial2014/B11/S1.026.

Smith, P. K., Mahdavi, J., Carvalho, M., Fisher, S., Russell, S., & Tippett, N. (2008). Cyberbullying: Its nature and impact in secondary school pupils. *Journal of Child Psychology and Psychiatry,* 49(4), 376—385.

Steinberg, L., Icenogle, G., Shulman, E. P., Breiner, K., Chein, J., Bacchini, D., et al. (2018). Around the world, adolescence is a time of heightened sensation seeking and immature self-regulation. *Developmental science,* 21(2), e12532.

Suler, J. (2004). The online disinhibition effect. *Cyberpsychology & Behavior,* 7(3), 321—326.

Tandon, A., Dhir, A., Almugren, I., AlNemer, G. N., & Mäntymäki, M. (2021). Fear of missing out (FoMO) among social media users: a systematic literature review, synthesis and framework for future research. *Internet Research,* 31(3), 782—821.

Tokunaga, R. S. (2010). Following you home from school: A critical review and synthesis of research on cyberbullying victimization. *Computers in Human Behavior, 26*(3), 277−287. Available from https://doi.org/10.1016/j.chb.2009.11.014.

Tomczyk, Ł., & Selmanagic-Lizde, E. (2018). Fear of Missing Out (FOMO) among youth in Bosnia and Herzegovina—Scale and selected mechanisms. *Children and Youth Services Review, 88*, 541−549. Available from https://doi.org/10.1016/j.childyouth.2018.03.048.

Tsitsika, A., Janikian, M., Wójcik, S., Makaruk, K., Tzavela, E., Tzavara, C., Greydanus, D., Merrick, J., & Richardson, C. (2015). Cyberbullying victimization prevalence and associations with internalizing and externalizing problems among adolescents in six European countries. *Computers in Human Behavior, 51*, 1−7.

Twyman, K., Saylor, C., Taylor, L. A., & Comeaux, C. (2010). Comparing children and adolescents engaged in cyberbullying to matched peers. *Cyberpsychology, Behavior, and Social Networking, 13*(2), 195−199. Available from https://doi.org/10.1089/cyber.2009.0137.

UK Safer Internet Centre. (2018). *Age Restrictions on Social Media Services | Safer Internet Centre.* Available from https://www.saferinternet.org.uk/blog/age-restrictions-social-media-services.

Van Geel, M., Vedder, P., & Tanilon, J. (2014). Relationship between peer victimization, cyberbullying, and suicide in children and adolescents: A meta-analysis. *JAMA Pediatrics, 168*(5), 435−442.

Wachs, S., Wright, M. F., & Vazsonyi, A. T. (2019). Understanding the overlap between cyberbullying and cyberhate perpetration: Moderating effects of toxic online disinhibition. *Criminal Behaviour and Mental Health, 29*(3), 179−188. Available from https://doi.org/10.1002/cbm.2116.

Wang, X., Zhao, F., Yang, J., & Lei, L. (2019). School climate and adolescents' cyberbullying perpetration: A moderated mediation model of moral disengagement and friends' moral identity. *Journal of Interpersonal Vsiolence, 36*(17−18), NP9601−NP9622.

Wells, M., & Mitchell, K. J. (2008). How do high-risk youth use the Internet? Characteristics and implications for prevention. *Child Maltreatment, 13*(3), 227−234.

WhatsApp. (2021). *Terms of Service.* WhatsApp.Com. Available from https://www.whatsapp.com/legal/terms-of-service/?lang = en.

Willard, N. E. (2007). *Cyberbullying and cyberthreats: Responding to the challenge of online social aggression, threats, and distress.* Research Press.

Wood, M. A., Bukowski, W. M., & Lis, E. (2016). The digital self: How social media serves as a setting that shapes youth's emotional experiences. *Adolescent Research Review, 1*(2), 163−173. Available from https://doi.org/10.1007/s40894-015-0014-8.

Wright, M. F., & Li, Y. (2012). Kicking the digital dog: A longitudinal investigation of young adults' victimization and cyber-displaced aggression. *Cyberpsychology, Behavior and Social Networking, 15*(9), 448−454. Available from https://doi.org/10.1089/cyber.2012.0061.

Wright, M. F., & Wachs, S. (2021). Does empathy and toxic online disinhibition moderate the longitudinal association between witnessing and perpetrating homophobic cyberbullying? *International Journal of Bullying Prevention, 3*(1), 66−74. Available from https://doi.org/10.1007/s42380-019-00042-6.

Yang, C., Sharkey, J. D., Reed, L. A., & Dowdy, E. (2020). Cyberbullying victimization and student engagement among adolescents: Does school climate matter? *School Psychology, 35*(2), 158−169. Available from https://doi.org/10.1037/spq0000353.

Zhu, C., Huang, S., Evans, R., & Zhang, W. (2021). Cyberbullying among adolescents and children: A comprehensive review of the global situation, risk factors, and preventive measures. *Frontiers in Public Health, 9.* Available from https://doi.org/10.3389/fpubh.2021.634909.

Zsila, Á., Urbán, R., Griffiths, M. D., & Demetrovics, Z. (2019). Gender differences in the association between cyberbullying victimization and perpetration: The role of anger rumination and traditional bullying experiences. *International Journal of Mental Health and Addiction, 17*(5), 1252–1267. Available from https://doi.org/10.1007/s11469-018-9893-9.

Zych, I., Baldry, A. C., Farrington, D. P., & Llorent, V. J. (2019). Are children involved in cyberbullying low on empathy? A systematic review and meta-analysis of research on empathy versus different cyberbullying roles. *Aggression and Violent Behavior, 45*, 83–97. Available from https://doi.org/10.1016/j.avb.2018.03.004.

Zych, I., Beltrán-Catalán, M., Ortega-Ruiz, R., & Llorent, V. J. (2018). Social and emotional competencies in adolescents involved in different bullying and cyberbullying roles. *Revista de Psicodidáctica (English Ed.), 23*(2), 86–93. Available from https://doi.org/10.1016/j.psicoe.2017.12.001.

## Further reading

Campbell, M., Spears, B., Slee, P., Butler, D., & Kift, S. (2012). Victims' perceptions of traditional and cyberbullying, and the psychosocial correlates of their victimisation. *Emotional and Behavioural Difficulties, 17*(3–4), 389–401.

CHAPTER TWO

# Cyberbullying: problematic internet behaviors among children and youths

**Seda Gökçe Turan**[1,2]
[1]Department of Educational Sciences, Bahçeşehir University, Turkey
[2]Department of Cyberpsychology, Bournemouth University, Poole, United Kingdom

## Contents

Despite the benefits of Internet and social media for children and youths, it is considered a risky environment in terms of cyberbullying, problematic Internet use, digital harassment, and digital addiction (Vlaanderen et al., 2020: 1). Moreover, pathological online behaviors (digital addiction, cyberbullying, cyberstalking, etc.) are evaluated as public health concern with regard to adverse cognitive, developmental, psychological, and physical consequences (Lee et al., 2019:568). Understanding problem behaviors in online environments is vital for protecting children and youths in both online and offline environments. According to research (Schimmenti et al., 2019: 328), there is a strong correlation between online and offline behaviors, especially in terms of cyberbullying and other digital harassment behaviors. It means that cyberbullying and other problematic Internet use are global psychosocial problems; they are not only related with online environments, they also need to be addressed in depth.

In the light of the information in the literature, dimensions, nature, and consequences of problematic Internet behaviors, digital harassment and cyberbullying among children and youths will be discussed.

*Handbook of Social Media Use Online Relationships, Security, Privacy, and Society, Volume 2*
DOI: https://doi.org/10.1016/B978-0-443-28804-3.00004-1

## Methodology

In order to discuss problematic Internet use and cyberbullying, "Narrative Review" will be used as research method. Rother (2007: 1) defined scientific literature review articles as "methodological studies which use database searches to retrieve results of research and have as their main goal to objective and theoretical discussion of a specific topic or theme." Accordingly, the general literature about children and youths' problematic Internet behaviors and cyberbullying has been searched.

## Research literature

### Problematic internet use

In order to understand cyberbullying and digital harassment, problematic Internet use among children and youths should be explained. Problematic Internet use is an issue related with mental health, offline problematic and aggressive behaviors, and psychopathological and health problems. In general, problematic Internet use is defined as failure to control excessive urges or behaviors regarding Internet use (Weinstein, Feder, Rosenberg, & Dannon, 2014: 99). Other researchers (Sela, Zach, Amichay-Hamburger, Mishali, & Omer, 2020: 2) frame problematic Internet use as an excessive use of the Internet, which is associated with impaired functioning.

Problematic Internet use has three dimensions, which are neglect, obsession, and control disorder (Kuss & Griffiths, 2011: 3528; Asam, Samara, & Terry, 2019: 428). According to findings (Asam et al., 2019: 428), problematic Internet use is associated with conduct problems, hyperactivity, depressive symptoms, and negative impact on daily functions and physical health of children and adolescents. These findings are like cyberbullying behaviors' consequences (Cao, Khan, Ali, & Khan, 2020: 1343), which we will discuss soon.

In terms of factors that trigger problematic Internet use, findings (Smahel et al., 2008; Sela et al., 2020) show that family environment and social lives of youths have a great impact on children and youths' problematic Internet use. Sela et al. (2020) noted that especially families characterized with low expressiveness, low cohesion, and intense conflicts are correlated with problematic Internet use of children and youths. In addition, according to the same study, a positive family environment could decrease depressive symptoms among adolescents, and it could lead to diminishing problematic Internet use and time spent online. There is another factor that affect problematic Internet use: gender. However, there are different findings about the relationship between gender and problematic Internet use. Asam et al. (2019: 428) noted that males are more likely than females to develop problematic Internet use. However, (Gomez, 2017) (2017) found that females are more likely to experience problematic Internet use. In addition, problematic Internet use and behaviors have different subtitles like cyberstalking and revenge pornography and image-based abuse, which are also the subject of this chapter.

Cyberstalking encompasses repeated threats, harassments, or pursuit of an individual through electronic devices, which make the victim fear for his or her safety (DreBing, Bailer, Anders, Wagner, & Gallas, 2014: 61; Strawhun, Adams, & Huss, 2013: 176). Basically, cyberstalking is characterized with repeated unwanted electronic communication in which the perpetrator wants to make victim alarm or distress (Livingstone et al., 2019: 44). According to findings (Livingstone et al., 2019: 40), most of the victims of cyberstalking are female, whereas most of the perpetrators are male.

The impact of cyberstalking on victims includes a continued state of anxiety or fear, paranoia, hurt, anger, and depression (DreBing et al., 2014; Golladay & Holtfreter, 2017; Jansen van Rensburg, 2017; Worsley, Wheatcroft, Short, & Corcoran, 2017). Additionally, Maran and Begotti (2019) defined not only emotional but also physical symptoms such as sleep disorders, agoraphobia, tiredness, and headaches. Some victims reported that they felt powerless and socially isolated after cyberstalking. According to Livingstone et al. (2019: 44), victims of cyberstalking mostly reported anger and irritation. For defending themselves, victims noted that they would change their addresses or phone number and deactivate their social media accounts (Nobles, Reyns, Fox, & Fisher, 2014: 986).

The other digital harassment type is revenge pornography, which encompasses nonconsensual sharing of sexual images. Most of the adolescent women were threatened by their ex-partner to share their private videos or images at social media. The motivation of the perpetrator is "revenge," and the perpetrator can create sexual images and videos or share sexual images of the victim without permission (Scheller, 2015;

Scott & Gavin, 2018; Walker & Sleath, 2017). In some cases, the motivation of the perpetrator can change, and the perpetrator would want to control or exact the victim both physically and financially (Livingstone et al., 2019: 45). In order to quickly go viral, perpetrators mostly post the sexual images on porn websites (Griftith, 2016). Due to characteristics of porn websites, those images can be reposted, and for the victims, it is impossible to erase porn sites because it may spread to one site to another (Kamal & Newman, 2016).

The impacts of revenge porn on victims are similar sexual harassment. The perpetrators mostly post the sexual images, contact details, and personal information of victims on porn websites, which may lead to secondary victimization or sexual victimization (Franklin, 2014; Souza, 2016).

There are some digital harassments different from revenge porn. They are image-based abuse. In this type of harassment, perpetrators take a picture up a young women's skirt at public places (transportation, university, supermarket, etc.) and post those photos on porn sites or social media. Maybe they cannot spread personal information of young women, but women feel fear or anxiety when they are at public places (McGlynn & Rackley, 2017). Additionally, some type of image-based abuse some victim's experiences further victimization through perpetrators doctor their online photograph and spread in digital environments (D'Amico & Steinberger, 2015).

Researchers warn about implications of revenge porn for victims (Franklin, 2014; Kamal & Newman, 2016; Livingstone et al., 2019; McGlynn & Rackley, 2017; Scheller, 2015). Because revenge porn makes victims embarrassed and ashamed, they mostly lose their control and damage their mental health. From a psychological perspective, victims of revenge porn suffer from anger, isolation, and powerlessness. Moreover, being a victim of revenge porn may have a damaging effect on their dignity, self-esteem, or self-worth, which may lead to deterioration of education, employment, or career (Bustamante, 2017; Kamal & Newman, 2016; D'Amico & Steinberger, 2015) As a result of this, they experience depression, self-blame, or even suicide. Walker and Sleath (2017) also noted that substance abuse is highly associated with revenge porn, which could be reflected in Bustamante (2017: 364)'s description of revenge porn as "mental torture."

To conclude, in contrast to young male victims, young female victims describe digital harassment as being an extremely and very upsetting experience. The impacts of digital harassment on young women can range from mental or emotional stress to financial loss. The most "seen" consequence of digital harassments (cyberstalking, cyberbullying, or revenge porn) is anxiety (Livingstone et al., 2019).

There are some serious consequences of digital harassment on young women. As consequences of image-based abuse, women's reputation and dignity may be damaged. As Bloom (2014: 242) noted, sexual online photographs or images can destroy a young woman's career, education, or employment at her adult ages.

As result of cyberstalking and revenge porn, victims cannot feel free both at public places and in their private house (Bloom, 2014; McGlynn & Rackley, 2017). Revenge porn victims reported ruination of their self-image and future relationships and may be subjected to offline harassment (Livingstone et al., 2019: 59). In order to fight against digital harassment toward children and adolescents, we should not forget that these harassments do not occur only in online environments. They also occur at public environments and real world. Besides the problematic Internet use, there is another one, which is so common among children and adolescents.

## Cyberbullying behaviors among children and youths

Despite the fact that Internet has become an integral part of daily life and people have concern about effects of Internet, there is still a gap between understanding serious consequences of Internet and positive effects of it. Firstly, we should underline the positive benefits of the Internet. It provides easy access to information, which is vital for education, global communication, and provision of entertainment (Sela et al., 2020: 1). Despite the role of Internet's positive effects on individuals' lives, the frequent use of Internet also brings new risks and challenges like cyberbullying and digital harassment into children and youths' lives (Yang, Wang, Gao, & Wang, 2021: 1). Before defining the frame of cyberbullying, it would be better to define digital harassment, which is an umbrella term for cyberbullying.

Digital harassment includes a broad spectrum of intentional and repeated abusive and annoying behaviors, which are conducted by technological devices and used to target a specific user or users (Blackwell, Dimond, Schoenebeck, & Lampe, 2017). Digital harassment encompasses some behaviors such as flaming, doxing, and impersonation. Flaming is kind of behavior that is characterized by using provocative language toward a victim, such as name calling or being insulting. Doxing, which is another type of digital harassment, includes identifiable personal information of victims such as home or work addresses or private telephone number at public places and digital environments. The last type of digital harassment is impersonation, in which a perpetrator tries to harm the reputation of the victim though using the victim's photo or video without consent (Blackwell et al., 2017).

The main types of digital harassment are offensive name calling, purposeful embarrassment, physical threats, sustained harassment, cyberstalking, and sexual harassment. Moreover, according to the same report, younger adults are more likely to be victims of digital harassment. Researchers argued that it would be linked with the time spent online (Livingstone et al., 2019: 21).

It has been observed that online harassment has increased over time (Powell, Scott, & Henry, 2018; Rodriguez-Rodriguez & Heras-Gonzalez,2020; Megarry, 2014). As result of this, efforts have been made to try to find prevention strategies for online harassment. Firstly, as researchers noted (D'Amico & Steinberger, 2015), victims of online harassment are more likely to be subjected to real-world harassments. So strategies should be developed and applied not only for digital environments but also for real life. Moreover, the characteristics of groups which are more likely to be subject to online harassment both as victim and perpetrator are an important issue. Perpetrators of digital harassment are usually somebody that victim knows (Megarry, 2014). Also, there are other perpetrators who only have a relationship with the victim through social media or other digital tools. The umbrella term of digital harassment is composed of different types of harassment such as cyberbullying.

Cyberbullying is a form of aggressive behavior that is acted intentionally and repeatedly carried out in digital environments against a person or group who cannot easily defend themselves (Kowalski, Giumetti, Schroeder, & Lattanner, 2014). Willard (2007) framed cyberbullying with eight categories. These categories are as follows: Flaming, denigration, impersonation, outing, trickery, exclusion, harassment, and stalking.

Under the umbrella of cyberbullying, most common behaviors are sending offensive e-mails and posting on social media defamatory gossip or victims' private or personal details (Oksanen, Oksa, Savela, Kaakinen ve Ellonen, 2020: 1; Livingstone et al., 2019: 38; Zapf & Gross, 2001: 498). Cyberbullying is a source of possible serious psychological, emotional, and social disturbances (Canet, Blais, Lavoie, Caron, & Hebert, 2018; Golladay & Holtfreter, 2017). When taking into consideration the developmental characteristics, these effects could lead to even suicide among teenagers due to dramatization of most of the peer acts. Additionally, these effects increase the risks of revictimization and bullying (Maran & Begotti, 2019; Patchin & Hinduja, 2006).

Cyberbullying is associated with many different factors, so overall findings of research may not cover every child and youth. For example, according to the different studies, cyberbullying is related to empathy, anger management, and low self-esteem in terms of perpetrators of cyberbullying. This means that perpetrators are not only empathizing with their victims but also with other people, while experiencing difficulties in anger control, and their self-esteem is lower than their peers. Not only characteristics of victims and perpetrators but also peers are effective for cyberbullying behaviors. Yang et al. (2021) noted that deviant peer affiliation is an important factor to predict cyberbullying perpetration, which is very important for peer relationships. As developmental characteristics, youths give importance to peer relationships and can copy the behaviors of others. So, their deviant peer affiliation could affect their perception and action related with cyberbullying.

When taking into consideration effects of cyberbullying among children and youths, researchers noted that (Oksanen, Oksa, Savela, Kaakinen, & Ellonen, 2020: 1; Farley, Coyne, & D'Cruz, 2018: 3; Forssell, 2020: 454) victims of cyberbullying can experience the same feelings such as fear, intimidation, and stress with victims of face-to-face bullying. Moreover, cyber-victims suffer more from depression, substance abuse (Ybarra, Boyd, Korchmaros, & Oppenheim, 2012), school failure, bringing sharp or dangerous tools (weapons, knives, etc.) to school, academic underachievement, lower self-esteem, and social isolation (Ybarra et al., 2012). In terms of cyberbullying perpetrators (Wright, Wachs, & Harper, 2018; You & Lee, 2019), they suffer from physical and mental health problems, depression, stress, and sleep disturbances (Aktepe, 2013; Deheu, Bolman, & Völlink, 2008). There is another point also: duality of cyberbullying, which means two completely opposite roles, being a cyber-victim and cyber-bully at the same time (Lozano-Blasco, Cortes-Pascual, & Latorre-Martinez, 2020: 1). It was found that this status of being both a perpetrator and victim of cyberbullying was typically found in females with unstable family links, and this duality lead to anxiety, depression, and aggression. When we consider the physical and psychological consequences of cyberbullying, digital harassment, and problematic Internet use, they are similar: sleep disturbance, depression, anxiety, or fear.

There is another important dimension of cyberbullying: humor. Humor is generally seen as a trigger factor in traditional/face-to face bullying. However, Steer, Betts, Baguley, and Binder (2020) argued that young people have a shared understanding of online humoristic aggressive behaviors such as online banter. These types of behaviors are ambiguous and difficult to interpret. This means that both perpetrators and victims cannot easily understand that they are subject to cyberbullying.

Because of the nature of cyberbullying, like most of the other online harassments, generally perpetrators know the victims (Craker & March, 2016), and this acquaintance can be interpreted that youths are mostly cyberbullied by the perpetrators that they knew from school or real life. Although cyberbullying is generally characterized among students and youths (Livingstone et al., 2019: 36; Smith *et al.* 2008: 376), according to recent studies, cyberbullying is quite common among young adults also (Ramos & Bennett, 2016). According to findings (Kwan et al., 2020: 1), 20%–40% of adolescents had experienced cyber-victimization at least once. So, while searching about cyberbullying among children and youths, we have to take into consideration that these cyberbullying behaviors could be last till adulthood of the victims. To conclude, cyberbullying is a psychosocial phenomenon that has psychological and physical consequences for both victims and perpetrators.

## Solutions and conclusion

Problematic Internet use such as Internet addiction, cyberbullying, trolling, or online gambling can adversely affect psychological development of children and youths in the context of maladaptive personality features, insecure attachment dispositions, and difficulties in development physical health (Schimmenti, Musetti, Costanzo et al., 2019: 447). Not only problematic Internet use but also long hours of Internet use can negatively affect daily lives of children and adolescents in terms of school, family interactions, psychological well-being, and physical health (Smahel, Blinka, & Ledabyl, 2008; Young & De Abreu, 2011 cited in Asam et al., 2019: 429). So, it is normal that parents and researchers have concerns about the effects of Internet use.

For protection of children and youths from cyberbullying and other problematic Internet use, "digital citizenship" could be considered as a solution. However, firstly, the bystander effect should be explained.

Beginning from early ages, if pupils know how to survive and use digital environments, it would be helpful in their adulthood. Learning how to survive in the digital environments and protect themselves from perpetrators are effective protection methods and can be gained through digital citizenship skills. However, digital harassment is a phenomenon that cannot be explained just with "technical" or "social" factors. It has a psychological layer that is related to victims' personal characteristics. Digital citizenship skills provide an opportunity to users to involve in digital environments and build their self-identity. Not as a short-term, but as a long-term protection method, digital citizenship skills would be useful for reducing digital harassment impacts (Emejulu, McGregor, 2019; Gleason & Gillern, 2018). According to Vlaanderen et al. (2020), it is beneficial and effective to increase children's awareness about intervening cyberbullying in order to combat with a cyberbullying event. They argued that it in order to make children to intervene in cyberbullying events, their digital citizenship skills should be empowered. Jones and Mitchell (2016: 2063) also stated that digital citizenship has a key role in understanding youths' online behaviors and protecting them from risks and danger of online environments. Regarding the education setting, Hollandsworth, Donovan, and Welch (2017: 524) noted the need for awareness and education of digital citizenship issues to begin in the early grades. Gleason and Gillern (2018: 200) have made it clearer which digital citizenship skills to teach. In their opinion, it is critical for children and youths to develop digital citizenship skills to find, evaluate, and share information responsibly and engage in constructive conversation with others from diverse backgrounds. Moreover, with better digital citizenship skills, adults and teachers can ensure their online participation is safe, ethical, and legal.

It is obvious that information and communication technologies make our lives easier, but these technologies also make it easier to harass others. So, researchers in this field advice developing digital citizenship skills in order to protect children and youths from cyberbullying through gaining awareness about them in the digital world, trolls, perpetrators, and digital law.

## References

Aktepe, E. (2013). Cyberbullying and cybervictimization among adolescents. *New Symposium Journal*, *51*(1), 31–36.

Asam, A. E., Samara, M., & Terry, P. (2019). Problematic Internet use and mental health among British children and adolescents. *Addictive Behaviors, 90*, 428−436.

Blackwell, L., Dimond, J., Schoenebeck, S., & Lampe, C. (2017). Classification and Its consequences for online-design insights from heartmob. *PACM on Human-Computer Interaction, 1*(24), 1−19.

Bloom, S. (2014). No vengeance for revenge porn victims: Unravelling why this latest female-centric, intimate-partner offense is still legal, and why we should criminalized it. *F Fordham University School of Law Journal, 42*, 233−289.

Bustamante, D. (2017). Analysis of Florida's new anti-revenge porn law. *FIU Law Review, 12*(2), 357−390.

Craker, N., & March, E. (2016). The dark side of facebook: The dark tetrad, negative social potency, and trolling behaviors'. *Personality and Individual Differences, 102*, 79−84.

Canet, J. M., Blais, M., Lavoie, F., Caron, P. O., & Hebert, M. (2018). Cyberbullying victimization and substance use among Quebec high schools students: The mediating role of psychological distress. *Computer in Human Behavior, 89*, 207−212.

Cao, X., Khan, A. N., Ali, A., & Khan, N. A. (2020). Consequences of cyberbullying and social overload while using SNSs: A study of users' discontinuous usage behavior in SNSs. *Information Systems Frontiers, 22*, 1343−1356.

D'Amico, D., & Steinberger, L. (2015). Fighting for online privacy with digital weaponry: Combating revenge pornography. *NYSBA Entertainment, Arts and Sports Law Journal, 26*(2), 24−36.

Deheu, F., Bolman, C., & Völlink, T. (2008). Cyberbullying: Youngsters' experiences and parental perception. *Cyberpsychology & Behavior, 11*(2), 217−223.

DreBing, H., Bailer, J., Anders, A., Wagner, H., & Gallas, C. (2014). Cyberstalking in a large sample of social network users: Prevalence, characteristics, and impact upon victims. *Cyberpsychology, Behavior, and Social Networking, 17*(2), 61−67.

Emejulu, A., & McGregor, C. (2019). Towards a radical digital citizenship in digital education. *Critical Studies in Education, 60*(1), 131−147.

Farley, S., Coyne, L., & D'Cruz, P. (2018). Cyberbullying at work: Understanding the influence of technology. In D'Cruz (Ed.), *Concepts, approaches and methods, handbooks of workplace bullying, emotional abuse and harassment 1* (pp. 1−31). Springer Nature Singapore Pte Ltd.

Forssell, R. C. (2020). Gender and organisational position: Predicting victimisation of cyberbullying behaviour in working life. *The International Journal of Human Resource Management, 31*(16), 2045−2064.

Franklin, Z. (2014). *Justice for revenge porn victims: Legal theories to overcome claims of civil immunity by operators of revenge porn websites* (pp. 1303−1335). California Law Review.

Gleason, B., & Gillern, S. V. (2018). Digital citizenship with social media: Participatory practices of teaching and learning in secondary education. *Journal of Educational Technology & Society, 21*(1), 200−212.

Golladay, K., & Holtfreter, K. (2017). The consequences of identity theft victimization: An examination of emotional and physical health outcomes. *Victims & Offenders, 12*(5), 741−760.

Gomez, P., et al. (2017). Screening of problematic internet use among Spanish adolescents: prevalence and related variables. *Cyberpsychol Behav Soc Netw, 20*(4), 259−267, In this issue. Available from https://doi.org/10.1089/cyber.2016.0262.

Griftith, V. N. (2016). Smartphones, nude snaps, and legal looholes: Why pennsylvania needs to amend its revenge porn statute. *Pittsburgh Journal of Technology Law and Policy, 16*(2), 1−21.

Hollandsworth, R., Donovan, J., & Welch, M. (2017). Digital citizenship: You can't go home again. *TechTrends, 61*, 524−530.

Jansen van Rensburg, S. (2017). Unwanted attention: The psychological impact of cyber-stalking on its survivors. *Journal of Psychology in Africa*, *27*(3), 273–276.

Jones, L. M., & Mitchell, K. J. (2016). Defining and measuring youth digital citizenship. *New Media & Society*, *18*(9), 2063–2079.

Kamal, M., & Newman, W. J. (2016). Revenge pornography: Menatl health implications and related legistation. *Journal of the American Academy of Psychiatry and Law Online, 44* (3), 359–367.

Kowalski, R., Giumetti, G., Schroeder, A., & Lattanner, M. (2014). Bullying in the digital age: A critical review and meta-analysis of cyberbullying research among youth'. *Psycohological Bulletin*, *140*(4), 1073–1137.

Kuss, D. J., & Griffiths, M. D. (2011). Online social networking and addiction- A review of the psychological literature. *International Journal of Environmental Research and Public Health, 8*, 3528–3552.

Kwan, I., Dickson, K., Richardson, M., MacDowall, W., Burchett, H., Stansfield, C., … Thomas, J. (2020). Cyberbullying and children and young people's mental health: A systematic map of systematic reviews. *Cyberpsychology, Behavior, and Social Networking*. Available from https://doi.org/10.1089/cyber.2019.0370.

Lee, S. Y., Kim, M. S., & Lee, H. K. (2019). Prevention strategies and interventions for internet use disorders due to addictive behaviors based on an integrative conceptual model. *Current Addiction Reports, 6*, 303–312.

Livingstone, S., Jenkins, S., Gekoski, A., Choak, C., Ike, T., & Philips, K. (2019). *Adult online hate, harassment and abuse: A rapid evidence assessment*. London, UK: UK Council for Child Internet Safety.

Lozano-Blasco, R., Cortes-Pascual, A., & Latorre-Martinez, M. P. (2020). Being a cyber-victim and a cyberbully — The duality of cyberbullying: A meta-analysis. *Computers in Human Behavior, 111*, 1–10.

Maran, D. A., & Begotti, T. (2019). Prevalence of cyberstalking and previous offline victimization in a sample of Italian University Students. *Social Sciences, 8*(30), 1–10.

McGlynn, C., & Rackley, E. (2017). Image-based sexual abuse. *Oxford Journal of Legal Studies, 37*(3), 534–561.

Megarry, J. (2014). Online incivility or sexual harassment? Conceptualising Women's experiences in the digital age. *Women's Studies International Forum, 47*, 46–55.

Nobles, M. R., Reyns, B. W., Fox, K. A., & Fisher, B. S. (2014). Protection against pur-suir: A conceptual and emprical comparison of cyberstalking and stalking victimization among a national sample. *Justice Quarterly, 31*(6), 986–1014.

Oksanen, A., Oksa, R., Savela, N., Kaakinen, M., & Ellonen, N. (2020). Cyberbullying victimization at work: Social media identity bubble approcah. *Computers in Human Behavior, 109*, 1–11.

Powell, A., Scott, A. J., & Henry, N. (2018). Digital harassment and abuse: Experiences of sexuality and gender minority adults. *European Journal of Criminology*, 1–25.

Ramos, M., & Bennett, D. (2016). *Cyberbullying: Who hurts and why* (pp. 20–25). Psychiatric Times.

Rodriguez-Rodriguez, I., & Heras-Gonzalez, P. (2020). How are universities using information and communication technologies to face sexual harassment and how can they improve? *Technology in Society, 62*, 1–8.

Rother, E. T. (2007). Systematic literature review X narrative review. *Acta Paul Enferm, 20*(2).

Schimmenti, A., Musetti, A., Costanzo, A., Terrone, G., Maganuco, N. R., Rinella, C. A., & Gervasi, A. M. (2019). The unfabulous four: Maladaptive personality functioning, insecure attachment, dissociative experiences, and problematic internet use among young adults. *International Journal of Mental Health and Addiction, 19*, 447–461.

Scheller, S. H. (2015). A picture is worth a thousand words: The legal implications of revenge porn. *North Carolina Law Review*, *93*(2), 551−595.

Scott, A. J., & Gavin, J. (2018). Revenge pornography: The influence of perpetrator-victim sex, observer sexting experience on perceptions of seriousness and responsibility. *Journal of Criminal Psychology*, *8*(2), 162−172.

Sela, Y., Zach, M., Amichay-Hamburger, Y., Mishali, M., & Omer, H. (2020). Family environment and problematic internet use among adolescents: The mediating roles of depression and fear of missing out. *Computers in Human Behvaior*, *106*, 1−9.

Smahel, D., Blinka, L., & Ledabyl, O. (2008). Playing MMORPGs: Connections between addiction and identifying with a character. *Cyberpsychology & Behavior*, *11*(6), 715−718.

Smith, P. K., Mahdavi, J., Carvalho, M., Fisher, S., Russell, S., & Tippett, N. (2008). Cyberbullying: Its nature and impact in secondary schools pupils. *Journal of Child Psychology and Psychiatry*, *49*, 376−385.

Souza, E. (2016). For his eyes only: Why federal legislation is needed to combat revenge porn. *UCLA Women's Law Journal*, *23*, 101−129.

Strawhun, J., Adams, N., & Huss, M. T. (2013). The assessment of cyberstalking: An expanded examination including social networking, attachment, jealousy, and anger in relation to violence and abuse. *Violence and Victims*, *28*(4), 715−730.

Vlaanderen, A., Bevelander, K. E., & Kleemans, M. (2020). Empowering digital citizenship: An anti-cyberbullying intervention to increase children's intentions to intervene on behalf of the victim. *Computers in Human Behavior*, *112*, 1−11.

Walker, K., & Sleath, E. (2017). A systematic review of the current knowledge regarding revenge pornography and non-consensual sharing of sexually explicit media. *Aggression and Violent Behavior*, *36*, 9−24.

Weinstein, A., Feder, L. C., Rosenberg, K. P., & Dannon, P. (2014). Internet addiction disorder: Overview and controversies. In K. P. Rosenberg, & L. C. Feder (Eds.), *Behavioral addictions: Criteria, evidence, and treatment* (pp. 99−116). London, UK: Elsevier.

Willard, N. E. (2007). *Cyberbullying and cyberthreats: Responding to the challenge on online aggression, threats, and distress*. Chicago: LLC.

Worsley, J.D., Wheatcroft, J., Short, E., & Corcoran, R. (2017). Victims' voices: Understanding the emotional impact of cyberstalking and individuals' coping responses, DOI: 10.1177/2158244017710292.

Wright, M. F., Wachs, S., & Harper, B. D. (2018). The moderation of empathy in the longitudinal association between witnessing cyberbullying, depression, and anxiety. *Cyberpsychology: Journal of Psychosocial Research on Cyberspace*, *12*(4), 1−6, Article 6.

Yang, J., Wang, N., Gao, L., & Wang, X. (2021). Deviant peer affiliation and adolescents' cyberbullying perpetration: Online disinhibition and perceived social support as moderators. *Children and Youth Services Review*, *127*, 1−8.

Ybarra, L. M., Boyd, D., Korchmaros, J. D., & Oppenheim, J. K. (2012). Defining and measuring cyberbullying within the larger context of bullying victimization. *Journal of Adolescent Health*, *51*, 53−58.

You, L., & Lee, Y. H. (2019). The bystander effect in cyberbullying on social network sites: Anonymity, group size, and intervention intentions. *Telematics and Informatics*, *45*, 1−13.

Zapf, D., & Gross, C. (2001). Conflict escalation and coping with workplace bullying: A replication and extension. *European Journal of Work and Organizational Psychology*, *10*(4), 497−522.

## Further reading

Anderson, K. E. (2018). Getting acquainted with social networks and apps: Combating fake news on social media. *Library HiTech News*, *35*(3), 1−6.

Blaauw, E., Winkel, F. W., Arensman, E., Sheridan, L., & Freeve, A. (2002). The toll of stalking: The relationship between features of stalking and psychopathology of victims. *Journal of Interpersonal Violence, 17,* 50−63.

Borrajo, E., Gamez-Guadiz, M., & Calvete, E. (2015). Justification beliefs of violence, myths about love and cyber dating abuse. *Psicothema, 27*(4), 327−333.

Edwards, K., Desai, A. D., Gidyez, C. A., & VanWynsberghe, A. (2009). College women's aggression in relationships: The role of childhood and adolescent victimization. *Psychology of Women Quarterly, 33,* 255−256.

Flynn, D. J., Nyhan, B., & Reifler, J. (2017). The nature and origins of misperceptions: Understanding false and unsupported beliefs about politics. *Political Psychology, 38,* 127−150.

Frenda, S. J., Knowles, E. D., Saletan, W., & Loftus, E. F. (2013). False memories of fabricated political events. *Journal of Experimental Social Psychology, 49*(2), 280−286.

Frommholtz, I., Al-Khateeb, H. M., Potthast, M., Ghasem, Z., Shukla, M., & Short, E. (2016). On textual analysis and machine learning for cyberstalking detection. *Datenbank- Spektrum, 16*(2), 127−135.

Ghosn-Chelala, M. (2019). Exploring sustainable learning and practice of digital citizenship: Education and place-based challenges. *Education, Citizenship and Social Justice, 14* (1), 40−56.

Gómez, P., Rial, A., Braña, T., Golpe, S., & Varela, J. (2017). Screening of problematic internet use among spanish adolescents: Prevalence and related variables. *Cyberpsychology, Behavior, and Social Networking, 20*(4), 259−267.

Hasan, H. R., & Salah, K. (2019). Combating deepfake videos using blockchain and smart contracts. *IEEE Access, 7,* 41596−41606.

Hinduja, S., & Patchin, J. (2010). *Sexting: A brief guide for educators and parents* (pp. 1−4). Cyberbullying Research Center.

Hintz, A., Dencik, L., & Wahl-Jorgensen, K. (2017). Digital citizenship and surveillance society. *Internation Journal of Communication, 11,* 731−739.

Kim, M., & Choi, D. (2018). Development of youth digital citizenship scale and implication for educational setting. *Journal of Educational Technology & Society, 21*(1), 155−171.

Kowalski, R. M., & Limber, S. P. (2007). Electronic bullying among middle school students. *Journal of Adolescent Health, 41*(6), S22−S30.

Laar, E. V., Deursen, A. J. A. M. V., Dijk, J. A. G. M. V., & Haan, J. D. (2017). The relation between 21st-century skills and digital skills: A systematic literature review. *Computers in Human Behavior, 72,* 577−588.

Livingstone, S., Olafsson, K., Helsper, E. J., Lupinaz-Villanueva, F., Veltri, G. A., & Folkvord, F. (2017). Maximizing opportunities and minimizing risks for children online: The role of digital skills in emerging strategies of parental mediation. *Journal of Communication, 67,* 82−105.

Mitchell, K. J., Ybarra, M., & Finkelhor, D. (2007). The relative importance of online victimization in understanding depression, delinquency and substance use. *Child Maltreatment, 12*(4), 314−324.

Mossberger, K., Tolbert, C. J., & McNeal, R. S. (2008). *Digital citizenship: The internet, society and participation.* The MIT Press USA.

Ohler, J. (2011). Digital citizenship means character education for the digital age. *Kappa Delta Pi Record, 47*(1), 25−27.

Raskauskas, J., & Stoltz, A. D. (2007). Involvement in traditional and electronic bullying among adolescents. *Developmental Psychology, 43,* 564−575.

Ribble, M. (2012). Digital citizenship for educational change. *Kappa Delta Pi Record, 48* (4), 148−151.

Tarzia, L., Cornelio, R., Forsdike, K., & Hegarty, K. (2018). Women's experiences receiving support online for intimate partner violence: How does it compare to face-to-face support from a health professional? *Interacting with Computers, 30*(5), 433–443.

Twyman, K., Saylor, C., Taylor, L. A., & Comeaux, C. (2010). Comparing children and adolescents engaged in cyberbullying to matched peers. *Cyberpsychology, Behavior and Social Networking, 13*(2), 195–199.

Vaccari, C., & Chadwick, A. (2020). Deepfakes and disinformation: Exploring the impact of synthetic political video on deception. *Uncertainty, and Trust in News, Social Media + Society,* 1–13.

Vromen, A. (2017). *Digital citizenship and political engagement. Digital citizenship and political engagement. interest groups, advocacy and democracy series.* London: Palgrave Macmillan.

Walters, M. G., Gee, D., & Mohammed, S. (2019). A literature review: Digital citizenship and the elementary educator. *International Journal of Technology in Education (IJTE), 2* (1), 1–21.

Whyte, C. (2020). Deepfake news: AI-enabled disinformation as a multi-level public policy challenge. *Journal of Cyber-Policy, 5,* 199–217.

Woodlock, D. (2017). The abuse of technology in domestic violence and stalking. *Violence Against Women, 23*(5), 584–602.

Xu, S., Yang, H. H., Macleod, J., & Zhu, S. (2019). Social media competence and digital citizenship among college students, convergence. *The International Journal of Research into New Media Technologies, 25*(4), 735–752, 2019.

Yue, A., Nekmat, E., & Beta, A. R. (2019). Digital literacy through digital citizenship: Online civic participation and public opinion evaluation of Youth Minorities in Southeast Asia. *Media and Communication, 7*(2), 100–114.

CHAPTER THREE

# Participation and nonparticipation in cyberbullying: a semiotic exploration on a Twitter encounter among young digital natives

## Charity T. Turano[1] and Jean A. Saludadez[2]
[1]University of San Carlos, Cebu City, Philippines
[2]University of the Philippines — Open University, Los Baños, Laguna, Philippines

## Contents

## Introduction

With the rise of social media such as Facebook, Instagram, Twitter, and other emerging cyberspace communication platforms, digital communication has become a prevalent topic of interest by a number of scholars. Themes of these studies cover both benefits and risks in cyberspace interactions.

*Handbook of Social Media Use Online Relationships, Security, Privacy, and Society, Volume 2*
DOI: https://doi.org/10.1016/B978-0-443-28804-3.00012-0

One of the popularly identified negative communicative acts happening in social media and which continues to be a major concern investigated by a number of scholars is cyberbullying (e.g., Asanan, 2017; Athanasiades, 2016; Hase, 2015; Hinduja & Patchin, 2012; Navarro, 2017). These studies define cyberbullying as any aggressive, intentional act carried out by a group or individual, using electronic forms of contact, against a victim who cannot easily defend oneself. Cyberbullying is stereotypically carried out continually and over time where imbalance of power is present among individuals. The one who is seemingly more powerful by authority, economic status, physical attributes, and other superior abilities is the usual perpetrator of the act.

However, alongside the evolution of human activities, there is a likelihood of communication events to go through alterations of accepted views of certain communicative acts such as cyberbullying. For instance, contrary to the popular definition, which emphasized that the more "powerful" is the initiator, someone who is not necessarily more "superior" in status compared to the victim may instigate cyberbullying. As for frequency, this attack may not necessarily be repeated, but may be a one-time mob event. Bullying in social media is known to be common among young people who target their peers or even someone who is known to be more powerful by status.

A popular communication tradition used as a lens to examine cyberbullying among young individuals is the Sociopsychological Tradition of Communication Theory, where the individual as a social being, one's social behavior, the psychological variables constituting the individual personalities, perception, and cognition are the focus of the study. Examples of these investigations explore impacts of cyberbullying on health, aggression as a behavior, self-esteem, association with loneliness and depression, emotional consequences, and moral identity.

Ang (2015) explored Internet usage, psychosocial problems and challenges, *proactive aggression* characteristics and normative beliefs about the tolerability of hostility. In the study, the parent—adolescent relationship variables, such as poor emotional bond, lack of knowledge about the adolescent's online activities, and lack of adequate parental monitoring and parental mediation were identified to be related to cyberbullying.

Balakrishman (2017), in his study, aimed at designing a cyberbullying behavioral model and determined the antecedents to cyberbully. Sociocultural (social influence and social acceptability) had the strongest impact on the intention to cyberbully, followed by technology (availability and ease of use) and psychology (entertainment) according to the research.

Also, a study by Hase (2015) sought to find out whether cyberbullying creates new victims or is merely a new means of victimization and whether cyberbullying uniquely contributes to negative outcomes above and beyond those of traditional bullying. In a survey that was conducted among students, it was found out that majority of the students who were bullied online were also victims of in-person bullying.

Nixon (2014: 1), in her research, found that adolescents who are targeted via cyberbullying reported increased *depressive effect, anxiety, loneliness, suicidal behavior,* and *somatic symptoms,* and perpetrators of cyberbullying are more likely to report increased *substance use, aggression,* and *delinquent behaviors.*

Yen et al. (2014) used a huge sample ($N = 1893$) of secondary school students in Hong Kong. Their study examined "gender differences in mean levels of traditional school bullying and cyberbullying behaviors and psychosocial characteristics (i.e., self-efficacy, empathy, prosocial behavior, family bonding, perception of a harmonious school, sense of belonging in school, and positive school experiences and involvement)." Findings indicated that the enactments of traditional school bullying and cyberbullying behaviors are positively correlated, and male adolescents reported higher levels of bullying perpetration than female adolescents.

In the investigations of cyberbullying, the Sociopsychological Tradition of Communication Theory has been the most dominantly used lens, leaving scholarly discourses within cybernetics, critical, phenomenological, sociocultural, rhetorical, and semiotic traditions of communication as underutilized frameworks. For this current investigation, the researcher attempted to add to the limited number of studies on cyberbullying framed through the Semiotic Tradition of Communication.

The researcher sees this study as an opportunity to inquire further into the dynamics of the cyberspace and cyberbullying that occurs in this space, the symbols or signs associated with the platform, and how these signs define the digital natives' participation or nonparticipation of this virtual communicative act, cyberbullying.

This study intends to comprehend the young digital natives' virtual communication propensities to either act conscientiously or otherwise thus support worldwide attempts of fostering responsible online communication and online safety by some organizations such as the government, schools, and family units. Gaining insights about how these young individuals are actually engaging themselves in virtual interactions specifically on Twitter may pave the way to more enlightened policies, campaigns, programs, and media literacy curriculum.

## Methods

A qualitative paradigm was employed in this study since the focus is on the exploration of meanings and interpretations of human online social interactions. Specifically, this study is grounded on the Semiotic Communication Tradition Theory and particularly made use of Peirce's Sign Theory or Semiotic as a lens in examining the data.

Peirce's Semiotic theory emphasized the interrelations between the sign or the signifier, an object (the signified), and an interpretant and its interpretation. "The basis of semiotic thinking is the concept of the triad of meaning and this maintains that meaning comes from the relationship between the object (referent), the interpretation, and the sign."

The Lens: Peirce's Semiotic Theory explained.

The triad relationship of sign, object, and interpretant.

The sign or signifier.

In one of his many definitions of a sign, Peirce writes:

I define a sign as anything which is so determined by something else, called its Object, and so determines an effect upon a person, which effect I call its interpretant, that the latter is thereby mediately determined by the former (EP2, 478 in Stanford Encyclopedia of Philosophy, 2010: 1).

To elaborate, the sign according to Peirce is the signifier which can be in the form of a written word, an utterance, and an act and can be verbal or nonverbal, a concept, or something material. For instance, a form that a sign takes is smoke as a sign of fire (Peirce's Theory of Signs, 2010). A smoke can have certain characteristics—volume, color, velocity, and density. Thin, black, fast smoke means that a well-ventilated fire is nearby, while a slow, white, dissipating smoke (first thick but thinning quickly) is a sign of steam and indicates early stage heating (Firefighternation, 2013). Not every characteristic necessarily plays a primary part in indicating the presence of a signifier. The color black as a characteristic, for instance, does not immediately indicate the presence of smoke. However, the connections between some features of a smoke—black color and fast velocity—and the one signified according to Peirce make smoke the qualified representamen or signifier. He stressed further that a sign signifies only when it is interpreted and that the sign has signifying elements or features that are crucial in its functioning or role as a signifier. These elements are also known as sign-vehicles. In this study, cyberspace is the identified signifier, which carries with it certain signifying elements, hence making it a capable signifier.

## The object

The object (a thing, concept, condition, an act), on the one hand, is the one signified. These objects have certain characteristics relevant to signification. "For Peirce, the connection between the object of a sign and the sign that represents it is one of determination: the object determines the sign" (Stanford Encyclopedia of Philosophy, 2010, p.1). This means that it is the object that enforces certain constraints that "a sign must fall within if it is to represent an object."

## The interpretant

The interpretation is the understanding or the thought that one has on the sign/object relation. This is the translation of the sign. As emphasized by Peirce, the sign determines the interpretant. In this paper, the interpretation is determined by the cyberspace as the signifier. These interpretations then mediated communicative acts such as participation or nonparticipation in cyberbullying.

Semiotic as a theory and communication tradition as a framework used in examining the data of this study viewed how the young digital natives understand the cyberspace, the associations they ascribe to the cyberspace, and how these representations mediate the communicative act, participation, or nonparticipation in cyberbullying.

Cyberspace and cyberbullying as a virtual communication act was examined in the researcher's guided conversations with the young people. Through the Semiotic Tradition of Communication Theory, the individual thoughts and interpretations of the young digital natives about the cyberspace and the communicative act, cyberbullying, have been underscored. Through the Semiotic Tradition of Communication Theory, details of the young virtual participants' representations and exemplifications of the cyberspace, which could signify concepts, words, or objects that mediate certain acts such as participation or nonparticipation in the communication situation have been revealed.

## The research participants

Senior high school students who were 16–17 years old, both male and female, who are digital natives participated in the study. Digital natives are those young people who are highly comfortable using communication technologies and have been frequently participating in virtual interactions for at least 2 years. These young digital natives were students from a private academic institution in Cebu City, Philippines. Eleven young people were interviewed and engaged in in-depth conversations regarding their thoughts on cyberbullying as a communicative act: what they associate cyberspace and cyberbullying with and how these representations mediated their act of participation or nonparticipation in cyberbullying.

These young individuals should have been directly or indirectly involved (either as participants or readers of the *tweet*, respectively) with the communication phenomenon on Twitter that went viral among senior high school students. To protect the real identities of the 11 participants, these fictitious names were assigned to them: *Shyna, Ana, Mitsy, Karleen, Gio, Susan, PJ, Thomas, Hanz, Leslie,* and *Amie.*

Letters of consent were given to the participants for clear understanding of the research objectives and to gain students' sincere cooperation in the inquiry. Also, permissions from the respective school director and the teacher concerned were sought before the researcher engaged the participants in a semistructured interview and conversations. Dialogs were recorded in order to explore the meanings, descriptions, and interpretations of the Twitter encounter.

In analyzing the data, this research made use of the modified van Kaam method, as described by Moustakas (1994), which follows the seven-step approach: (1) Listing and preliminary grouping, wherein responses were grouped according to themes. In this stage, the researcher transcribed verbatim everything that has been recorded. (2) Reduction and elimination, which involves excluding answers that were not necessarily relevant to the topic at hand and reducing the data to units of meaning. (3) Clustering and thematizing was done to achieve more general themes. (4) Final identification of the invariant constituents and themes by application. This involves checking the central themes against the whole transcript to see whether the themes align to the entire text. (5) Construction of the individual textural description for each participant using the validated themes. (6) Construction of the individual structural description. This presents the structural description of the overall experience guided by the textural description. (7) Construction of a textural-structural description, which is the combination of the participants' viewpoints. The data were then further examined using the semiotic frame (sign/signifier-object/signified-interpretation) of Charles Sanders Peirce. The data gathered went through rigorous methods of transcribing, coding, interpreting, and analyzing of themes and trends.

**Table 3.1** Summary of interrelations between object, sign, interpretant, and action.

| Object/signification | Interpretant/action | |
|---|---|---|
| | Participation | Nonparticipation |
| Cyberspace is a platform for | Friendship, alliance | Friendship, alliance, sympathy |
| Community building | Sympathy for good or bad | |
| Cyberspace is a platform for freedom of expression | Grievances, criticisms | Disrespect, immaturity, recklessness, aggression, *spread*, impact |

## Results and discussions

Table 3.1 presents a summary of interrelations between object, sign, interpretant, and action.

## The sign and the signified: what the cyberspace signifies for the senior high school students

### The cyberspace interpreted as a platform for community building

Some digital natives interpret the cyberspace as a platform for *community building*, wherein nuances of friendships, alliances, and sympathy are demonstrated in the cyberspace communications. These significations of the cyberspace clearly mediate acts of participation in cyberbullying.

*In Shyna's story, elements of community building such as friendship and show of support to a friend are highlighted, "... In Twitter you can find friends, you can find a lot of people who will agree to what you stand for...I think in that tweet, she was looking for people to side on her...and you can see that a girl was really getting a lot of people on her side."*

*Another participant, Susan saw friendship and support in the cyberspace, as she narrated, "...She had many friends and expectedly they supported her. And* those other students who did not know the whole story they also commented and they sided with the girl even if they didn't know the whole story..."

*On the other hand, the story of Gio is an honest admission of his sympathy for a friend,* "...I was also triggered because the one who tweeted was my friend so I also co-tweeted to be honest because I felt for my friend...I participated because I also wanted to defend my friend ..."

*Thomas thought that an alliance among the cyberspace community members is demonstrated,* "...I think she tweeted about it because she presumed that many other students do not like the teacher and she wanted for others to validate what she feels towards the teacher...."

*Hanz's narrative emphasized how the messages of other members of the community impelled him to join in the Twitter interactions to support a friend,* "...I was kind of brainwashed so I got carried away. I agreed that the teacher was rude, like that and he was not able to handle the student properly. That was the first thing that came to my mind so I sided with the student."

*Amie said that support for a friend was also seen in the communication event,* "Perhaps she felt that social media was a great outlet because people would be able to even support her arguments especially people who didn't know the real story so maybe it becoming viral was in her favor...."

The participants view the cyberspace as a setting where people with similar thought constructs can show support and sympathy with one another as manifested in the exchange of messages. For these young individuals, the cyberspace, specifically Twitter, has its own purpose, appreciated by the citizens of the digital space. The platform has allowed these young people to congregate as a community, verbalizing care, sympathy, and empathy for its members. In the cyberspaces, those who hold the same views and share similar experiences are able to validate each other's opinions and form alliances through their interactions.

As the interconnections between the characteristics of a smoke as a whole—black color and fast velocity—and the one signified according to Peirce make smoke the qualified representamen or signifier, in the context of cyberspace communications, friendship, alliances, and sympathy are the crucial elements of the object, *community building* in the cyberspace. Under

Peirce's semiosis principle, this feature of the object, *community building*, makes the cyberspace a qualified signifier in the Twitter encounter being studied.

The young digital natives' interpretation of communication in the cyberspace appears to be mutually agreed upon as the participants gave a shared definition to the Twitter encounter. This sharing of the same *sense* or *thought* regarding discourses in the virtual arena depicts a communal meaning adequate for a signifier such as the cyberspace to mediate acts of participation or nonparticipation in cyberbullying.

## The cyberspace interpreted as a platform for freedom of expression

Other than the cyberspace being viewed as platform of community building, the young digital natives thought of the cyberspace as a podium for freedom of expression. In the cyberspace, young people are able to voice out opinions, disapprovals, and complaints about certain issues. In the students' narratives, it is highlighted that the tweet and some of its corresponding comments were expressions of grievances toward a perceived unfavorable act done upon the one who started the conversation and to the other students who participated in the Twitter interaction.

Some of the research participants suggested that the tweets of those who supported the student maybe interpreted as a retribution and a defense, not an offense.

*Mitsy shared about how expressive the young people are in the cyberspace,* "Actually as a millennial, a lot of us are actually careless about our posts because social media becomes like a freedom wall wherein we feel free to post what we want. . ."

*Susan also views the millennials to be very outspoken,* ". . .I think, people now, especially millennials my age are too vocal. . . Twitter is your own account and you can express anything in Twitter but this should be used in a good way and not to talk bad things about people just because you are mad about that person."

"If you try to look at it, it's quite cyberbullying at some point but we can also say that it's an expression at some point or just merely expressing one's grievance. . ." *as told by PJ.*

*Thomas' story presents his views on how young people could bravely speak their minds regardless of being incorrect,* "As a millennial, we tend to express a lot especially on Twitter and we tend to think that we are protected by the screen so we feel that we can say anything we want to say even if they are wrong... In social media we can release our anger, our hatred, our heavy feeling so in that sense if you tweet like personally I tweet a lot about how I feel even if sometimes it's for a specific person, it's in a way relieving..."

*In the story of Leslie, the cyberspace can be a venue where everyone is equal,* "...we can't really retaliate much we can't really fight him about it so instead of confronting him head on because everyone is scared of him they go to Twitter and rant about their frustrations...."

*In the story of Amie, she saw the cyberspace as an opportunity of expressing feelings,* "...it's a platform to express your emotions maybe to people or to other people, things about ourselves that we don't necessarily want other people to know about or maybe we do want them to know but we don't want to tell them directly...."

These students found the cyberspace to be a leveling ground, where no authorities can restrict straightforward views and sentiments.

*The story of Shyna points out that young individuals are upfront in the cyberspace,* "The thing about tweeting especially teenagers tweet is that, we're not afraid to be direct..."

*Karleen thought that the cyberspace provides an avenue for honest confessions of ill feelings,* "...I mean everyone's ill feelings towards the teacher that were bottled up were tweeted and the tweet was somehow boosted since others opened up on their feelings against the teacher."

*In the story of Leslie, the cyberspace is seen to be a safe place for students to express frustrations,* "...he's a teacher so we can't really retaliate much... we can't really fight him about it so instead of confronting him head on because everyone is scared of him they go to Twitter and rant about their frustrations..."

*The young digital natives see the cyberspace as a platform where the attention of even those in the authority can be called. This freedom of expression is something they believe to be not normally afforded them on a face-to-face (FtF) encounter.*

*Leslie's story conveyed that expressions of criticisms in the cyberspace change other people's behavior, "...I didn't want to personally attack the teacher, I just wanted to say that sometimes, he's too much for us and should control himself so that's why I didn't participate cause I didn't want to attack him personally...I just wanted his behavior to change. That's all that I want."*

*In the cyberspace, one could feel safer compared to offline encounters, and calling out people's attention is done easier than on a personal interaction as the story of Amie emphasized, "...because social media is like, there's a screen, you can't really tell the consequences of your actions or you can't really tell immediate responses from the person you are tweeting about so it can almost feel safer compared to personal interactions...I tweeted in favor of the student, I called out the teacher for some other things that I felt he was lacking in or he was doing wrong.."*

Compared with FtF interactions, tweeting has been seemingly a very accessible and most convenient way of sharing what one thinks or feels, irrespective of whether it is positive or negative, with those who may share the same outlook, sentiment, passion, frustration, and other human emotions.

*Susan's story underscored Twitter's communicative affordances, "...Twitter is your own account and you can express anything in Twitter but this should be used in a good way and not to talk bad things about people just because you are mad about that person...Maybe I can relate because I'm also like them... I let out frustrations..."*

*Leslie in her story again emphasizes that the cyberspace is a place of free expressions, "...the students didn't really know who to go to and who to tell their issues and I guess they were outraged considering the issue behind it so I guess it was really just that, a venting place..."*

Viewing the cyberspace as a platform for various expressions of communications such as dissatisfactions, frustrations, protests, and so forth mediates actions of participation in virtual interactions. The signifying elements identified earlier such as grievances and criticisms acted as the signifying vehicles, the presence of which, according to Peirce, makes a sign, in this case the cyberspace, a capable signifier for freedom of expression.

These young individuals believe that the platform gives them the liberty to speak openly and candidly about anything, albeit recklessly sometimes. The platform has become a venting place, a freedom wall to the young people.

The narratives provide perspectives as to how the cyberspace is seen by the young digital natives as a ground where people could gather as a community, and where issues can be openly discussed in a venue free from power structures. The cyberspace, specifically Twitter, for these young digital natives has its own purpose enjoyed and valued by its users and participants. They are able to express freely some thoughts that they may not be able to easily or comfortably share with others in an FtF context. The cyberspace provides a venue for them to participate in discussions they deem important, an arena where no authorities can intimidate them and where they can freely and fearlessly speak to anyone regardless of age or status.

The participants appreciate and value the use of Twitter in terms of revealing what their hearts genuinely feel; sharing what their strong convictions are and communicating these views to a large audience; and facilitating interactions, which may be convenient to hold only in the virtual arena but not in their classrooms and in their respective family settings. This representation of the cyberspace hence defined the participation in cyberbullying by some young digital natives.

This signification of the cyberspace as a platform for freedom of expression, wherein the highlighted shared meaning constructed by the young individuals is that the cyberspace affords them a sense of emancipation from the highly structured FtF communications and allows them to exercise democratic discourses with the other communication participants, is observed. This, therefore, has mediated their act of participation.

The stories of the participants provided a context for the deeper views of the young digital natives about their participation or nonparticipation in the communicative act, cyberbullying. The participants' contextualization of the Twitter encounter provides a depiction of the constituents or the surrounding elements (friendship, alliances, and sympathy) of the shared understanding of the situation. The narratives portray multiple cognitions of the situation interacting with each other as well as the common understanding of the Twitter dialogs in the cyberspace. This common consciousness of the tweeting circumstance as well as the divergent views of the situation has provided equilibrium in recognizing the presence of a signifier, cyberspace, that arbitrated the communicative acts of participation or nonparticipation.

## The signifier: how the signification of the cyberspace mediates the senior high school students' participation or nonparticipation in cyberbullying

### Nonparticipation in cyberbullying

The participants who have regarded the cyberspace as an avenue where aggression in the freedom of expression can be exhibited conveyed that they did not participate. Aggression as one of the characteristics of the object, freedom of expression in the cyberspace, has clearly mediated their act of nonparticipation.

*Shyna's story speaks of offensiveness or aggression in the tweets, "...it's defi-nitely offensive...* You can see it's directed to someone and you can see it's actually meant to offend someone because you know it has like screenshots...For sure, it's not right. It's something very explicit. It's some-thing that is like over the line offensive..."

*Mitsy commented, "...Maybe it makes them happy to hurt others... What she did was cyberbullying because she posted something online that humil-iated the person... He's a human being, people make mistakes but I don't think they should be judged for their mistakes and being talked about online..."

*Susan's story underscored the destructiveness or aggressiveness of the messages encountered on Twitter,* "They just destroyed the reputation of the teacher... She then tweeted very negative comments and then she shared her conver-sation with the teacher in Twitter."

The statements of the participants confirm previous studies (Ang, 2015; Balakrishman, 2017; Doanne et al., 2014; Gualdo et al., 2015; Hemphill & Heerde, 2014; Lee & Shin, 2017; Palermiti et al., 2017; Yen et al., 2014; Wang, et al., 2017, etc.) that describe cyberbullying as an aggressive behavior demonstrated in the communicative act. Participants described what they saw in the comments of the tweet as destructive, pro-vocative, and violent. In this current study, *aggression* in the cyberspace is cogitated as one of the signifying elements of the signifier intermediated the students' act of nonparticipation.

Also, the young digital natives' interpretations of the cyberspace as a platform with a massive audience for self-expressions have mediated an act of nonparticipation.

*As told in Shyna's story,* "It's something very explicit. It's something that is like over the line offensive because it's online and what you put online you can't. . .It's just there even if you delete the tweet people would know you actually tweeted it. It's involving everyone in the world because everyone can actually see it. . ."

*Mitsy emphasized in her story the "double publicity" of the message,* "If you bully a student in school at least not everybody knows about it unlike what was done. She posted it online for everybody to see and it didn't just include the school, it also included everybody because everybody saw the post even those from other schools so it became a double publicity. The audience was doubled. . ."

The enormity of the audience and the far-reaching scope of the cyberspace are highlighted in the narratives of some of the young digital natives. Taking into consideration the social media as a platform, what makes the action cyberbullying exceptionally humiliating according to those who did not participate is its large audience and the extent of reach. One of the participants called it "double publicity." Many of them mentioned, "having the whole world" as the audience. In this case, the young digital natives see the cyberspace as a platform with the entire globe as its audiences and whatever unconstructive messages for an individual are broadcasted on this space could be accessed by a huge number of spectators, thus resulting in potentially severe destructive impact on the subject. This view of the exercise of freedom of expression clearly mediated the act of nonparticipation as relayed in the narratives of the students.

Similar to the claims of other studies (Gualdo et al., 2015; Dempsey et al., 2009; Hase, 2015; Holfeld & Sukhawathanakul, 2017; Reio & Ledesma Ortega, 2016), typically, cyberbullying could have serious outcomes on the victim. The participants thought that the tweeting event, which turned into cyberbullying, humiliated the person and seriously destroyed the target's character, given the whole world as its viewers.

*Ana in her story speaks of the embarrassment of the subject spoken of in the tweets,* "I think that it's shameful for the subject because obviously the girl tweeted a screen shot of their conversation and the subject was not properly aware about the tweet. It's very inappropriate for the subject because he was simply being put to shame. . .."

*Mitsy thought of the hurt and humiliation experienced by the authority being criticized on the cyberspace as her story goes, "If I were in the teacher's place, I would really get hurt even if I wasn't in his place, I was really hurt because I'm also human and even if you think he made mistakes, he doesn't deserve that kind of publicity... What she did was cyberbullying because she posted something online that humiliated the person."*

*Susan judged the act of cyberbullying as wrong as she expressed her views, "I think it was wrong for the students to post negative things online... They just destroyed the reputation of the teacher... Cyberbullying can cause depression on the victims. There's a negative impact. I was also bullied before and I was depressed.."*

The elements mentioned such as aggression, audience, reach, and impact constitute the characteristics of the communication phenomenon in the cyberspace. Peirce refers to these features or gradations of freedom of expression in the cyberspace as signifying elements. These signifying elements play a crucial part in signifying the presence of a signifier or a sign. These rudiments are important in the functioning of the sign because the existence of their connection is the one responsible for signification. These signifying elements according to Peirce play a critical part in representing the presence and authenticity of a sign or signifier.

For those who did not participate, a communal signification about the cyberspace (demonstrations of aggression, scope and reach of the platform, and gravity of impact) in the practice of freedom of expression has intersubjectively mediated their communicative response. Although these young individuals mutually share the view of those who participated that the cyberspace is a platform for freedom of expression, one can remarkably note that within this universal thought is a differing belief that is governed by certain principles of social interactions. Interestingly, the like-mindedness of these individuals in terms of how they perceive the elements of freedom of expression in cyberspace has coregulated their nonparticipation.

### Interpreting the cyberspace as a platform for offensive, disrespectful, immature, and reckless exercise of freedom of expression mediating nonparticipation in cyberbullying

The research participants provided interesting further interpretations of the cyberspace. There were participants who interpreted the cyberspace as a platform for disrespectful, immature, and reckless expressions. These interpretations of the cyberspace thus determined the participants' act of nonparticipation.

*Ana in her story emphasized the "unsuitability" of the tweet, "... It's very inappropriate for the subject because he was simply being put to shame...It's not okay to put someone to shame, like anyone to shame even though like you have grudges on that person, personal stuff should stay personal. It's not okay because they do not have the right..."*

*"... It was a wrong thing to do. She should not have tweeted about it... It's cyberbullying and any kind of cyberbullying is wrong. No matter what your status is, no one should talk bad things about you... It was inappropriate because I think cyberbullying is bad in itself." As told by Susan.*

The abovementioned statements *highlight* the offensiveness of the communicative act, cyberbullying. They emphasized that hurtful and disrespectful statements are wrong and unreasonable in every sense.

In addition, for those participants who did not participate, they believe that there was a display of disrespect in the Twitter encounter. Apparently, in that tweeting encounter, some of the student participants viewed the cyberspace as a platform for freedom of expression, which could exhibit disrespect on certain occasions. For most of the participants, this view of the cyberspace as a platform for this unlikely exercise of freedom of expression determined their communicative act of nonparticipation in the Twitter conversations, again exemplifying Peirce's "sign/object/interpretant relation."

*Shyna's story spoke of disrespect among those who exercised their freedom of expression to an extreme, "It was disrespecting authority for sure and you know authorities will always be higher ...I guess for that, I wouldn't disrespect, I wouldn't go that far 'cause I also think that the subject also had his you know his kind of rationale as to why he chose to make that decision for the student and I guess that's kind of the main reason why I didn't really get into it..."*

*Ana believes that, "... cyberbullying is a sign of disrespect because even 'though you're holding grudges, you can't just put anyone to shame. Many people have seen it, many people will have copies and you know it will put that person, it may give him fears. It's a sign of disrespect and it's cyberbullying.."*

*Karleen saw that there was disrespect in the tweets of those who criticized the teacher, "It was somehow disrespectful towards the teacher...If you try to post bad comments about other people and share to others these comments you are disrespecting someone because you hurt the person's feelings."*

The cyberspace, due to its signifying elements or conditions mentioned earlier, therefore becomes a clear signifier or ground of the object. Interestingly, the young individuals who did not participate perceive the communicative act of those who participated as a display of immaturity and recklessness other than disrespect.

As Peirce suggests, smoke as a signifier of fire can have certain characteristics—volume, color, velocity, and density. Thin, black, fast smoke means that a well-ventilated fire is nearby while a slow, white, dissipating smoke (first thick but thinning quickly) is a sign of steam and indicates early stage heating (Firefighternation, 2013). Not every characteristic necessarily plays a primary part in indicating the presence of a signifier. The color black as a characteristic, for instance, does not immediately indicate the presence of a smoke. However, the connections between the characteristics of a smoke as a whole—black color and fast velocity—and the one signified according to Pierce make smoke the qualified signifier.

In the context of the cyberspace, audience as a feature taken alone does not immediately imply any signification; neither does *reach* or *spread* of the message in the exercise of freedom of expression. However, the presence of other characteristics such as aggression, disrespect, immaturity, and thoughtlessness in the exercise of freedom of expression in the cyberspace makes the cyberspace a qualified signifier and when given interpretations, mediated an act of nonparticipation.

*Shyna in her story speaks of the teens' carelessness in her cyberspace expressions, "It's expected because you know it's a teenager so teenagers you know, we're carefree and we'd say whatever we want and stuff and not really caring about what they think..."*

*Ana saw the situation as a display of immaturity on the virtual platform, "...She is just humiliating someone who may not really care about her so like there's no point really...I didn't comment. I think because I've gone through those stuff already. I find it immature..."*

*As told by Mitsy in her story, she also saw immaturity demonstrated on the cyberspace, "I don't mean to insult the person (the one who tweeted) but I* think she is like a brat who threw a tantrum because she didn't get what she wanted and so she posted things online to seek for sympathizers, something like that. It was immature of her to post online..."

The tendencies of young people to *abuse* the Twitter platform and to be careless in their communications are seen by some of these young people who suggest that tweeting should be done more thoughtfully.

While young individuals are able to coconstruct interpretations of the cyberspace as a platform wherein communications are viewed as a vehicle that enable people to build communities and facilitate *exercises* of freedom of expression, other views which are shaped by individual ethical standards such as notions of respect, conscientiousness, maturity, and sensitivity toward other communication participants could further mediate actions of nonparticipation in cyberbullying.

## Participation in cyberbullying

Interestingly, those who participated in the incident shared the same views with those who thought that the Twitter encounter manifested characteristics of cyberbullying. However, the participants view the cyberspace as a venue where sympathy, honesty, and forthright interactions dominantly mediated their participation in cyberbullying.

*Gio in his story emphasized that friendship mediated his participation in cyberbullying*, "...I was also triggered because the one who tweeted was my friend so I also co-tweeted to be honest because I felt for my friend. However, I wasn't able to think before I tweeted because I got carried away by the negative comments."

*PJ viewed the situation more of an expression of grievance than cyberbullying*, "If you try to look at it, it's quite cyberbullying at some point but we can also say that it's an expression at some point or just merely expressing one's grievance... the line is blurry between those things and you just can't categorize that thing in one context because it can be in every context, it depends on how you look at it...."

*Thomas in his story stressed that sympathy for a friend in the cyberspace made him participate in the communicative act, cyberbullying*, "The situation itself, if you look at it, it's a bit like in a way rude especially for our adviser but I cannot also blame the one who posted it in a sense that the teacher was also somewhat disrespectful in the way he replied..."

*As told by Hanz in his narrative, "...*I was kind of brainwashed so I got carried away. I agreed that the teacher was rude, like that and he was not able to handle the student properly... Almost all students gave negative comments so my brain sort of sided with the majority especially that I didn't know the whole story yet. For me, tweeting about the situation was a careless move because first of all the conversation between the teacher and the student was private so for you to share it especially on Twitter wherein so many people can view so it was a careless act..."

*Leslie, who participated in the cyberbullying incident believed that it was more of a call for a change of behavior than a baseless attack to a personality,* "I just saw students ranting about a particular teacher whom we've had and this teacher has caused a lot of problems for us as students. The tweets were simply complaints for the experiences they had about the teacher, observations they have about him... What makes it not okay is when people start going overboard with criticism and the hate and people are jumping into it and becomes kind of like a sort of trend as you can see and some people don't even mean what they say, they just go along with it so, but the good thing about tweeting about these sort of things is, it gives people awareness, it gives them some background info on what the students are going through..."

*Amie sympathized for a costudent in the cyberspace as she speaks,* "I saw a student who felt perhaps victimized maybe in a wrong sense and then she found the opportunity to express herself on social media... I don't think it was the most appropriate thing especially since the names could be seen in the picture and I didn't think it was appropriate but perhaps in the heat of the moment that's the only way that she felt she could gain support. I joined because there were instances when I also felt, or I was also caught up by my emotions. You have no time to think about things, you know it's social media it's, we would have talked to the person face to face... I would have thought about it a lot more but since it's social media then I went ahead."

Emergent in the young digital natives' narratives is the view that even if they share the *thought construct* that bullying in the cyberspace is an undesirable online behavior, it is also understood by other individuals that this communicative act is something that may address a wrongdoing. People's interpretation of the cyberspace where expressions of criticisms for someone or a situation are freely facilitated spurs one to get involved in bullying without necessarily being conscious of its wrongness and its adverse effect on the target person. On the other hand, in a Twitter community, people may feel obliged to support an ally who is seemingly transgressed.

For some participants, their participation has been mediated by seeing the platform as a setting where freedom of expression can be exercised. These expressions of grievance and objective criticisms are aimed at rectifying certain injustices done. For these young digital natives, this is one way of calling the attention of the "transgressor" in the hope that he might take heed of the crowd's clamor for a change of behavior. The cyberspace in this aspect has played a significant role, as this setting is viewed to have facilitated no-holds-barred interactions. In the cyberspace, egalitarianism and autonomy are enjoyed and practiced by these young individuals.

Like the sign vehicles of the smoke—volume, color, velocity and density—and the interconnections of these constituents, the components or sign vehicles such as friendship and alliances in community building and expressions of grievances and criticisms in the freedom of expression, how they are interweaved in the cyberspace, and their interpretations mediated an act of participation.

The *construct* that cyberspace is a platform for community building where there are coalitions of those who share the same sentiment toward a situation has undoubtedly mediated an act of participation. Some participants confessed that "they got carried away" or they yielded to the community's judgment thus expressed their agreement with the other members of the community.

Signifying the cyberspace as a platform for community building where like-minded beings are able to unreservedly converge and voice out stances without being restricted by power structures becomes the intersubjective mediation of participation or nonparticipation in cyberbullying. Those who participated, albeit admittedly, also viewed the cyberspace as a platform where unlikely expressions of disrespect and display of immaturity and recklessness occur and may suspend this view during the actual communication event and allow other sign vehicles such as expressions of grievance, alliance, and so forth to offset the more affirmative signifying elements of the sign, hence determining the young digital natives' communication participation.

The authentic narratives of the senior high school students have clearly established that signs, when interpreted, mediate communication actions. In this study, the shared constructs of meanings of the sign have meaningfully mediated actions of participation or nonparticipation.

It is interesting to note, however, that despite the shared view of a communicative action, it is possible that some sign vehicles could compete with each other and that dominant signifying elements or sign characteristics identified will not initially mediate a person's communicative response but may only influence or mediate a delayed communicative act.

The cyberspace, specifically, social media, has in one way or another fostered community building, self-expressions, and public discussions. This has led to a good outcome in several aspects, such as people being more politically, socially, and environmentally aware and involved (Effing et al., 2011; Mangold & Faulds, 2009; Moorhead, 2013). Expressions in the cyberspace, however, may not always bring about positive outcomes, especially when these are used to exploit, deceive, harass, and damage reputations, whether intentionally or unintentionally done, such as in the case of this current study. Efforts such as promotions of responsible and ethical social media use, therefore, must be given emphasis in schools and other human organizations.

## References

Ang, R. (2015). Adolescent cyberbullying: A review of characteristics, prevention and intervention strategies. *Aggression and Violent Behavior, 25*(Part A), 35–42. Available from http://dx.org/10.1016/j.avb.2015.070.011.

Asanan, Z. Z. T., et al. (2017). A study on cyberbullying: Its forms, awareness, and moral reasoning among youth. *International Journal of Media and Communication, 2*(5), 54–58. Available from https://doi.org/10.11648/j.ijics.20170205.11.

Athanasiades, C., et al. (2016). The "net" of the Internet: Risk factors to cyberbullying among secondary-school students in greece. *European Journal on Criminal Policy and Research, 22*(2), 301–317.

Balakrishnan, V. (2017). Unraveling the underlying factors Sculpting cyberbullying behaviors among Malaysian young adults. *Computers in Human Behavior, 75*, 194–205.

Dempsey, A., Sulkowski, M., & Nichols, R. (2009). Differences between peer victimization in cyber and physical settings and associated psychosocial adjustment in early adolescence. *Psychology in the Schools, 46*(10), 962–971.

Doane, A. N., Pearson, M. R., & Kelley, M. L. (2014). Predictors of cyberbullying perpetration among college students: An application of the Theory of Reasoned Action. *Computers in Human Behavior, 36*, 154–162.

Effing, R., van Hillegersberg, J., & Huibers, T. (2011). Social media and political participation: Are facebook, twitter and youtube democratizing our political systems? In E. Tambouris, A. Macintosh, & H. de Bruijn (Eds.), *ePart 2011, LNCS 6847* (pp. 25–35). 2011. © IFIP International Federation for Information Processing 2011.

Gualdo, G., Hunter, A. N., Durkin, K., Arnaiz, P., & Maquilon, J. J. (2015). The emotional impact of cyberbullying: Differences in perceptions and experiences as a function of role. *Computers & Education, 82*, 228–235.

Hase, C., et al. (2015). Impacts of traditional bullying and cyberbullying on the mental health of middle school and high school students. *Psychology in the Schools, 52*(6), 607–617.

Hemphill, S., & Heerde, J. (2014). Adolescent predictors of young adult cyberbullying perpetration and victimization among Australian Youth. *Journal of Adolescent Health, 55* (4), 580–587.

Hinduja, S., & Patchin, J. (2012). Bullying beyond the schoolyard: Preventing and responding to cyberbullying. *Security Journal, 25,* 88–89. Available from https://doi.org/10.1057/sj.2011.25.

Holfeld, B., & Sukhawathanakul, P. (2017). Cyber victimization, and internalizing symptoms among adolescents. *CyberPscyhology, Behavior, and Social Networking, 20*(2), 91–95. Available from https://doi.org/10.1089/cyber2016.0194.

Lee, C., & Shin, N. (2017). Prevalence of cyberbullying and predictors of cyberbullying perpetration among Korean adolescents. *Computers in Human Behavior, 68,* 352–358.

Mangold, A. & Faulds, D. (2009). Social media: The new hybrid element of the promotion mix. Kelley School of Business, Indiana University. Available from https://doi.org/10.1016/j.bushor.2009.03.002.

Moorhead, A., et al. (2013). A new dimension of health care: A systematic review of the uses, benefits, and limitations of social media for health communication. *Journal of Medical Internet, 15*(4), e85. Available from https://doi.org/10.2196/jmir.1933.

Moustakas, C. (1994). *Phenomenological research methods.* Thousand Oaks, CA: Sage.

Navarro, J., et al. (2017). One step forward, two steps back: Cyberbullying within social networking sites. *Security Journal, 30*(3), 844–8581.

Nixon, C. (2014). Current perspectives: The impact of cyberbullying on adolescent health. *Adolescent Health Med Ther, 5,* 143–158. Available from https://doi.org/10.2147/AHMT.S36456.

Palermiti, A. L., Servidio, R., Bartolo, M. G., & Costabile, A. (2017). Cyberbullying and self-esteem: An Italian study. *Computers in Human Behavior, 69,* 136–141.

Reio, T. G., & Ledesma Ortega, C. C. (2016). Chapter 8: Cyberbullying and Its Emotional Consequences: What We Know and What We Can Do. Emotions. *Technology and Behaviors,* 145–158.

Stanford Encyclopedia of Philosophy (2010). Peirce's Theory of Signs. Retrieved, July 19, 2018 Available from https://plato.stanford.edu/entries/peirce-semiotics.

Wang, Xingchao, Yang, Ling, Yang, Jiping, Wang, Pengcheng, & Lei, Li (2017). Trait anger and cyberbullying among young adults: A moderated model of moral disengagement and moral identity. *Computers in Human Behavior, 73,* 519–526.

Yen, C., Chou, W., Liu, T., Ko, C., & Hu, H. (2014). Cyberbullying among male adolescents with attention-deficit/hyperactivity disorder: Prevalence, correlates, and association with poor mental health status. *Research in Developmental Disabilities, 35*(12), 3543–3553.

CHAPTER FOUR

# Bystander intervention to cyberbullying on social media

**Peter J.R. Macaulay[1], Oonagh L. Steer[2] and Lucy R. Betts[2]**
[1]School of Psychology, University of Derby, Derby, United Kingdom
[2]Department of Psychology, Nottingham Trent University, Nottingham, United Kingdom

## Contents

## An introduction to cyberbullying

The landscape of social interaction has continually evolved since information communication technologies (ICTs) was made available to the general population. The internet has pervasively advanced over the past two decades, which has led the internet to become a more accessible commodity within society. For instance, in a 2011 Ofcom report, 76% of British adults had access to the internet within their home. Nearly a century later, internet access for British adults had increased to 94% (Ofcom, 2020). For young people, ICT development and internet access has led to a shift toward a virtual environment in terms of how they communicate and attain information. ICT expansion has involved the development of varying mediums, such as smart technology, to access the internet, which has enabled overall convenience and speed. Smartphone usage and ownership for young people has gradually increased over the last decade. For instance, 95% of American teenagers aged 13 to 17 have been reported to own a smartphone (Anderson & Jiang, 2018), which is a relatively large increase from 73% reported 2014/2015 (Lenhart, 2015). Similarly, a study conducted in the United Kingdom found that 83% of 12- to 15-year olds own a smartphone, with a significant rise of smartphone ownership occurring around the age of 10 (Ofcom, 2019). Anderson and Jiang (2018) also report that smartphones in America are not restricted by gender, race, ethnicities, or socioeconomic backgrounds, implying that the majority of young people have the means to connect with others online. For young people, this increase of ICT access will have provided a wide range of positive opportunities. General benefits include communication and networking (Boyd, 2014), using online support services (Rice et al., 2014), creative attributes (Notley & Tacchi, 2005), and e-learning (Chen et al., 2010). The affordances made available by the internet have become a part of everyday living, especially for young people (Anderson & Jiang, 2018).

Alongside the positive features of the internet are the risks that it presents to young people. One experience that has gained a great deal of research attention is cyberbullying. The phenomenon of cyberbullying from a research standpoint can be viewed from alternative perspectives, which are yet to reach a consensus (Kofoed & Staksrud, 2019). The prevailing definition views cyberbullying as an extension of traditional bullying (Calvete et al., 2010; Kowalski et al., 2014; Olweus & Limber, 2018; Perren & Gutzwiller-Helfenfinger, 2012). The traditional bullying definition outlines three criteria: (1) intent to cause harm, (2) power imbalance between the victim and perpetrator; and (3) repetition of an act (Olweus, 1993, 2013). Therefore, cyberbullying has been defined as "an aggressive, intentional act carried out by a group or individual, using electronic forms of contact, repeatedly and over time against a victim who cannot easily defend him or herself" (Smith et al., 2008: p. 376). The singular difference between the former, traditional bullying, and latter, cyberbullying, definitions is the inclusion of technology.

An understanding of each of the traditional bullying criteria outlined by Olweus (1993, 2013) can be contextually helpful when considering this definition in the digital environment. Firstly, intentionality is the desire to cause unwanted harm upon a victim. Intentionality can be indicated by evaluating if the perpetrator knew that their actions would cause harm, especially if this is also concluded by the victim. A power imbalance between victim and perpetrator is evaluated based on the perception of the victim and how likely they can defend themselves. A power imbalance can also be identified by aspects such as greater physicality or greater number of bullies, popularity, and status. Repetitiveness signifies that an aggressive act must occur more than once for it to be deemed as bullying. Repeated attacks can also reinforce intentionality as it indicates that a perpetrator has decided to repeat their aggressive act despite being aware that their first offense caused harm to the victim.

Cyberbullying, for some researchers and academics (Corcoran et al., 2015; Grigg, 2010; Kofoed & Staksrud, 2019), is considered as a singular phenomenon separated from traditional bullying by the idiosyncratic affordances provided by the internet (Barlett et al., 2017; Hutson, 2016). The argument for observing cyberbullying as a distinct behavior is grounded in the contextual differences between the online and offline environments. Online communication and interaction exchanges are different from face to face situations in varying ways, one distinct characteristic being the audience. The internet allows users to present interactions to an audience of choice, which includes the size of the audience. In the context of cyberbullying, a singular incident of cyberbullying by one perpetrator can be viewed publicly by any amount of witnesses (Kowalski et al., 2012), who may share or like the incident and therefore carry on the perpetration (Ševčíková et al., 2012; Slonje, et al., 2013). Public cyberbullying, as opposed to private cyberbullying, has been reported to be more severely perceived by a victim (Sticca & Perren, 2013), suggesting that audience may conceptually need to be accounted for in the cyberbullying definition. The affordance of publicly posting social interactions is problematic for the definitional criterion of repetition as one act of cyberbullying can, in some instances, be severely impactful act upon the victim (Vandebosch & Van Cleemput, 2008; Ybarra, Diener-West, et al., 2007). This suggests that repetition of an incident may have less emphasis in cyberspace and therefore may not characterize cyberbullying behavior. In support of this argument, Menesini et al. (2012) conducted experimental research to explore how young people (aged 11–17) perceived cyberbullying. The criterion of repetition was reported to be less reliable as a definitional criterion to other key characteristics (i.e., intentionality and power imbalance).

Perceiving an incident of online aggression as cyberbullying can be a difficult and misleading process. This is mainly due to the remote communication aspect of online interactions, which exclude social indicators such as facial expression, body language, gestures, and prosody of voice (Baruch, 2005; Kiesler et al., 1984). The lack of social indicators can create ambiguity during an online interaction, making it more difficult to evaluate and perceive an interaction that may, for instance, involve sarcasm, irony, banter, and satire (Baas et al., 2013; Steer et al., 2020). This ambiguity can cloud clarity concerning the intentions of the perpetrator (Langos, 2012) and perhaps lead to a user feeling victimized despite the perpetrator having no intention to harm, or vice versa (O'Dea & Campbell, 2012; Vandebosch & Van Cleemput, 2008). Without social indicators, users are also unaware of the impact their behavior may have had on others unless the recipient clearly states that they are offended by the actions of the unknowing perpetrator (Dehue et al., 2008). The issues which stem from the remote online environment, which can alter how aggressive acts are perceived by victims, do present issues around the definitional criterion of intent to cause harm. Intentionality is not only distorted by limited social indicators; in some situations, it also cannot be reinforced by the characteristic of repetition. For example, as previously mentioned, one act of cyberbullying can be viewed by a large audience, which can potentially be more harmful for the victim (Sticca & Perren, 2013). If one act of aggression is perceived by a victim as cyberbullying due to a large audience witnessing the incident, then potentially limited indicators remain to aid the evaluation of an act having the intention to cause harm and therefore cyberbullying.

Recognizing a power imbalance between the victim and perpetrator in cyberspace can be complex (Grigg, 2010; Barlett et al., 2017). An individual's physical size or strength presents a low threat for an online user (Barlett et al., 2017; Slonje et al., 2013). However, some evidence suggests that popularity and status can contextually translate to cyberbullying behavior and has been reported to contribute to an imbalance of power between a victim and perpetrator. Wegge et al. (2016) found in their study with 12- to 14-year-old adolescents that cyberbullying perpetrators were longitudinally associated with an increase of perceived popularity. An imbalance of power has also been linked with a higher degree technology skill or the ability to be anonymous online (Kowalski et al., 2014; Slonje et al., 2013). Perpetrators of cyberbullying can be anonymous online, which is a key contextual difference between traditional bullying and cyberbullying. The implications of not knowing the perpetrator's identity can lead to a victim feeling helpless and fearful and therefore can automatically place them in a position of lesser power (Menesini et al., 2012; Slonje et al., 2013). Limited research conceptually defines how imbalance of power contextually relates across the various forms of cyberbullying. Further research is needed in this research area for clarification concerning the function of asymmetric power roles within cyberbullying.

## Prevalence and impact of cyberbullying

There is huge variation in the reported prevalence rates of cyberbullying. For example, the reported prevalence rates of experiencing cyberbullying as a victim range from 1.5% for Spanish 12- to 18-year-olds (Ortega et al., 2009) to 72% for American 12- to 17-year-olds (Juvonen & Gross, 2008). For those who engage in cyberbullying as a bully, the reported prevalence rates range from 0% for 12- to 19-year-olds from the Netherlands (Didden et al., 2009) to 60% for University students from Hong Kong (Xiao & Wong, 2013). The reported prevalence rates for those who fulfill the bully/victim role in cyberbullying range from 6% for Spanish 12- to 18-year-olds (Ortega et al., 2009) to 62% for Australian 17- to 25-year-olds (Brack & Caltabiano, 2014). Despite the variation in the prevalence rates, some researchers argue that reported prevalence rates tend to converge between 20% and 40% (Aricak et al., 2008; Dehue et al., 2008), with variations attributed to participants' age (Kowalski et al., 2019) and methodological differences.

There are three main methodological reasons for the reported variability in the prevalence rates of cyberbullying, and it is important that we consider them when thinking about the reported prevalence rates of cyberbullying. First, the reported prevalence rates of cyberbullying vary according to how cyberbullying is defined and conceptualized in the measures used to assess cyberbullying. For example, asking participants about specific forms of cyberbullying behaviors is likely to provide lower prevalence rates compared to asking participants about whether they have experienced cyberbullying at a more general level. Second, prevalence rates also vary according to the time frame an individual is asked to reflect on when reporting their experiences. Specifically, there is likely to be variation according to whether an individual is asked to reflect on experiences over a tightly defined timeframe (e.g., a week, month) versus a much longer timeframe (e.g., a year, in their lifetime). Third, prevalence rates also vary according to whether cut off criteria are used to classify individuals into particular participant roles (e.g., bully, victim) and how stringently these criteria are applied. For example, when strict cut off criteria are used to determine a particular role, fewer individuals are likely to fall into this group than when more lenient criteria are applied (Gradinger et al., 2010). Indeed, some researchers have argued that because of the limitations associated with cut off points, utilizing a person-centered approach to identify experiences gives a clearer understanding of experiences (Betts & Houston, 2012; Betts, Gkimitzoudis et al., 2017; Betts et al., 2019). In addition to these methodological reasons for the variation in the reported prevalence rates of cyberbullying, it is also important to acknowledge that social desirability may influence an individual's propensity to disclose involvement in cyberbullying (Chun et al., 2020), many of the samples used in research to explore cyberbullying are self-selecting in nature (Chisholm, 2014), and biases may arise when recalling experiences of bullying (Bovaird, 2010).

Cyberbullying can take many forms. Bauman (2011) described seven forms of cyberbullying: (1) flaming—hostile or aggressive acts directed toward an individual; (2) harassment; (3) denigration—putting the target down or being disrespectful; (4) masquerading—pretending to be someone else when engaging in harmful behaviors directed toward the target; (5) outing and trickery—gaining confidential information from the target and then sharing it with a wider audience; (6) social exclusion—deliberately excluding the target from a group or activities; and (7) cyber stalking. Researchers have also conceptualized cyberbullying in terms of whether it is direct or indirect (Menesini et al., 2011). Direct cyberbullying includes physical (e.g., sending a virus), verbal, nonverbal (i.e., image based), and social (e.g., excluding the target). Indirect forms include sharing gossip and deformation. It is important to acknowledge that the same behavior can be experienced through multiple platforms such as instant messengers, social networking sites, email, small text messages, websites, voting booths, chat rooms, and bash rooms (Beale & Hall, 2007). When considering the types of cyberbullying that bystanders are likely to encounter, research suggests that bystanders are more likely to witness cyberbullying behaviors that include public and private comments, photographs, and status updates (Bordy & Vangelisti, 2017).

Although some research suggests that involvement in cyberbullying tends to peak around the age of 14 (Ortega et al., 2009), there is evidence that cyberbullying is potentially experienced by a much wider age range, albeit decreasing with age (Kim et al., 2017; Wang et al., 2019). Research that has explored the consequences of involvement in cyberbullying has tended to focus on the consequences of those who fulfill the victim role during adolescence for psychosocial adjustment. Adolescents who are victims of cyberbullying also report experiencing elevated levels of anxiety (Juvonen & Gross, 2008), depression (Foody et al., 2019), negative emotions (Ortega et al., 2009; Raskauskas & Stoltz, 2007), poorer mental health, and suicidal ideation (Sampasa-Kanyinga et al., 2014). There is also evidence that experiencing cyberbullying as a victim has consequences that extend beyond psychosocial adjustment including influencing peer relationships and school adjustment (Betts, Spenser, et al., 2017). Focusing on peer relationships, sixth graders who reported experiencing cyberbullying as a victim had lower rates of optimism about peer relationships, had fewer friends, and lower levels of social acceptance (Jackson & Cohen, 2012). In terms of constructs aligned to school adjustment, research has highlighted that those who are victims of cyberbullying also report that they are afraid to go to school (Raskauskas & Stoltz, 2007), like school less (Betts, Houston, et al., 2017), and were more likely to carry weapons to school (Ybarra, Espelage, et al., 2007).

There is also evidence that fulfilling other participant roles in cyberbullying has consequences for an individual's adjustment. Focusing on those individuals who fulfill the cyber bully role, they report engaging in other forms of aggressive behavior, including proactive aggression (Calvete et al., 2010), fights, and liking school less (Carvaldho et al., 2021). Although fewer studies have focused on those individuals who fulfill the bully/victim role, there is evidence that the consequences of being a bully/victim include experiencing elevated levels of depression and somatic symptoms and engaging in other forms of aggressive acts (Gradinger et al., 2009) and consuming more alcohol (Carvalho et al., 2021). Relatively few studies have examined the consequences of witnessing cyberbullying in terms of adjustment. One such study found that those who witnessed greater levels of cyberbullying were more likely to report elevated levels of depressive symptoms and social anxiety (Doumas & Midgett, 2020).

Although there is evidence of the consequences of involvement in cyberbullying, it is important to recognize that not everyone who experiences cyberbullying goes on to experience the same consequences and that, in some cases, consequences vary according to the medium through which the cyberbullying occurred (Nixon, 2014). One of the reasons for this variation is that many of the relationships between involvement in cyberbullying and the psychosocial consequences are mediated and moderated by other variables. For example, social support has been identified as a protective buffer to mitigate against the relationship between experiencing cyberbullying as a victim and bully/victim and anxiety (Hellfeldt et al., 2020). Additionally, gender has been found to moderate relationships between experiencing cyberbullying as a victim and behavioral and emotional outcomes such that being a victim of cyberbullying was a stronger predictor of emotional outcomes for adolescent females, whereas being a victim of cyberbullying was a stronger predictor of behavioral outcomes for adolescent males (Kim et al., 2018). There is also evidence that variations in the size of the audience that witnesses the cyberbullying influence the severity of the social and emotional consequences (Dooley et al., 2009). In addition to the role that other variables may play in the relationship between involvement of cyberbullying and the consequences for adjustment, it is important to acknowledge that much of the research to date has been cross-sectional in nature and the longer-term consequences of involvement in cyberbullying are not well understood because of the lack of longitudinal studies in this area (Jenaro et al., 2018; Kowalski et al., 2019). Further, the lack of longitudinal research also means that it is hard to determine the causal nature of the relationship relating to the consequences of cyberbullying. For example, Kwan et al. (2020) argued that there is a lack of clarity over whether mental health outcomes are the consequence or antecedent of cyberbullying.

## Bystander intervention to cyberbullying

Cyberbullying often occurs in group-based situations, and therefore, how young people respond when they witness cyberbullying is important to the process of combating the issue (Bauman, 2013). Individuals involved in a cyberbullying situation can be classified broadly into three major roles: the instigators of the incident known as "perpetrators," receivers of the targeted insult known as "victims," and observers that are present when the incident takes places also known as "bystanders." Bystanders of cyberbullying can either respond positively by supporting the victim (e.g., comforting the victim, challenging the bully, etc.) or negatively by supporting the perpetrator (encouraging the perpetrator, joining in, ignoring the situation, etc.). Salmivalli et al. (1996: p. 117) suggested that "bystanders were trapped in a social dilemma," where young people recognize the behavior they observe as inappropriate, but fear to intervene to support the victim due to the perceived impact on their social status and safety.

The reactive behaviors of these bystanders play a crucial role in the permanence of cyberbullying incidents and the consequences it may have to the victim and perpetrator. For instance, reactive behaviors focused on victim supportive strategies (e.g., telling the perpetrator to stop) is effective in alleviating the negative consequences for the victim (Salmivalli, 2010). Equally, reactive behaviors centered on supporting the perpetrator (e.g., encouraging the perpetrator to assault the victim) can escalate the severity of the incident on the victim. A focus on bystander processes is warranted not least because peer support can help alleviate victims' suffering (Sainio et al., 2011). However, bystanders are often reluctant to step in and help (Dillon & Bushman, 2015), so there is a crucial need to explore different factors associated with bystander intervention on social media. Young people that use social media can be confronted with cyberbullying both within and outside their social members. This is attributed to the characteristics of social media. For example, users of social media can see public content accessible to anyone, content only accessible to the user's friends, but also content available from "friends of friends". This suggests that bystanders have more of a complex role in the realm of social media, as bystanders may have different types of relationships with other people on social media, which creates different dynamics when choosing if to intervene or not. Specific characteristics of social media allow bystanders to intervene in a variety of ways. For instance, bystanders can intervene using text- and picture-based communication or simply by clicking a button (e.g., like) or "reporting" the incident on the social media channel. As social media is the most common place for cyberbullying to occur (Chen et al., 2017; Whittaker & Kowalski, 2015), it is important to consider different factors that may influence bystander intervention to cyberbullying on social media.

The literature has established that bystanders play a critical role when they witness acts and forms of bullying (Cowie, 2014; Machackova, 2020; Pepler et al., 2021). Even though the online environment is characterized by increased anonymity and autonomy, studies from Poland and the Republic of Korea still report a lack of positive intervention of bystanders in the online domain (Barlińska et al., 2013; Song & Oh, 2018). Young people may choose not to intervene in a positive way due to a fear of retaliation or becoming the next victim (Bauman, 2013), and young people may lack the skills and awareness on how to respond to cyberbullying when they witness it (Gini et al., 2008; Kowalski & Limber, 2007). For example, in a study of 1158 adolescents from Malaysia, 61.5% reported they positively intervened to support the victim (Balakrishnan, 2018). However, a large proportion (40%) still reported not intervening due to fear of retaliation. Reacting in a way that provides support and help for the victim can increase feelings of self-esteem, whereas ignoring an act due to severity or lack of personal responsibility can lead to feelings of social shame and injustice (Bastiaensens et al., 2014; Cowie, 2014). This suggests that it is important to consider different factors that may play a role in bystander intervention to cyberbullying on social media.

One factor associated with bystander intervention is perceived severity. Encouraging bystanders who witness bullying to take responsibility to do something positive is important since they are often reluctant to do so (Caravita et al., 2009; Gini et al., 2008; Song & Oh, 2018). Young people are known to make evaluations about the likely impact of different types of bullying on victims (Chen et al., 2015) and so can respond in a negative or positive manner as they weigh up the risks and benefits according to different courses of action. For instance, research in Taiwan has highlighted the importance of perceived severity of cyberbullying, which can influence how young people respond as a bystander based on their perception on the potential or practical harm (Chen & Cheng, 2017). Some studies conducted in Belgium have reported that when young people evaluate incidents of cyberbullying as severe, they are more motivated to positively intervene to support the victim (Bastiaensens et al., 2014; Desmet et al., 2012; 2014). Recent research with 868 11- to 13-year-olds in the United Kingdom found that bystanders reported that they would provide emotional support to the victim and intervene to address the bully when they evaluated the incident to be severe, characterized by the intensity of the cyberbullying, frequency of the victimization, and extent the victim was upset (Macaulay et al., 2019). In addition, qualitative work has found that young people are more likely to respond positively as a bystander as bullying severity increases (Forsberg et al., 2014; Pepler et al., 2021; Thornberg et al., 2018). For instance, Pepler et al. (2021) interviewed 16 15–16-year olds in Canada and found the when students regard the incident to be more severe, this triggers an emotional response and so are more inclined to step in and intervene to help the victim. As such, bullying severity is considered an important factor for bystander intervention to social media.

Bystander intervention to cyberbullying is also characterized by the public nature of social media. As discussed earlier, the nature of cyberbullying means there could be an infinite amount of witnesses online (Kowalski

et al., 2012), and so the factor of publicity is important for bystander intervention. Research has suggested that cyberbullying behavior may vary
according to publicity, often distinguished across public (i.e., visible to anyone), semipublic (i.e., visible to those in a group), and private (i.e., visible
by the bully and victim only) (Dooley et al., 2009; Macaulay et al., 2022).
The public nature associated with cyberbullying means that young people
online are more likely to witness these incidents (Macaulay et al., 2021;
Mishna et al., 2009). For instance, a study of 10 focus groups with 63 teachers in England found that teachers perceived incidents of cyberbullying in
the public domain would encourage young people to step in and help the
victim, attributed to the increased severity and impact on the victim
(Macaulay et al., 2021). In a similar vein, interviews across 25 Australian
15- to 24-year-olds found that public instances of cyberbullying and those
where the perpetrator had concealed their identity were regarded as more
severe (Dredge et al., 2014). Such findings pertaining to publicity are consistent across young people in Italy, Germany, and Spain (Nocentini et al.,
2010). These findings were attributed to the increased distress and anxiety
when exposed in the public domain (Pieschl et al., 2015; Ševčíková et al.,
2012) and feelings of loneliness and fear when the victim did not know the
identity of the perpetrator (Corby et al., 2016; Dredge et al., 2014). The
nature of social media means that cyberbullying can be perpetrated privately
or publicly. The development of digital technology means that users can
adjust the visibility of their posts on social media. For example, a post that
is visible to a wider number of people has higher visibility than the same
post which may only be visible to friends of the users' social network. The
former is characterized by an increased publicity, allowing more people to
view and react to the post. This suggests that the publicity of cyberbullying
is an important factor to consider when examining bystander intervention
on social media. As young people perceive private and semipublic forms of
cyberbullying to be less severe than incidents in the public domain, this
suggests that young people could choose to ignore these incidents
(Barlińska et al., 2013; Bastiaensens et al., 2014; Koehler & Weber, 2018;
Macaulay et al., 2022). The publicity element of social media also affords
bystanders to intervene in a private or public manner. For example, bystanders to a cyberbullying incident on social media can either send a private
message asking the perpetrator to stop or post the same message more visi-
bly on the original content so friends of the bystander can also see. The latter may encourage other bystanders to also take positive action and so may
be important when mobilizing bystander support on social media.

In addition to bullying severity and publicity, friendship status between the bystander and victim is also an important factor which determines how the bystander intervenes. Jones et al. (2011) found that children's group membership predicted likelihood of intervention with children not intervening to support the victim if they do not identify with them or have a good relationship with the perpetrator. This suggests that bystander friendships with the perpetrator may act as a barrier to positive intervention. On the other hand, studies have shown that friendship between the bystander and victim encourages bystanders to act and help the victim (Byers & Cerulli, 2020; DeSmet et al., 2012; 2014; Jones et al., 2011; Price et al., 2014). For instance, in the qualitative research of Price et al. (2014), young people discussed how friendship is characterized by mutual support for each other and so bystanders that are friends with the victim would not want to betray the trust and social convention of friendship by not intervening. In addition, intervening to support friends that are being bullied outweighs the cost of becoming the next victim (DeSmet et al., 2014). This is in line with more recent findings reporting that friendship ties were important for reasoning to intervene to help the victim (Byers & Cerulli, 2020).

There are also moral implications for not intervening to help friends (e.g., being excluded from a friendship group). However, DeSmet et al. (2012) found young people have a preference to support victims indirectly, as this can be easier than direct intervention online. Positive relationships with the victim may prompt bystander intervention to support the victim due to the emotional arousal the bystander experiences from witnessing the incident. For example, a study of 800 children from the Netherlands found that emotional arousal to a victim of bullying was a function of bullying severity, with greater levels of bullying severity inducing higher levels of emotional arousal (van Noorden et al., 2016). In addition, emotional arousal to intervene may also be promoted by relationship status to the victimized peer (Byers & Cerulli, 2020; DeSmet et al., 2014). For instance, DeSmet et al. (2014) found that bystanders expressed more willingness to intervene when the victim was a friend, even though they recognized the costs associated with intervention: personal costs of being isolated for not intervening outweighed risks for intervening.

Another contextual factor that influences bystander intervention to cyberbullying is centered on a unique characteristic with social media, the number of virtual onlookers. The greater number of passive individuals that witness something online and choose to do nothing, the less likely any will step in and help the victim, via diffusion of responsibility (i.e., the perception that individuals do not need to take responsibility to intervene as someone else will). Previous research using a sample of 333 derived from online communities has provided empirical support that group size online does influence response behavior (Voelpel et al., 2008). As such, there is growing tendency to use the theoretical notion of diffusion of responsibility to explain incidents of cyberbullying (e.g., Machackova et al., 2015; Obermaier et al., 2016; You & Lee, 2019). For example, Obermaier et al. (2016) found that participants in Germany did report less responsibility when witnessing cyberbullying in the presence of more bystanders, and so were less likely to intervene to support for the victim. However, You and Lee (2019) found that the relationship between number of bystanders and willingness to intervene to support the victim is not a linear one. You and Lee (2019) examined how the number of bystanders present on Facebook influenced bystander intervention intentions from a sample of 253 participants aged between 25−35 years. Specifically, this study showed that as the number of other bystanders present on Facebook increased from 6−24 to 224, bystander intentions to intervene to help the victim decreased. However, when the number of bystanders' present increased from 224 to 5025, bystander intentions to support the victim increased. This suggests that there is a critical point where bystanders choose to intervene to support the victim despite the number of other bystanders' present. The nature of social media means that bystanders can intervene directly (i.e., telling the perpetrator to stop) or indirectly (i.e., reporting the incident via the social media moderator). One study looking at how bystanders intervene on social media reported that bystanders prefer to take indirect forms of supportive intervention compared to direct forms (Dillon & Bushman, 2015). More recently, an experimental study exposing cyberbullying messages on Twitter to undergraduate students found that bystanders were more likely to directly intervene when there were multiple perpetrators involved in the incident (Kazerooni et al., 2018). Despite this, bystanders were less willing to intervene when they witnessed content on Twitter that had been retweeted compared to the original content.

The social environment on social media may also influence how bystanders intervene. The nature of the social environment relates to how young people are expected to behave in different settings and the attitudes and behaviors of those within the group. For instance, one study of 525 adolescent bystanders to cyberbullying found that perceived approval from friends or family for approving cyberbullying predicted likelihood for bystanders to join in and support the perpetrator, attributed to social pressure (Bastiaensens et al., 2016). Regarding victim support, young people are motivated to help when they receive an appropriate response from the adults and the approval of their peers, as well as the expectation of reciprocal behavior if they are bullied in the future (Thomas et al., 2012). The nature of social media means that bystanders may not know if the victim needs help or not, so aligned to the social environment, bystanders may receive a direct request for help (Machackova, 2020; Macháčková et al., 2013). Holfeld (2014) reported that active responses from victims (such as asking for help) or reactive ones (such as the victim confronting the offender) mean that an incident is more likely to be viewed as a serious situation from which the victim is trying to escape, which could help mobilize bystanders to offer support.

Evaluation of the cyberbullying incident on social media also influences intervention. Despite young people recognizing cyberbullying as a serious issue (Bryce & Fraser, 2013), a majority continue to do nothing (Balakrishnan, 2018; Song & Oh, 2018). Van Cleemput et al. (2014) attributed this to a lack of knowledge regarding the situation. For instance, bystanders may perceive that other people are helping the victim so the situation may already be resolved. In addition, bystanders may also not intervene if they blame the victim for what has happened or are not aware of the serious consequences cyberbullying can lead to (DeSmet et al., 2012; 2014). As such, it is important to promote the serious consequences of cyberbullying, as this can act as a facilitator for bystander intervention (Thomas et al., 2012).

Personal factors have also been attributed to explaining cyberbystander intervention on social media. For instance, empathy has been discussed as an important trait in promoting bystander intervention, with higher empathy levels associated with bystander victim supportive behaviors (Barlińska et al., 2018; Erreygers et al., 2016; Machackova et al., 2015; Price et al., 2014; Van Cleemput et al., 2014; Wang & Kim, 2021). In a recent study examining bystander intervention to cyberbullying on social media, empathy was found to influence if bystanders would act or not (Wang, 2020). Those individuals that reported higher levels of empathy when witnessing a cyberbullying incident on social media were more likely to privately and publicly step in to support the victim. The latter is important because if bystanders can be encouraged to offer support in the presence of others, this may mobilize other bystanders to also step in and help the victim. Other personal factors like gender have also been linked to bystander intervention to cyberbullying. On the one hand, some research suggests that gender is not associated with bystander intervention to cyberbullying (Barlińska et al., 2015). On the other hand, a more consistent line of research suggests that girls compared to boys are more likely to step in and support the victim (Bastiaensens et al., 2016; DeSmet et al., 2016; Macaulay et al., 2019). For instance, Macaulay et al. (2019) explored the role of bullying severity on victim defending and found that girls compared to boys are more likely to provide victim support regardless of how severe the bullying context was. It has been suggested that girls view bullying in general as more serious than boys and so may feel a greater responsibility to do something positive to help the victim (Maunder et al., 2010; Molluzzo & Lawler, 2012).

Taken together, there are a variety of factors at play that influence bystander intervention to cyberbullying on social media. Future research should endeavor to further explore the contextual and personal factors responsible for mobilizing bystanders to help the victim. Such findings can be applied to antibullying initiatives when combating the challenge of cyberbullying.

## Theoretical explanations of bystander behavior

One recognized theoretical explanation for why young people may or may not intervene is the bystander effect (Latané & Darley, 1970). This theoretical notion argues that in emergencies, people in groups are less likely to help in an emergency compared to individuals. This intervention in an emergency is inhibited by diffusion of responsibility (i.e., the reduction of feeling responsible when others are present), audience inhibition, and pluralistic ignorance (i.e., looking to others for cues about how to behave, while they are looking to you; collective misinterpretation). The bystander effect and research on diffusion of responsibility is the most widely used theoretical framework to help explain online behavior when responding to cyberbullying (Allison & Bussey, 2016; You & Lee, 2019). When it comes to cyberbullying, bystanders have the option to positively intervene anonymously; however, despite the physical absence of other bystanders, the perceived virtual onlookers of an incident imply an element of diffusion of responsibility (Barlińska et al., 2013; DeSmet et al., 2014). The social psychological work by Latané and Darley (1970) outlines the importance of being able to notice the event and interpret the event as something serious that merits intervention. Normally, bystanders would look to others to see how they physically respond via diffusion of responsibility. However, in the online environment, this notion is much more ambiguous, as bystanders may be unaware of how many virtual "onlookers" there are.

In addition, the arousal: cost−reward model (Dovidio et al., 1991; Piliavin et al., 1981) can also be used to explain bystander helping behavior on social media. The model consists of two factors that influence bystander intervention: arousal and cost−reward. The first factor of arousal is a fundamental construct as it focuses on the emotional response of witnessing a distressing incident where others are in need of help. In the context of bystander intervention on social media, bystanders witnessing cyberbullying elicits emotional arousal associated with unpleasant emotions, subsequently motivating bystanders to intervene to reduce such unpleasant emotions. The second factor of cost−reward involves the cognitive component of bystanders weighing up the risks and the benefits of different course of action. For example, costs for a bystander include personal costs for intervening to support the victim (e.g., embarrassment and retaliation from the perpetrator), but also the negative consequences for the victim if the bystander chooses not to intervene (e.g., feelings of guilt and perceived evaluation from others). On the other hand, rewards refer to the positive outcomes associated with intervention. So, the arousal: cost-reward model (Dovidio et al., 1991; Piliavin et al., 1981) assumes that bystander intervention to cyberbullying on social media is heightened when costs are minimized and rewards are maximized.

Finally, the online disinhibition effect has also been used to understand bystander intervention to cyberbullying (Suler, 2004). Due to the minimization of authority in the online domain and the notion of asynchronicity as actions have no immediate consequences online, it is possible that young people are more likely to encourage the bully and escalate the situation (Bryce & Fraser, 2013; Suler, 2004). The notion of online disinhibition suggests that young people separate their actions online to real-life interactions. For example, this suggests that young people are more likely to encourage the bully online because they have the invisible barrier of anonymity, allowing young people to feel more confident online to do things they would not necessarily do in the physical world (Bryce & Fraser, 2013;

Suler, 2004). As a result, young people may inaccurately misjudge how the victim is feeling. On the other hand, this absence of authority figures in the online domain may suggest that young people are less likely to actively seek help from an adult and/or provide emotional support to the victim.

## Recommendations

This chapter has presented an overview of cyberbullying and discussed different factors associated with bystander intervention to cyberbullying on social media. From the factors discussed in this chapter, the following suggestions should be considered when devising strategies to address cyberbullying and mobile prosocial bystander behavior.

It is recommended that strategies to combat cyberbullying should focus on working with young people to develop empathy. Involving young people in the development of antibullying initiatives would ensure that these initiatives also acknowledge the perceptions of young people and solutions to promote bystander intervention. For example, antibullying initiatives could focus more on building empathy through role play activities and reflections to facilitate bystander intervention to cyberbullying. This would encourage bystanders to intervene to support victims and provide emotional support, in the hope of alleviating the negative consequences of cyberbullying. This is important because providing emotional support for the victim is an effective strategy young people adopt when they witness cyberbullying online (Bastiaensens et al., 2019; Machackova et al., 2015). When young people provide emotional support, they discuss the cyberbullying incident with the victim and provide the victim coping strategies (Bastiaensens et al., 2019) to help them overcome the negative consequences.

In addition, strategies to address cyberbullying should focus on promoting a school climate that advocates bullying and emphasizes the importance of victim support. For instance, whole-school approaches to bullying have been widely advocated in the literature (Altundağ & Ayas, 2020; Ttofi & Farrington, 2011), and so the voices of young people need to be acknowledged in the development of antibullying initiatives. From a theoretical viewpoint, the social psychological work by Latané and Darley (1970) outlines the importance of being able to notice the event and interpret the event as something serious that merits intervention when deciding whether to intervene. Normally, bystanders would look to others to see how they physically respond via diffusion of responsibility. However, in the online environment, this notion is much more ambiguous, as bystanders may be unaware of how many virtual "onlookers" there are. In this case, it is important that strategies addressing cyberbullying work with young people to promote the idea that all forms of cyberbullying are serious, and despite the ambiguity the online environment affords, victim support should be at the forefront of bystander actions. Indeed, severity of the situation has been implicated in reducing diffusion of responsibility (Macaulay et al., 2019), so it is suggested that cyberbullying initiatives inform young people on the serious consequences of being a cyberbullying victim to mobilize prosocial bystander support.

Interventions to address cyberbullying and promote bystander intervention on social media should encourage social support and fostering strong friendships within the school. An important element to promote positive bystander actions is the expectation of appraisal and social support. Therefore, the educational community, parents, and social media companies need to implement social support and recognition for bystander intervention, as this will increase perceived self-efficacy to intervene to support the victim and confront the perpetrator (DeSmet et al., 2014; Price et al., 2014; Thomas et al., 2012). For example, if teachers recognize and appraise positive bystander intervention, this will make young people more motivated to act in this manner when the witness cyberbullying online. In addition, educating young people that some victims may suffer in silence and can experience negative consequences from cyberbullying even if the perpetrator has/has not concealed their identity may reinforce the message that all incidents of cyberbullying are serious. As such, young people will be more inclined to intervene to support the victim and seek help to address the situation. For example, teachers can implement reflection discussions and role play scenarios to help build empathy, so young people are more likely to see cyberbullying as serious when the victim is upset (Machackova & Pfetsch, 2016). However, it is also important that interventions addressing bystander behavior implement adult support to avoid "unhelpful" responses from young people. Research suggests that young people are more likely to positively intervene when they exhibit higher levels of empathy and perceive supportive relationships with their peers and teachers within the school (Barlińska et al., 2013; Machackova & Pfetsch, 2016). This suggests that schools and teachers play an important role in promoting the notion of positive intervention and building a positive school climate. In addition, while it is important to support bystanders of cyberbullying, this should be systematically addressed alongside parent, school, and community support to address the issue.

## Conclusion

The universal presence of digital technologies and accessibility to the internet enables children and adolescents to benefit from fast and efficient communication, but also presents numerous online dangers, specifically cyberbullying. This chapter has provided an overview on cyberbullying, discussing the definitional characteristics, prevalence, and the impact it can have. Specifically, this chapter has provided an overview on the different factors that influence bystander intervention to cyberbullying on social media. It is clear that bystanders play a prominent role in cyberbullying and should be at the forefront of intervention efforts. This chapter has shown how different contextual and personal factors may precipitate rather than attenuate prosocial bystander responses. Future research on bystander behavior should endeavor to further understand the mechanism that facilitates prosocial bystander action to cyberbullying on social media.

## References

Allison, K. R., & Bussey, K. (2016). Cyber-bystanding in context: A review of the literature on witnesses' responses to cyberbullying. *Children and Youth Services Review, 65,* 183–194. Available from https://doi.org/10.1016/j.childyouth.2016.03.026.

Altundağ, Y., & Ayas, T. (2020). Effectiveness of the whole school-based program for Equipping High School Counselors with strategies of coping with cyberbullying and cyberbullying awareness. *Education & Science/Egitim ve Bilim, 45*(201).

Anderson, M., & Jiang, J. (2018). Teens, social media & technology 2018. Pew Research Center. Retrieved from <http://www.pewinternet.org/2018/05/31/teens-social-media-technology-2018/>.

Aricak, T., Siyahhan, S., Uzunhasanoglu, A., Saribeyoglu, S., Ciplak, S., & Memmedov, C. (2008). Cyberbullying among Turkish adolescents. *Cyberpsychology & Behavior, 11,* 253–261. Available from https://doi.org/10.1089/cpb.2007.0016.

Baas, N., de Jong, M. D., & Drossaert, C. H. (2013). Children's perspectives on cyberbullying: Insights based on participatory research. *Cyberpsychology, Behavior, and Social Networking, 16,* 248–253. Available from https://doi.org/10.1089/cyber.2012.0079.

Balakrishnan, V. (2018). Actions, emotional reactions and cyberbullying—From the lens of bullies, victims, bully-victims and bystanders among Malaysian young adults. *Telematics and Informatics, 35*(5), 1190–1200. Available from https://doi.org/10.1016/j.tele.2018.02.002.

Barlett, C. P., Prot, S., Anderson, C. A., & Gentile, D. A. (2017). An empirical examination of the strength differential hypothesis in cyberbullying behavior. *Psychology of Violence*, 7(1), 22.

Barlińska, J., Szuster, A., & Winiewski, M. (2013). Cyberbullying among adolescent bystanders: Role of the communication medium, form of violence, and empathy. *Journal of Community & Applied Social Psychology*, 23(1), 37–51. Available from https://doi.org/10.1002/casp.2137.

Barlińska, J., Szuster, A., & Winiewski, M. (2015). The role of short-and long-term cognitive empathy activation in preventing cyberbystander reinforcing cyberbullying behavior. *Cyberpsychology, Behavior, and Social Networking*, 18(4), 241–244. Available from https://doi.org/10.1089/cyber.2014.0412.

Barlińska, J., Szuster, A., & Winiewski, M. (2018). Cyberbullying among adolescent bystanders: Role of affective versus cognitive empathy in increasing prosocial cyberbystander behavior. *Frontiers in Psychology*, 9, 799. Available from https://doi.org/10.3389/fpsyg.2018.00799.

Baruch, Y. (2005). Bullying on the net: Adverse behavior on e-mail and its impact. *Information and Management*, 42, 361–371.

Bastiaensens, S., Van Cleemput, K., Vandebosch, H., Poels, K., DeSmet, A., & De Bourdeaudhuij, I. (2019). *"Were you cyberbullied? Let me help you." Studying adolescents' online peer support of cyberbullying victims using thematic analysis of online support group fora. Narratives in research and interventions on cyberbullying among young people* (pp. 95–112). Cham: Springer. Available from https://doi.org/10.1007/978-3-030-04960-7_7.

Bastiaensens, S., Pabian, S., Vandebosch, H., Poels, K., Van Cleemput, K., DeSmet, A., & De Bourdeaudhuij, I. (2016). From normative influence to social pressure: How relevant others affect whether bystanders join in cyberbullying. *Social Development*, 25(1), 193–211. Available from https://doi.org/10.1111/sode.12134.

Bastiaensens, S., Vandebosch, H., Poels, K., Van Cleemput, K., Desmet, A., & De Bourdeaudhuij, I. (2014). Cyberbullying on social network sites. An experimental study into bystanders' behavioural intentions to help the victim or reinforce the bully. *Computers in Human Behavior*, 31, 259–271. Available from https://doi.org/10.1016/j.chb.2013.10.036.

Bauman, S. (2011). *Cyberbullying: What counselors need to know*. Alexandria, VA: American Counseling Association.

Bauman, S. (2013). Cyberbullying: What does research tell us? *Theory into Practice*, 52(4), 249–256. Available from https://doi.org/10.1080/00405841.2013.829727.

Beale, A. V., & Hall, K. R. (2007). Cyberbullying: What school administrators (and parents) can do. *The Clearing House*, 81, 8–12. Available from https://doi.org/10.3200/TCHS.81.1.8-12.

Betts, L. R., Baguley, T., & Gardner, S. (2019). Examining adults' participant roles in cyberbullying. *Journal of Social and Personal Relationships*, 36, 3362–3370. Available from https://doi.org/10.1177/0265407518822774.

Betts, L. R., Gkimitzoudis, T., Spenser, K. A., & Baguley, T. (2017). Examining the roles young people fulfil in five types of cyber bullying. *Journal of Social and Personal Relationships*, 34, 1080–1098. Available from https://doi.org/10.1177/0265407516668585.

Betts, L. R., & Houston, J. E. (2012). The effects of cyberbullying on children's school adjustment. In J. Jia (Ed.), *Educational stages and interactive learning: From kindergarten to workplace training* (pp. 209–230). Hershey, PA: IGI Global.

Betts, L. R., Houston, J. E., Steer, O. L., & Gardner, S. E. (2017). Adolescents' experiences of victimization: The role of attribution style and generalized trust. *Journal of School Violence*, 16, 25–48. Available from https://doi.org/10.1080/15388220.2015.1100117.

Betts, L. R., Spenser, K. A., & Gardner, S. E. (2017). Adolescents' involvement in cyber bullying and perceptions of school: The importance of perceived peer acceptance for female adolescents. *Sex Roles*, 77, 471–481. Available from https://doi.org/10.1007/s11199-017-0742-2.

Bordy, N., & Vangelisti, A. L. (2017). Cyberbullying: Topics, strategies, and sex differences. *Computers in Human Behavior*, 75, 739–748. Available from https://doi.org/10.1016/j.chb.2017.06.020.

Bovaird, J. A. (2010). Scales and surveys: Some problems with measuring bullying behavior. In S. R. Jimerson, S. M. Swearer, & D. L. Espelage (Eds.), *International handbook of school bullying: An international perspective* (pp. 277–292). New York, NY: Routledge.

Boyd, D. (2014). *It's complicated: The social lives of networked teens.* Yale University Press.

Brack, K., & Caltabiano, N. (2014). Cyberbullying and self-esteem in Australian adults. *Journal of Psychosocial Research on Cyberspace, 8,* article 7.

Bryce, J., & Fraser, J. (2013). "It's common sense that it's wrong": Young people's perceptions and experiences of cyberbullying. *Cyberpsychology, Behavior, and Social Networking,* 16(11), 783–787. Available from https://doi.org/10.1089/cyber.2012.0275.

Byers, D. S., & Cerulli, M. (2020). Staying in their own lane: Ethical reasoning among college students witnessing cyberbullying. *Journal of Diversity in Higher Education.* Available from https://psycnet.apa.org/doi/10.1037/dhe0000180.

Calvete, E., Orue, I., & Estévez, A. (2010). Cyberbullying in adolescents: Modalities and aggressors' profile. *Computers in Human Behavior,* 26, 1128–1135. Available from https://doi.org/10.1016/j.chb.2010.03.017.

Caravita, S. C., Di Blasio, P., & Salmivalli, C. (2009). Unique and interactive effects of empathy and social status on involvement in bullying. *Social Development,* 18(1), 140–163. Available from https://doi.org/10.1111/j.1467-9507.2008.00465.x.

Carvalho, M., Branquinho, C., & Gasper de Matos, M. (2021). Cyberbullying and bullying: Impact on psychological symptoms and well-being. *Child Indicators Research, 14,* 435–452. Available from https://doi.org/10.1007/s12187-020-09756-2.

Chen, L., Ho, S. S., & Lwin, M. O. (2017). A meta-analysis of factors predicting cyberbullying perpetration and victimization: From the social cognitive and media effects approach. *New Media & Society,* 19(8), 1194–1213. Available from https://doi.org/10.1177/1461444816634037.

Chen, L. M., Cheng, W., & Ho, H. C. (2015). Perceived severity of school bullying in elementary schools based on participants' roles. *Educational Psychology,* 35(4), 484–496. Available from https://doi.org/10.1080/01443410.2013.860220.

Chen, L. M., & Cheng, Y. Y. (2017). Perceived severity of cyberbullying behaviour: Differences between genders, grades and participant roles. *Educational Psychology,* 37(5), 599–610. Available from https://doi.org/10.1080/01443410.2016.1202898.

Chen, P. S. D., Lambert, A. D., & Guidry, K. R. (2010). Engaging online learners: The impact of web-based learning technology on college student engagement. *Computers & Education,* 54(4), 1222–1232.

Chisholm, J. F. (2014). Review of the status of cyberbullying and cyberbullying prevention. *Journal of Information Systems Education,* 25, 77–87.

Chun, J., Lee, J., Kim, J., & Lee, S. (2020). An international systematic review of cyberbullying measurements. *Computers in Human Behavior,* 106485. Available from https://doi.org/10.1016/j.chb.2020.106485.

Corby, E. K., Campbell, M., Spears, B., Slee, P., Butler, D., & Kift, S. (2016). Students' perceptions of their own victimization: A youth voice perspective. *Journal of School Violence,* 15(3), 322–342. Available from https://doi.org/10.1080/15388220.2014.996719.

Corcoran, L., McGuckin, C. M., & Prentice, G. (2015). Cyberbullying or cyber aggression?: A review of existing definitions of cyber-based peer-to-peer aggression. *Societies,* 5(2), 245–255.

Cowie, H. (2014). Understanding the role of bystanders and peer support in school bullying. *International Journal of Emotional Education,* 6(1), 26–32.

Dehue, F., Bolman, C., & Völlink, T. (2008). Cyberbullying: Youngsters' experiences and parental perception. *CyberPsychology & Behavior, 11,* 217—223. Available from https://doi.org/10.1089/cpb.2007.0008.

DeSmet, A., Bastiaensens, S., Van Cleemput, K., Poels, K., Vandebosch, H., & De Bourdeaudhuij, I. (2012). Mobilizing bystanders of cyberbullying: An exploratory study into behavioural determinants of defending the victim. In B. K. Wiederhold, & G. Riva (Eds.), *Annual review of cybertherapy and telemedicine 2012: Advanced technologies in the behavioral, social and neurosciences* (pp. 58—63). Amsterdam: IOS Press BV. Available from https://doi.org/10.3233/978-1-61499-121-2-58.

DeSmet, A., Bastiaensens, S., Van Cleemput, K., Poels, K., Vandebosch, H., Cardon, G., & De Bourdeaudhuij, I. (2016). Deciding whether to look after them, to like it, or leave it: A multidimensional analysis of predictors of positive and negative bystander behavior in cyberbullying among adolescents. *Computers in Human Behavior, 57,* 398—415. Available from https://doi.org/10.1016/j.chb.2015.12.051.

DeSmet, A., Veldeman, C., Poels, K., Bastiaensens, S., Van Cleemput, K., Vandebosch, H., & De Bourdeaudhuij, I. (2014). Determinants of self-reported bystander behavior in cyberbullying incidents amongst adolescents. *Cyberpsychology, Behavior, and Social Networking, 17*(4), 207—215. Available from https://doi.org/10.1089/cyber.2013.0027.

Didden, R., Scholte, R. H. J., Korzilius, H., de Moor, J. M. H., Vermeulen, A., O'Reilly, M., Lang, R., & Lancioni, G. E. (2009). Cyberbullying among students with intellectual and developmental disability in special education settings. *Developmental Neurorehabilitation, 12,* 146—151. Available from https://doi.org/10.1080/17518420902971356.

Dillon, K. P., & Bushman, B. J. (2015). Unresponsive or un-noticed?: Cyberbystander intervention in an experimental cyberbullying context. *Computers in Human Behavior, 45,* 144—150. Available from https://doi.org/10.1016/j.chb.2014.12.009.

Dooley, J., Pyżalski, J., & Cross, D. (2009). Cyberbullying versus face-to-face bullying: A theoretical and conceptual review. *Journal of Psychology, 217,* 182—188. Available from https://doi.org/10.1027/0044-3409.217.4.182.

Doumas, D. M., & Midgett, A. (2020). The association between witnessing cyberbullying and depressive symptoms and social anxiety among elementary school students. *Psychology in the Schools, 58,* 622—637.

Dovidio, J. F., Piliavin, J. A., Gaertner, S., et al. (1991). The arousal: Cost-reward model and the process of intervention: A review of the evidence. In M. S. Clark (Ed.), *Review of personality and social psychology* (pp. 86—118). Thousand Oaks, CA: SAGE.

Dredge, R., Gleeson, J. F., & De la Piedad Garcia, X. (2014). Risk factors associated with impact severity of cyberbullying victimization: A qualitative study of adolescent online social networking. *Cyberpsychology, Behavior, and Social Networking, 17*(5), 287—291. Available from https://doi.org/10.1089/cyber.2013.0541.

Erreygers, S., Pabian, S., Vandebosch, H., & Baillien, E. (2016). Helping behaviour among adolescent bystanders of cyberbullying: The role of impulsivity. *Learning and Individual Differences, 48,* 61—67. Available from https://doi.org/10.1016/j.lindif.2016.03.003.

Foody, M., McGuire, L., Kuldas, S., & O'Higgins Norman, J. (2019). Friendship quality and gender differences in association with cyberbullying involvement and psychological well-being. *Frontiers in Psychology, 10,* 1723. Available from https://doi.org/10.3389/fpsyg.2019.01723.

Forsberg, C., Thornberg, R., & Samuelsson, M. (2014). Bystanders to bullying: Fourth-to seventh-grade students' perspectives on their reactions. *Research Papers in Education, 29* (5), 557—576. Available from https://doi.org/10.1080/02671522.2013.878375.

Gini, G., Albiero, P., Benelli, B., & Altoe, G. (2008). Determinants of adolescents' active defending and passive bystanding behavior in bullying. *Journal of Adolescence, 31*(1), 93—105. Available from https://doi.org/10.1016/j.adolescence.2007.05.002.

Gradinger, P., Strohmeier, D., & Spiel, C. (2009). Traditional bullying and cyberbullying: Identification of risk groups for adjustment problems. *Journal of Psychology, 217,* 205–213. Available from https://doi.org/10.1027/0044-3409.217.4.182.

Gradinger, P., Strohmeier, D., & Spiel, C. (2010). Definition and measurement of cyberbullying. *Cyberpsychology: Journal of Psychosocial Research on Cyberspace, 4,* 1–13.

Grigg, D. W. (2010). Cyber-aggression: Definition and concept of cyberbullying. *Australian Journal of Guidance & Counselling, 20*(2), 143–156. Available from https://doi.org/10.1375/ajgc.20.2.143.

Hellfeldt, K., López-Romoero, L., & Andershed, H. (2020). Cyberbullying and psychological well-being in young adolescence: The potential protective mediation effects of social support from family, friends, and teachers. *International Journal of Environmental Research and Public Health, 17,* 1–16. Available from https://doi.org/10.3390/ijerph17010045.

Holfeld, B. (2014). Perceptions and attributions of bystanders to cyber bullying. *Computers in Human Behavior, 38,* 1–7. Available from https://doi.org/10.1016/j.chb.2014.05.012.

Hutson, E. (2016). Cyberbullying in adolescence. A concept analysis. *Advances in Nursing Science, 39,* 60–70.

Jackson, C. L., & Cohen, R. (2012). Childhood victimization: Modeling the relation between classroom victimization, cyber victimization, and psychosocial functioning. *Psychology of Popular Media Culture, 1,* 254–269. Available from https://doi.org/10.1037/a0029482.

Jenaro, C., Flores, N., & Frías, C. P. (2018). Systematic review of empirical studies on cyberbullying in adults: What we know and what we should investigate. *Aggression and Violent Behavior, 38,* 113–122. Available from https://doi.org/10.1016/j.avb.2017.12.003.

Jones, S. E., Manstead, A. S., & Livingstone, A. G. (2011). Ganging up or sticking together? Group processes and children's responses to text-message bullying. *British Journal of Psychology, 102*(1), 71–96. Available from https://doi.org/10.1348/000712610X502826.

Juvonen, J., & Gross, E. F. (2008). Extending the school grounds?–Bullying experiences in cyberspace. *Journal of School Health, 78,* 496–505.

Kazerooni, F., Taylor, S. H., Bazarova, N. N., & Whitlock, J. (2018). Cyberbullying bystander intervention: The number of offenders and retweeting predict likelihood of helping a cyberbullying victim. *Journal of Computer-Mediated Communication, 23*(3), 146–162. Available from https://doi.org/10.1093/jcmc/zmy005.

Kiesler, S., Siegel, J., & McGuire, T. W. (1984). Social psychological aspects of computer-mediated communication. *American Psychologist, 39*(10), 1123.

Kim, S., Boyle, M. H., & Georgiades, K. (2017). Cyberbullying victimization and its association with health across the life course: A Canadian population study. *Canadian Journal of Public Health, 108,* e468–e474. Available from https://doi.org/10.17269/CJPH.108.6175.

Kim, S., Colwell, S. R., Kata, A., Boyle, M. H., & Georgiades, K. (2018). Cyberbullying victimization and adolescent mental health: Evidence of differential effects by sex and mental health problem type. *Journal of Youth and Adolescence, 47,* 661–672. Available from https://doi.org/10.1007/s10964-017-0678-4.

Koehler, C., & Weber, M. (2018). "Do I really need to help?!" Perceived severity of cyberbullying, victim blaming, and bystanders' willingness to help the victim. *Cyberpsychology: Journal of Psychosocial Research on Cyberspace, 12*(4). Available from https://doi.org/10.5817/CP2018-4-4.

Kofoed, J., & Staksrud, E. (2019). 'We always torment different people, so by definition, we are no bullies': The problem of definitions in cyberbullying research. *New Media & Society, 21*(4), 1006–1020.

Kowalski, R., Giumetti, G., Schroeder, A., & Lattanner, M. (2014). Bullying in the digital age: A critical review and meta-analysis of cyberbullying research among youth. *Psychological Bulletin*, *140*(4), 1073−1137. Available from https://doi.org/10.1037/a0035618.

Kowalski, R. M., Limber, S. E., & Agatston, P. W. (2012). *Cyberbullying: Bullying in the digital age* (2nd ed.). Malden, MA: Wiley-Blackwell.

Kowalski, R. M., & Limber, S. P. (2007). Electronic bullying among middle school students. *Journal of Adolescent Health*, *41*(6), S22−S30. Available from https://doi.org/10.1016/j.jadohealth.2007.08.017.

Kowalski, R. M., Limber, S. P., & McCord, A. (2019). A developmental approach to cyberbullying: Prevalence and protective factors. *Aggressive and Violent Behavior*, *45*, 20−32. Available from https://doi.org/10.1016/j.avb.2018.02.009.

Kwan, I., Dickson, K., Richardson, M., MacDowall, W., Burchett, H., Stansfield, C., Brunton, G., Sutcliffe, K., & Thomas, J. (2020). Cyberbullying and children and young people's mental health: A systematic map of systematic reviews. *Cyberpsychology, Behavior, and Social Networking*, *23*, 72−82. Available from https://doi.org/10.1089/cyber.2019.0370.

Langos, C. (2012). Cyberbullying: The challenge to define. *Cyberpsychology, Behavior, and Social Networking*, *15*(6), 285−289.

Latané, B., & Darley, J. M. (1970). *The unresponsive bystander: Why doesn't he help?* Appleton-Century-Crofts.

Lenhart, A. (2015). Teens, social media, and technology overview. Pew Research Center.

Macaulay, P. J., Betts, L. R., Stiller, J., & Kellezi, B. (2021). 'The more public it is, the more severe it is': Teachers' perceptions on the roles of publicity and severity in cyberbullying. *Research Papers in Education*, 1−28. Available from https://doi.org/10.1080/02671522.2020.1767183.

Macaulay, P. J., Betts, L. R., Stiller, J., & Kellezi, B. (2022). Bystander responses to cyberbullying: The role of perceived severity, publicity, anonymity, type of cyberbullying, and victim response. *Computers in Human Behavior*, *131*, 107238. Available from https://doi.org/10.1016/j.chb.2022.107238.

Macaulay, P. J., Boulton, M. J., & Betts, L. R. (2019). Comparing early adolescents' positive bystander responses to cyberbullying and traditional bullying: The impact of severity and gender. *Journal of Technology in Behavioral Science*, *4*(3), 253−261. Available from https://doi.org/10.1007/s41347-018-0082-2.

Machackova, H. (2020). Bystander reactions to cyberbullying and cyberaggression: Individual, contextual, and social factors. *Current Opinion in Psychology*. Available from https://doi.org/10.1016/j.copsyc.2020.06.003.

Machackova, H., Dedkova, L., & Mezulanikova, K. (2015). Brief report: The bystander effect in cyberbullying incidents. *Journal of Adolescence*, *43*, 96−99. Available from https://doi.org/10.1016/j.adolescence.2015.05.010.

Machackova, H., & Pfetsch, J. (2016). Bystanders' responses to offline bullying and cyberbullying: The role of empathy and normative beliefs about aggression. *Scandinavian Journal of Psychology*, *57*(2), 169−176. Available from https://doi.org/10.1111/sjop.12277.

Macháčková, H., Dedkova, L., Sevcikova, A., & Cerna, A. (2013). Bystanders' support of cyberbullied schoolmates. *Journal of Community & Applied Social Psychology*, *23*(1), 25−36. Available from https://doi.org/10.1002/casp.2135.

Maunder, R. E., Harrop, A., & Tattersall, A. J. (2010). Pupil and staff perceptions of bullying in secondary schools: Comparing behavioural definitions and their perceived seriousness. *Educational Research*, *52*(3), 263−282. Available from https://doi.org/10.1080/00131881.2010.504062.

Menesini, E., Nocentini, A., & Calussi, P. (2011). The measurement of cyberbullying: Dimensional structure and relative item severity and discrimination.

*Cyberpsychology, Behavior, and Social Networking, 14,* 267−274. Available from https://doi.org/10.1089/cyber.2010.0002.

Menesini, E., Nocentini, A., Palladino, B. E., Frisén, A., Berne, S., Ortega-Ruiz, R., & Naruskov, K. (2012). Cyberbullying definition among adolescents: A comparison across six European countries. *Cyberpsychology, Behavior, and Social Networking, 15*(9), 455−463.

Mishna, F., Saini, M., & Solomon, S. (2009). Ongoing and online: Children and youth's perceptions of cyber bullying. *Children and Youth Services Review, 31*(12), 1222−1228. Available from https://doi.org/10.1016/j.childyouth.2009.05.004.

Molluzzo, J. C., & Lawler, J. (2012). A study of the perceptions of college students on cyberbullying. *Information Systems Education Journal, 10*(4), 84.

Nixon, C. L. (2014). Current perspectives: The impact of cyberbullying on adolescent health. *Adolescent Health, Medicine and Therapeutics, 2014*(5), 143−158. Available from https://doi.org/10.2147/AHMT.S36456.

Nocentini, A., Calmaestra, J., Schultze-Krumbholz, A., Scheithauer, H., Ortega, R., & Menesini, E. (2010). Cyberbullying: Labels, behaviours and definition in three European countries. *Australian Journal of Guidance and Counselling, 20*(2), 129.

van Noorden, T. H., Bukowski, W. M., Haselager, G. J., Lansu, T. A., & Cillessen, A. H. (2016). Disentangling the frequency and severity of bullying and victimization in the association with empathy. *Social Development, 25*(1), 176−192. Available from https://doi.org/10.1111/sode.12133.

Notley, T., & Tacchi, J. (2005). Online youth networks: Researching the experiences of 'peripheral' young people in using new media tools for creative participation and representation. *Journal of Community, Citizen's and Third Sector Media, 1*(1), 73−81.

Obermaier, M., Fawzi, N., & Koch, T. (2016). Bystanding or standing by? How the number of bystanders affects the intention to intervene in cyberbullying. *New Media & Society, 18*(8), 1491−1507. Available from https://doi.org/10.1177/1461444814563519.

O'Dea, B., & Campbell, A. (2012). Online social networking and the experience of cyber-bullying. *Annual Review of Cybertherapy and Telemedicine, 181,* 212−217.

Ofcom. (2020). Adults' Media Use and Attitudes report 2020/21. Retrieved from <https://www.ofcom.org.uk/research-and-data/media-literacy-research/adults>.

Ofcom. (2019). *Children and parents: Media use and attitudes report* 2019. Retrieved from <https://www.ofcom.org.uk/research-and-data/media-literacy-research/adults>.

Olweus, D. (1993). *Bullying at school. What we know and what we can do.* Malden, MA: Wiley-Blackwell.

Olweus, D. (2013). School bullying: Development and some important challenges. *Annual Review of Clinical Psychology, 9,* 751−780.

Olweus, D., & Limber, S. P. (2018). Some problems with cyberbullying research. *Current Opinion in Psychology, 19,* 139−143.

Ortega, R., Elipe, P., Mora-Merchán, J. A., Calmaestra, J., & Vega, E. (2009). The emotional impact on victims of traditional bullying and cyberbullying: A study of Spanish adolescents. *Journal of Psychology, 217,* 197−204. Available from https://doi.org/10.1027/0044-3409.217.4.197.

Pepler, D., Mishna, F., Doucet, J., & Lameiro, M. (2021). Witnesses in cyberbullying: Roles and dilemmas. *Children & Schools, 43*(1), 45−53. Available from https://doi.org/10.1093/cs/cdaa027.

Perren, S., & Gutzwiller-Helfenfinger, E. (2012). Cyberbullying and traditional bullying in adolescence: Differential roles of moral disengagement, moral emotions, and moral values. *European Journal of Developmental Psychology, 9,* 195−209.

Pieschl, S., Kuhlmann, C., & Porsch, T. (2015). Beware of publicity! Perceived distress of negative cyber incidents and implications for defining cyberbullying. *Journal of School Violence, 14*(1), 111−132. Available from https://doi.org/10.1080/15388220.2014.971363.

Piliavin, J. A., Dovidio, J. F., Gaertner, S. L., et al. (1981). *Emergency intervention*. New York: Academic Press.

Price, D., Green, D., Spears, B., Scrimgeour, M., Barnes, A., Geer, R., & Johnson, B. (2014). A qualitative exploration of cyber-bystanders and moral engagement. *Journal of Psychologists and Counsellors in Schools*, 24(1), 1−17.

Raskauskas, J., & Stoltz, A. D. (2007). Involvement in traditional and electronic bullying among adolescents. *Developmental Psychology*, 43, 564−575. Available from https://doi.org/10.1037/0012-1649.43.3.564.

Rice, S. M., Goodall, J., Hetrick, S. E., Parker, A. G., Gilbertson, T., Amminger, G. P., Davey, C., McGorry, P., Gleeson, J., & Alvarez-Jimenez, M. (2014). Online and social networking interventions for the treatment of depression in young people: A systematic review. *Journal of Medical Internet Research*, 16(9), e206.

Sainio, M., Veenstra, R., Huitsing, G., & Salmivalli, C. (2011). Victims and their defenders: A dyadic approach. *International Journal of Behavioral Development*, 35(2), 144−151. Available from https://doi.org/10.1177/0165025410378068.

Salmivalli, C. (2010). Bullying and the peer group: A review. *Aggression and Violent Behavior*, 15(2), 112−120. Available from https://doi.org/10.1016/j.avb.2009.08.007.

Salmivalli, C., Lagerspetz, K., Björkqvist, K., Österman, K., & Kaukiainen, A. (1996). Bullying as a group process: Participant roles and their relations to social status within the group. *Aggressive Behavior: Official Journal of the International Society for Research on Aggression*, 22(1), 1−15. Available from https://doi.org/10.1002/(SICI)1098-2337 (1996)22:1 < 1::AID-AB1 > 3.0.CO;2-T.

Ševčíková, A., Šmahel, D., & Otavová, M. (2012). The perception of cyberbullying in adolescent victims. *Emotional and Behavioural Difficulties*, 17(3-4), 319−328.

Sampasa-Kanyinga, H., Roumeliotis, P., & Xu, H. (2014). Associations between cyberbullying and school bullying victimization and suicidal ideation, plans and attempts among Canadian schoolchildren. *PLoS One*, 9, e102145. Available from https://doi.org/10.1371/journal.pone.0102145.

Slonje, R., Smith, P. K., & Frisén, A. (2013). The nature of cyberbullying, and strategies for prevention. *Computers in Human Behavior*, 29(1), 26−32.

Smith, P. K., Mahdavi, J., Carvalho, M., Fisher, S., Russell, S., & Tippett, N. (2008). Cyberbullying: Its nature and impact in secondary school pupils. *Journal of Child Psychology and Psychiatry*, 49(4), 376−385. Available from https://doi.org/10.1111/j.1469-7610.2007.01846.

Song, J., & Oh, I. (2018). Factors influencing bystanders' behavioral reactions in cyberbullying situations. *Computers in Human Behavior*, 78, 273−282. Available from https://doi.org/10.1016/j.chb.2017.10.008.

Steer, O. L., Betts, L. R., Baguley, T., & Binder, J. F. (2020). "I feel like everyone does it"- adolescents' perceptions and awareness of the association between humour, banter, and cyberbullying. *Computers in Human Behavior*, 108, 106297.

Sticca, F., & Perren, S. (2013). Is cyberbullying worse than traditional bullying? Examining the differential roles of medium, publicity, and anonymity for the perceived severity of bullying. *Journal of Youth and Adolescence*, 42(5), 739−750. Available from https://doi.org/10.1007/s10964-012-9867-3.

Suler, J. (2004). The online disinhibition effect. *Cyberpsychology & Behavior*, 7(3), 321−326. Available from https://doi.org/10.1089/1094931041291295.

Thomas, L., Falconer, S., Cross, D., Monks, H., & Brown, D. (2012). *Cyberbullying and the Bystander* (Report prepared for the Australian Human Rights Commission). Perth, Australia: Child Health Promotion Research Centre, Edith Cowan University. Retrieved from: https://bullying.humanrights.gov.au/sites/default/files/content/bullying/ bystanders/ bystanders_results_insights_report.pdf.

Thornberg, R., Landgren, L., & Wiman, E. (2018). 'It Depends': A qualitative study on how adolescent students explain bystander intervention and non-intervention in bullying situations. *School Psychology International, 39*(4), 400−415. Available from https://doi.org/10.1177/0143034318779225.

Ttofi, M. M., & Farrington, D. P. (2011). Effectiveness of school-based programs to reduce bullying: A systematic and meta-analytic review. *Journal of Experimental Criminology, 7*(1), 27−56. Available from https://doi.org/10.1007/s11292-010-9109-1.

Vandebosch, H., & Van Cleemput, K. (2008). Defining cyberbullying: A qualitative research into the perceptions of youngsters. *Cyberpsychology & Behavior, 11*(4), 499−503.

Van Cleemput, K., Vandebosch, H., & Pabian, S. (2014). Personal characteristics and contextual factors that determine "helping," "joining in," and "doing nothing" when witnessing cyberbullying. *Aggressive Behavior, 40*(5), 383−396. Available from https://doi.org/10.1002/ab.21534.

Voelpel, S. C., Eckhoff, R. A., & Förster, J. (2008). David against Goliath? Group size and bystander effects in virtual knowledge sharing. *Human Relations, 61*(2), 271−295. Available from https://doi.org/10.1177/0018726707087787.

Wang, M.-J., Yogeeswaran, K., Andrews, N. P., Hawi, D. R., & Sibley, C. G. (2019). How common is cyberbullying among adults? Exploring gender, ethnic, and age differences in the prevalence of cyberbullying. *Cyberpsychology, Behavior, and Social Networking, 22*, 736−741. Available from https://doi.org/10.1089/cyber.2019.0146.

Wang, S. (2020). Standing up or standing by: Bystander intervention in cyberbullying on social media. *New Media & Society, 23*(6), 1461444820902541. Available from https://doi.org/10.1177/1461444820902541.

Wang, S., & Kim, K. J. (2021). Effects of victimization experience, gender, and empathic distress on bystanders' intervening behavior in cyberbullying. *The Social Science Journal,* 1−10. Available from https://doi.org/10.1080/03623319.2020.1861826.

Wegge, D., Vandebosch, H., Eggermont, S., & Pabian, S. (2016). Popularity through online harm: The longitudinal associations between cyberbullying and sociometric status in early adolescence. *The Journal of Early Adolescence, 36*(1), 86−107.

Whittaker, E., & Kowalski, R. M. (2015). Cyberbullying via social media. *Journal of School Violence, 14*(1), 11−29. Available from https://doi.org/10.1080/15388220.2014.949377.

Xiao, B. S., & Wong, Y. M. (2013). Cyber-bullying among university students: An empirical investigation from the social cognitive perspective. *International Journal of Business and Information, 8*, 34−69.

Ybarra, M. L., Diener-West, M., & Leaf, P. J. (2007). Examining the overlap in Internet harassment and school bullying: Implications for school intervention. *Journal of Adolescent Health, 41*(6), S42−S50.

Ybarra, M. L., Espelage, D. L., & Mitchell, K. J. (2007). The co-occurrence of internet harassment and unwanted sexual solicitation victimization and perpetration: Associations with psychosocial indicators. *Journal of Adolescent Health, 41*, S31−S41. Available from https://doi.org/10.1016/j.jadohealth.2007.09.010.

You, L., & Lee, Y. H. (2019). The bystander effect in cyberbullying on social network sites: Anonymity, group size, and intervention intentions. *Telematics and Informatics, 45*, 101284. Available from https://doi.org/10.1016/j.tele.2019.101284.

CHAPTER FIVE

# Interpreting ambiguous online messages: the case of banter

**Lucy R. Betts, Sarah L. Buglass, Loren Abell and Oonagh L. Steer**
Department of Psychology, Nottingham Trent University, Nottingham, United Kingdom

## Contents

## Introduction

Over the last decade, the number of social network users worldwide has risen from 0.97 billion to 3.6 billion (Clement, 2020). Social media use offers users many benefits, including facilitating social interactions, providing peer support, promoting engagement, and participation in mental health services (Naslund et al., 2020). However, one of the challenges associated with increased social media use is understanding how users interpret and respond to content that may be ambiguous in nature. Online communication lacks many of the cues that typically would be available in face-to-face communications. For example, cues such as gestures, tone of voice, and facial expressions can be used in physical interactions to signal the intent of communications (Kruger et al., 2006) are not present in the same way in the virtual world. Communications may be formal or informal, with coordination, socialization, and awareness being key elements of online communication (Dittrich & Giuffrida, 2011). How individuals interpret ambiguous communications is central to their understanding and may impact how users engage with messages and content such as the news (Wei & Wan, 2017). This chapter will explore a particular type of online communication that is often open to misinterpretation in everyday settings: banter.

With reference to online banter, this chapter will discuss how the lack of cues that may be available in the offline world to help those on the receiving end of banter (sometimes called targets) understand and interpret potentially ambiguous messages. Therefore cues such as intent, audience, and speaker characteristics will be discussed and how these characteristics may be used by individuals to determine whether an online communication is banter or cyberbullying (Buglass et al., 2021; Steer et al., 2020). This chapter will also consider the impact of the potential misinterpretation of ambiguous messages and give some suggestions about how to frame and interpret ambiguous messages and exchanges of banter to avoid some of the potential pitfalls of misinterpretation.

## Theoretical accounts for how individuals process ambiguous messages

Yang et al. (2011) argued that *"ambiguity is a phenomenon inherent in natural language and occurs when linguistic expression may be understood in two or more different ways"* (p. 163). Ambiguity in the actions or words of others is part of everyday life, and this means that when several people witness the same event or act, they may take different meanings from the situation (Schoth & Liossi, 2017). To help us make sense of the ambiguous situations that we encounter, we make use of the available cues to help guide our interpretations. Depending on the context of the situation, these cues can include the use of words, images, facial expressions, behaviors, and comments from others (Schoth & Liossi, 2017). Early research suggests that during childhood, we develop an awareness that some messages can be ambiguous in nature and that how we respond to these messages does not change the quality of the message (i.e., the message still remains unclear irrespective of how we chose to interpret it; Singer & Flavell, 1981). Children also learn to revise their knowledge when other alternatives are presented when interpreting ambiguous messages (Beck &

Robinson, 2001). However, as adults, we may reserve judgment until we get additional information, consider a range of interpretations until there is clarity, or make a judgment which may be revised when additional information becomes available (Beck & Robinson, 2001).

There are several theoretical perspectives that offer insight into how ambiguous messages are interpreted. The social information processing (SIP) model (Crick & Dodge, 1994) outlines the process individuals go through when interpreting social situations and behaviors in the social world. Originally applied to children's social decision making, the SIP model has five stages. In the first stage the cues surrounding the behavior or event are encoded, and this involves trying to make sense of the social world, the situation, and any internal cues. In the second stage, the cues are interpreted, and this involves considering both causal and intent attributions along with evaluations of the situation. The third stage, clarification of goals, involves considering the goal of the behavior within the context of the situation and the goal of the other individual. In the next stage, individuals consider the range of responses that could be relevant to the situation or behavior. Following this process of reflection, a response decision is made, which involves considering how the response will be received and an individual's self-efficacy. Finally, a behavior is enacted that is consistent with the individual's response selection. Crick and Dodge argue that this process is cyclic in nature and is informed by an individual's memory and the knowledge of the social context, social schemas, and rules.

The SIP model has been used as a theoretical framework to explore how individuals respond to ambiguous behaviors and messages. Runions et al. (2013) provided a discussion of how the SIP model can be adapted to consider the structural and functional aspects of information and communication technology (ICT). Specifically, relating to cue encoding, permanence of social cues and paucity of social sematic cues are recognized. For the interpretation of cues stage, ICT structural properties include emoticon use and internet slang. Privacy vulnerability of online identity related to the goal clarification stage, and the response construction stage is influenced by the perceived audience in one-to-many modes. Finally, paucity of inhibitory cues and continuous access to the technologies inform the response decision and behavioral enactment stages, respectively.

Research suggests that someone with a hostile attribution bias is more likely to interpret an ambiguous message as hostile and experience a more negative emotional reaction (van den Berg & Lansu, 2020). Further, in the presence of ambiguous situations, having a hostile attribution bias is a recognized risk factor for aggression (Bondü, 2018). Although there is a wealth of evidence supporting the SIP model, recent research by Zajenkowska et al. (2020) highlights cultural variations in how ambiguous messages are interpreted. Zajenkowska et al. argued that their findings are particularly significant to the online world because of the increasing frequency of cross-cultural interactions.

Expectancy violation theory (Burgoon & Jones, 1976) provides another theoretical lens through which to understand how individuals interpret ambiguous messages from the perspective of the recipient and audience. Expectancy violation theory suggests that in the context of communication, we have a sense of the pattern of likely behavior. This pattern is guided by the norms of the society in terms of what is acceptable and typical (Burgoon, 1993). These expectations are guided by the communicator, the relationship, and contextual characteristics. Burgoon argues that characteristics of the communicator include personal characteristics, personality style, and communication style that helps understand how the communicator will act. Relationship characteristics reflect the qualities of the relationship between the individuals involved in the communication (e.g., familiarity, similarity, and status). Contextual characteristics denote the situation in which the communication is taking place (e.g., publicly versus privately) and prescribe certain behaviors. Together, the communicator, the relationship, and the contextual characteristics influence the expectancies for a particular interaction. When expectancy violations occur (i.e., the norms of the interaction are not followed), individuals evaluate the communication and the person engaging in that communication (Bachman & Guerrero, 2006).

Bevan et al. (2014) applied the expectancy violation theory to Facebook unfriending. Bevan et al.'s research found that unfriending was regarded by participants as an expectancy violation that was negative and important. Expectancy violation theory has also been used to understand how individuals engage in impression management on Facebook (Rui & Stefanone, 2018). Rui and Stefanone reported that when posts that may challenge the public image of an individual are carried out privately, this is less likely to be perceived as threatening to the individual's image than if the post was public. Further, if a friend was responsible for the behavior, this was identified as a clear violation of what was expected. Together, these studies provide evidence of how the expectancy violation theory can be applied to social media use and provide an account of how users may interpret ambiguous communications.

Superiority theory has its origins in the work of Plato, Aristotle, and Hobbes, who argued that humor is a form of aggression that individuals use to make themselves feel better over another (Martin & Ford, 2018) and, as such, can inform individuals how to interpret potentially ambiguous interactions, especially banter. Specifically, individuals may make jokes about others or make fun of them to make themselves feel more superior than the target (Banas et al., 2011). Consequently, according to superiority theory, humor is used as a way to restore the balance in relationships and simultaneously increase relational power (Vallade et al., 2013) with laughter seen as a triumph over another (Duncan, 1985). However, Pahl (2016) argued that humor in the context of superiority theory can be used as a mechanism to classify individuals into categories (e.g., right or wrong). Vallade et al. reported that when individuals experienced relational transgressions, they were more likely to use humor to show their superiority. Further, this tendency was stronger when the hurt associated with the relational event was higher and the recipient felt more insulted by the transgression.

Considering the online world, the reduced social cues theory (Sproull et al., 1991) provides further insight into how ambiguous online behaviors may be interpreted. Reduced social cues theory argues that computer-based communication provides users with a different social sphere. Specifically, when compared to the face-to-face world, the online world is potentially much more restricted in terms of social cues and shared experiences. Sproull et al. argued that because individuals often engage in online communication on their own, the conventions of communications are weaker than if someone is physically present. Also, the lack of a physical presence may result in individuals engaging in communication with less social awareness and more social posturing (Sproull et al., 1991). Consequently, as highlighted by the reduced social cues theory, the cues available to interpret ambiguous behavior online are likely to be reduced and, as such, this is likely to influence interpretation.

Similar to the reduced social cues theory (Sproull et al., 1991), the online disinhibition effect (Suler, 2004) indicates that when individuals engage in online communication, they self-disclose more or act more intensely and frequently compared to how they would behave in offline settings. Suler proposes a dichotomy ranging from benign disinhibition to toxic disinhibition. Benign disinhibition is characterized by instances of individuals disclosing personal traits, emotions, or experiences or engaging in helping behaviors directed toward others. On the other hand, toxic disinhibition involves engaging in harsh criticism, directing anger, threats, or inappropriate language toward others and engaging in behavior that they would not do so offline. Suler argues that it is the combination of dissociative anonymity (i.e., the ability to remain anonymous), invisibility (i.e., the individual engaging in the behavior is not "seen" as they would be in the offline world), asynchronicity (i.e., communications may not occur in real time), solipsistic introjection (i.e., due to the context, an internal representation of the communicator may be developed), dissociative imagination (i.e., through creating representations of online interaction partners, there is a perception that they operate in a different space), and minimization of authority (i.e., the lack of cues related to authority figures being present) that together result in the observed disinhibition. Recent research has highlighted that toxic disinhibition is a predictor of cyberbullying (Huang et al., 2020), and it is possible that these factors may influence how online ambiguous behaviors are interpreted.

In sum, the SIP model, expectancy violation theory, superiority theory, reduced social cues theory, and the online disinhibition effect together provide a theoretical framework to understand how ambiguous behaviors and communications are interpreted. The next section of this chapter will introduce banter as a case study of how ambiguous communications can be interpreted.

## Banter

With age, social aggression such as teasing, pranking, banter, or drama is regarded something that is playful and exciting (Burnett Heyes, 2020). Banter is something that we see, hear, and experience everywhere across a range of interactions. Banter is defined as an *"interactional bonding game"* that is designed to promote social relationships (Dynel, 2008: p. 246). Often characterized as jocular humor between individuals, banter may appear to be aggressive in nature, but it is interpreted with a friendly effect in the context of relationships (Plester & Sayers, 2007). For example, friendly banter occurs between friends and is not intended to cause offense. It is important to acknowledge that banter is distinct from other forms of relational aggression such as teasing; banter is a reciprocal form of communication that has a shared context, whereas teasing is regarded as one-sided (Rivers & Ross, 2021). With friendly banter, there is no intent to harm, but rather this form of banter is used as a mechanism to promote and maintain social relationships (Plester & Sayers, 2007) and facilitate social cohesion (Alexander et al., 2012). Plester and Sayers suggest that the main functions of banter include making a point, reducing boredom, promoting socialization, celebrating differences, displaying culture, and highlighting and defining status. Considering the dyadic interactions when both parties engage in banter exchanges and respond appropriately to the exchange, Alexander et al. (2012) argue that in these circumstances, it means that the person who is the subject of the banter is accepted by their social circle. Banter is also used as a way of ensuring high functioning, cohesive teams in some professional settings (Alexander et al., 2012) and is regarded as a shared language of belonging, acceptance, fitting in, and being part of the group (Giousmpasoglou et al., 2017).

A recent publication by Whittle et al. (2019) suggests that banter can have several functions within social exchanges. First, banter can be used as a mechanism to negotiate the process of "othering," where those involved attempt to mediate their status within a group (Whittle et al., 2019), specifically, using banter to negotiate acceptance and status in the ingroup and a rejection of the outgroup. Second, when banter is confrontational in nature and the exchange occurs between friends, Whittle et al. argue that banter can be used to explore social boundaries. Finally, banter can also be used as a mechanism of performing masculinity and male bonding. Banter that occurs in male-to-male bonding interactions tends to be underpinned by a desire for individuals to maintain their ego (Rivers & Ross, 2021) but can also be used as a way to exclude women in the advertising industry (Topić, 2020). Relatedly, banter is regarded as a central part of "lad culture" which is characterized by a *"mix of boorish socialising, drinking, sport and pack behaviour"* (Jeffries, 2020, p. 908). It is also important to acknowledge that the norms around the acceptability and use of banter can evolve. For example, Duncan (2019) argues that sledging (described as verbal barbs)/trash talk in sport has moved beyond *"light hearted, good nature banter"* (p. 183) to something that is *"characterised as hurtful, insulting, offensive and intimidating"* (p. 184).

Previously, researchers have tended to study banter in the context of professional settings such as information technology, hospitality, and the advertising industry. Banter in the context of the information technology industry was seen as an important mechanism for developing and maintaining organizational culture (Plester & Sayers, 2007). Plester and Sayers' research highlighted that banter occurred between colleagues who were popular, and the banter exchanges were an accepted part of the organizational culture.

Focusing on the hospitality industry, it has been argued that banter serves an important function in the high stress environment of a professional kitchen (Alexander et al., 2012). In this context, banter is seen as multifaceted. The professional chefs who participated in Alexander et al.'s research suggested that banter facilitated team cohesion and comradeship. Further, the aggressive and defamatory language that was characteristic of most banter exchanges was seen as the most effective way for the chefs to get their message across to fellow team members and denoted the urgency in the situation. Banter was regarded as so important in this context, and the participants argued that an absence of banter was viewed as a clear indicator that relationships and communications between individuals had broken down. Therefore, in this professional context, banter was seen to be indicative of a "happy team" (Alexander et al., 2012, p. 1253) and without this banter the team was not working effectively. More recent research with professional chefs has also provided further evidence that banter is regarded as a central part of a chef's occupational culture and socialization within the context of a professional kitchen (Giousmpasoglou et al., 2017).

The ambiguity surrounding the interpretation of banter may influence whether banter is interpreted as bullying and researchers have talked about a fine line between banter and bullying (Betts & Spenser, 2017; Buglass et al., 2021; Steer et al., 2020). Understanding the intent of a communication or act is key to determining whether the behavior is interpreted as bullying or banter (Kruger et al., 2006), with Duncan (2019) arguing that how banter is interpreted depends on the "*eye of the beholder*" (p. 193). In other words, how a message is interpreted by the recipient in terms of intent means that a message intended to be benign in nature could be regarded by the target as hurtful. Returning to the example of banter in professional kitchens, Giousmpasoglou et al. (2017) argue that although academics and practitioners regard banter as potential bullying, the professional chefs that engage in banter see this as part of the organizational culture that promotes high performance. However, not all forms of banter are received as positively with the term banter being used to excuse harmful, bullying behaviors toward individuals or groups. For example, when the banter is characterized by verbal comments that are critical in nature or are demeaning, Middlemiss (2017) argues that this type of communication is bullying. Further, banter can also be used to continue to disempower individuals if the recipient of the banter is a minority group or individual (Wardman, 2020). Steer et al.'s work with adolescents suggests that when banter involves referencing another person's family member, appearance or self-harm, comments about someone or something that has died, or behaviors that would constitute hate crimes, the banter is not acceptable.

## Interpreting online banter and ambiguous behaviors

With the prominence and central nature that social media plays in many individuals' lives, we are increasingly playing out our lives on social media and online contexts (Boyd & Ellison, 2007) in a way that previous generations have not done so. The greater internet accessibility and use also increases the potential to encounter ambiguous messages (Miers et al., 2020). To illustrate the potential ambiguity in messages, Miers et al. use the example of an individual receiving a message saying "K" as short hand for ok. This message could be interpreted as being sent by someone who was short of time and who was not able to write a full message or could be interpreted as lack of enthusiasm on the part of the sender.

Online banter can take many forms including one-to-one and group exchanges between friends (Steer et al., 2020) and through tagging individuals in online photographs and images (Whittle et al., 2019). Crucial to this form of online banter is the shared relationship between the individuals engaging in the banter to ensure that the target is aware of why they have been tagged in the image (Whittle et al., 2019). As previously outlined, it is not always easy to determine the intent in banter (Buglass et al., 2021) and this challenge is likely to be exacerbated in the online world. Specifically, because of the nature of online environments which may promote ambiguity in online banter interactions, it means that such ambiguous exchanges could easily be interpreted as cyberbullying (Steer et al., 2020). Further, when adolescents shared private online posts beyond the intended audience, such behavior was interpreted as inappropriate banter (Steer et al., 2020). The role of banter for framing online interactions between younger users has yet to be fully explored in the research literature (Whittle et al., 2019).

Kingsbury and Coplan (2016) argue that while nonverbal cues in face-to-face interactions can be the source of the ambiguity, with online communication, the lack of cues creates a different type of ambiguity. There are several reasons as to why ambiguous messages in the online world may be more likely to be interpreted differently to the intent. One of the main differences between the online and offline worlds that likely impacts the interpretation of ambiguous messages is the availability of cues to facilitate interpretation of intent. For example, cues that may be available in face-to-face interactions such as tone of voice, facial expressions, and gestures are not available when trying to determine the intent of an interaction that may be considered to be banter. Cumulatively, on the one hand, the reduced social cues available online that assist in the interpretation of an ambiguous message may mean that behaviors that were intended as banter are regarded by the recipient as offensive. On the other hand, the term banter can be used to euphemistically label behavior that was cyberbullying. Consequently, individuals turn to other cues to help them to determine the intent of ambiguous messages and banter online. For example, audience and speaker characteristics are factors used to facilitate interpretation of the intent of banter and ambiguous messages (Buglass et al., 2021; Steer et al., 2020). When banter behaviors extend beyond private friendship groups to public social media, this larger audience creates an environment where the banter can become offensive because the expectations around banter occurring between friends has been violated (Steer et al., 2020). So, an exchange that might be regarded as light-hearted and humorous between friends might result in embarrassment and reputational damage when visible to a wider (potentially unknown) audience. The presence of a larger audience may also lead to the target of the banter experiencing a great level of embarrassment because of the public nature of the exchange.

The social context of the banter and ambiguous messages is important when individuals determine how to interpret such communication. Specifically, the interpretation of the same act that could be interpreted as aggressive is likely to be interpreted differently according to whether the act was directed toward a disliked peer rather than a friend (Burnett Heyes, 2020). When directed toward a disliked peer, the potentially aggressive act is more likely to be interpreted as aggressive, whereas when the same act is directed toward a friend, it is more likely to be interpreted as banter, playful, or affection.

A further example of how relationships are important in the context of interpreting ambiguous online messages was provided by Cohen et al. (2014). Cohen et al. explored the impact of ambiguous messages sent to a romantic rival and the impact of audience and context. In the study, undergraduates were asked to report how they would respond to seeing an ambiguous message ("hey you ☺") that their partner had posted to a romantic rival either: (1) as a private Facebook message to the rival or (2) posted publicly on the rival's Facebook wall. In terms of exclusivity of the audience, the private Facebook message was highly exclusive, whereas the public post was less exclusive because it was accessible to a much wider audience. When the participants were asked to rate the private message to the rival, they reported more negative emotions and said that they would be more likely to be confrontational than if the same message was posted publicly to the rival. Therefore the findings from Cohen et al.'s research highlight that in the context of romantic rivals, ambiguous messages are interpreted to be more threatening if they are private where the audience is highly exclusive underscoring the importance of context and audience. Cohen et al. suggest that ambiguous messages may be interpreted as more threatening for relationships when they are sent in the context of private messages because of the limited audience and the direct nature of the message. Further, by posting the same message to a public forum, it suggests that there is little to hide. The size and type of the audience was also highlighted by participants in Buglass et al., (2021) study as a key factor in determining the appropriateness and impact of banter. Banter shared with larger audiences was regarded as crossing the line of acceptability because the audience was more likely to be contextually collapsed, including individuals from many social spheres, and may not adhere to the same rules and values (Vitak, 2012).

Characteristics of the recipient such as their gender and humor style may also influence how ambiguous online messages and banter are interpreted. Focusing on the interpretation of offline written scenarios that could be interpreted as humorous, Futch and Edwards (1999) explored how an individual's sense of humor influenced their interpretation of ambiguous communication following physical acts (i.e., nearly falling over, misfiling documents, or dropping groceries) and appearance-related acts (i.e., comments about clothes, hair, or food consumption). There was evidence of gender differences in how the ambiguous communications were interpreted. Males interpreted the ambiguous comments following a physical act as less humorous than females. However, there were no gender differences in the interpretation of the ambiguous communication following appearance-related acts. In addition to some evidence of gender differences associated with the interpretation of the ambiguous communication, there were also gender differences associated with who the communication was attributed to and how the speaker was evaluated. When the ambiguous communication was attributed to males, both males and females interpreted the ambiguous messages as more humorous than when the same communication was attributed to females.

Based on their findings, Futch and Edwards (1999) suggest that the content of communications may change how ambiguous communications are interpreted. Although Futch and Edwards' research was in an offline context and focused on potentially humorous acts, it is likely that humor style has a similar impact in interpreting messages in online settings and banter. Specifically, parallels can be drawn with this research and the work on banter because, like banter, humor has beneficial impacts for relationships and can buffer against stressful events (Futch & Edwards, 1999).

More recent research by Kingsbury and Coplan (2016) has explored how university students interpret ambiguous text messages. Using scenarios based on findings from focus groups, Kingsbury and Coplan developed text messages that could be interpreted in multiple ways (e.g., "*The day after attending a party, you get this message from a friend "I heard about last night""* p. 378), and participants were asked to rate the extent to which two possible interpretations came to mind (e.g., "*S/he heard about something interesting that happened at the party,*" "*S/he heard about something embarrassing I did or said*" p. 378). When the messages were attributed to a female sender, they were rated as more negative and less benign than when the same messages were attributed to male senders and this effect was stronger for male participants. Kingsbury and Coplan argue that this pattern of results concerning the gender of the sender may reflect the norms around how females are expected to communicate and, as such, when these norms are violated, the sender is rated more harshly.

## Graphical emotional cues

A specific example of the cues that can be used to help with the interpretation of online banter and ambiguous communication are graphical emotional cues. Steer et al. (2020) reported that adolescents said that they use emojis as a way of helping them to express themselves and signal their intent to the target of the communication. Specifically, the adolescents used emojis as a way of overcoming the lack of social cues online and to reduce the chance that their banter would be misinterpreted. For example, while emojis are frequently used to signal intent of ambiguous messages (Buglass et al., 2021) and reduce uncertainty in how the message is perceived (Teng & Hew, 2019), these cues have the potential to be misinterpreted (Runions et al., 2013). Further, emojis and the associated ambiguities are sometimes a feature of text-based banter exchanges, for example, to try and better convey the supposed meaning of the banter itself or excuse the banter. Emojis can of course also be used, alongside gifs and memes to poke fun or tease people. However, emojis can also be used as a way to mask potential cyberbullying behaviors and the behavior euphemistically labeled as banter to avoid the potential offense caused (Steer et al., 2020). Further, the use of cues such as emojis to denote banter is dependent on the audience's ability to interpret and understand these cues (Buglass et al., 2021).

Another type of graphical cue is stickers, but unlike emojis, stickers contain animation, diverse gestures, and multiple characters and objects and, as such, are regarded as more expressive (Cha et al., 2018). Like emojis, there is the potential for sticker use to be misinterpreted. Cha et al. reported that 22% of sticker use was misinterpreted with those involved in the communication interpreting the intended use of the sticker differently. In the majority of cases, the difference occurred because the recipient of the sticker did not interpret the ambiguous nature of the sticker in the same way as the sender had done and this tended to most frequently happen with animated stickers. Together, these studies highlight how graphical emotional cues that are designed to facilitate communication can, in fact, prompt ambiguity and misinterpretation. The next section of the chapter will consider the impact of such misinterpretation for social media users.

## Impact of misinterpretation of ambiguous messages/banter

Previous research suggests that when graphical emotional cues are misinterpreted, this tends to happen because of their potential ambiguous nature, and such misinterpretations have been associated with elevated levels of anxiety and reduced well-being (Lansford et al., 2006). Social anxiety has also been linked to misinterpretation of ambiguous communication in both online and offline settings (Miers et al., 2020). Miers et al. also found that for university students, online interpretation bias predicted self-reported peer victimization and avoidance behaviors in an online context, when social anxiety was controlled for.

Considering ambiguous communications in the form of banter, although banter has been highlighted as an important part of organizational culture and identifying whether new staff can cope with the demands of the job role in high pressured environments (Giousmpasoglou et al., 2017), when the banter occurred between individuals who were not part of the group, it was experienced as insulting, painful, and exclusionary (Plester & Sayers, 2007). More recent research by Yuan et al. (2020) has examined passive email incivility as a form of ambiguous messages. Passive email incivility is defined as a lack of decent interpersonal treatment or the omission of respect in an email. A sample of working employees rated passive email incivility as more ambiguous than other forms of communication. There was also evidence that experiencing passive email incivility was associated with insomnia and heightened the negative affect at the start of the working day.

In summary, there is emerging evidence that the misinterpretation of ambiguous online communications and banter can impact an individual's well-being and their workplace performance. The next section of the chapter will use the findings from the literature to provide some recommendations about how social media users should frame and interpret ambiguous messages and exchanges of banter to avoid some of the potential pitfalls of misinterpreting ambiguous messages.

## Practical implications: how to frame and interpret ambiguous messages and online banter

There are three main areas for social media users to focus on when framing and interpreting ambiguous online messages and banter: (1) the nature of the relationship between individuals in the interaction, (2) the content of the message, and (3) the audience.

Central to framing and interpreting ambiguous messages online is considering the social relationship between the individuals involved in the interaction because social context has been identified as a key factor in how ambiguous messages and banter are perceived (Burnett Heyes, 2020; Plester & Sayers, 2007). Further, it is important to acknowledge the role of shared history between individuals and consider how these can be used to shape the interpretation of online banter (Whittle et al., 2019). For example, if the individuals are well known to each other, the nature of the intent of the communication could be different than if they were more loosely connected.

In addition to considering the nature of the social relationship between individuals, when framing and interpreting banter, it is important to consider the content of the message or act. For example, Plester and Sayers (2007) suggest focusing on a habit, trait, or characteristic when the exchange is anticipated to be equal between individuals. Further, it is important to acknowledge the significance of reciprocity and the shared confidence between individuals but also to be mindful of the fact that comments intended as banter can be hurtful for the target (Plester & Sayers, 2007). Relatedly, when framing and interpreting online banter and ambiguous messages tone of communication, timing, facial expressions, and body language are cues that could be used to determine intent but may be missing in online exchanges (Whittle et al., 2019).

The nature of the audience is also a key consideration when framing and interpreting online banter and ambiguous messages. For example, messages posted to a wider audience may be more likely to be misinterpreted and, as such, risk the reputation of those who are involved (Buglass, 2020). Additionally, a larger audience may mean that potential witnesses to the messages may join in, resulting in potentially elevated levels of harm and distress for the target (Myers & Cowie, 2016). Also, when the audience is larger, it is also more likely to be contextually collapsed, in that the audience may comprise of members who may not share the same rules and values (Vitak, 2012). However, there is evidence that when an ambiguous message is to a romantic rival, it is regarded less negatively when posted publicly compared to private messages (Cohen et al., 2014). Therefore it is important to recognize that when considering the audience of ambiguous messages and online banter, the context of the message or act also potentially shapes how it is perceived.

Drawing together these three areas, from a practical perspective, before engaging in banter type behavior, it is important that social media users think about who they are interacting with including thinking about how long they have known them and how well they know them. In terms of the message, social media users should think about what they are saying and how the message is framed to avoid any potential ambiguity. Finally, social media users should think about who else may see the message and how big and diverse the audience is.

## Conclusion

In summary, this chapter has discussed, using the case of online banter, how ambiguous messages are perceived. The chapter has introduced the SIP model (Crick & Dodge, 1994), expectancy violation theory (Burgoon & Jones, 1976), superiority theory (Martin & Ford, 2018), reduced social cues theory (Sproull et al., 1991), and online disinhibition effect (Suler, 2004) as potential accounts for how individuals construct and interpret ambiguous messages. This chapter has also highlighted how online banter lacks many of the contextual cues that are available when individuals engage in offline banter and how emojis and stickers can be used to further confound the ambiguity in communications. Finally, this chapter has provided a brief review of the impact of misinterpreting ambiguous communications and online banter and has provided some suggestions about how to frame and interpret communications to try to ameliorate some of these impacts.

## References

Alexander, M., MacLaren, A., O'Gorman, K., & Taheri, B. (2012). "He just didn't seem to understand the banter": Bullying or simply establishing social cohesion. *Tourism Management*, *33*, 1245−1255. Available from https://doi.org/10.1016/j.tourman.2011.11.001.

Bachman, G. F., & Guerrero, L. K. (2006). Relational quality and communicative responses following hurtful events in dating relationships: An expectancy violations analysis. *Journal of Social and Personal Relationships*, *23*, 943−963. Available from https://doi.org/10.1177/0265407506070476.

Banas, J. A., Dunbar, N., Rodrigues, D., & Liu, S.-J. (2011). A review of humor in educational settings: Four decades of research. *Communication Education*, *60*, 115−144. Available from https://doi.org/10.1080/03634523.2010.496867.

Beck, S. R., & Robinson, E. J. (2001). Children's ability to make tentative interpretations of ambiguous messages. *Journal of Experimental Child Psychology*, *79*, 95−114, 0022-0965/01.

van den Berg, Y. H. M., & Lansu, T. A. M. (2020). It's not just what you say, it's how you say it too. Adolescents' hostile attribution of intent and emotional responses to social comments. *Aggressive Behavior*, *46*, 425−436. Available from https://doi.org/10.1002/ab.21910.

Betts, L. R., & Spenser, K. A. (2017). "People think it's a harmless joke": Young people's understanding of the impact of technology, digital vulnerability and cyberbullying in the United Kingdom. *Journal of Children and Media*, *11*(1), 20−35. Available from https://doi.org/10.1080/17482798.2016.1233893.

Bevan, J. L., Ang, P. C., & Fearns, J. B. (2014). Being unfriended on Facebook: An application of expectancy violation theory. *Computers in Human Behavior*, *33*, 171−178. Available from https://doi.org/10.1016/j.chb.2014.01.029.

Bondü, R. (2018). Is bad intent negligible? Linking victim justice sensitivity, hostile attribution bias, and aggression. *Aggressive Behavior*, *44*(5), 442−450. Available from https://doi.org/10.1002/ab.21764.

Boyd, D. M., & Ellison, N. B. (2007). Social network sites: Definition, history, and scholarship. *Journal of Computer-mediated Communication, 13*(1), 210–230. Available from https://doi.org/10.1111/j.1083-6101.2007.00393.x.

Buglass, S. L. (2020). Banter: Are we crossing the line? *Psychology Review, 26,* 32–33.

Buglass, S. L., Abell, L., Betts, L. R., Hill, R., & Saunders, J. (2021). Banter versus bullying: A University student perspective. *International Journal of Bullying Prevention, 3,* 287–299. Available from https://doi.org/10.1007/s42380-020-00085-0.

Burgoon, J. K. (1993). Interpersonal expectations, expectancy violations, and emotional communication. *Journal of Language and Social Psychology, 12,* 30–48. Available from https://doi.org/10.1177/0261927X93121003.

Burgoon, J. K., & Jones, S. B. (1976). Toward a theory of personal space expectations and their violations. *Humman Communication Research, 2,* 131–146.

Burnett Heyes, S. (2020). Just banter? Friendship, teasing and experimental aggression in adolescent peer networks. *Developmental Science, 2020*(23), e12926. Available from https://doi.org/10.1111/desc.12926.

Cha, Y., Kim, J., Park, S., Yi, M. Y., & Lee, U. (2018). Complex and ambiguous: Understanding sticker misinterpretations in instant messaging. *Proceedings of the ACM on Human-Computer Interaction, 2*(CSCW), 1–22.

Clement, J. (2020). *Most popular social network worldwide as of January 2020, ranked by number of active users.* Available from: https://www.statista.com/statistics/272014/global-social-networks-ranked-by-number-of-users/.

Cohen, E. L., Bowman, N. D., & Borchert, K. (2014). Private flirts, public friends: Understanding romantic jealousy responses to an ambiguous social network site message as a function of message access exclusivity. *Computers in Human Behaviour, 35,* 535–541. Available from https://doi.org/10.1016/j.chb.2014.02.050.

Crick, N. R., & Dodge, K. A. (1994). A review and reformulation of social information-processing mechanisms in children's social adjustment. *Psychological Bulletin, 115*(1), 74–101. Available from https://doi.org/10.1037/0033-2909.115.1.74.

Dittrich, Y., & Giuffrida, R. (2011). Exploring the role of instant messaging in a global software development project. *2011 IEEE Sixth International Conference on Global Software Engineering,* 103–112. Available from https://doi.org/10.1109/ICGSE.2011.21, IEEE.

Duncan, S. (2019). Sledging in sport-playful banter, or mean-spirited insults? A study of sledging's place in play. *Sport, Ethics and Philosophy, 13,* 183–197. Available from https://doi.org/10.1080/17511321.2018.1432677.

Duncan, W. J. (1985). The superiority theory of humor at work: Joking relationships as indicators of formal and informal status patterns in small, task-oriented groups. *Small Group Behavior, 16*(4), 556–564. Available from https://doi.org/10.1177/104649648501600412.

Dynel, M. (2008). No aggression, only teasing: The pragmatics of teasing and banter. *Lodz Papers in Pragmatics, 4*(2), 241–261. Available from https://doi.org/10.2478/v10016-008-0001-7.

Futch, A., & Edwards, R. (1999). The effects of sense of humor, defensiveness, and gender on the interpretation of ambiguous messages. *Communication Quarterly, 47,* 80–97. Available from https://doi.org/10.1080/01463379909370125.

Giousmpasoglou, C., Marinakou, E., & Cooper, J. (2017). "Banter, bollockings and beatings" The occupational socialisation process in Michelin-starred kitchen brigades in Great Britain and Ireland. *International Journal of Contemporary Hospitality Management, 30,* 1882–1902. Available from https://doi.org/10.1108/IJCHM-01-2017-0030.

Huang, C. L., Zhang, S., & Yang, S. C. (2020). How students react to different cyberbullying events: Past experience, judgment, perceived seriousness, helping behavior and the effect of online disinhibition. *Computers in Human Behavior, 110,* 106338.

Jeffries, M. (2020). 'Is it okay to jo out on the pull without it being nasty?: Lads' performance of lad culture. *Gender and Education, 32,* 908–925. Available from https://doi.org/10.1080/09540253.2019.1594706.

Kingsbury, M., & Coplan, R. J. (2016). RU mad @me? Social anxiety and interpretation of ambiguous messages. *Computers in Human Behavior, 54*, 368−379. Available from https://doi.org/10.1016/j.chb.2015.08.032.

Kruger, J., Gordon, C. L., & Kuban, J. (2006). Intentions in teasing: When "just kidding" just isn't good enough. *Journal of Personality and Social Psychology, 90*(3), 412. Available from https://doi.org/10.1037/0022-3514.90.3.412.

Lansford, J. E., Malone, P. S., Dodge, K. A., Crozier, J. C., Pettit, G. S., & Bates, J. E. (2006). A 12-year prospective study of patterns of social information processing problems and externalizing behaviors. *Journal of Abnormal Child Psychology, 34*(5), 709−718. Available from https://doi.org/10.1007/s10802-006-9057-4.

Martin, R. A., & Ford, T. E. (2018). *The psychology of humor: An integrative approach* (2nd ed). London: Academic Press.

Middlemiss, S. (2017). "Another nice mess you've gotten me into" employers' liability for workplace banter. *International Journal of Law and Management, 59*, 916−938. Available from https://doi.org/10.1108/IJLMA-07-2016-0063.

Miers, A. C., Sumter, S. R., Clark, D. M., & Leigh, E. (2020). Interpretation bias in online and offline social environments and associations with social anxiety, peer victimization, and avoidance behavior. *Cognitive Therapy and Research, 44*, 820−833. Available from https://doi.org/10.1007/s10608-020-10097-1.

Myers, C. A., & Cowie, H. (2016). How can we prevent and reduce bullying amongst University Students? *International Journal of Emotional Education, 8*(1), 109−119, ISSN: EISSN-2073-7629.

Naslund, J. A., Bondre, A., Torous, J., & Aschbrenner, K. A. (2020). Social media and mental health: Benefits, risks, and opportunities for research and practice. *Journal of Technology in Behavioral Science, 5*(3), 245−257. Available from https://doi.org/10.1007/s41347-020-00134-x.

Pahl, B. (2016). Pussy Riot's humour and the social media: Self-irony, subversion, and solidarity. *The European Journal of Humour Research, 4*(4), 67−104. Available from https://doi.org/10.7592/EJHR2016.4.4.pahl.

Plester, B. A., & Sayers, J. G. (2007). Taking the piss: The functions of banter in three IT companies. *Humor: International Journal of Humor Research, 20*(2), 157−187. Available from https://doi.org/10.1515/HUMOR.2007.008.

Rivers, D. J., & Ross, A. S. (2021). "This channel has more subs from rival fans than Arsenal fans": Arsenal fan TV, football fandom and banter in the new media era. *Sports in Society, 24*(6), 867−885. Available from https://doi.org/10.1080/17430437.2019.1706492.

Rui, J. R., & Stefanone, M. A. (2018). That tagging was annoying: An extension of expectancy violation theory to impression management on social network sites. *Computers in Human Behavior, 80*, 49−58. Available from https://doi.org/10.1016/j.chb.2017.11.001.

Runions, K., Shapka, J. D., Dooley, J., & Modecki, K. (2013). Cyber-aggression and victimisation and social information processing: Integrating the medium and the message. *Psychology of Violence, 3*, 9−26. Available from https://doi.org/10.1037/a0030511.

Schoth, D. E., & Liossi, C. (2017). A systematic review of experimental paradigms for exploring biased interpretation of ambiguous information with emotional and neural associations. *Frontiers in Psychology, 8*, 171. Available from https://doi.org/10.3389/fpsyg.2017.00171.

Singer, J. B., & Flavell, J. H. (1981). Development of knowledge about communication: Children's evaluations of explicitly ambiguous messages. *Child Development, 52*, 1211−1215.

Sproull, L., Kiesler, S., & Kiesler, S. B. (1991). *Connections: New ways of working in the networked organization*. MIT Press.

Steer, O. L., Betts, L. R., Baguley, T., & Binder, J. F. (2020). "I feel like everyone does it" — adolescents' perceptions and awareness of the association between humour, banter, and cyberbullying. *Computers in Human Behavior, 108*, 106297. Available from https://doi.org/10.1016/j.chb.2020.106297.

Suler, J. (2004). The online disinhibition effect. *Cyberpsychology & Behavior, 7*(3), 321–326.

Teng, Y., & Hew, K. F. (2019). Emotion, emoji, and sticker use in computer-mediated communication: A review of theories and research findings. *International Journal of Communication, 13*, 2457–2483, 1932-8036/20190005.

Topić, M. (2020). It's something that you should go to HR about — banter, social interactions and career barriers for women in the advertising industry in England. *Employee Relations: The International Journal, 43*, 757–773. Available from https://doi.org/10.1108/ER-03-2020-0126.

Vallade, J. I., Booth-Butterfield, M., & Vela, L. E. (2013). Taking back power: Using superiority theory to predict humor use following a relational transgression. *Western Journal of Communication, 77*(2), 231–248. Available from https://doi.org/10.1080/10570314.2012.669018.

Vitak, J. (2012). The impact of context collapse and privacy on social network site disclosures. *Journal of Broadcasting & Electronic Media, 56*(4), 451–470. Available from https://doi.org/10.1080/08838151.2012.732140.

Wardman, N. P. (2020). Humour or humiliation? When classroom banter becomes irresponsible sledging in upper-primary school contexts. *Discourse: Studies in the Cultural Politics of Education*. Available from https://doi.org/10.1080/01596306.2019.1707777.

Wei, W., & Wan, X. (2017). *Learning to identify ambiguous and misleading news headlines*, 06031. Available from https://doi.org/10.1007/s00766-011-0119-y, *arXiv preprint arXiv:1705*.

Whittle, J., Elder-Vass, D., & Lumsden, K. (2019). There's a bit of banter': How male teenagers 'do boy' on social networking sites. In K. Lumsden, & E. Harmer (Eds.), *Online othering: Exploring the dark side of the web* (pp. 165–186). Cham: Palgrave Macmillan. Available from 10.1007/978-3-030-12633-9_7.

Yang, H., De Roeck, A., Gervasi, V., Willis, A., & Nuseibeh, B. (2011). Analysing anaphoric ambiguity in natural language requirements. *Requirements Engineering, 16*(3), 163–169.

Yuan, Z., Park, Y., & Sliter, M. T. (2020). Put you down versus tune you out: Further understanding active and passive e-mail incivility. *Journal of Occupational Health Psychology, 25*, 330–344. Available from https://doi.org/10.1037/ocp0000215.

Zajenkowska, A., Bower Russa, M., Rogoza, R., Park, J., Jasielska, D., & Skrzypek, M. (2020). Cultural influences on social information processing: Hostile attributions in the United States, Poland, and Japan. *Journal of Personality Assessment*, 1–9. Available from https://doi.org/10.1080/00223891.2020.1774380.

# Politics and influence

CHAPTER SIX

# Netnography of YouTube as an open space for a vlogger advocate

**Jea Agnes Taduran-Buera[1] and Jean A. Saludadez[2]**
[1]University of the Philippines Los Bañ, Los Baños, Laguna, Philippines
[2]University of the Philippines Open University, Los Baños, Laguna, Philippines

## Contents

## Background

YouTube "vlogosphere" is situated in a performative and an open space created through programming and communicative interaction (Vrooman, 2002). To this day, the community of YouTube video creators, video bloggers, or vloggers is growing each day as more technology becomes available. This is why there is a shift of YouTube byline from

*Handbook of Social Media Use Online Relationships, Security, Privacy, and Society, Volume 2*
DOI: https://doi.org/10.1016/B978-0-443-28804-3.00003-X

"Your Digital Video Repository" to "Broadcast Yourself," which is paving way to a new generation of communicators.

In the Philippines, advocacies such as veganism have a limited place for discussion anywhere except in cyberspace or social media platforms which can be considered a free and open space for any advocacy. Thus, the study analyzes how advocacy of veganism is shared through vlogging on YouTube.

Unlike public speaking or any face-to-face interactions, video blogging or vlogging veganism is a "distinctly original" form of communication that is emblematic of the amateur videos found on YouTube (Tolson as cited in Savage, 2015). The process of vlogging starts by picking and facing a handheld video camera or phone camera to your face and "naturally," without a script and in one take, narrating your experiences in a conversational tone with the intent of sharing the video to a wider audience. Vlogs contain a person narrating a story, thought, or expertise to an online and international audience. YouTube vloggers can be attributed to what Richarson (as cited in Suler, 2016) mentioned as "verbalizers of the online world" who are drawn to the more thoughtful, effective, and deliberate style of asynchronous communication. In YouTube's context, this can be attributed to Walter Ong's work on "technologization of verbal communication" or the shift from orality to literacy and the impact of this shift on culture and education (Wahl, 2013) from the earliest forms of human communication such as stories, songs, folklore, and public speeches to written tradition to social networking. Given its growing user base, it is no wonder that social networking is changing communication as we know it. Although mostly asynchronous, YouTube now has a live feature that allows a vlogger to have active and dialogic communication with the viewers.

With modern technology and mobility, connecting with others through YouTube has become easier than ever. We communicate in a dynamic and intricate system of personal and social relationships, and each of us is linked to all others by fewer degrees of separation than ever before. These technological advancements have revolutionized how we communicate. The evolution of media to social media became the fulcrum that links and influences the modern world (Baym, 2015). However, merely connecting is not sufficient, as communication studies also require engagement or the act of sharing in the activities of the group. One specific way to engage in communication activism is through direct action in support of needed social change for individuals or groups (Frey and Carragee, 2007).

Successful content creators such as the vloggers become social influencers and advocates with a lot of persuasive influence. Through YouTube, vloggers are given a space to present their arguments for or against a particular issue to influence attitudes and beliefs as well. This rise in social media has also created a cluttered message environment and advocacy groups have to be creative in their social media messages delivered.

With a YouTube vlogger's strong influence over his or her viewers, it is interesting to know an advocacy is communicated to the viewers, especially when the message is not the convention. An observational netnographic analysis was conducted to study the social interactional dynamics in an open space that allow a YouTube vlogger to advance an advocacy. Specifically, the purpose of the study is to answer the following questions:

1. What are the opportunities that an open space provides for a YouTube vlogger to advance veganism as an advocacy?
2. What is the nature of YouTube vlogging in an open space?

## Literature review

Due to the relative newness of the topic, the corpus of literature on netnographic analysis on YouTube vegan vlogging is still limited. Through netnography, Kozinets (2010) found five major themes that emerged within the online vegan community related them to other social and subculture movements.

A number of scholars studying veganism focus on various practices, motivations, and/or barriers of transitioning to veganism. Through an online ethnographic approach (netnography), Nolasco (2016) examined how Spanish vegans perceive barriers of veganism and how they can be solved by using Facebook groups. Frawley's (2017) thesis on veganism employed ethnography techniques to focus on the adaptation and transition to veganism through the experiences of 19 interviewees to interpret veganism as a cultural phenomenon. Her research questions answered how societal, moral, and physical environments both shape and inform a sense of meaning and action behind an individual's decision to become vegan. Hirschler's (2008) dissertation on vegan's beliefs and experiences using critical theory and autoethnography explored the initial force of becoming vegan, the sustaining motivation to persist, the impact the diet and associated practices have had on the participant, and vegan's assessment of omnivore's eating practices.

While studies on veganism generally focus on motivations and identity creation, studies on YouTube focus on video comments and YouTube vloggers' influence on consumer brand perceptions, intention, and identity formation (Simonsen, 2012). Several scholars found that YouTube challenged the received concepts of the audience. Napoli (2010) examined audience studies in a new direction by calling for a reconceptualization of the idea of the mass, particularly as it functions in the two-way communication of YouTube. In a study of YouTube España viewers, Camacho and Alonso (as cited in Soukup, 2014) found that "Internet users who watch videos on-line have adopted the passive attitude that is inherent in the behavior of viewers of unidirectional and traditional media."

YouTube vlogging has been largely overlooked in rhetorical and netnographic scholarship. Thus, it is highly relevant to have a broader scholarly conversation and extend the existing studies for digital rhetoric and the use of netnography as a method of analysis as there is a lack of scholarly attention given to it. By examining YouTube video blogs through netnography, this study aims to provide new opportunities to interrogate the culture of communication of a YouTube vlogger in advancing an advocacy.

## Methodology

With online communities becoming important fields for qualitative research with its diverse and open cultural spaces, this study provides the distinctive cultural and rhetorical features of YouTube vlog entries as qualitative data and explains the process of netnography that has been developed in this research.

Netnography originated from ethnography, which is defined as "the study of people in their own time and space, in their own everyday lives" (Burawoy et al., 1991, as cited by Hallet & Barber, 2013). Ethnographers must study people in their "natural habitat" to understand the fissures between practices and discourses and to situate the microworkings of everyday life within larger social structures.

Ethnography is centered on an extended period of immersion in a field setting, allowing the researcher to understand the activities and relationships of a culture or subculture from an emic perspective (Denzin, 1997). An ethnographer is described as someone who inhabits somewhat of a strange no-man's land or stranger in a strange land, but trying to live as a native.

With the technological advancements in society, Denzin (1997) articulated that ethnography needed to adapt. Kozinets (2015) argues that the mass adoption of networked personal computing since the mid-1990s has seen the development of new cultural formations that are novel due to their online context and so consequently require new research methodologies.

Before the term netnography gained usage as the term referring to a virtual or internet ethnography (Kozinets, 2015), a number of terms have emerged in the literature, including digital ethnography, ethnography on/of/through the internet, connective ethnography, networked ethnography, hypermedia ethnography, digital ethno-, and cyber-ethnography, to coin the new research method.

Although other researchers perceived netnography and the above terms as synonymous, the more established view is that netnography is a distinct research method, with its own set of guidelines. Digital ethnography, online ethnography, virtual ethnography, and cyber-ethnography, however, are not characterized by any specific practices, and thus they are considered much more general approaches to online research (Kozinets, 2015).

Rokka (2010) distinguished netnography from the other research methods by providing several benefits starting with the netnographic data, which are often described as "rich and naturalistic, with the ability to accurately depict the lived realities of customers" or users. Another distinct quality of netnography is that it can be conducted in an "unobtrusive manner, offering researchers a view of customers' everyday lives especially in the case of sensitive research topics" (Kozinets, 2015).

Netnography has the advantage of being faster, simpler, and much less expensive than traditional ethnography. It is an adaptable and flexible qualitative method that has proven to be useful in various research settings (Kozinets, 2015). It is also compatible with other research methods such as rhetorical analysis.

According to Heinonen and Medberg's (2018) metaanalysis, more than half of the netnographic studies combined netnography with other qualitative or quantitative methods or as a complement to larger studies. Netnography, as a qualitative and interpretive research methodology, adapts ethnographic research techniques to the study of the online environment to form an understanding of a cultural phenomenon (Kozinets, 2010). It aims to understand that our social worlds are increasingly digital. Today, anyone with a computer or a smartphone and a reliable internet connection has the potential to become a social media influencer. More and more people are creating YouTube content such that for every five seconds, 35 hours of video are uploaded (http://www.everysecond.io/youtube). With YouTube's 1.9 billion users worldwide, there is a highly active, engaged, and potential viewers to tap into committing to an advocacy (Clement, 2019). This results in emerging new conditions on how people communicate and influence each other which is the focus of the study. Netnography is vital in the study since it allowed us as researchers to be active participants in the culture of the YouTube community through the following steps as recommended by Kozinets (2015):

## Online community identification

Before restructuring or studying the context of the vlog and the background of the vlogger to establish understanding of the artifact, the audience for the artifact, and why the artifact is engaging in the particular rhetoric, a netnographic analysis was conducted to study the social interactional dynamics of a vlogosphere that allows a YouTube vlogger to advance an advocacy.

Traditionally, vegan advocates make use of a variety of measures to influence people to take steps in eliminating animal products from their diet and lifestyle. Forms of activism include handing out pamphlets, producing documentaries, initiating talks and debates, organizing campus vegan activities, sharing vegan recipes, opening vegan food places, working for and building animal sanctuaries, and protesting or discouraging meat consumers out in the streets.

Nowadays, YouTube channels are used as communicative platforms for plant-based advocates, medical doctors advocating plant-based, vegan diet, vegans, and vegan activists to upload videos online to discuss their expertise and advocacy and get maximum and swift exposure for their videos to build audience and authority on veganism.

## Engagement and immersion

Before collecting the data, immersing in the YouTube community was important to learn and understand its language and context. My personal YouTube channel, created almost 10 years ago, was reactivated to have content access and contribute to the community.

To be immersed in the community and the advocacy, subscribing and following vegan YouTube vloggers became part of the daily routine for over a year. Voluntary informed consent is essential before proceeding to the data selection. Electronic mails were sent to the selected YouTube vlogger to introduce myself, explain the purpose of and procedures involved in the study, and seek permission for him to be part of the research.

## Data collection

The videos analyzed fulfilled the four requirements:
1. The vlogs offered at least two events, which can be active or stative.
2. The vlogs were organized by time, which means that the vlog had a sequence of events arranged chronologically or had flashbacks or flash-forwards.
3. The vlogs depicted a relationship between earlier and later events in the vlog.
4. The vlogs presented a unified subject. The setting, vloggers, and their actions were connected in ways that together tell a story.

To provide a context of understanding of why the YouTube vlogs were created and uploaded for public consumption, describing the rhetorical situation is vital. Aside from answering the research questions, field notes from a netnographic perspective are important in collecting relevant data, personal observations, introspective reflections, and questions such as:
1. What is meaningful in the vlogs?
2. Where is the vlogger coming from?
3. What is it like to connect to the YouTube community members?
4. What is absent from the findings that you expected to find?
5. What do I not understand in the vlog?

This process gave me an opportunity to understand and document my learning of the YouTube community culture—its architecture, practices, language, members, uses, reach, and resonance. As netnographers, our decisions of what to analyze were documented. Through participation within the YouTube community, the netnographer also becomes vital in the creation and analysis of data (Kozinets, 2015). By employing netnography as a research method, the YouTube channels of vegan vloggers were viewed and the selection of the research subject was purposely made based on Kozinets' (2010) list of recommendations in choosing the subject. His six criteria are as follows:
1. The online site must be relevant to the research focus and questions.

2. The online site must be active or with recent and regular communications.
3. The online site must be interactive.
4. The online site must be substantial in terms of numbers of users.
5. The online site must be heterogeneous, involving different participants
6. The online site must be data-rich.

Earthling Ed's YouTube channel was the chosen research subject, as it was substantial in the total number of vlogs uploaded about veganism, relevant to the research questions, active in both posts and comments, heterogeneous in terms of the number of people/viewers involved, and potentially data-rich.

## Selection of vlogging entries

The community of YouTube is held up by the content but also the viewership, likes, comments, and subscriptions. Before collecting the data, immersing in the YouTube community was important to learn and understand its language and context. The main author created a personal YouTube channel to have an access to curate own content and contribute to the community. To be immersed in the community and the advocacy, subscribing and following vegan YouTube vloggers became part of the daily routine for over a year. Voluntary informed consent is essential before proceeding to the data selection. Electronic mails were sent to the selected YouTube vlogger to identify self, explain the purpose of and procedures involved in the study, and seek permission for him to be part of the research.

Ed Winters' YouTube channel, Earthling Ed, has over 424,000 subscribers with almost 250 uploaded videos about veganism as of September 2019. Ed Winters has devoted himself to participating in all forms of animal rights activism after becoming a vegan. According to his personal website https://earthlinged.org/, he is the cofounder and codirector of an animal rights organization named Surge that aims to "create a world where compassion towards all animals is the norm." He used his website as a platform for people to be educated and be committed to going vegan. In a year, 33,248 people signed up to go vegan through Earthling Ed's online content. As proof of his social media influence, Ed Winters was invited to teach a class entitled "animals as commodities" at Harvard University as a guest lecturer. He will be speaking at other universities including Brown, Cornell, Columbia, Yale, and Rutgers about veganism.

For this study, we selected five more popular vlogs of the 30-video series on Earthling Ed's YouTube channel, which mainly addressed fallacies people have or excuses people make to avoid going vegan. The five vlogs analyzed for the study are: (1) It's my personal choice to eat animals; (2) Can you love animals and eat animals?; (3) I love how animals taste!; (4) It's cultural and traditional to eat animals; and (5) Everything in moderation.

After selecting vlogs to be analyzed, we transcribed each of the videos and started to compile themes of how the YouTube vlogger communicated veganism to the viewers. By coding and highlighting the sentences or ideas on how the vlogger explained the consequences of animal consumption, the common themes emerged after the sentences have been categorized under each theme. Making abstractions, checking and refining, generalizing, and theorizing were employed to complete the analytical coding. Through this method, it revealed the nature of YouTube vlogging in an open space.

## Thematic analysis

After selecting vlogs to be analyzed, transcriptions were made and themes of how the YouTube vlogger communicated veganism to the viewers were compiled. The field notes gathered were used to organize themes that emerged from the analysis of the online community. The data were analyzed using qualitative and ethnographic thematic content analysis techniques. Qualitative content analysis extends the scope of inquiry to examine meanings, themes, and patterns that may be apparent or concealed in a text (Grbich, 2017).

As netnography involves an inductive approach to the analysis of qualitative data, thematic content analysis was deemed an acceptable method for a textual inquiry. Thematic content analysis is the detailed examination of coding and categorizing textual information into constituent trends of consensus.

In qualitative research, coding captures the essence of a piece of language-based or visual data (Saldaña, 2015). It derives from interpretation of the data, rather than using preconceived codes as in quantitative research. By coding and highlighting the sentences or ideas on how the vlogger explained the consequences of animal consumption, the common themes emerged after the sentences have been categorized under each theme.

Before coding, the vlog was viewed a couple of times (including the other 29 vlogs on misconceptions about veganism) before it was transcribed and viewed multiple times again for me to be immersed in the data. Often you are not looking to place a value judgment on the piece, and if there is an implicit or implied argument, you may not be ultimately taking a side.

As a vital phase of netnography, making abstractions, checking and refining, generalizing, and theorizing were employed to complete the analytical coding.

## Results and discussion

After the analytical coding of the five YouTube blogs addressing common misconceptions or fallacies of veganism, results revealed YouTube as an open space that provides three opportunities and the processes for a YouTube vlogger to advance an advocacy: interaction, inclusion, and influence through a dialogic performance.

### Interaction

YouTube is used as a communicative platform for plant-based advocates, medical doctors advocating plant-based, vegan diet, vegans, and vegan activists in getting maximum and swift exposure for their videos to build audience and authority on veganism. In the five videos of Earthling Ed, continual interaction with the audience was evident. To engage the viewers, interactive dialog was apparent not only in the vlogs but also offline.

Earthling Ed provided moral arguments on the value of animal lives and their welfare in persuading the viewers to commit to veganism. This was a deliberate attempt to highlight the abuses animals experience due to animal agriculture. His shift from "we" to "you" point of view is a persuasive way of addressing the audience as it calls for action. The second person "you," "your," or "yours" are usually in the context of providing instructions or advice, thus the shift to better engage the viewers. It drew on the areas of Burke's consubstantiation to identify with the viewers since differences are inevitable among people and human interaction is far more complex than simply persuading online. Vloggers like Earthling Ed share far more personal experiences with their fans, or "friends" as most of them refer to their fan base. They open up their homes and invite viewers into their lives by sharing their ways of living making it much easier to identify with them.

In this context, the vlogger's attempt to interact with the viewers by identifying with them is a necessary step to communicate with anyone online or offline. As Burke (1969) stated, people are "both joined and separate, at once a distinct substance and consubstantial with one another."

In this sense, there is a need to link the animals' sentience and intelligence to humans as we feel more connected to those who are like us. Larsson et al. (2003)'s echoes this emphasis when they observed that vegans tend to cite moral concerns regarding animal welfare as the key motivation for pursuing veganism. Accepting that animals experience pain and identifying with them should become one of the greatest motivations for going vegan.

Earthling Ed and the other YouTube vloggers can be attributed to what Richarson (as cited in Suler, 2016) mentioned as "verbalizers of the online world" who are drawn to the more thoughtful, effective, and deliberate style of communication. One of the rhetorical effects of the digital world has been the ways in which the globally accessible messages posted to it can address particular audiences. By analyzing underlying messages that advocate a particular viewpoint, the viewers become critical and interactive consumers, making educated choices regarding whether or not to embrace such messages. In the study's selected vlogs, the vlogger has intended for an interactive digital dialog for the viewers to seize a moral high ground by committing to veganism.

Although the multimodal form of interaction between the vlogger and the viewers is asynchronous, there is still a discursive exchange, wherein the vlogger and the viewers mutually engage with one another that will lead toward a better position. This is why the motive that impels the kind of discourse is more cooperative than competitive. Many of the most engaging vlog content is aimed at informing or persuading viewers. When creating such content, it is critical to consider how best to present the information or advocacy. The most effective way to gain insight into the viewership's attitude is to engage with them.

## Inclusion

Forms of moral argumentation that were observed in the vlogging entries are claim-reason points based on moral norms as premises. Motivated by moral and ethical principles, the vlogger advocacy takes on a special role in serving both the interests of justice and the rights and privileges of his "clients" (the animals, the environment, and the people) by pleading a case, supporting a cause, or recommending a course of action and seeking to influence policies by pleading or arguing within political, economic, and social systems.

When presenting a moral argument, the vlogger deeply employs the concept of identification rather than persuasion per se to facilitate understanding of how his way of communicating unites or separates him from the viewers through the choices of words and overall vlog content.

Connecting with the viewers was apparent in the articulation of the advocacy. It is a clear indication of Burke's identification since the vlogger connects with and persuades the viewers by identifying with them in certain ways. In this context, persuasion may occur after the viewers have identified with the vlogger. Burke stated that people, by nature, are responsive to symbolic expressions that can unite them in purpose and action when a persuasive message such as the vlog is skillfully crafted. Veganism is most often perceived as an alternative lifestyle since it challenges mainstream conventions about food, health, and morality. There is an increasingly high rate of engagement among young people with YouTube, the majority of whom are either avid fans, critics, or spectators of the vegan lifestyle. The YouTube vlogging community provides viewers means for acquiring feelings of inclusion, especially among people who seek the company of like-minded people. At the heart of this community, there exists a quality of commonality. After all, a person might be the only one who practices veganism in a small town, but there are many across the globe who advocate the same lifestyle that he or she can meet online. Thus, a YouTube vlogging community allows people to transcend geographic boundaries and unite with others who share common interests.

Connection is the power of communication that helps a vlogger relate to people, groups, communities, social institutions, and cultures. The YouTube vlogging community provides an open space where viewers have means for acquiring feelings of inclusion, especially among people who seek the company of like-minded people. Earthling Ed constantly included the viewers in his message. At the heart of this community, there exists a quality of commonality. After all, a person might be the only one who practices veganism in a small town, but there are many across the globe who advocate the same lifestyle that he or she can meet online.

Thus, a YouTube vlogging's open society allows people to transcend geographic boundaries and unite with others who share common interests.

## Influence

As a YouTube vegan advocate, Earthling Ed made use of a variety of measures to influence people to take steps in eliminating animal products from their diet and lifestyle. Forms of activism on YouTube include production of documentaries, initiating talks and debates, organizing campus vegan activities, sharing vegan recipes, opening vegan food places, working for and building animal sanctuaries, and protesting or discouraging meat consumers out in the streets, among many others.

Before the explicit mention of the call for action to commit to veganism, the statements below indirectly stated the harmful effects of animal consumption:

> "As vegans, we respect the environment and everyone who is affected by climate change because consuming animals is responsible for causing some of the worst environmental calamities that we're currently facing as a species."

In this utterance, the vlogger appealed to his audience as he emphasized on the negative effects of animal consumption on the environment, specifically climate change.

Through YouTube, Earthling Ed is given an open space to present arguments for veganism and consequences of meat consumption. Through the open space, he is able to present his experiences as a vegan while commanding international access, appeal, and following.

Earthling Ed's influential role as a YouTube vlogger has an impact in how the world is interpreted since vlogging, although primarily a form of entertainment, can both reflect and shape what people believe in and how they behave. A vlogger's rhetoric has the power to influence the behavior and attitudes which can help in directing the action of the targeted viewers toward committing to veganism. Particularly, vlogging has played an influential role in addressing a common misconception about veganism.

With YouTube's influence on the viewers' behavior through the videos uploaded, rhetoric has evolved to include the process of "adjusting ideas to people and people to ideas" in messages of all kinds. Once clicked, the uploaded vlog is continually persuading, shaping people's perspectives about the world of veganism, and providing firsthand accounts, as no other conventional speaker could.

The study affirms Fogg's (2008) mass interpersonal persuasion or the "power of interpersonal persuasion with the reach of mass media" to create the most significant advance in persuasion since radio was invented in the 1890s.

YouTube has fostered a community of advocates worldwide such as vegan creators that produce videos dedicated to their advocacy and lifestyle. Although veganism is most often perceived as an alternative lifestyle since it challenges mainstream conventions about food, health, and morality, there is an increasingly high rate of engagement among young people, the majority of whom are either avid fans, critics, or spectators of the vegan lifestyle.

After analyzing the themes or opportunities and the processes for a YouTube vlogger to advance an advocacy, the nature of YouTube vlogging emerged: multidirectional or complex, multitemporal or continuous, and multisituational or contextual.

## Multidirectional or complex

Vlogging occurs under complex conditions that are ever changing as it recognizes intricacies of communicating advocacies online. YouTube vlogging in an open space occurs under complex conditions that are ever changing, which make the communication process multidirectional. It may occur in a variety of places and under different circumstances. The vlog is not just a simple output in which a YouTube video creator forward to the recipient. One YouTube video will be viewed and received by 2–200 viewers differently or simultaneously worldwide. The viewers' educational background, upbringing, beliefs, values, needs, ideals, motives, and physical surroundings, as well as the video creator's character, speech, and competence all affect the communication process.

Unlike the traditional processes of public speaking, monologue, or soliloquy, vlogging is more complex because it originated in a setting that is also similar to a face-to-face interaction except for the "missing" interlocutor needed for turn taking. Unlike in a public speaking situation where most students approached the topic with nervous excitement or just plain nervousness, recognizing the power of articulating thoughts and advocacies, and taking into consideration the content of speech, pace, voice, audience rapport, nonverbal cues, and delivery to a room full of audience/critics, vloggers need not now worry about facing a crowd at least not while filming the vlog. However, it is still necessary to deliver a vlog in a clear, articulate, and engaging manner since what will be presented online will be seen and critiqued. The vlog is automated, making persuasion much easier to be shared among friends and viewers on YouTube, quickly distributing content to millions of people across the globe.

## Multitemporal or continuous

YouTube vlogging is continuous. Baym (2015) pointed out that the change has been rapid, as digital technologies remove the barriers associated with the traditional media such as the format, location, distance and time, and the transfer of content, which make it more effective and efficient in sending a message across. She added that our engagement online is becoming a requirement for "successful participation in society."

YouTube vlogging is continuous, as there are no definable beginnings and endings in the process of persuasive performance as it is all up to the viewers when and how they will be possibly taken in the vlogs. Prior events in the viewers' lives also affect how the message is received. A set of interactions of many new and existing stimuli led to a vlog's characterization as a process. Thus, a vlog is a dynamic and an ongoing event. Similarly, communication in YouTube is not something the users do, but something in which they engage.

## Multisituational or contextual

Lastly, YouTube vlogging is contextual, as there are a variety of factors that affect the creation, persuasion, dissemination, and interpretation of a vlog. Communication through a YouTube vlog should be studied from a cultural perspective. This is in the context that a vlog is produced under complex circumstances that are ever changing. The YouTube vlogger is someone for whom the viewers have their own set of evaluations. Its language and delivery are unique to the event, and all this occurs with one or more people involved in the online interaction. Problems or exigency also come to exist based on how people perceive and define them in interaction.

## Summary and conclusion

This study explored a particular type of performance—advocating veganism on YouTube vlogs. Evident in the videos was the role of the vlogger as someone who intended to engage with the audience from the very start. He had different ways of interacting with the viewers and employed communicative strategies to identify with and include the viewers in the online dialog.

This study analyzed vegan YouTube vlogs to discuss how veganism is presented to their viewers. Ed Winters' influential role was asserted when he made use of rhetorical appeals to address the common misconceptions or fallacies about veganism. After the initial analysis, it has been inferred that YouTube vlogging in an open space occurs under complex conditions that are ever changing, as it recognizes the intricacies of communicating advocacies online. Contrary to a previous study by Camacho and Alonso (as cited in Soukup, 2014) who concluded that online viewers have adopted the passive attitude that is inherent in the behavior of viewers of unidirectional and traditional media, YouTube vlogs are multidirectional, especially when more viewers are affected by the vlogger and the viewers' comments. Vlogging is also a continuous process since there are no definable beginnings and endings and it is contextual, as there are a variety of interactional features that influence the creation, dissemination, and interpretation of a vlog.

Articulating an advocacy through YouTube vlogging is a dialogic act. With the viewers' support and performance through their social media presence and engagement, they themselves are part of the rhetorical act. Although the multimodal form interaction between the vlogger and the viewers are asynchronous, there is still a discursive exchange wherein the vlogger and the viewers mutually engage with one another that will lead toward a better position. The advocacy vlogs' rhetorical acts of directly addressing viewers' comments through more vlogs distinguish the mode of interaction dominated by user-generated content from those dominated by traditional media.

Netnography revealed how the YouTube vlogger used interpersonal communication strategies by interacting, including, and influencing the viewers to commit to veganism. As a dialogic performance, vlogging serves as a powerful instrument for the advancement of any advocacy. Bitzer (1968) stated that a fitting rhetorical response is, therefore, determined by the way the situation is presented and statements that are arranged to comprise each situation. The vlogger's dialogic responses to the viewers would not have been elicited without today's health, animal, human, and environmental crises.

Although the multimodal form interaction between the vlogger and the viewers are asynchronous, there is still a discursive exchange wherein the vlogger and the viewers mutually engage with one another that will lead toward a better position. The advocacy vlogs' dialogic process of directly addressing viewers' comments through more vlogs distinguish the mode of interaction dominated by user-generated content from those dominated by traditional media.

Netnography of YouTube vloggers led to a better understanding of the opportunities and process of a YouTube vlogger in communicating an advocacy such as veganism. The study's methodological contribution is employing netnography in gaining insights from the YouTube vlogging community through identification, selection, engagement, immersion, data collection, analysis, and iterative interpretation. The method is described as unobtrusive as it is of major significance to netnography to respect the vlog as itself without intervening with the vlogger and/or the viewers.

## References

Baym, N. (2015). Personal connections in the digital age. Retrieved from https://www.hs-heilbronn.de/16580627/2015-baym-nancy-personal-connections-in-a-digital-age-pdf.pdf.

Bitzer, L. (1968). The rhetorical situation. *Philosophy and Rhetoric, 1*(January), 1−14.

Burke, K. (1969). *A rhetoric of motives*. Berkeley: University of California Press. (Original work published 1950).

Clement, J. (2019). *Social media - statistics & facts*, Retrieved from. Available from https://www.statista.com/topics/1164/social-networks/.

Denzin, N. K. (1997). *Interpretive ethnography: Ethnographic practices for the 21st century*. SAGE Publications, Inc. Available from https://doi.org/10.4135/9781452243672.

Earthling Ed. Retrieved from https://earthlinged.org/.

Fogg, B. J. (2008). Mass interpersonal persuasion: An early view of a new phenomenon. In H. Oinas-Kukkonen, P. Hasle, M. Harjumaa, K. Segerståhl, & P. Øhrstrøm (Eds.), *Persuasive technology. PERSUASIVE 2008. Lecture notes in computer science* (vol 5033). Berlin, Heidelberg: Springer. Available from https://doi.org/10.1007/978-3-540-68504-3_3.

Frawley, E. (2017). Veganism as a cultural phenomenon (Undergraduate honors thesis). Retrieved from https://digitalcommons.bucknell.edu/cgi/viewcontent.cgi?article = 1392& context = honors_theses.

Frey and Carragee. (2007). Communication for social change. Retrieved from https://www.semanticscholar.org/paper/Communication-for-social-change-Frey-Carragee/f2b1fe1f4ff8110f7961b94c04231568f08199ff.

Grbich, C. (2017). Qualitative data analysis: An introduction. Retrieved from https://www.researchgate.net/publication/234779440_Qualitative_Data_Analysis_An_Introduction.

Hallet, R., & Barber, K. (2013). Ethnographic research in a cyber era. *Journal of Contemporary Ethnography, 43*(3 August), 306−330. Available from https://doi.org/10.1177/0891241613497749.

Heinonen, K., & Medberg, G. (2018). Netnography as a tool for understanding customers: Implications for service research and practice. *Journal of Services Marketing, 32*(6), 657–679. Available from https://doi.org/10.1108/JSM-08-2017-0294.

Hirschler, C. (2008). An examination of vegan's beliefs and experiences using critical theory and autoethnography (Doctoral dissertation, Cleveland State University). Retrieved from https://etd.ohiolink.edu/rws_etd/document/get/csu1211977933/inline.

Kozinets, R. (2010). *Netnography: Doing ethnographic research online.* London: Sage.

Kozinets, R. (2015). *Netnography: Redefined* (2nd ed.). London: Sage.

Larsson, C., Ronnlund, U., Johansson, G., & Dahlgren, L. (2003). Veganism as status passage: The process of becoming vegan among youths in Sweden. *Appetite, 41*(1), 61–67. Available from https://doi.org/10.1111/j.1440-172X.2006.00580.x.

Napoli, P. M. (2010). Revisiting "mass communication" and the "work" of the audience in the new media environment. *Media, Culture & Society, 32*(3), 505–516. Available from https://doi.org/10.1177/0163443710361658.

Nolasco, N. (2016). Vegan lifestyle on Facebook: An online ethnography study. Retrieved from https://www.diva-portal.org/smash/get/diva2:946093/FULLTEXT01.pdf.

Rokka, J. (2010). Netnographic inquiry and new translocal sites of the social. *International Journal of Consumer Studies, 34,* 381–387. Available from https://doi.org/10.1111/j.1470-6431.2010.00877.x.

Saldaña, J. (2015). *The coding manual for qualitative researchers.* Thousand Oaks, CA: Sage.

Savage, K. (2015). Understanding and engaging YouTube communities (Master's thesis). Retrieved from https://pdfs.se.

Simonsen, T.M. (2012). Identity-formation on YouTube: Investigating audiovisual presentations of the self.

Soukup, P. A. (2014). Looking at, with, and through YouTube[TM]. *Communication Research Trends, 33*(3), 3. Available from https://link.gale.com/apps/doc/A385069098/AONE?u = anon ~ b02ee8e2&sid = googleScholar&xid = 07ad7a13.

Suler, J. (2016). *Psychology of the digital age.* New York, USA: Cambridge University Press.

Vrooman, S. (2002). The art of invective: Performing identity in cyberspace. Retrieved from https://journals.sagepub.com/doi/10.1177/14614440222226262.

Wahl, S. (2013). *Persuasion in your life.* New Jersey: Pearson Education Inc.

Winters, Ed. [Earthling Ed]. (2018, January 8). It's Cultural and Traditional to Eat Animals [Video File]. Retrieved from https://www.youtube.com/watch?v = 0tItNLwMT_g.

Winters, Ed. [Earthling Ed]. (2018, January 3). Can You Love Animals and Eat Them? [Video File]. Retrieved from https://www.youtube.com/watch?v = 7mjVwVDDI8E&t = 13s.

Winters, Ed. [Earthling Ed]. (2018, January 4). It's My Personal Choice To Eat Animals! [Video File]. Retrieved from https://www.youtube.com/watch?v = LseSfTA1BMw.

Winters, Ed. [Earthling Ed]. (2018, January 5). I Love How Animals Taste! [Video File]. Retrieved from https://www.youtube.com/watch?v = w7sn6gyxMvE.

Winters, Ed. [Earthling Ed]. (2018, January 19). Everything in Moderation [Video File]. Retrieved from https://www.youtube.com/watch?v = Z-S21l0Xa_s.

# CHAPTER SEVEN

# Trolling and fake news diminish critical analysis and morality: insights from Philippine newspapers and trolling narratives

**Nimrod L. Delante**
School of Humanities, Nanyang Technological University, Singapore

## Contents

Traditionally speaking, we produce and reproduce knowledge based on the intellectual discourse maintained by our fundamental institutions such as the newspapers, television, and universities, in which the public is given an opportunity to participate freely in shaping public opinion (Demetrious, 2013; Habermas, 1989). Discourse is open, participative, and intended for social growth, as it offers tremendous possibilities for the creation of

DOI: https://doi.org/10.1016/B978-0-443-28804-3.00002-8

knowledge (Foucault, 1972; Mumby, 1997) that encourages us to share and create meaning systems, allowing us to gain truths and define and organize both ourselves and our social world (Pinkus, 1996). Fair and equitable participation in discourse among the members of the public, including attempts to disrupt social norms and traditions and deconstruct the central authority, is key to social progress, intellectual development, and emancipation (Mumby, 1997).

However, in this day and age, knowledge and its sources are constantly disrupted by the rapid advancement in technology, the internet, social media, and smartphones (Contreras, 2017; Demetrious, 2013). Knowledge creation no longer resides among intellectuals who represent, protect, and uphold these traditional institutions. Rather, knowledge has transcended to those in the periphery who are gaining traction in the fight against marginalization, oppression, and silencing (Contreras, 2017; Demetrious, 2013). The marginals have destabilized social norms and traditional structures due to the immense power of social media (Demetrious, 2013). This outcome is worthwhile because it promotes democratic thinking and free speech and allows voices and grievances to be heard (Demetrious, 2013), as people practice their democratic freedom and advance their liberalist mindsets in the public sphere through open discourse (Habermas, 1989).

However, the progress of social media does not come without impediments. Disinformation, rumor mongering, fraudulence, and falsity continue to emerge, spreading hate, hostility and violence, destroying critical thinking, and diminishing public morality, making the fight for truth much more difficult (Kavanagh & Rich, 2018). The list of related terms can be long, but in the public eye, all these terms that gain recognition and legitimacy in the literature cascade down to a common terminology: *fake news*. Fake news has become highly politicized (Kalsnes, 2018); it emerges in many forms, is alarmingly dangerous, and pervades on social media because of social groups with ill intentions and political agendas. Fake news is "...orchestrated, funded, planned. In politics, it is run by professionals," argued Professor Clarissa David of the University of the Philippines Diliman (as cited in Quilinguing, 2019, para. 4). These orchestrators and perpetrators of fake news are called trolls. Some of these trolls are considered white trolls: those perceived to have good intentions for facts and discourse to prevail in the public sphere and who could be more proactive in disclosing vulnerabilities so that harmful attacks on people can be reduced (Matthews & Goerzen, 2019), but majority of them are wicked. Harmful trolls are those that start flame wars or upset people by spreading inflammatory, digressive, attacking, derogatory, violent, extraneous or off-topic messages, videos, attacks, assaults, and contemptuous remarks (Hardaker, 2017) in news platforms, forums, chats, social media posts, and video blogs with the intention to provoke the public into displaying strong emotional responses and normalize tangential discussion either for the trolls' amusement and self-gratification or for economic gains (Hopkinson, 2013; March, 2020; Ong & Cabanes, 2019). One example of this is profit-driven trolling, whereby financial gain is made possible by pay-per-click (clickbait model) with the intention to spread digital disinformation (Cabanes, 2020). Another example is trolling for amusement driven by people's inner desire to have fun or to feel good when they mock other people (Bishop, 2012; March & Steele, 2020). Patriotic trolling comes next, which is pivoted to increase the popularity, relevance, and credibility of a politician that trolls are paid for and at the same time demonize the opposition party and its leaders (Chanco, 2021; Valderama, 2017), while destroying authentic political discourses and distorting public opinion, leading to a decadence in critical thought and morality (Contreras, 2017; Kavanagh & Rich, 2018).

## Review of literature

Three major drivers of trolling are associated with patriotism or political partisanship, socioeconomic needs, and self-gratification.

### Patriotic trolling

A key driver of trolling strongly resides in the minds of the public where ideological beliefs grow: *partisan politics* or *patriotic trolling*. Partisan politics happens when two major opposing groups are fighting against each other in words, in views of power and influence, in ideology, in reason, and in action in defense of the political figure or a cause that they believe in and share with that political figure, often without thinking carefully about the matter of contention (Gundersen et al., 2000; Klein, 2020; Oscarsson & Holmberg, 2020). On social media, those individuals or groups who create fake accounts and show strong support to their politician are called patriotic trolls. They imbue loyalty, trust, and fanaticism to one politician. Their nationalism is based on the beliefs, ideals, and causes of that politician, rather than on the collective consciousness and fundamental ideals of the nation, curbing democracy, civil rights, and civic consciousness (Sombatpoonsiri, 2018). Either way, political trolls who support their politician (whether representing the government or the opposition) are fighting with each other by expressing their deeply polarized views entrenched within the complexity of social, economic, and political issues that confront the people (Rivera, 2020; Saludo, 2018), which, in turn, diminish civic space and civic action (Sombatpoonsiri, 2018). In most cases, their attacks to their targets and defense of their politician are primarily based on nostalgia, regionalism and blind fanaticism, less with historical facts, available data, or leadership credentials (Heydarian, 2022; as cited in Amanpour, 2022). Even if such sentimental longing or wistful affection is tilted to a dark period of history in which their politicians are implicated, these trolls support their politicians blindly and are willing to revise narratives in defense of their politicians (Levinger, 2018) or engage in strategic distractions to benefit their clients and ignore pressing issues that affect the greater majority (King et al., 2017; Steinfield, 2018).

Exacerbating divide, trolls are allegedly paid, thrive on a huge network of social media to promulgate pro-government messages, monitor and report civic defiance, bully and threaten critics online, and orchestrate fake news that can lead to harassment and mockery of an opposition's standard bearer (Sombatpoonsiri, 2018). These happen because these keyboard armies are blinded by patriotism, bravely defending their politician even if the politician's stand is illogical, unreasonable, distorted, or immoral. Tamalayan (2020) argued that repression persists in the Philippines' internet world because a huge network of cyber troll armies continues to operate in that space by trying to maneuver internet traffic, silence dissent, distort public opinion, and spread terror and trauma. These cyber trolls seem to project their virtuous self-image online operating within a cloak of invisibility or disguise (Fahey, 2020) in the name of patriotism, progress, and growth (King et al., 2017), making patriotic trolling rampant in many countries, further dividing the people politically and morally. In China, King et al. (2017) reported that hundreds of thousands of trolls are hired to distract the public, ignore controversial issues, and cheer for China's robust economic identity, worsening political divide and making the fight for critical dialogue, civic activism, moral ascendancy, and truth much more difficult.

## Trolling for economic gain

Another driver of trolling behavior is entrenched in what trolls do: they spread fake news and discredit a politician they dislike yet gain something from it economically. Trolls are monetarily rewarded. The clickbait model explains this profit-making goal that is usually double-edged, that is, trolls can be influenced by their political beliefs so they manufacture fake news to discredit their client's rival, yet they are driven by profit that can grow via pay-per-click through media commoditization (Ong & Cabanes, 2019; Marantz, 2020; Sillisen, 2014). The cost-per-click economy is the most politically agnostic and commercially driven model of digital disinformation (Ong & Cabanes, 2019). Using a cat-and-mouse game of manipulating platform algorithms to optimize reach of defamatory and salacious content, the clickbait model emerges to be highly profitable for the trolls and cognitively rewarding for end users consuming content (Ong & Cabanes, 2019; Scott, 2021). Political pundits and digital influencers take advantage of it by sharing highly emotional but factually misleading narratives to ensure that their names remain popular and relevant (Levinger, 2018; Ong & Cabanes, 2019). State-sponsored trolls will continue to emerge, manipulating public opinion (Savvas et al., 2019) and cheering for the progress and development of the country's leadership (King et al., 2017) to conceal those socioeconomic problems that need critical attention.

In the Philippines, it is not difficult for fresh university graduates to be enlisted as trolls creating fake accounts to support a political candidate, said Jonathan Ong, a Professor of global digital media at the University of Massachusetts Amherst (as cited in Bengali & Halper, 2019). They have fleeting loyalties politically speaking, but they are also equally attracted to the cash they are getting. Those big scale consultancy firms who are running these troll farms in the Philippines could do an outright betrayal of their clients' trust (Mallik, 2018) at any time, for instance, in the middle of elections depending on who is potentially winning. This is because cash matters to them (Bengali & Halper, 2019). In an increasingly vicious online gaming industry and virulent social media, trolls are driven by amorality, apathy, and neglect (Sparrow et al., 2021). Guilt may not be something that trolls worry about (March, 2020). They would almost always have moral, ethical, and political backing for their online expression despite how distorted it can be (Phillips, 2011). Money, to the trolls, is the most appealing factor that motivates them to continually engage in the act of trolling no matter the consequences.

## Trolling for self-gratification

The third driver of trolling behavior is innately personal and behavioral. Some trolls create content for the "lulz" of it, that is, for the fun of it (Bishop, 2012), to unleash certain impulses not deemed appropriate in face-to-face interactions (Escartin, 2015). They are satisfied with the act of trolling, they feel a level of gratification when they spread hate speech that spins the public in different directions, and many of them do not show a tinge of guilt for doing this form of hostility (March, 2020). Trolls spread fake news and feel tremendous gratification when they victimize thousands of vulnerable social media users. March (2020) argued that trolls do not just enjoy hurting others emotionally because of their malevolent behavior, but also feel good about themselves when they troll. March (2020) and March and Steele (2020) found that sadism was the most powerful predictor of trolling. Hurting others online due to trait sadism can feed on people's self-esteem and amour propre (March & Steele, 2020). The more someone enjoys hurting others, the more it is likely that they will troll, and it feeds on their self-esteem, self-confidence, and ego—an indication that they have an appetite for cruelty and madness (Buckels et al., 2013). According to Cheng, Mizil, et al. (2017), this feel-good behavior of trolling highly depends on people's moods. This means that people who are experiencing negative moods that could persist inside them for a long time will highly likely engage in trolling, and this gives them tremendous satisfaction. A negative mood such as annoyance, anger, or resentment can become the troll's weapon to mock people on social media, which is a self-gratifying act.

In this article, I have attempted to answer two research questions:

1. Why do trolls do what they do?
2. How can trolling and fake news diminish critical analysis and moral values, and what can be done to fight this phenomenon?

## Context, data collection, and method of analysis

I utilized two sets of data for this study. Firstly, I collected 25 newspaper articles published in 2016 through 2021 by five Philippine newspaper organizations as the main textual data utilized in thematic analysis, namely, The Philippine Star, Philippine Daily Inquirer, The Manila Times, Manila Bulletin, and Rappler. These news articles reported about "trolling behavior," "trolling," "troll farms," "social media," "cyberbullying," "troll armies," "manufactured facts," and "fake news" in the Philippines. Secondly, I conducted online interviews with observants and victims of trolling and fake news and used the textual data from these interviews to supplement my thematic analysis of newspaper articles using the constant comparison method.

## Casual interviews

Casual conversations are core to qualitative research in an attempt to understand human experience through open, honest, uncoerced, spontaneous, and respectful exchange of ideas. In this study, I conducted online interviews using Zoom and Messenger with seven individuals who happened to be my connections on Facebook (three males and four females). Two of them witnessed several troll activities online, while five of them confessed that they became victims of trolling (named Mr M, Mr P, Ms R, Ms X, Mr B, Ms Q, and Ms Y). I sought their verbal consent prior to conducting our casual conversations. No screenshots of their names were captured. All call histories and recordings in my Zoom and Messenger profiles were deleted. Transcriptions of conversations (from Cebuano and Tagalog to English) were also deleted after completing the results and discussion. My goal of reaching out to them was to solicit ideas about dealing with trolling and fake news from a first-person account. These casual interviews helped me in substantiating the insights emerging from thematic analysis of newspaper articles. Our conversations mirrored those mundane day-to-day human conversations. They understood my research goals, and we maintained confidentiality, openness, fairness, and mutual respect. Three questions guided our online conversations: (1) What is trolling and why do trolls do what they do? (2) What are the effects of trolling? (3) What can be done or how can we respond to trolling behavior?

## Thematic analysis

My sensemaking of qualitative data was guided by the principles of thematic analysis. As a grounded theory methodology (Glaser & Strauss, 1967), thematic analysis requires qualitative researchers to code, a process of assigning value to a foundational text of words, an interaction, or conversation (Anderson, 2008). Coding invokes researchers to engage in a tedious process of reading and rereading narrative texts so that concepts, patterns, themes, even anomalies will come to the fore. Such concepts, patterns, and themes can be broken down into subthemes, or that these can be brought to a higher level of categorizing by coalescing them and creating overarching themes. Anderson (2008) and Lindlof and Taylor (2011) called this process axial coding, in which researchers dig deep into textual data, make further categorization of subthemes emerging from the data, build connections, and decide as to which major themes warrant a space in the analysis. In the Results and Discussion section, some authors of newspaper articles were cited in text due to relevance of interpretation. These authors also appeared in the References.

## Results and discussion

Trolls do what they do because of the following: (1) they are driven by partisan politics that widens public polarization, (2) they have profit-driven goals, and (3) they have an innate characteristic of viciousness, callousness, or sadism, offering them entertainment and self-gratification. These results echo the findings in the literature and confirm the devastating impact of trolling and fake news, that is, as critical analysis and moral values diminish, truths are distorted, social progress is obstructed, social consciousness is impaired, and social justice is crippled.

### Patriotism and partisanship

Patriotic trolling emerged as the topmost reason for trolling in the Philippines. It is hideous, and trolls are becoming more aggressive on social media trying to assassinate the characters of their client's rivals in politics (Chanco, 2021; Ong & Cabanes, 2019; Viray, 2019). Patriotic trolls share nationalistic and proadministration sentiments due to their undying loyalty and fanaticism to a politician whom they think share their own causes and beliefs, while attacking dissent by targeting individuals who criticize their politicians through hate speech, verbal abuse, attack on identity, and death threats (Hardaker, 2017; Matsuzawa, 2017) and by attempting to revise historical narratives in defense of their politicians (Levinger, 2018). In the 2016 elections in the Philippines, Rivera (2020) reported that patriotic trolling was rampant on Facebook where a huge ecosystem of fake news emerged in support of a strong political candidate who, at that time, won in the national elections. Facebook became a war machine, creating a climate of hostility where trolls attacked ordinary citizens and opposition parties with no remorse (Rivera, 2020), and most of them did not feel guilty of their act (Phillips, 2011); it is all for the "lulz" of it (Bishop, 2012).

Political trolling is a state-sponsored online hate campaign to silence dissent, intimidate citizens, and manipulate public opinion (Avendano, 2018; Cabanes, 2020; Ong & Cabanes, 2019; Tubeza, 2018) by operating within a cloak of invisibility or disguise (Fahey, 2020). As troll armies create click parties, they can systematically distort political discussions and turn fake news into reality. Their emotionally charged campaigns can tap into populist sentiments of anger and resentment and unleash uncivil expressions of misogyny, antiintellectualism, and other forms of offensive speech and distorted logic into the public discourse (Saludo, 2018), suppressing civil rights and civic action (Sombatpoonsiri, 2018) and distracting the public from attending to the crucial issues of the country (King et al., 2017; Steinfield, 2018).

Social media, particularly Facebook, continues to be a hegemonic platform in the Philippines through which trolls spread false narratives and counternarratives (Romulo, 2021), and it has become a powerful tool for social control and manipulation (Matsuzawa, 2017). In propagating fake news, intelligent ploy and deception is key (Saludo, 2018). Because anyone can say whatever they want to say, including those in power (Valderama, 2017), ideological and political polarization widens (Gundersen et al., 2000; Klein, 2020; Oscarsson & Holmberg, 2020), affecting the way the citizens, as a collective consciousness, think critically and make informed decisions about how they respond to trolling and fake news. Indeed, trolling and fake news has contributed significantly to the degradation of morality and ethics.

Leximancer enabled me to confirm the outcomes of my sensemaking: that trolling and fake news (85% relevance based on hits or counts) constitutes as one of the 21st century evils that is optimizing the power of social media as its weapon in continually destroying the national consciousness of the Philippines and its people. By making sense of conceptual maps, key words, and percentage reporting of key sentences, I confirmed one key outcome of patriotic trolling: that it is evil, highly divisive, and it does more harm than good (Fig. 7.1).

Additionally, a simple sentiment analysis of the terminologies mentioned in textual data from newspaper articles and interviews revealed that the news writers' and participants' overall feeling toward the terms "fake

## KEY SENTENCES AS WARNINGS TO SOCIAL MEDIA USERS

■ Fake news is evil  ■ Trolls/trolling is divisive  ■ Social media/media is weaponized  ■ Public must be aware

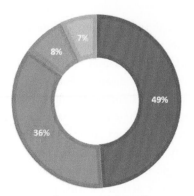

**Figure 7.1** Key sentences as warnings to social media users.

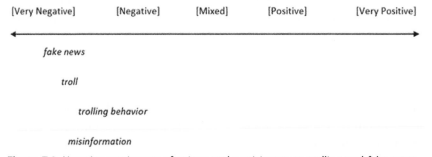

**Figure 7.2** Negative sentiments of writers and participants on trolling and fake news.

news," "troll," "trolling behavior," and "misinformation" is leaning toward the very negative spectrum. This means that the authors and the interview participants detest the phenomenon of fake news and trolling. Trolls proliferate like gremlins, distorting authentic political discourses, destabilizing credible sources and institutions of knowledge, and expanding polarization of ideas among the members of the public (Contreras, 2017; Gundersen et al., 2000; Klein, 2020; Oscarsson & Holmberg, 2020). Social media users must therefore be vigilant, curate activism, be more discerning (Torregoza, 2021), and have the courage to speak the truth and say what is right and just no matter how difficult and dangerous it can be (Ruperto Santos, as cited in Hermoso, 2021), in an attempt to triumph against trolls (Fig. 7.2).

If little is done on a personal, social, community, and governmental level with regard to trolling and the machination of fake news, and if the culture of impunity continues in the government alongside draconian tactics that impair activism, then, it is highly likely that autocracy and the silencing of dissent will prosper, and this will have tremendous implications on decision making, democratic thinking, social consciousness, moral ascendancy, and free speech (Billing, 2020; Kavanagh & Rich, 2018).

## Profit

The second reason why trolling is rampant in the Philippines and elsewhere in the world is due to profit. The Philippine Star (2017) and Rappler (2017) reported that a huge sum of money was used by the camp of Nic Gabunada to create farm trolls and attack opposition candidates in the 2016 presidential elections. Fake accounts were created in forms of bots flooding the social media with spams, phishing, and fake news, inflating likes and shares and creating momentum, popularity, and relevance to a former presidential candidate who eventually won the elections (Matsuzawa, 2017). Hundreds of thousands of fake accounts were created, which angered the public due to identity theft and public anxiety (Rivera, 2020), where trolls could betray their clients' trust at any time (Mallik, 2018). Why? Because there is profit in trolling (Inventor-Miranda, 2020), which can grow via pay-per-click through media commoditization (Ong & Cabanes, 2019; Marantz, 2020; Sillisen, 2014). Money is an enormous motivation (Bengali & Halper, 2019), especially in a country with endemic corruption where millions of people continue to suffer from poverty as an outcome of corruption. Social media influencers who are supporting politicians while operating in their echo chambers will contribute to the growth of profit-driven trolling, making it more difficult to combat.

When asked about why trolls become trolls, Mr M responded:

*Primarily for income. Many were jobless during the pandemic... They can hide their identity, right? With hungry mouths to feed, what choice do they have? I read somewhere that trolls don't need to come clean and act like a saint. They are faced with the reality of having nothing to eat. So, they troll. (03 June 2020)*

Mr M continued:

*Many companies have retrenched workers. If you are a parent with no job, it is very painful to see your kids hungry. So, people become trolls because there is money in trolling... Morality seems to be out of the equation. Morality jumps out of the window when people have nothing to eat. (03 June 2020)*

Mr P's response mirrors that of Mr M's. When asked about why trolls do what they do, Mr P declared:

*What is there to feel guilty about? Aren't all political candidates lying to us? These politicians embezzle people's money from the taxes they pay. What is there to defend them? As trolls post deceitful comments targeting political candidates, the higher the engagement from the public. Money is easy when a troll's post invites traffic and becomes viral. You know, these politicians are corrupt. So, is it wrong to mess with these politicians? Whatever has this country done to the Filipino people? (05 June 2020)*

Mr M and Mr P showed so much anger and resentment toward the government. They are not trolls, but they seemed to support trolls trying to attack traditional politicians who have nothing but selfish interests. They seemed to have lost faith in the country's leadership and governance.

## Self-gratification

The third reason why people troll is deeply ingrained in their character and personality. March (2020) and March and Steele (2020) argued that trolls do not just enjoy hurting others emotionally because of their malevolent behavior, but also feel good about themselves when they troll (Bishop, 2012). March (2020) found that sadism was the most powerful predictor of trolling. This means that the more someone enjoys hurting others, the more that they will troll, and it feeds on their ego. Billing (2020) echoed this by reporting that trolls can create tweets lauding their politician's humility and service to the country while attacking those who oppose their politician's sentiments, and this act of atrocity makes them feel good. With an appetite for abomination, cruelty, and madness (Buckels et al., 2013), trolls proliferate hate speech, threats of violence, personal attacks, character assassination, manufactured reality, and evil intentions (Hardaker, 2017), and they are gratified by these acts, while at the same time enjoy the economic benefits it brings (Hofilena, 2016; March, 2020). Mr P expressed:

*I feel bad about how innocent people would react to a post by a troll, but I chuckle when I see them engage in online tirades. I'm not happy about what is happening in the country, but with trolling, people make money and are entertained. You don't pay anything to feel good. It's right in front of your screen. I would rather enjoy the moment. (03 June 2020)*

Mr P did not hesitate to express his ideas openly. There was no tinge of guilt in his language. To him, the political candidates, as victims of trolling in a country of extreme corruption, deserve it. Mr M echoed similar sentiments:

> What change there is for the Philippines whose educational system and leadership are flawed and deeply problematic? I am hopeless and I don't care about what trolls do. Is there hope in this country with billions of loans from the World Bank? What I am concerned about is what the government is doing to our country! The Filipino people deserve better! (05 June 2020)

Mr P added:

> I feel bad when people believe those fake posts on Facebook. Are they even thinking? You feed them s\*\*\*, they would just open their mouths. They don't use their minds. Where is critical consciousness? I think these people should feel guilty to have allowed trolls to manipulate their minds, right? (05 June 2020)

"Why feel guilty in a country led by corrupt leaders?" emerged as their common predicament. On the one hand, Mr M and Mr P expressed amusement about what trolls are doing to Philippine politicians or leaders in government; on the other hand, they showed no remorse in finding pleasure from the trolls' activities. Noteworthy in their responses, though, is their deep concern and care for the Filipino people who remain victims of the ills of bad governance. "The Filipino people deserve better," said Mr M with a tone of resentment.

## How trolling and fake news diminish critical analysis and moral values

Trolling can demoralize their targets, distort truths, impede social progress, destroy social justice, and diminish moral compass and social consciousness. Trolls engage in the doxing enterprise to gain profit. Doxing is the act of publicly revealing or sharing intimate photos of target individuals as attack to their identities, credibility, and dignity (Avendano, 2018; Rivera, 2020). Because individuals want to protect their identity and reputation, they are more likely to give in to the financial demands of the trolls. This is demoralizing to these victims and seeking help seems to be their last resort because of fear of being singled out. Moral panic ensues. Sexual violence becomes rampant with trolling and fake news in which individuals are degraded into sexual objects (Avendano, 2018; United Nations, Educational, Scientific and Cultural Organisation, 2018) and opposition activists are turned into demons (Casayuran, 2020; Sombatpoonsiri, 2018). A troll who woke from trolling regretted in pursuing her irrationality in defense of a leader of her country that she had degraded herself with her own act (Mahinay, 2019). As a woke, she argued that it is not a sin to point out the flaws of the government, and that politicians do not deserve loyalty; the country does (Mahinay, 2019). She argued that trolling destroys authentic political discourses and distorts public opinion, leading to a decadence in critical thinking and morality (Kavanagh & Rich, 2018). This echoes the sentiments of Mr M and Mr P who expressed sadness about the fate of their country. "Aren't Filipinos gifted with intellect and critical thought? Why are they quick to fall for deception and trick? My fear is that when fake news gets into their mind, it can be difficult to erase. It can metamorphose into reality. Are people even thinking?" asked Mr M. It was a rhetorical question worth pondering. He was unsure if he would still cling to hope because he had already lost his faith in the government. Engaging in lies and conspiracies is rampant in his country, and this should worry the fundamental institutions and leaders of the land. Ms R shared:

> The troll who made me a target of insult and mockery really got into my head. They can change minds of vulnerable people, you know. They have the power to normalize wrong thinking and actions. I feel demoralized. I feel bad that until now, the police and our local government officials have done nothing to identify this troll. He/she is attacking people's character in town, you know. But he/she is there, free to spread hate online. (07 June 2020)

Ms X echoed the same sentiment:

> The troll did not hesitate to insult me online. I feel ashamed of myself for being called out as a prostitute. I lost face you know, and I was depressed because of what happened. That troll deserves all the punishment for having no values. The problem lies with the fact that people on Facebook are quick to believe the trolls and judge the victims. Are we losing our public morals? Maybe. (07 June 2020)

Ms Q shared the same sentiment:

> I became a victim of character assassination. I felt demoralized. That troll has no balls. He was hiding his true colors. He is dangerous. The problem is when your friends on Facebook will believe in the troll. Many of them are happy to see you in misery. It's sad, you know. (08 June 2020)

Ms R's, Ms X's, and Ms Q's statements resonate March's (2020) assertion that trolls, and those who inflate trolls' concoctions, are gratified to see their victims' afflictions. Their responses illustrate that trolling can tremendously diminish morality and critical thinking. Worse, as Ms R, Ms X and Ms Q were embarrassed and demoralized, the public commentators were enjoying the mockery they have experienced, and nothing was done. "What can I do, sir? The police and the government seem complacent to what these trolls are doing. Are these trolls even tracked down? They are diffused all over social media" argued Ms Q.

There is no common ground for people to engage further with trolls because trolls can deny data or facts outright (Chapman, 2015). "Gone are the days when majority of the public engage in conversations driven by facts," said Mr B. Knowledge created by the fundamental institutions that build a country—newspapers, television, community organizations, and universities (Demetrious, 2013)—seem to be revoked by trolls. As social media is becoming a war machine for trolls to sow falsity and deceit (Rivera, 2020), people should start asking themselves: "What can we do to stop trolling and fake news from destroying our moral tenets? What actions are worth trying?" added Mr B.

## Some feasible actions

Ramos (2020) and Saludo (2018) posited that people must be responsible users of social media, which means reading credible sources of information for fact checking (Saludo, 2018). Fact checking will have tremendous long-term impact in debunking misleading claims, educating the public, and opening their consciousness (Billing, 2020). Social media users can ignore and block trolls (Centre for Countering Digital Hate, 2022; Heritage, 2019; Dupuis and Williams, 2019) but report their bad behavior to relevant authorities, seek follow-up action, and ensure oversight and moderation (Cheng, Bernstein, et al., 2017; Rainie et al., 2017). Casayuran (2020), Hofilena (2016), and Valderama (2017) discouraged the idea of engaging trolls in online debate as it will put the latter in an advantaged position due to the prevalence of pay-per-click economy (Ong & Cabanes, 2019), where inflaming emotions (March, 2020) is what they are good at. Trolls must be punished through legal statutes and laws; if not, trolling might be perceived as a normal activity freeing trolls from repercussions (Golf-Papez & Veer, 2017). Social media users must reclaim their spaces of power to promote truths and guide people to choose good, conscientious leaders. They should mimic the trolls' strategy, that is, using compelling stories to promote truths because it is in these stories that people might pause and listen (Savvas et al., 2019); and that they will become wiser electorates. Impactful storytelling must be core to media literacy to subjugate the harmful tactics of trolls. Storytelling can be an effective and more meaningful alternative to the problematic strategy of challenging social media manipulation solely by doubling down on objectivity and facts (Cabanes, 2020).

Discernment, deep reflections, meaningful engagement, and citizenship activism are highly encouraged for social media users to challenge their consciousness and fight trolls more effectively to reduce polarization, increase access to information, and enliven free speech (Rainie et al., 2017), whereby openness, transparency, and mutual respect are valued. With the increasing levels of demagoguery on social media, Anderson and Rainie (2020) propounded that those technocrats (e.g., Facebook, Twitter, and YouTube) must improve online ethos, promote an enabling culture of dissent, and exhaust efforts to work for justice through citizenship activism and media literacy. Global technocrats such as Facebook, Twitter, and YouTube should be held responsible for the unprecedented use of social media spreading disinformation. One cannot create something and forget their social responsibility when something goes wrong. The public must also be more discerning of what is happening on social media (Valderama, 2017) and be bold to resist deceitful campaign tactics (Torregoza, 2021). Amplifying their voices through social media is a way of winning over paid trolls operating outside their echo chambers (Lardizabal-Dado, 2020). People should always question the veracity of information and perform rigorous fact-checking. Expressing deep concern about the diminishing moral compass of the people, Torregoza (2021) was advocating enhanced media literacy to fight fake news and put a stop to this vicious cycle (Lardizabal-Dado, 2020; S. B. Rosenthal, personal communication, December 17, 2020). Whatever has happened to our connection with our lifeworld, our sense of being and our active consciousness (Habermas, 1989), if we do not advocate media literacy and let it triumph in people's minds and practices?

People should have courage, valor, and bravery to speak the truth (Pangue & Serafica, 2020). Trolls will triumph in sowing deceit and misinformation annihilating public opinion and destroying critical thought if people do not speak up. Viray (2019) advised to create committees of transparency and accountability along with policies and regulations providing social safety nets to citizens. The government must penalize perpetrators of false and alarming reports that create confusion (Inventor-Miranda, 2020). Ms Y remarked:

*I think the NBI should investigate this troll who, I believe, lives in our town because she knows a lot of people in our town. She drops their names in her posts on Facebook. It is alarming yet I did not see any action or intervention from the local government. (08 June 2020)*

Mr B added:

*I hope the government will trace them and put them in jail. We have created many laws in the country, but are they implemented? I don't care if these trolls will rot in jail or die. What they do is abhorrent. They sow deceit and they seem to be invincible. Are they protected? (08 June 2020)*

Legal amendments, statutory reforms, and electoral laws must be implemented strongly in support of transparency and accountability in business, leadership and governance. These laws will help regulate bad behavior of social groups that are increasingly shifting their operations to social media sowing deceit and falsity using troll armies (Ong & Cabanes, 2019). In the Philippines, Facebook must affirm its role in public discourse and social justice; if not, Facebook must be held accountable for the ways it has gravely impacted politics and degraded discourse in the country (Rivera, 2020).

Better journalism and reasoned public deliberation must also prevail (Tubeza, 2018). Citizens must have a concerted voice pressuring governments to adjudicate reported cases of alleged misinformation for truth and justice to prevail (Recuenco, 2020). In democratic nations, citizens must not stop exercising their freedom to vote and become more educated voters. To stop voting is to view them as weak, suggesting defeat to autocracy and draconian leadership (Romulo, 2021). Furthermore, abandoning social media and not challenging fake news peddlers is losing by default to the trolls and black propagandists. If social media users do not act on the trolling problem, they may find themselves no different from the desensitized frog slowly cooked in the heat (Hofilena, 2016). Realization is late, regret surfaces, and the vicious cycle persists diminishing critical thought and morality.

## Conclusion

The journey toward justice and truth where social media is weaponized to spread lies and machinate fake news remains a constant challenge to the leadership and governance in the Philippines and elsewhere in the world. Without strong political will, social media will soon break a country beset by endemic corruption and rampant distortion of truths.

With trolls sowing falsity and disinformation, fake news will continue to appear as reality to many people along with the increasing disagreement about facts, differing analytical interpretations of facts and data, and the increasing relative volume and resulting influence of opinion and personal experience over data, evidence, and facts (Kavanagh & Rich, 2018). Civic discourse and morals will continue to erode, many more individuals will be alienated and disenfranchised from participating in discourse with political and civic institutions, and political paralysis will continue with aggressive trolls trying to destroy public discourse, morality and critical thought (Kavanagh & Rich, 2018).

Capable of intellectual discourse (Habermas, 1989), people must not fret or surrender to trolling and fake news. They must continue to engage in meaningful discourse and activism to generate wisdom and promote truth. Finding common ground in meaningful discourses will lead to critical thought, strong morals, and social cohesion. Social media users must activate their critical consciousness and citizenship to become courageous in the fight for truth, justice, and the common good. They must claim social media as a space of influence and an avenue to amplify their voice to fight trolls and make communities better. They must harness the power of media literacy and civic education to make positive change. They must also challenge political leaders to crystallize proactive, authentic, transparent, and transformative leadership to sustain a culture of trust, dissent, respect, and justice necessary to fight the evil that is trolling and fake news.

Kavanagh and Rich (2018) made this call: that people should revisit national narratives and collate lessons from history that they can use in their midst and learn from behavioral economics and behavioral psychology to understand these trolls better, open their minds, and persuade them to change. It may be a difficult challenge to change the trolls for the better, but as human beings, we can start by believing that behind their orchestrated (or imagined) identities lies a person with the capacity to think, feel, reflect, and reason driven by the power of human consciousness and the fundamental pursuit of a meaningful existence. We can always try.

# References

Amanpour, C. (2022). Back to the future in the Philippines? CNN. Available from https://edition.cnn.com/audio/podcasts/amanpour/episodes/e9ef469b-2f5e-4142-94ee-ae8d00d671c4, May 6.

Anderson, J., & Rainie, L. (2020). Hopeful themes and suggested solutions. *Pew Research Centre*. Available from https://www.pewresearch.org/internet/2020/02/21/hopeful-themes-and-suggested-solutions/, February 21.

Anderson, J. A. (2008). Thinking qualitatively: Hermeneutics in science. In D. W. Stacks, & M. B. Salwen (Eds.), *An integrated approach to communication theory and research* (pp. 40–58). Routledge.

Avendano, C. O. (2018). Rappler links Duterte 2016 campaign to certain fake news. *Philippine Daily Inquirer*. Available from https://newsinfo.inquirer.net/964969/rappler-links-duterte-2016-campaign-to-certain-fake-news, January 31.

Bengali, S., & Halper, E. (2019). Troll armies, a growth industry in the Philippines, may soon be coming to an election near you. *The Los Angeles Times..* Available from https://www.latimes.com/politics/story/2019-11-19/troll-armies-routine-in-philippine-politics-coming-here-next, November 19.

Billing, L. (2020). Duterte's troll armies drown out COVID-19 dissent in the Philippines. *Rappler*. Available from https://www.rappler.com/technology/features/philippine-troll-armies-coda-story, July 22.

Bishop, J. (2012). The psychology of trolling and lurking: The role of defriending and gamification for increasing participation in online communities using seductive narratives. In H. Li (Ed.), *Virtual community participation and motivation: Cross-disciplinary theories* (pp. 160–176). IGI Global. Available from https://doi.org/10.4018/978-1-4666-0312-7.ch010.

Buckels, E. E., Jones, D. N., & Paulhus, D. L. (2013). Behavioural confirmation of everyday sadism. *Psychological Science, 24*(11), 2201–2209. Available from https://doi.org/10.1177/0956797613490749.

Cabanes, J. V. (2020). Digital disinformation and the imaginative dimension of communication. *Journalism & Mass Communication Quarterly, 97*(2), 435–452. Available from https://doi.org/10.1177/1077699020913799.

Casayuran, M. (2020). De Lima denounces increase of fake news against opposition. *Manila Bulletin*. Available from https://mb.com.ph/2020/03/21/de-lima-denounces-increase-of-fake-news-against-opposition/, March 21.

Centre for Countering Digital Hate. (2022). DM abuse: Instagram negligent over misogynist harassment of women in the public eyes, study finds. Available from https://counter-hate.com/blog/dm-abuse-instagram-negligent-over-misogynist-harassment-of-women-in-the-public-eye-study-finds/, April 6.

Chanco, B. (2021). *The trolls have it. The Philippine Star*. Available from https://www.philstar.com/business/2021/05/31/2101927/trolls-have-it, May 31.

Chapman, S. (2015). Why I block trolls on Twitter. *The Conversation*. Available from https://theconversation.com/why-i-block-trolls-on-twitter-36120, January 12.

Cheng, J., Bernstein, M., Danescu-Niculescu-Mizil, C., & Leskovec, J. (2017). Anyone can become a troll: Causes of trolling behaviour in online discussions. *PMC PubMed Central*. Available from https://doi.org/10.1145/2998181.2998213.

Cheng, J., Mizil, C. D. N., Leskovec, J., & Bernstein, M. (2017). Our experiments taught us why people troll. *The Conversation*. Available from https://theconversation.com/our-experiments-taught-us-why-people-troll-72798, March 2.

Contreras, A. (2017). Trolls, fake news and the crisis of political representation in cyberspace: A post-modern theoretical perspective. *The Manila Times*. Available from https://www.manilatimes.net/2017/05/11/opinion/analysis/trolls-fake-news-crisis-political-representation-cyberspace-post-modern-theoretical-perspective/326583, May 11.

Demetrious, K. (2013). *Public relations, activism, and social change: Speaking up*. Routledge.

Dupuis, M. J., & Williams, A. (2019). The spread of disinformation on the web: An examination of memes on social networking. 2019 IEEE SmartWorld, Ubiquitous Intelligence & Computing, Advanced & Trusted Computing, Scalable Computing & Communications, Cloud & Big Data Computing, Internet of People and Smart City Innovation (SmartWorld/SCALCOM/UIC/ATC/CBDCom/IOP/SCI), Leicester, UK, 2019, pp. 1412−1418. Available from https://doi.org/10.1109/SmartWorld-UIC-ATC-SCALCOM-IOP-SCI.2019.00256.

Escartin, M. C. P. D. (2015). Rogue cops among rogues: Trolls and trolling in social networking sites. *Philippine Sociological Review*, *63*(2), 169−190. Available from http://www.jstor.org/stable/24717164.

Fahey, R. (2020). Internet trolls: Monsters haunting the world wide web. *University of Notre Dame*. Available from https://sites.nd.edu/manuscript-studies/2020/04/20/internet-trolls-monsters-haunting-the-world-wide-web/, April 20.

Foucault, M. (1972). *The archaeology of knowledge and the discourse on language*. Random House.

Glaser, B. G., & Strauss, A. L. (1967). *The discovery of grounded theory: Strategies for qualitative research*. Aldine Transaction.

Golf-Papez, M., & Veer, E. (2017). Don't feed the trolling: Rethinking how online trolling is being defined and combated. *Journal of Marketing Management*, *33*(15/16), 1336−1354. Available from http://sro.sussex.ac.uk/id/eprint/82176/.

Gundersen, A. G., Portis, E. B., & Shively, R. L. (2000). *Political theory and partisan politics*. State University of New York Press.

Habermas, J. (1989). *The structural transformation of the public sphere*. Polity Press.

Hardaker, C. (2017). Flaming and trolling. In C. Hoffman, & W. Bublitz (Eds.), *Pragmatics of social media* (pp. 493−522). de Gruyter.

Heritage, S. (2019). The best way to deal with online trolls? Do like Rachel Riley − starve them for oxygen. *The Guardian*. Available from https://www.theguardian.com/commentisfree/2019/sep/18/the-best-way-to-deal-with-online-trolls-do-like-rachel-riley-starve-them-of-oxygen, September 18.

Hermoso, C. (2021). To fight fake news, always speak the truth − bishop. *Manila Bulletin*. Available from https://mb.com.ph/2021/01/27/to-fight-fake-news-always-speak-the-truth-bishop/, January 27.

Hofilena, C. F. (2016). Fake accounts, manufactured reality on social media. *Rappler*. Available from https://www.rappler.com/newsbreak/investigative/fake-accounts-manufactured-reality-social-media, October 9.

Hopkinson, C. (2013). Trolling in online discussions: From provocation to community building. *BRNO Studies in English*, *39*(1), 5−26. Available from http://hdl.handle.net/11222.digilib/129149.

Inventor-Miranda, W. C. (2020). Trolls − behind the mask. *Manila Bulletin*. Available from https://mb.com.ph/2020/07/20/trolls-behind-the-mask/, July 20.

Kalsnes, B. (2018). *Fake news*. Oxford University Press. Available from https://oxfordre.com/communication/communication/view/10.1093/acrefore/9780190228613.001.0001/acrefore-9780190228613-e-809.

Kavanagh, J., & Rich, M. D. (2018). *Truth decay: An initial exploration of the diminishing role of facts and analysis in American public life*. RAND Corporation. Available from https://www.rand.org/pubs/research_reports/RR2314.html.

King, G., Pan, J., & Roberts, M. E. (2017). How the Chinese government fabricates social media posts for strategic distraction, not engaged argument. *American Political Science Review*, *111*(3), 484−501. Available from https://gking.harvard.edu/50C.

Klein, E. (2020). *Why we're polarised*. Profile Books Limited.

Lardizabal-Dado, N. (2020). The fake news provision in the Bayanihan Act. *The Manila Times*. Available from https://www.manilatimes.net/2020/04/05/business/sunday-business-i-t/the-fake-news-provision-in-the-bayanihan-act/709855, April 05.

Levinger, M. (2018). Master narratives of disinformation campaign. *Journal of International Affairs*. Available from https://jia.sipa.columbia.edu/master-narratives-disinformation-campaigns.

Lindlof, T. R., & Taylor, B. C. (2011). *Qualitative communication research methods*. Sage Publications.

Mahinay, K. (2019). From troll to woke gal. *Philippine Daily Inquirer*. Available from https://opinion.inquirer.net/119826/from-troll-to-woke-gal, February 28.

Mallik, P. (2018). Of jotnar-gygjars and hulderfork-huldras: Just look through the trolls. *Liberal Studies*, *3*(7). Available from https://heinonline.org/HOL/LandingPage?handle = hein.journals/libs3&div = 6&id = &page = .

Marantz, A. (2020). Big swinging brains and flashy trolls: How the world fell into the clickbait death spiral. *The Guardian*. Available from https://www.theguardian.com/technology/2020/feb/07/big-swinging-brains-fashy-trolls-clickbait-death-spiral-internet-media, February 7.

March, E. (2020). New research shows trolls don't just enjoy hurting others, they also feel good about themselves. *The Conversation*. Available from https://theconversation.com/new-research-shows-trolls-dont-just-enjoy-hurting-others-they-also-feel-good-about-themselves-145931, September 16.

March, E., & Steele, G. (2020). High esteem and hurting others online: Trait sadism moderates the relationship between self-esteem and internet trolling. *Cyberpsychology Behaviour and Social Networking*, *23*(7), 441−446. Available from https://doi.org/10.1089/cyber.2019.0652.

Matsuzawa, M. (2017). Duterte camp spent $200,000 for troll army, Oxford study says. *The Philippine Star*. Available from https://www.philstar.com/headlines/2017/07/24/1721044/duterte-camp-spent-200000-troll-army-oxford-study-finds, July 24.

Matthews, J., & Goerzen, M. (2019). Black hat trolling, white hat trolling, and hacking the attention landscape. *WWW '19: Companion Proceedings of the 2019 World Wide Web Conference*, New York, NY. Available from https://dl.acm.org/doi/abs/10.1145/3308560.3317598?casa_token = w5oGUzLf3Q0AAAAA%3As5gXp0HRAgUqUOT-I8lP-CBsknynsVOk4Qgf67NejHYE1k0sGn8dpkRJWn0giyyD6ZK3OjBgtCt1Ys, May 13−17.

Mumby, D. K. (1997). Modernism, postmodernism, and communication studies: A rereading of an ongoing debate. *Communication Theory*, *7*(1), 1−28. Available from https://doi.org/10.1111/j.1468-2885.1997.tb00140.x.

Ong, J. C., & Cabanes, J. V. (2019). Politics and profit in the fake news factory: Four work models of political trolling in the Philippines. *NATO Strategic Communications Centre of Excellence*. Available from https://stratcomcoe.org/cuploads/pfiles/5december-ber_report_philippines.pdf.

Oscarsson, H., & Holmberg, S. (2020). *Research handbook on political partisanship*. Edward Elgar Publishing. Available from https://www.e-elgar.com/shop/gbp/research-handbook-on-political-partisanship-9781788111980.html.

Pangue, J., & Serafica, R. (2020). Who is Joie Cruz and why are Duterte fanatics and trolls attacking her? *Rappler*. Available from https://www.rappler.com/moveph/things-to-know-joie-cruz-trolls-attack, August 14.

Phillips, W. (2011). Meet the trolls. *Index on Censorship*, *40*(2), 68−76, https://doi.org/10.1177/0306422011409641.

Pinkus, J. (1996). Foucault. Available from https://www.massey.ac.nz/ ∼ alock/theory/foucault.htm#: ∼ :text = Discourse%2C%20as%20defined%20by%20Foucault,of%20thinking%20and%20producing%20meaning, August.

Quilinguing, K. I. M. G. (2019). *The problem with fake news: UP experts speak on the impact of disinformation on politics, society and democracy.* Diliman, Quezon City: University of the Philippines. Available from https://up.edu.ph/the-problem-with-fake-news-up-experts-speak-on-the-impact-of-disinformation-on-politics-society-and-democracy/.

Rainie, L., Anderson, J., & Albright, J. (2017). The future of free speech, trolls, anonymity and fake news online. *Pew Research Centre.* Available from https://www.pewresearch.org/internet/2017/03/29/the-future-of-free-speech-trolls-anonymity-and-fake-news-online/, March 29.

Ramos, C. M. (2020). Gov't warns public vs false info after 'fake news' on holiday 'lockdown' circulates online. *Philippine Daily Inquirer.* Available from https://newsinfo.inquirer.net/1368641/govt-warns-public-vs-false-info-after-fake-news-on-holiday-lockdown-circulates-online, December 06.

Recuenco, A. (2020). PNP to run after troll cops who spread fake news. *Manila Bulletin.* Available from https://mb.com.ph/2020/02/26/pnp-to-run-after-troll-cops-who-spread-fake-news/.

Rivera, K. (2020). The problem with Facebook. *Philippine Daily Inquirer.* Available from https://opinion.inquirer.net/130576/the-problem-with-facebook, June 08.

Romulo, R. R. (2021). The social media imperative. *The Philippine Star.* Available from https://www.philstar.com/business/2021/05/14/2098018/social-media-imperative, May 14.

Saludo, R. (2018). Fake news in PH: Here's the real story. *The Manila Times.* Available from https://www.manilatimes.net/2018/02/15/opinion/columnists/topanalysis/fake-news-ph-heres-real-story/380295, February 15.

Savvas, Z., Caulfield, T., Setzer, W., Sirivianos, M., Stringhini, G., & Blackburn, J. (2019). Who let the trolls out? Towards understanding state-sponsored trolls. *WebSci '19: Proceedings of the 10th ACM Conference on Web Science.* Available from https://doi.org/10.1145/3292522.3326016.

Scott, K. (2021). You won't believe what's in this paper! Clickbait, relevance and the curiosity gap. *Journal of Pragmatics, 175*(6), 53–66. Available from https://doi.org/10.1016/j.pragma.2020.12.023.

Sillisen, L. B. (2014). Trolls make good clickbait. *Columbia Journalism Review.* Available from https://archives.cjr.org/behindthenews/trollsmakegoodclickbait-t.php, August 21.

Sombatpoonsiri, J. (2018). Manipulating civic space: Cyber trolling in Thailand and the Philippines. *GIGA German Institute of Global and Area Studies, 3*, 1–12. Available from https://www.ssoar.info/ssoar/handle/document/57960.

Sparrow, L. A., Gibbs, M., & Arnold, M. (2021). The ethics of multiplayer game design and community management: Industry perspectives and challenges. *CHI 2021: Proceedings of the 2021 CHI Conference on Human Factors in Computing Systems, Australia, 325*, 1–13. Available from https://doi.org/10.1145/3411764.3445363.

Steinfield, J. (2018). The new "civil service" trolls who aim to distract: the government in China is using its civil servants to act as internet trolls. It's a hard management task generating 450 million social media posts a year. *Index on Censorship, 47*(4). Available from https://doi.org/10.1177/0306422018819361.

Tamalayan, F. (2020). Policing cyberspace: Understanding online repression in Thailand and the Philippines. *Journal of ASEAN Studies, 34*(2), 129–145. Available from https://journal.binus.ac.id/index.php/jas/article/view/6769/3950.

Torregoza, H. (2021). Troll farms, fake news spoiling voters' ability to make right choice — Lacson. *Manila Bulletin.* Available from https://mb.com.ph/2021/05/12/troll-farms-fake-news-spoiling-voters-ability-to-make-right-choice-lacson/, May 12.

Tubeza, P. C. (2018). Malacañang: Penalising fake news unconstitutional. *Philippine Daily Inquirer.* Available from https://newsinfo.inquirer.net/965234/malacanang-penalizing-fake-news-unconstitutional, February 01.

United Nations, Educational, Scientific and Cultural Organisation. (2018). *Journalism, fake news and disinformation: Handbook for journalism, education and training.* UNESCO Press. Available from https://en.unesco.org/sites/default/files/journalism_fake_news_disinformation_print_friendly_0.pdf.

Valderama, T. C. (2017). ). Trolling takes its toll on the truth. *The Manila Times.* Available from https://www.manilatimes.net/2017/07/31/opinion/analysis/trolling-takes-its-toll-on-the-truth/341563, July 31.

Viray, P. L. (2019). Philippines' 'fake news' farms thrive due to politicians, industry players — report. *The Philippine Star.* Available from https://www.philstar.com/headlines/2019/12/06/1974832/philippines-fake-news-farms-thrive-due-politicians-industry-players-report, December 06.

**CHAPTER EIGHT**

# Modes and meanings of language use in social media

## Lenis Aislinn C. Separa[1,2] and Anna Ruby P. Gapasin[1]

[1]Office of the Vice President for Research, Extension, Planning and Development, Polytechnic University of the Philippines, Manila, Philippines
[2]School of Communication, Journalism and Marketing, Massey University, Wellington, New Zealand

## Contents

*Handbook of Social Media Use Online Relationships, Security, Privacy, and Society, Volume 2*
DOI: https://doi.org/10.1016/B978-0-443-28804-3.00006-5

With the advent of technology, a lot of innovations to communication have arisen. One of the newest means of computer-mediated communication (CMC) is social media. This kind of mass medium is being utilized through people's voluntary inclusion to an online community. Social networking sites such as Facebook, Twitter, LinkedIn, Pinterest, and Google Plus + are now being utilized by a number of people all over the world to connect with their families, relatives, friends, and even acquaintances using the internet. Users of this application provide information about themselves, which can be viewed by not only those known to them, but also by those whom they do not.

Since it is a known fact that the young generation is hooked to a variety of gadgets together internet connectivity, social media has been an everyday part of their lives. Posting of both verbal and nonverbal messages in their own profile pages becomes now an integral means of self-expression in the cyber community worldwide. Once tagged as a "text country," the Philippines is known for being a wide consumer of technology, both gadgets and connectivity. With this known fact, it is expected that Filipinos of all ages are predisposed to online interaction through utilizing social networking sites, or what is now termed as social media. The Philippines has even been called the social media capital of the world since millions of Filipinos spend four hours per day on an average on social media sites like Facebook (Pablo, 2018).

An individual's ability to verbally express oneself through posting status updates and sharing infographics mirrors how language is used in the context of this platform. However, what is alarming in this new media is that no matter how individuals carefully choose words to best describe their thoughts, some people may view and interpret them differently, as pointed out by Finegan and Niko (1989). It would also be worthy to focus on the linguistic features of the emerging themes in the usage of social media to further enrich the practice of corpus linguistics in the Philippines, which could then unleash the unknown characteristics of our usage of both Filipino and English languages.

Social media consist of internet-based sites and services that promote social interaction among its participants (Page et al., 2014). Among the most utilized social media in interacting with the online community is Facebook. This has been a part of every person's life in socializing with individuals whom they have already known in person or have just met online. With the default question in the status, "What's on your mind, Lenis?," this social networking site is encouraging people to verbalize their thoughts through typing it in their respective Facebook pages. Not to mention the other platforms where Facebook users can express themselves that include but not limited to pictures, videos, and graphics.

Looking at the Facebook status posts, we can observe that there exist writings that do not actually conform to the usual conventions of writing. Some of these are written in complete statements with correct punctuation, spelling, and capitalization, but there are those which are written based on the thoughts and preferences of the users without giving much importance to the usual rules of language. With Facebook becoming one of the most utilized social networking sites across different countries, there has been a language culture that emerged, as users engage themselves in the online community. This language is said to be one's guide to social reality (Sapir, 1929).

In schools, the proper usage of words is emphasized in language classes. The usage of the correct form of words, phrases, and sentences when writing is given emphasis in instruction. Though this is one of the goals of language classes, a variety of writing styles in social media can be observed, as this online community creates and recreates a culture of language use in Facebook. A content analysis of Facebook status posts of millennials in the Philippines characterizes different features of syntax that are present in their profiles.

## Literature review

### Social networking

In Boyd and Ellison (2007), social network sites are defined as web-based services that allow individuals to construct a public or semipublic profile within a bounded system, articulate a list of other users with whom they share a connection, and view and traverse their list of connections and those made by others within the system. People access these social network sites or social media through the usage of the computer and internet connectivity. Thus, this process can be considered one form of CMC.

CMC includes human communication and information shared through communication networks (Pearson et al., 2008). When we engage in CMC, we can "meet and talk to anonymous individuals at a distance and in relative safety" (Trenholm & Jensen, 2011). She further added in her book *Interpersonal Communication*, engaging in CMC frees us from obvious status markers and from being judged for our nonverbal characteristics.

In this study of 800 adolescents between ages 12 and 17 led by Lenhart et al. (2010), it was revealed that "older online teens are more likely to report using online social networks than younger teens." Moreover, teenagers who go online daily are also more likely to utilize social network websites. Teens from lower income families (those earning less than $30,000 annually) are more likely to use online social networks than teens from wealthier households.

## Motivations for social media use

Individuals use social media for varied reasons. The seven unique uses and gratifications of social media users include social connection, shared identities, content, social investigation, social network surfing, and status updating (Joinson, 2008). College students use Facebook for about 30 minutes throughout the day as part of their daily routine (Pempek et al., 2009). They spend more time viewing content on Facebook than posting any verbal or nonverbal content. These have been the result of a qualitative and quantitative study among 92 undergraduate students who have accomplished a daily diary and a survey afterward.

Building relationships is also one reason for using social media. In a survey among 286 undergraduate students, there is a strong association between use of Facebook and the three types of social capital, with the strongest relationship being to bridging social capital (Ellison et al., 2011). In this study, Facebook is considered to maintain existing offline relationships or solidify offline connections, as opposed to meeting new people. Dwyer et al. (2007) also mentioned that maintaining contact with high school friends and getting to know new classmates better are motivations for social media use.

Aside from relationships among schoolmates, Facebook plays an important role in learning. Among first year Belgian students who are language learners of English, the integration of Facebook in the language learning curriculum backed by a proper approach to encourage scaffolded support gives way to new opportunities for stimulating learners in higher education (Peeters, 2019). Meanwhile, Hong Kong university students used blogs and Facebook as a common space for reflective writing and interaction where messages of emotional expressions and social support are evident (Cheong et al., 2017).

## Creation of online personalities

Individuals may consider socialization as the goal of using social media and not to realize the desire to represent themselves. Nevertheless, these individuals need to construct self-representations to participate in the practice of Facebook (Enli & Thumim, 2012). Social media users tend to present themselves positively on social networking sites. Through focusing on one's presented positive self-image, beneficial outcomes are usually expected, whereas focusing on others' idealized images typically leads to harmful outcomes (Vogel & Rose, 2016).

In creating one's profile in social media, a user considers self-image. This is the picture one has for oneself and the kind of person one believes he or she is (Pearson et al., 2008). In her book *Human Communication*, she discussed three types of feedback from others, which indicate other people's perception of us. These are confirmation, rejection, and disconfirmation.

*Confirmation* happens when others treat a person consistent with one's self-image. On the other hand, *rejection* happens when other people treat a person in a manner that is inconsistent with one's self-definition. The last type of feedback is *disconfirmation*, which happens when others are not able to respond to one's notion of self through being neutral about it.

Disclosing one's self-image through social media has both advantages and disadvantages. According to DeVito (2002), "self-disclosure contributes to self-knowledge; it helps you gain a new perspective on yourself and a deeper understanding of your own behavior." However, he also stressed that self-disclosure can also effect to personal and social rejection, and even material losses.

The issue of *over attribution* can also be involved in the perceptual process of a social media user. In DeVito (2002), it is defined as "the tendency to single out one or two obvious characteristics of a person and attribute everything that person does to these one or two characteristics." If this is the case, it works positively to someone who has a dominantly good characteristic but works otherwise to someone who had been identified with even a single negative trait.

It is stated in National Broadcasting Corporation's (NBC) article entitled *Facebook's Online Rudeness Ruins Offline Relationships* that "many of those surveyed believed that people are much ruder online than in real life." 80% of the respondents stopped having a face-to-face interaction with the person who had been rude to them online. This study has been the result of a survey among 2698 Americans in February.

Building one's identity online provides opportunity for a social media user to build one's positive image. One way in which participants reconciled their conflicting needs for positive self-presentation and accuracy was to create profiles that described a potential future version of self (Ellison et al., 2011). These individuals who are active on a large online dating site described how they or others created profiles that reflected an ideal as opposed to actual self. The concept of "foggy mirror" or unintentional misrepresentation of oneself is said to be triggered by the limits of self-knowledge.

Finding a partner is one reason for creating online personality in social media. Individuals manage their online presentation of self to be able to find a romantic partner through attending to small cues online, mediating the tension between impression management pressures, and the desire to present an authentic sense of self. Creation of a profile that reflected their ideal self and attempted to establish the veracity of their identity claims is considered one of the tactics (Ellison et al., 2011).

Social media can also be a platform for seeking advice from others. In a Facebook Group dedicated for Black fathers, conversations on advice include family expansion, financial matters, maternal gate-keeping, navigating family relationship conflict, and raising children and child development (McLeod, 2020).

The attractiveness of the social media users' online friends affected their own in an assimilative pattern (Walther et al., 2008). Favorable or unfavorable statements about the respondents interacted with gender. Negative posts about certain moral behaviors increased male profile owners' perceived physical attractiveness, but decreased attractiveness of females.

## Self-disclosure in social media

The variety of audience in online causes individuals to manage impressions on the topics they choose to share and prefer to say. Schlosser (2019) explains that social media posts have become performers who present an edited version of Facebook users, which the latter believe will be best received by others. This is the way of managing individuals' reputations through what they post and what other people post about them.

Since social media is an online platform for self-disclosure, privacy issues are inevitable. There are Facebook members who divulge a lot of personal information and are not very aware of privacy options or who can actually view their profile (Acquisti & Gross, 2006). Although privacy can be an issue among social media users, individuals still choose to share online. Social media users are usually inspired by expressions of kindness and overcoming obstacles (Dale et al., 2019). This quantitative content analysis done in the United States show that inspirational Facebook posts contain similar frequencies of hope and appreciation of beauty and excellent elicitors when compared with other forms of media and social media.

## Language use in social media

The recognition of emotions and feelings in Facebook through computer technology has been commonly explored in recent years. According to Farina (2015), status updates in Facebook can be examined as tellings using the conversation analysis approach. These tellings varies in formats which include textual messages only, combinations of textual messages with either photos or hyperlinks, photos only, or hyperlinks only. Using an ad hoc build crawler, Facebook posts can be classified based on a set of predefined categories and can be detected as being positive, negative, or neutral (Terrana et al., 2014; Iram, 2019). Giuntini et al. (2019) investigated whether the emoticons chosen by users in social network news express the emotions they wish to express, having as indicative the polarity of the emotions and the six basic emotions, and found that use of reactions in feelings analysis algorithms can increase the confidence in defining the emotion attached to the content, as well as the emotional state of the Facebook users.

Based on the language used in one's social media, the personality traits of an individual can also be determined. Using the Facebooks posts of Chinese using Chinese texts, an experiment made using a Chinese text segmentation tool suggests that extraverts seem to write more sentences and use more common words than introverts, making the former more willing to express their feelings and life with others than introverts (Peng et al., 2015).

Grounded on Searle's (1969) speech act (SA) framework, together with Grice (1975) theory of cooperative maxims and implicature, the language used online in the Facebook status updates and posts of individuals in Egypt is seen as a form of social interaction (Khalaf, 2019). Though individuals differ in the manner of expressing themselves though language, Facebook has been a way to record their daily events, activities, and experiences in the assertive statements in their posts. This is made possible through users' representation of themselves using the language and frameworks of Facebook (Enli & Thumim, 2012).

Youth in Nepal use social networking to redefine the role of English to their existing social relationships, code-switch English and Nepali to construct bilingual identities, and embed English with other texts to recontextualize both local and global media content (Sharma, 2012). Meanwhile, Filipino multilingual Facebook users are found to code-switch when they discuss a specific topic, provide emphasis on a message, express group identity, clarify speech content, meet a real lexical need, exclude others, indicate emotion, express their emotions, and keep up with linguistic trend (Banuag, 2020).

Humor orientation of individuals can also be traced from Facebook posts. The cues for a humorous disposition include status updates on relational talk, humor in profile pictures, humor in quotes, number of times online friends "liked" status updates, and number of friends who commented on status updates (Pennington & Hall, 2014). Conversely, sarcasm in language is also detected in Facebook, which can be studied through a supervised machine learning-based approach that focuses on the contents of posts and users' interaction on those posts on Facebook (Das & Clark, 2018). Aside from humor, Facebook posts can also be a venue in expressing mourning and grief. Individuals post memories and condolences, as well as interact with friends and family members in the deceased user's network (Willis & Ferrucci, 2017).

## Theories on social media communication

There are communication theories that present perspectives on how Facebook users' online personalities are being formed. These include the following: (1) Dramaturgical Approach to Interactionist Perspective (Goffman, 1959); (2) Sapir–Whorf Theory (Sapir & Whorf, 1958); and (3) Hyperpersonal communication (Walther, 1996).

The *Dramaturgical Approach to Interactionist Perspective* (Goffman, 1959) states that the actions of people are dependent on time, place, and audience. A human being presents themselves to another human based on cultural values, norms, and expectations. This theory compares everyday life to the setting of the theater and stage. It further assumes that "just as actors project images, all of us seek to present particular features of our personalities while we hide other qualities."

In creating one's profile on social media, people post messages, both verbal and nonverbal, which they think would be positively perceived by other users. Such contents become their online identity with the belief that these suggest how they really are in person.

The next theory considers language as culturally determined and results to different interpretations of reality based on a certain phenomenon. Specifically, the Sapir—Whorf Theory (1958) assumes that "we see and hear and otherwise experience very largely as we do because the language habits of our community predispose certain choices of interpretation." It further explains that, "the "real world" is to a large extent unconsciously built upon the language habits of the group."

This theory clearly explains the emerging social media terminologies based on how they are being used in context. Words, phrases, and even expressions which are contained in the posts of other users become part of the reality of another user and later represent the similar thoughts for other users. This can be attributed to the possibility of accepting the new language as the best way of representing a shared idea.

Hyperpersonal communication (Walther, 1996), the third theory considered in this study, assumes that "individuals are better able to express themselves in mediated environments than they are in face-to-face conversation." This framework includes four interdependent factors: the *sender*, the *receiver*, the *channel*, and *feedback*. The sender is believed to possess greater control of self-presentation to others and therefore is able to create an even more idealized self-image. On the other hand, the receiver can over attribute qualities of the people at the other end of a message. In terms of channel, the asynchronous communication which exists in social media "allows individuals to overcome the limitations of copresence and to construct messages in a more deliberative manner." Feedback in CMC can result to an *intensification loop* "where the confirming messages of each partner reinforce the behavior of the other."

This model describes the phenomena of creating one's profile in the social media and the perception created by the viewers of others' profile as well. Social media users can freely post verbal and nonverbal messages according to how they wanted to create their identity online. However, this intended self-image may not be the same perception that other users can have on another user and the acceptance of one's projected image also depends on the existing personal relationship outside the online community.

## Methods and procedure

### Research design

To gather empirical data for this study, the qualitative research design was used. With an interpretative approach in looking through the phenomenon of posting status updates on one's Facebook wall, content analysis of posts enabled a thorough description of the language features evident in this social networking site. Adapting this framework, the qualitative research design was primarily used with the aim of deriving meaning from the verbal and nonverbal posts and later come up with integrative insights on the results which can add knowledge to language awareness education. It is a descriptive type of research, which according to Rubin et al. (1996) "seeks to identify or describe events or conditions." Specifically, *corpus linguistics* is used in investigating the language use of the students in CMC.

### Procedure

With the nature of the qualitative design of this study, the *homogenous purposeful* sampling technique was employed. This procedure aims to target a certain group of respondents which have a similar background. To investigate online behavior of students which belong to a group with similar academic experiences in colleges, Facebook posts of 83 Filipino university students were chosen as the source of data for this study. Their status updates in their Facebook account pages for 6 months served as the unit of analysis.

## Results and discussion

### Hashtag it

When respondents want their post to be viewed easily by other social network users, they label them with a "#" or hashtag. By doing so, other people who would enter the same code they use can access the post they have created. Various manners of labeling posts can be observed in the corpus of their status posts. In the study of Rauschnabel et al. (2019), there are 10 identified motivations in using hashtags in social media, which include amusing, organizing, designing, conforming, trendgaging, bonding, inspiring, reaching, summarizing, and endorsing. However, it is also worth noting that there are those who do not use hashtags since they become aware that hashtags are vulnerable to interventions by platforms and third parties (Gerrard, 2018).

Since hashtags can only be registered by continuous characters, it has been a practice that compound words are separated not by character spacing, but by the capitalization of the first letter of the succeeding word/s. It is observed in the hashtags *#waybackWednesday*, *#BeBetterNotBitter*, and *#MyJourneywithHim*.

In the language of the social media users, the invention of terminologies which becomes common among them or what is referred to as *coined words* can also be observed. Coined words articulate one's emotions and opinions fittingly and directly relates with the social emotion of a person (Yang & Chung, 2019). Instead of traditionally expressing a thought in a series of words, social media users create hashtags to represent the same intention. For instance, when someone wants to mean having a date with a special someone on a Thursday, *#Thursdate* is rather used. A person who intends to express a well-spent vacation with the family labels it with *#fambam*, which stands for family bonding.

Though there are social media users who value the need for word separation to make their thoughts understandable, hashtags require users not to use spaces to make the line recognizable. Posts like *#goodmorning*, *#lagotkasakin*, and *#capturethemoment* are actually sentences squeezed in one hashtag post. Momentary feelings can also be expressed through hashtags. A respondent posted, "*Ang sarap ng mag mura mo sa agahan grabe sxa #beastmode.*" When a not-so-favorable event occurred, resulting in the person being irritated or pissed off, *#beastmode* is used. Meanwhile, a showcase of pictures showing fun experiences is also marked with hashtags. An uploaded picture with friends on vacation is labeled with *#WhenInDavao* and a picture displaying a gathering of people in a coffee shop is tagged with *#kapekapekape*.

The intention of the Facebook user to include one's post in a pool of related topics is evident in this course of action when updating statuses. As how Sapir and Whorf (1958) assumes that "*the 'real world' is to a large extent unconsciously built upon the language habits of the group,*" so does the creation of this virtual world of hashtags.

## Letters speak

Laszlo and Federmeier (2007) studied the contribution of familiarity to single-word reading and found that there exists a similarity of brain response in familiar-but–illegal and unfamiliar-but–legal classes of stimuli. The repetition of its use in the online community suggests how people learn the meanings of these acronyms and adapt the same acronym in referring to the same concept.

Certain situations are described through acronyms. There are posts containing *ATM*, which means *at the moment*. Pictures of ongoing events or activities are being accompanied by this to express *present progressiveness* of their participation in such. Similarly, together with pictures of their romantic partners holding their hands, the *HH* acronym is used. The *I love you* message is expressed as *ily*, while the greeting *See you* is shortened as *cu*. To show online that somebody is currently traveling to a destination, *OTW* is used, which represents the phrase *on the way*. When a Facebook user wants the attention of another user to be directed to the head to foot attire, including accessories, of the person in the picture, the acronym *OOTD* is used to mean *outfit of the day*.

Aside from letters, numbers are used in minimization of characters of a word. In the Philippines, there are respondents who show their support to the incumbent President through the creation of *DU30* posts to refer to His Excellency Rodrigo Roa Duterte. As these acronyms spread in social media, the symbolisms become meaningful and acceptable among its users. The intelligibility of these morphemes can also be possible in other social media, for these terminologies become a common word to refer to concerned individuals.

## The shorter, the better

The existence of spelling alterations of some words can be attributed to the concept of *assimilation* in phonology. Certain letters in words are omitted in the verbal postings in statuses to make the word sound natural as if they are actually uttered. As how Poplack et al. (1988) puts it, the initial uses of borrowing and assimilation are meant to specify culturally or technologically novel concept. Gow (2001) made an experiment on assimilation, which suggests that listeners utilize assimilatory modification, as they anticipate the context of the next set of words.

A post to meant *sorry na* is expressed as *sorna*. In this post, the *ry* in the word is omitted as how it is said. Aside from this, the deletion of *we* in the word *pwede* can also be attributed in the assimilation of the word into /pede/, thus the post *pde* exists. This vowel deletion can also be traced in the prefix *mag* in Filipino in the word *mgpost*. The practice of omitting letters is not limited to a single character, but also involves an entire syllable and even word. The term *coz* is used in place of because. The first syllable *be* has been removed, while the syllable cause was written as it is pronounced.

Similarly, *nxt yr* (next year), *bby* (baby), *ur* (your), *wat* (what), and *pii* (happy) involve omission of parts that can be adjudged to be not that necessary in the intelligibility of the words. Like in the practice of texting using mobile phones, the post *nxt yr* and *bby* can be understood even without the inclusion of the vowels with just articulating the consonant sounds and gliding from one letter to the next. Meanwhile, *ur* and *wat* involve inclusion of letters that can best represent the sound of the words when articulated, giving weight to the vowel sounds.

The aspect of oral utterances being a basis for spelling a word can also be inferred from Facebook status posts. The conventional term *mommy*, which pertains to *mother*, is written differently in one of the posts— *"mame."* This can be attributed to the natural manner of speaking of the social media user when the term is uttered. It is also true in other Filipino terms *kain* as *kaen* and *kunwari* as *kunyare.*

The same principle can be associated with other terms spelled differently in the social media. There exists omission and substitution of consonant sounds to apply liaison in spelling, as it is sounded off in speaking. McCarthy and Smith (2003) refer to the articulatory gestures that are proper to one segment to intrude to another segment since it not possible to create perfect coordination of different articulators as *coarticulation*. The posts *"ansharap"* and *"ansarap"* both refer to the Filipino phrasal expression *Ang sarap*, meaning tasty or delicious. This style of writing has been the result of the disappearance of the sound /ng/ in the phrase and replacing /s/ with /sh/. Similarly, another phrase beginning with the Filipino determiner *ang*, in this case, *ang bitter*, which aims to describe a person who is sourgraping, is altered in writing based on the naturalness of speaking. The word *ang* is replaced by the syllable *am*, with which /m/ has the same positioning with /b/ being bilabial sounds.

However, it is a different case when the word *happy* is represented with just the sound of the last syllable of the word /py/ with the spelling *pii*. In this treatment of the word, the intelligibility depends on the language culture being shared by the Facebook users in a particular context.

The same is true when the Filipino affirmation expression *sige* is being downsized to *geh*. Notice that the first syllable has been omitted, but an additional letter is connected, which clearly represents the breath of air which a person produces when sounding out the syllable.

A suggested abbreviation for a concept is also clearly seen in the post of a respondent—*"Call me besty if you need a bestfriend."* Here, the addition of −y to the first root word of this compound word to make an acceptable shortened version of the term is suggested. The same is true when a respondent wanted her online friends to focus on the physical features of the person in the uploaded picture. Instead of using the Filipino term *itsura* to refer to *physical aspect*, a Facebook user preferred to express the concept with the word *"chura."* Kreidler (1979) refers to this kind of word shortening as *clipping*—subtraction of material which is not obviously morphemic. Though clipping is done in these words, there are no grammatical and semantic changes.

## Stress styling

Cutting short a word based on its articulation to simplify expression is not the only feature of the writing style of respondents in posting statuses. Rather, there are those who even lengthen the spelling of the words as a style of making themselves heard in the online community. Instead of the usage of the word *baby*, a respondent wrote, *"bheybii"* to refer to the concept. The Filipino term *dito* to refer to *here* is even twice written as *ditto*, while the 1980s expression *yo* is expressed as *"youw."* Berkovits (1994) explains that existing evidence for progressive utterance and final lengthening is based on the duration of segments in monosyllables or final stressed syllables.

White et al. (2020) studied final vowel strengthening and suggested that this is considered as a cue to an upcoming boundary that is universal in English but not in Italian and Hungarian. To provide readers with the intensity of feelings attached to the text of the post, the style of repetitively typing select vowel or consonant sounds to emphasize elongation of pronunciation is being utilized by Facebook users. A picture of weekend spent well with family members bear a text, *Family sundaaaaay!* Moreover, the heightened feeling brought about by a favorable event are expressed through the posts, *Omggggg (emoticon okay)* and *Strollingggggg! Wooooooooh!*

Aside from the application of repetition of letters in positive feelings, this is also used to express sadness toward a situation. Notice that the last vowel sound /u/ in, *"Puyatan nanaman ituuuu (emoticon sad)"*is also repeated to emphasize the stress and emotion attached to the statement.

Even the four-letter word *cute* which functions as an adjective to show appreciation of a person or a thing is spelled as *"cuuuuute"* in one of the posts. Brody and Diakopoulos (2011) worked on the idea that the common phenomenon of lengthening words though repeating letters is a substitute for increased duration or change of pitch, which is an indicator of important words that are emphasized. Not only that the vowel sounds were repeated four times to give stress to the word, but a social media user also even altered the spelling a more expanded manner and connected another word to add intensity to the level of cuteness of a person being loved with the post, *"cutie patootie."* Such forming of compound substitutes using rhyming words is called *reduplication* that is associated with child talk—*hypocoristic language* (Somanova, 2017).

The concept of mother, which is usually expressed in the terms *mama, mommy,* and *nanay* or *nay* in Filipino, is extended in the term used in the post, *mudrabels.* Though the term refers to a singular concept, notice that the preferred term ends with *s.* A respondent has also written the Filipino word *kumare* as *kumars,* replacing the vowel *e* with *s.* The *good evening* greeting is shortly expressed as *eve,* while *good night* is cut short as *nyt.* An assumption is clearly made that when the used words appear, the precedent word is always *good.* Notice that the term used is just the first syllable of the word evening since it may have been thought to bear the same meaning as *evening.* Clark and Araki (2011) refer to this phenomenon as *text normalization,* which describes how the use of social media gave birth to casual written English that does not conform to the traditional rules of spelling, grammar, and punctuation.

## Jargonizing community

Instances exist when different concepts represented by different words are being merged in a single expression, thus the birth of new terminologies used in social networking. Compounding is one process of word formation in social media where two or more words are joined to form an independent lexical term (Somanova, 2017). Possibly because of the usual usage of the word *mate* as someone we are with in a particular situation or place like schoolmate, classmate, or roommate, a respondent posted a picture with her classmates and labeled it with: *Hello Thesismate!* Creating impressions associated with beauty is a common thought in their posts. When a respondent posted her picture, she then labeled it as *FreshrunnerUp*. Since labeling a post is an option, putting such is a sign that she wants other users to associate her physical appearance with freshness and traits of a beauty contest title holder.

The relatively new term *mema* also holds place in the posts of users. This word which usually comes after insightful and inspirational posts which may be an original or adapted from other sources is the shortened version of the Filipino expression *may masabi lang*, which is conventionally spoken as /*memasabilang*/. As explained by Bauer (1983), the process where a word is shortened while still retaining the same meaning is called *clipping*. The meaning is retained for the social media users since the word remains intelligible.

Fillers in statements which previously do not have meaning in the Filipino vocabulary are gradually created to express a specific context while the post is made. In the status, *"Graduate tayo (emoticon kissed) HAHA (emoticon tears of joy, hat of graduation, camera) pampam ka e XD,"* the social media user mentioned the term *pampam* to describe herself being *papansin*—somebody who seeks attention from other people. As suggested in the content of the text, this term could have been used to describe a situation in which a person has expected and acted in contrary to what has actually happened with a dash of humor. This word formation is a form of clipping, wherein the initial part is retained and called *backclipping*. The usual Filipino expression *joke lang* being uttered when someone wants to retract a statement that is meant to give humor has already been replaced the word *choss!* which is the shortened version of the word *etchos* having the same meaning. In this second case of clipping, *foreclipping*, the last part is retained.

Putting together words which have a similar last syllable is also practiced. A respondent once posted, *"Sundate stroll,"* together with her picture in a mall. When analyzed, this term is the combination of the words *Sunday* and *date*. It is an innovation on how a situation can be called evolved through the Facebook user's creativity in combining words and creating a new concept. This is an example of *compounding*, that is, putting together two or more common words together to form a new word (Celce-Murcia & Larsen-Freeman, 2008).

When caught in an unexpected situation, the expression *"Diyos ko"* has been passed on from one generation to the next. The call to God, which is discussed in the section *Profession of Faith*, can also be said to be part of the usual expressions of Facebook users. Having assimilation of sounds as the basis of its spelling, a respondent has written it as *juskoo*. There is an intentional change in some letters in a word, which forms a new word that is misspelled on purpose and referred to as *creative spelling* (Somanova, 2017).

To express blissful feelings with other people, the terms used are *baliwan overload* and *happiness kulitan overload*. In these two expressions, *overload* has been a common term to emphasize the superlative level of the concept of happiness that is experienced at the point of making the post. The attachment of feelings or emotions attached to a word in the writing of this post can be characterized as *connotation* (Celce-Murcia & Larsen-Freeman, 2008). If happiness has its space in the posts of users, so are the unwanted ones. Being vocal in the foul thoughts in the form of writing can be observed the inclusion of the terms *taragis* and *wtf!* in their posts, usually in the beginning of statements.

Meanwhile, the eventual proliferation of android mobile phones that comes with the front camera feature led to the birth of another term, which is *selfie*. This term refers to the act taking a picture of oneself using the front camera of the mobile phone. Together with this concept, other nouns were also connected after the term, making the word *selfie* function as an adjective. From the original word self, there is a suffixation of -ie to form a new word with a new meaning (Park, 1988).

The post, *selfie time*, has emerged referring to the moment in a particular context, in which a person takes the opportunity to take a picture of self. Other terms which pertain to a person accompanying another person fond of taking a selfie were formed, that is, *selfie buddie* and *selfie buddy*. To form these new concepts incorporating the word selfie, social media users used *compounding*. The words *time* and *buddy* can be considered as *collocates*—words that often occur with another word (Yule, 2010).

## Space jam

As how Facebook users utilize hashtags, all characters, regardless of the number of words, must be written as one word only. Since content of hashtags include the common greetings, respondents must have adapted the practice of expressing them in just one word, thus the observed posts: *Thankyou, Happymorning, GoodMorning, Good Noon, GoodEvening, GoodEve, Goodnight,* and *ILOVEYOU*. This illustrates how the emergence of the culture of hashtags results in a bandwagon of writing phrases without leaving spaces per word with the intention to have one's post searchable online.

## Code name construction

The practice of representing people other than their names can also be observed in Facebook. As a term of endearment of a boyfriend, a user posted *Mr. Kilay*. In another post, *"To my dearest sugar cousin! Congratulations! Finally! Ikaw lang makakaranas satin ng Senior High kaya dapat maging masaya ka. . .,"* the respondent added *sugar* to describe the personality of her cousin, therefore generating a new concept of a *sugar cousin*.

Getting credit to the emergence of the word *selfie*, a label has been given to a person who does the act of *selfie-Ing*, that is, *SELFIECHIC*, as written by a respondent. In another post where a group picture was posted, a respondent labeled themselves with a post, *TraveLords XD (last last Saturday)*. They refer to themselves as *Lords*, which can suggest a concept of powerful beings, as they pose to a traveled destination. These examples of invention of new terms is called *coinage* (Yule, 2010).

*At ako na nga ang hugot queen:* When taken literally, the term *hugot* means *to pull out* in English. It is supposed to be an action verb, but in this case, *hugot* modifies the noun *queen* and forms a new concept. As used in the present times, *hugot queen* is a title given to oneself when a person is fond of reflecting about life and verbalizing the ideas in an impactful manner. This *coinage* suggests the innovativeness of Facebook users to present things in the best way they think they can. A feeling of nonrepresentativeness of a concept among the available standard words they have learned in school or in the community can be viewed from this.

Another group picture of friends is posted online, and a social media user shows appreciation of being around with her friends: *Thanks sa bonding blacksheeps*. In this caption, notice that the friends are labeled as *black sheeps*, a term that is known to refer to a sibling that emanate negative attitudes in a certain family. As contrary to this belief, such a term is used as a term of endearment for a clique. This is where the linguistic context plays a role in the meaning-making of a word based on how it is used.

## Of parallels and rhymes

In terms of the structural style of writing, the element of parallelism is considered in doing status posts. An example is the line, *"Sila may, Ako may (emoticon smile),"* which is written with the uploaded picture of the respondent with a friend. Aside from the clausal level, a Facebook user also applies *parallelism* in the sentence level in the form of one-word staccato statements. The post, *"Strollin. Chillin. Lovin.,"* suggests a relaxing environment one experiences at a given moment, which is believed to be best explained in those three words.

Aside from the parallelism in the clauses, notice the usage of rhyming words *BESTIE* and *BETSY*. Such a style is also true in another post where a noun with a common last syllable has been connected to the expression *well well well I* in the post, *"Well well well caramel!."* A social media user's phonological knowledge of the pattern of sounds in English words allows for the treatment of these forms as acceptable (Yule, 2010). The familiarity of the social media users on the principles of creative writing sets foot on these observations.

## Figure me out

Facebook users also go beyond the conventional manner of self-expression with their usage of figures of speech inserted to their statements. As written by one respondent: *"Anong meron ngayon? Andaming naka-glue ang mga kamay, sakit sa mata (What is with today? There are lots of glued hands, eyesore),"* the feelings of disappointment, irritability, and even envy are given emphasis with the use of the term *naka-glue*, instead of *magkahawak*. It can also be a way of avoiding using the concept, which the respondent despises. In social media posts where there are no visual markers for sarcasm, there is a need for strong linguistic markers to be perceived as sarcastic where hyperbole is usually considered a strong marker (Kunneman et al., 2015).

## Hyperbole

Describing a situation using exaggeration is one style of asserting oneself in Facebook. In the post, *"Nakakamiss yung panahong plastic ballon lang masaya kana (emoticon ballon),"* the idea of plastic balloon represents the usual object of joy of children which the respondent is trying to reminisce. In this case, the writer obviously misses certain things about her childhood.

There are times when hyperbole is used to add humor to a statement while making oneself the subject of entertainment. The *"My forehead is brighter that his future"* post clearly associates the forehead and future in relation to the common descriptor of the latter—*bright*. With this attempt for an analogy, the Facebook user suggests having a more than the usual size of forehead, which she uses as an object of humor online.

Issues on love life can also be traced in the status posts. In the writing, *"Hahaha mas malamig kappa kay lando! Hahaha Orayt (Emoticon Evil),"* there has been an association between the cold wind bought by one of the strongest typhoon in 2016 and someone's falling out of love. Meanwhile, another usage of hyperbole is seen in the exaggeration of the nervousness felt by a user in anticipation of a stressful situation in school through the usage of a term referring to a serious medical condition. This post reads: *"Yayy. Nervous breakdown."*

Sarcasm using hyperbole backed by a hashtag that connotes an activity that is not desirable can also be traced from this post: *I'm so excited for tomorrow! Why? Because tomorrow, I will see zombies walking in the hallways #thesis #defense.* Looking at the context of the writing, the figurative language is also used to exaggerate an expected not-so-favorable scenario in school. Comparing students to walking zombies also implies a lack of sleep due to the preparations done for the pertained event.

## Personification

Aside from the usage of hyperbole in status posts, associating human actions with things or *personification* is evident in some posts. Instead of directly saying that someone is sleepy, a descriptive statement can be read in one post: *"My pillows have been calling me for the night time."* Meanwhile in another status, a respondent has written a direct address to her hair: *"Hello short wavy hair! (emoticon smile) You made me look like a mature one. Haha (emoticon smile)."* A greeting has been made to one's own hair and even evaluated what it has done to oneself. Nizhehorodtseva-Kyrychenko (2015) explains that personification reflects an individual's picture of one's consciousness and experiences in the world in a reflective way.

Giving life to one's body part has also been evident in Facebook through the usage of *personification*. In the post, *"Hello short wavy hair! (emoticon smile) You made me look like a mature one. Haha (emoticon smile),"* the user appears to be talking to her hair and claiming an action intentionally or unintentionally done toward her, though it is a result of an intervention done by another person. Sung and Kim (2021) related personification in the social network in the context of an organization and suggested that interpersonal approaches of communication could be necessary in the perceived personality traits and relationship quality of organization with the publics.

## Metaphor

As observed in one post: *"You're the smile to my face and the beat of my heart,"* the Facebook user associates a certain person as the reason for happiness in the first idea *"smile to my face,"* whereas in the second idea, *"beat of my heart,"* the same person is referred to as someone who makes her alive and experience the feeling of loving. Piata (2016) established that the relationship of metaphor and humor in political ads are related concerning their function in discourse as evaluative devices that convey political criticism in a comprehensible and amusing way.

## Eponym

Though Filipinized in spelling, the term *hokuspokus* is attributed also to negativity, which in the situation of tallying numbers entails manipulation of data results. Considering the entire statement, *"Walang halong hokuspokus,"* the reverse is intended. It is an allusion to the 1993 Disney film Hocus Pocus, which narrates the story of villainous doings of three witches. This word is formed through adapting a real name, in this case, a movie, and is called an *eponym* (Somanova, 2017). Popescu and Şorcaru (2008) studied the presence of European eponyms in English and Romanian vocabularies and considered this as a special case of linguistic interculturality.

## Symbolism

The concept of an overconfident person is expressed as *makapal ang mukha* (*thick face*) in Filipino. However, in this case, the *kumapal ang mukha* refers not to somebody who has transformed to an extrovert and showy person, but to a state wherein a person had an allergy attack which manifests through skin rashes. This can be read in the post: *"Ansarap pa ng kaen ko na hipon aaay Hahahah ayaaaan literal na kumapal yun mukha."* Instead of literally saying that an allergy attack is felt, the Facebook user described the feeling of having the attack.

## Irony

Using words with opposite meaning in a single statement to add value to one's post is revealed in the line: *"Bakit ba kasi nagmahal ka ng taong dapat minura mo nalang?.*" *Mahal* and *mura* are antonyms in the Filipino context where the former means *expensive* while the latter means *cheap*. As a head word, these two are adjectives. However, when the prefix *nag-* was added to *mahal* and the infix *−in-* to *mura*, the words function as verbs in the sentence. *Nagmahal*, roughly translated, means fell in love, while *minura* pertains to the past aspect of telling foul words to another person. To express sarcasm, this social media post is made of irony, that is, an expression used in an opposite view (Perez, 2002).

## Oxymoron

Two contradicting concepts are also being put together to come up with a post that accompanies one's uploaded picture of oneself. The post, *Delightfully chaotic*, which can be qualified as an *oxymoron*, contains two words with different associations; *delightfully* is a positive adverb while *chaotic* is an adjective which means not organized. Flayih (2009) considers oxymoron as a lexical device which intentionally combines two ideas usually thought of as opposite or incompatible to provide emphasis.

## Presence of code-switching in status posts

Sankoff and Poplack (1981) explain that code-switching is not a result of incompetence in either of the two languages but rather an indication of knowledge of the rules of both. Shifting of language use from Filipino to English and vice versa in the status posts of respondents is practiced in the status posts of Facebook users. In the question, *Wala bang mag-iinvite dyan?(Is there anybody there who will invite me?)*, the respondent prefers the English term *invite* over the Filipino translation *imbita* as the root word in expressing futurity.

Terms used in technological innovations also have an impact on how people construct their thoughts online. The post with direct address, *Dear meek, Sana iaccept mo na yung friendrequest ko*, also shows how the term *accept* is more conventional for the respondent than using the Filipino term *tanggapin*. The usage of the term *friendrequest* is expected since it has no equivalency in Filipino in the context of usage in technology.

Aside from the code-switching in the sentence level, a series of it is observable in this status post:

*Pag may nagtext po sa inyo at ginagamit ang name ko, wag po kayo*

*maniniwala, or chat or call. Gumagamit po sya ng bastos na words. I don't know*

*why he/she used my name. Basta wag po kayo maniniwala! This is my only*

*account,I have 2 CP numbers, TM and TNT.*

Note that the words *nagtext, chat,* and *call* are naturally used since these are technology terms which can best describe their thoughts. However, the act of shifting to *words* instead of using term *salita* in the second statement suggests nonspontaneity of speech with its usage in an informal setup. Looking through the series of statements, the respondent also considers shifting of languages between statements as something normal in asserting oneself.

With the statement *Napakamapanlait na boyfriend,* the representation of someone who is romantically attached to another is no longer expressed in its traditional Filipino term, thus fossilizing the terms *nobyo* and *kasintahan.* Similarly, the *pamangkin* term is more naturally referred to as niece in the post, *Namimiss ko na niece ko.* Regardless of one's acceptance of the premise on fossilization of some Filipino terms, evidence of it can clearly be traced in how they have shifted to some English terms, which can have meaning equivalency to the source language.

Instead of the Filipino way of expressing romantic feelings to another person, *Mahal kita,* Facebook users felt more comfortable in using the English term as a basis of their posts. The *labyu* and *lab u* posts are derivatives of the term *I love you.* In the first derivative, the two words love and you became connected and the vowel *o* was replaced by *a,* the consonant *v* with *b,* and the vowel e was omitted in *love,* same with the vowel *o* in the word *you.* Meanwhile, the second derivative maintains love and you as two words but *you* is only expressed as *u* and love is also written as *lab.* In both cases, the pronoun *I* are omitted. Such instance of code-switching used compounding in the new word formation.

Even in describing a specific situation, words with a borrowed origin are being used. This is evident when a respondent made a verbal post together with a picture of a group of students doing schoolwork, *Praktis praktisan sila oh!.* The word *ensayo,* which is the closest translation of

English term practice in the context of the word's usage in this post, may also be considered a fossilized term for the generation of social media users. Also, as a way of giving new meaning of *praktis* aside from being a mere verb translated in Filipino, the repetition of the word itself connected with the suffix *−an* provides a new definition to the word as being an act of pretending.

The expression *Oh My God!*, used in both positive and negative situations, has also been contextualized. When a respondent posted: "*Ohmaygaad. We're done! FINALLY!*," the expression is used to show a feeling of relief and accomplishment while stressing the word God through *gaaad* with the repetitions of the vowel *a*.

Aside from the meaning of the words *call* and *text* brought about by the emergence of mobile telecommunication, there are other terms used in information technology, which respondents find to have no equivalency in the native language. Thus, in the statement "*I-filter mo pa hija..*," unlike in the discussion above, wherein words borrowed actually have equivalent terms in the target language (in this case, Filipino), the verb *filter*, which means an action to be taken in the operation of a technology or application, does not have.

Since there is no specific term in Filipino that can best represent the concept of being a *fan girl*, a respondent borrowed the actual term in the construction of a post—"*sa pagfafangirling nalang ako kikiligin (emoticon smile with heart).*" The respondent started her post in Filipino then shifted to borrowing the term while connecting prefixes and suffixes, making the term function as a verb, instead of being an adjective.

Based on how respondents normally assert themselves in this platform, the usage of what we refer to as *Taglish* presents to be a common practice to give the best representation to the meanings intended. Nonequivalence of English terms to Filipino words, as well as naturalness of discourse, explains this phenomenon of code–switching in status posts.

## Conclusion

The content of social media posts, specifically of Facebook users, is an important part of the linguistic culture of the online community. It reflects how users intend to present themselves to a countless number of people in the world through the verbalizing of their thoughts and feelings through their status posts. As part of this fast-changing community linked by internet connectivity, we are given an opportunity to have a deeper understanding of language and communication strategies of people in making sense of their worlds.

# References

Acquisti, A., & Gross, R. (2006). *Imagined communities: Awareness, information sharing, and privacy on the Facebook* (pp. 36—58). *Berlin, Heidelberg: Springer.* Available from http://doi.org/10.1007/11957454_3.

Banuag, L. L. (2020). Episodes of forms and reasons of code-switching in Facebook posts. *Asia Pacific Higher Education Research Journal, 7*(1).

Bauer, L. (1983). *English word formation.* Cambridge: Cambridge University Press.

Berkovits, R. (1994). Durational effects in final lengthening, gapping, and contrastive stress. *Language and Speech, 37*(3), 237—250. Available from https://doi.org/10.1177/002383099403700302.

Boyd, D. M., & Ellison, N. B. (2007). Social network sites: Definition, history, and scholarship. *Journal of Computer-Mediated Communication, 13*(1), article 11.

Brody, S., & Diakopoulos, N. (2011). Cooooooooooooooolllllllllllll!!!!!!!!!!!!! Using word lengthening to detect sentiment in microblogs. *Proceedings of the 2011 Conference on Empirical Methods in Natural Language Processing,* 562—570.

Celce-Murcia, M., & Larsen-Freeman, D. (2008). *The Grammar Book: An ESL/EFL Teacher's Course. 2nd ed.* Thomson Asian Edition, 35—39.

Cheong C., Hu, X., Chu, S., & Ng, N. (2017). A preliminary analysis on student postings on Facebook and blogs in an internship course in information management. iConference 2017 Proceedings, 517—524. Available from https://doi.org/10.9776/17225.

Clark, E., & Araki, K. (2011). Text normalization in social media: Progress, problems and applications for a pre-processing system of casual english. *Procedia - Social and Behavioral Sciences, 27,* 2—11. Available from https://doi.org/10.1016/j.sbspro.2011.10.577.

Dale, K. R., Raney, A. A., Ji, Q., Janicke-Bowles, S. H., Baldwin, J., Rowlett, J. T., & Oliver, M. B. (2019). Self-transcendent emotions and social media: Exploring the content and consumers of inspirational Facebook posts. *New Media & Society.* Available from https://doi.org/10.1177/1461444819865720, 146144481986572.

Das, D., & Clark, A.J. (2018). Sarcasm detection on Facebook. *Proceedings of the International Conference on Multimodal Interaction Adjunct - ICMI '18.* Available from https://doi.org/10.1145/3281151.3281154.

DeVito, J. A. (2002). *Essentials of human communication* (4th ed). Allyn and Bacon.

Dwyer, C., Hiltz, S. R., & Passerini, K. (2007). Trust and privacy concern within social networking sites: A comparison of Facebook and MySpace. *Conference Proceedings of 13th Americas Conference on Information Systems.*

Ellison, N. B., Steinfield, C., & Lampe, C. (2011). Connection strategies: Social capital implications of Facebook-enabled communication practices. *New Media & Society, 13* (6), 873—892. Available from https://doi.org/10.1177/1461444810385389.

Enli, G. S., & Thumim, N. (2012). Socializing and self-representation online: Exploring Facebook. *Observatorio Journal, 6*(1), 87—105.

Farina, M. (2015). Facebook first post telling. *Journal of Pragmatics, 90,* 1—11. Available from https://doi.org/10.1016/j.pragma.2015.10.005.

Finegan, E., & Niko, B. (1989). *Language: Its structure and use.* Harcourt Brace Jovanovich, Inc.

Flayih, R. M. (2009). A linguistic study of oxymoron. *Journal of Kerbala University, 7,* -3.

Gerrard, Y. (2018). Beyond the hashtag: Circumventing content moderation on social media. *New Media & Society*. Available from https://doi.org/10.1177/1461444818776611, 146144481877661.

Giuntini, F. T., Ruiz, L. P., Kirchner, L. D. F., Passarelli, D. A., Dos Reis, M. D. J. D., Campbell, A. T., & Ueyama, J. (2019). How do i feel? Identifying emotional expressions on Facebook reactions using clustering mechanism. *IEEE Access*, 7, 53909–53921. Available from https://doi.org/10.1109/access.2019.2913136.

Goffman, E. (1959). Dramaturgical approach to interactionist perspective.

Gow, D. W. (2001). Assimilation and anticipation in continuous spoken word recognition. *Journal of Memory and Language*, *45*(1), 133–159.

Grice, H. P. (1975). Logic and conversation. In P. Cole, & J. L. Morgan (Eds.), *Syntax and semantics* (3, pp. 41–58). Academic Press, Speech Acts.

Iram, A. (2019). Sentiment analysis of student's Facebook posts. *Intelligent Technologies and Applications*, 86–97. Available from https://doi.org/10.1007/978-981-13-6052-7_8.

Joinson, A. N. (2008). Looking at, looking up or keeping up with people?: Motives and use of Facebook. *Proceedings of the 2008 Conference on Human Factors in Computing Systems, CHI 2008*. Available from https://doi.org/10.1145/1357054.1357213.

Khalaf, Y.M. R.A. (2019). A Pragmatic Analysis of the Language of Facebook Posts and Status Updates. ‫ﻓﻲ اﻵداب‬ ‫,اﻟﺒﺤﺚ اﻟﻌﻠﻤﻲ‬ 19(‫اﻟﺜﺎﻣﻦ‬ ‫ﻋﺸﺮ اﻟﺠﺰء‬ ‫اﻟﺘﺎﺳﻊ‬ ‫,)اﻟﻌﺪد‬ 1–40. Available from https://doi.org/10.21608/jssa.2019.28726.

Kreidler, C. W. (1979). Creating new words by shortening. *Journal of English Linguistics*, *13*(1), 24–36. Available from https://doi.org/10.1177/007542427901300102.

Kunneman, F., Liebrecht, C., van Mulken, M., & van den Bosch, A. (2015). Signaling sarcasm: From hyperbole to hashtag. *Information Processing & Management*, *51*(4), 500–509. Available from https://doi.org/10.1016/j.ipm.2014.07.006.

Laszlo, S., & Federmeier, K. D. (2007). Better the DVL you know. *Psychological Science*, *18*(2), 122–126. Available from https://doi.org/10.1111/j.1467-9280.2007.01859.x.

Lenhart, A., Purcell, K., Smith, A., & Zickuhr, K. (2010). Social media & mobile internet use among teens and young adults. millennials. Pew internet & American life project.

McCarthy, J. J., & Smith, N. (2003). *Phonological processes: Assimilation. Oxford International Encyclopedia of Linguistics*. Retrieved from https://scholarworks.umass.edu/linguist_faculty_pubs/20.

McLeod, B. A. (2020). "Hello group, I need advice": A textual analysis of black fathers' help-seeking posts on Facebook. *Family Relations*, *69*(5), 944–955.

Nizhehorodtseva-Kyrychenko, L. (2015). *Personification of Mental Concepts*. Available from http://www.irbis-nbuv.gov.ua/cgi-bin/irbis_nbuv/cgiirbis_64.exe? C21COM = 2&I21DBN = UJRN&P21DBN = UJRN&IMAGE_FILE_DOWNLOAD = 1&Image_file_name = PDF/akpif_2015_3_22.pdf.

Pablo, M. C. (2018). Internet Inaccessibility Plagues "Social Media Capital of the World.". *The Asia Foundation*. Available from https://asiafoundation.org/.

Page, R., Barton, D., Unger, J. W., & Zappavigna, M. (2014). *Researching Language and social media: A student guide*. Available from https://doi.org/10.4324/9781315771786.

Park, C.B. (1988). A study on the rule of clipping with special reference to the phonological structure of english words. Available from https://s-space.snu.ac.kr/bitstream/10371/2135/3/englishstudiesv12168.pdf.

Pearson, J., Nelson, P., Titsworth, S., & Harter, L. (2008). *Human communication* (3rd ed.). McGraw-Hill Higher Education.

Peeters, W. (2019). The peer interaction process on Facebook: A social network analysis of learners' online conversations. *Education and Information Technologies*. Available from https://doi.org/10.1007/s10639-019-09914-2.

Pempek, T. A., Yermolayeva, Y. A., & Calvert, S. L. (2009). College students' social networking experiences on Facebook. *Journal of Applied Developmental Psychology, 30*(3), 227−238. Available from https://doi.org/10.1016/j.appdev.2008.12.010.

Peng, K.-H., Liou, L.-H., Chang, C.-S., & Lee, D.-S. (2015). Predicting personality traits of Chinese users based on Facebook wall posts. *2015 24th Wireless and Optical Communication Conference (WOCC) Proceedings.* Available from https://doi.org/10.1109/wocc.2015.7346106.

Pennington, N., & Hall, J. (2014). An analysis of humor orientation on Facebook: A lens model approach. *International Journal of Humor Research, 27*(1).

Perez, A. D. (2002). English: Its meanings. *Forms, and Functions,* 14.

Piata, A. (2016). When metaphor becomes a joke: Metaphor journeys from political ads to internet memes. *Journal of Pragmatics, 106,* 39−56.

Popescu, F., & Şorcaru, D. (2008). Eponyms: An instance of linguistic interculturality. *Culture, Subculture, and Counterculture. Romanian Society for English and American Studies,* 160. Available from https://doi.org/10.1006/jmla.2000.2764.

Poplack, S., Sankojf, D., & Miller, C. (1988). The social correlates and linguistic processes of lexical borrowing and assimilation. *Linguistics, 26,* 47−48.

Rauschnabel, P. A., Sheldon, P., & Herzfeldt, E. (2019). What motivates users to hashtag on social media? *Psychology & Marketing.* Available from https://doi.org/10.1002/mar.21191.

Rubin, R. B., Rubin, A. M., & Piele, L. J. (1996). *Communication research: Strategies and sources* (4th ed.). Wadsworth Publishing Company.

Sankoff, D., & Poplack, S. (1981). A formal grammar for code-switching1. *Paper in Linguistics, 14*(1), 3−45. Available from https://doi.org/10.1080/08351818109370523.

Sapir, E. (1929). The status of linguistics as a science. *Language, 5*(4), 207. Available from https://doi.org/10.2307/409588.

Sapir, E., & Whorf, B. (1958). *Sapir-Whorf hypothesis.*

Schlosser, A. (2019). Self-disclosure versus self-presentation on social media. *Current Opinion in Psychology.* Available from https://doi.org/10.1016/j.copsyc.2019.06.025.

Searle, J. R. (1969). *Speech acts: An essay in the philosophy of language.* Cambridge: Cambridge University Press.

Sharma, B. K. (2012). Beyond social networking: Performing global Englishes in Facebook by college youth in Nepal1. *Journal of Sociolinguistics, 16*(4), 483−509. Available from https://doi.org/10.1111/j.1467-9841.2012.00544.x.

Somanova, L. (2017). Words recently coined and blended: Analysis of new english lexical terms. *Faculty Of Education at Masaryk University in Brno.* Available from https://is.muni.cz/th/u9wo7/ANNOTATION.pdf.

Sung, K. H., & Kim, S. (2021). Do organizational personification and personality matter? The effect of interaction and conversational tone on relationship quality in social media. *International Journal of Business Communication, 58*(4), 582−606.

Terrana, D., Augello, A., & Pilato, G. (2014). Facebook users relationships analysis based on sentiment classification. *2014 IEEE International Conference on Semantic Computing.* Available from https://doi.org/10.1109/icsc.2014.59.

Trenholm, S., & Jensen, A. (2011). *Interpersonal communication* (7th ed.). Oxford University Press.

Vogel, E. A., & Rose, J. P. (2016). Self-reflection and interpersonal connection: Making the most of self-presentation on social media. *Translational Issues in Psychological Science, 2*(3), 294−302.

Walther, J.B. (1996). *Hyperpersonal communication.* Retrieved from Andrew F. Wood and Mathew J. Smith. Online Communication: Linking Technology, Identity, and Culture.

Walther, J. B., Van Der Heide, B., Kim, S. Y., Westerman, D., & Tong, S. T. (2008). The role of friends' appearance and behavior on evaluations of individuals on Facebook: Are we known by the company we keep? *Human Communication Research*, *34*(1), 28−49. Available from https://doi.org/10.1111/j.1468-2958.2007.00312.x.

White, L., Benavides-Varela, S., & Mády, K. (2020). Are initial-consonant lengthening and final-vowel lengthening both universal word segmentation cues? *Journal of Phonetics*, *81*, 100982. Available from https://doi.org/10.1016/j.wocn.2020.100982.

Willis, E., & Ferrucci, P. (2017). Mourning and Grief on Facebook: An examination of motivations for interacting with the deceased. *OMEGA - Journal of Death and Dying*, *76*(2), 122−140. Available from https://doi.org/10.1177/0030222816688284.

Yang, J. S., & Chung, K. S. (2019). Newly-coined words and emoticon polarity for social emotional opinion decision. *2019 IEEE 2nd International Conference on Information and Computer Technologies (ICICT)*. Available from https://doi.org/10.1109/infoct.2019.8711413.

Yule, G. (2010). *The study of language*. Cambridge: Cambridge University Press.

# Relationships and the self

> CHAPTER NINE

# Developing, nurturing, and expanding personal and professional relationships through social media

## Deborah A. Olson[1], Debora Jeske[2] and Kenneth S. Shultz[2]

[1]California State University, San Bernardino, CA, United States
[2]Department of Psychology, University College Cork, California State University, San Bernardino, CA, United States

## Contents

Social media and social networks (e.g., LinkedIn and Facebook) have expanded their impact and become essential pathways to establish, maintain, and build social connections, expand career opportunities, as well as sustain personal and professional relationships (Chen & Wei, 2020; Tijunaitis et al., 2019). The 2020 and 2021 COVID-19 pandemic accelerated the use of social media platforms and technology, both within and outside the work domain. These platforms have become a foundation for remote work, school, social connections, and healthcare (i.e., tele-health visits). Specifically, we are increasingly using technology to engage in education (remote learning), conduct business (across industries and locations), and reach out to nurture personal connections and foster professional relationships. In 2020 and 2021, this was primarily to remain physically distant to slow the spread of the COVID-19 virus and manage the stress caused by the pandemic for leaders and workers in many organizations working, learning, and living in remote contexts (Rudolph et al., 2020). For example, as the pandemic unfolded in early 2020, CEOs expanded their use of social media to communicate with a wide variety of constituents, from employees to shareholders. Liu (2020) found that in 2015, 39% of CEOs in Fortune 500 companies were on some social media platform, yet by August 2020, 62% of CEOs were actively engaged in one or more social media platform (e.g., LinkedIn, YouTube, Twitter, Facebook, and Instagram).

In this chapter, we use the term *social media* as an umbrella term to cover the full range of platforms that are available to create connections with others in one's offline and online relationships. These include social networking sites (e.g., LinkedIn, Facebook, Snapchat, and Instagram); blogging—micro and macro—(e.g., Twitter and Tumblr); instant messaging (e.g., WhatsApp and Facebook Messenger); along with virtual worlds (Second Life) and massively multiplayer online games (e.g., Minecraft and World of Warcraft). With the rapid expansion and popularity of social media tools and applications (e.g., Facebook having over 2.7 billion monthly active users and LinkedIn having over 740 million members in 200 countries with 260 million monthly active users [Osman, 2021]), relationships traditionally nurtured offline can be easily done online.

Our focus in this chapter is on the positive uses of social media and technology to build and expand constructive social relationships. While there are a plethora of examples and applications focused on the negative uses of social media (e.g., trolling, fake news, and hate posts), the primary aim of this chapter is to expand consideration of positive social media uses to build and nurture meaningful social connections both in one's personal and professional life. Each section also includes a critical discussion of conclusions based on prepandemic insights and what we are learning about social media benefits and disadvantages during the COVID-19 pandemic. At the end of the chapter, we offer practical actions that can be taken by individuals, teams, and organizational leaders to facilitate the development of positive social connections and amplify their positive resonance through intentional interactions and positive uses of social media tools and technology (Fredrickson, 2018).

# Personal relationships and social media

The following section focuses on several points. In the first segment, we introduce the concepts of social connectedness, social capital, and the evidence that social media engagement of individuals and communities can help expand and build our personal networks, as well as those within and across communities. The second segment also considers social capital as well as social connections but focuses here on the personal connections and relatedness among people in work settings.

## Connections among individuals and their social communities

Social connections are the foundation of organizations, communities, families, and individual effectiveness. Over time, and accelerated during the COVID-19 pandemic, social media use has become more deeply embedded into the fabric of our relationships as a primary mechanism for building and expanding social connections and sustaining social embeddedness in organizations, teams, and personal/community relationships (Lombardo et al., 2021). Social connectedness is characterized as a short-term experience of relatedness and belonging built on the individual's belief that they are part of a group and that investing energy in maintaining that group identity is important for well-being and overall success in work, school, and one's community (Mauss et al., 2011). Social capital refers to the advantages and support that emerge through building and maintaining relationships, for example, by sharing information that is helpful to others and providing social support to those in one's network. It is now well known that one's social media presence and engagement with others online can lead to better social integration in communities (Wei & Gao, 2017). For example, Ryan et al. (2017) found that active engagement in social media sites had a positive impact on building social capital, creating friendships and embedded communities of people with shared interests, and reducing feelings of loneliness.

Watching and observing others who are interacting in positive ways can be profoundly moving and positively impact the mood and feelings of the observers and recipients of the positive actions (Algoe et al., 2008). Researchers have found that positive emotions impact individuals in completely different ways when compared to the impact of negative emotions (Prinzing et al., 2020). Specifically, negative emotions narrow our focus and ability to generate alternatives and options, while positive emotions expand our peripheral vision, allowing us to be more open to alternatives and unique approaches. In addition, positive emotions motivate us to take action to build resources and recognize good things that are happening in our relationships and communities.

Social media applications and platforms provide an easily accessible tool for intentionally expressing gratitude and engaging in acts of kindness to share positive experiences and information to help and support others (Buchanan et al., 2021; Olson et al., 2012; Roy & Ayalon, 2021). In turn, social support from others positively impacts our well-being, even when expressed via social media. Research on the impact of virtual social support has demonstrated that when individuals were encouraged to engage in more autonomous actions and be more optimistic when facing challenging situations, virtual support made a positive impact on the actions and decisions (Layous et al., 2012). The key is to be intentional and focused on outcomes that contribute to positive communication, providing support, and expanding relationships. Expressions of gratitude can be readily amplified through use of social media. For example, a recent study used Instagram where participants posted pictures with captions of gratitude (experimental group) or just general pictures (control group) for a 7-day period. Results showed that posting pictures with positive captions that expressed optimistic emotions had a significant impact on the participant's experience of gratitude at the end of the 7-day period (Koay et al., 2020). Whether mediated by social media or through the quasi-face-to-face environment (e.g., via Zoom, WebEx, and FaceTime) in response to the pandemic, social media platforms became a tool to expand positive relationships.

In addition, the positive impacts on well-being that are accrued through providing support to individuals who are acquaintances has the same impact as supporting those who are friends and colleagues (see also Buchanan et al., 2021). For example, Tsang and Martin (2019) found that helping others who we do not know well increases gratitude and prosocial behaviors, which in turn motivates others to help and provide support, thereby creating upward spirals of prosocial behaviors.

It is noteworthy here to reference certain conditions under which social media use will be beneficial and enables users to transmit messages of support. While the abovementioned findings suggest that individuals who use social media in positive and productive ways in their personal lives will experience better mental health and interpersonal outcomes, not all users are necessarily aware what kind of social media use will be beneficial. "Doom scrolling" became a particularly common theme during the COVID-19 pandemic, as many social media sites were flooded with negative and divisive news (Buchanan et al., 2021; Price et al., 2021; Ytre-Arne & Moe, 2021). This suggests that the use of social media use can certainly generate certain benefits, but under the assumption that the users are also aware of how their own choices and filter bubbles may be affecting what they see, as well as who they connect with online. This suggests that a more reflective, conscious use of social media may be key for this communication channel to maintain the positive benefits for personal and communication relationships—particularly in situations where personal and community relationships may be strained (e.g., during Covid-19 lockdowns).

## Connections and work communities

The importance of social capital and social connections are not just limited to our personal interactions within our family or friend network. As people, we also thrive or struggle if we lack social connections in our work settings. Our workplaces are communities where we as individuals also find support, confidantes, friends, or even marital partners. As a result, in addition to regular neighborhood or social communities, the social behaviors that are exhibited and endorsed in our workplaces can have a significant impact on our social and mental well-being. Workplaces are heavily investing in social media and networking in order to provide connective tissues for employees, similar to how many people use social media to connect to their network of friends, family, and their community as a whole. The following segment outlines the role of social behaviors and how these often connect to social media use.

Prepandemic research has demonstrated the importance of social behaviors for our sense of belonging in the workplace. Psychologists have researched the impact of positive organizational citizenship behaviors (Ng & Feldman, 2011), or prosocial work behaviors, and their sustained impact on organizational and individual well-being for several decades now. Deci and Ryan (2000) asserted that prosocial work behaviors directly impact the social needs of connectedness, autonomy, and competence in relationships. Chancellor et al. (2018) extended this by asserting that prosocial behaviors impact connectedness through deepening social ties; autonomy through augmenting self-direction; and competence through the ability to take initiative to achieve meaningful outcomes.

Research on prosocial behaviors in the workplace has also found that it positively impacts empathy and performance, as well as reducing feelings of negative stress and burnout (Grant & Berry, 2011; Grant & Sonnentag, 2010). Chancellor et al. (2018) extended this area of research by focusing on understanding the impact of everyday prosocial actions on relationships at work. Their results indicated that merely observing others demonstrating prosocial behaviors inspired the observers to in turn act in prosocial ways toward others. Thus, positive interactions at work can arise spontaneously by observing others interact in prosocial ways creating an upward spiral of positive interactions.

The impact of prosocial behavior has also been explored in terms of relationship building and maintenance. For example, Fredrickson (2018) found a positive prosocial impact that expands and deepens relationships through investigating positivity resonance in relationships. Positivity resonance occurs among individuals who coexperience positive emotions through interactions that trigger feelings of connectedness. In this framework, the focus is on the connection that is created among individuals through the shared positive experience and is not an evaluative component of "Do I like you." Through short meaningful interactions, individuals experience positive affect and a relationship of mutual caring and support becomes reinforced. Individuals who experience more moments of positivity resonance reported higher daily well-being, which was in turn linked to positive physical and mental health outcomes (Majors et al., 2018). These positive outcomes can occur through both personal and professional social connections fostered via social media.

Similar to our personal relationships and our relationships within our local communities, our work communities were also impacted by the sudden move to remote work due to the COVID-19 pandemic. What is more, the often-necessary separation of key workers in the workplace due to health concerns separated colleagues from one another. Many employees worked for their companies for many months without ever meeting any of their fellow colleagues in person. These circumstances, and the lack of a sense of community, has highlighted the importance of providing connecting opportunities. The following examples highlight this further. For example, in their intervention, Prinzing et al. (2020) tasked individuals to engage in 35 daily micro actions to reinforce social ties with the intent to build and expand their network of positive relationships. Their results showed that individuals who experienced positivity resonance through their micro interactions (on social media and technology tools) actively provided more social support, demonstrated more humility, and were less self-focused in their interactions. In addition, within the context of the 2020/2021 COVID-19 pandemic, individuals' positivity resonance was manifested through their prosocial tendencies linked to positive community related behaviors (e.g., mask wearing and hand washing) and the intention to be vaccinated to reduce the spread of COVID-19 within one's community (West et al., 2021).

Social media was often a means by which workplaces tried to connect and offer new opportunities to their often geographically scattered workforce. This is demonstrated by research during the COVID-19 pandemic that shows the positive impact of using social media as a vehicle for taking micro actions to share positive experiences and gratitude as an important tool for sustaining relationships in the context of physical distancing. In addition, Ma et al. (2021) found that in a sample of 1020 Chinese workers aged 55 and older, using social media at work resulted in increased perceptions of both emotional and informational social support. This suggests that social media during COVID-19 pandemic presented an important channel for certain parts of communities that may not have sought social support online. There is also evidence that the conscious effort to build and maintain social connections by social media users enabled these users to maintain and nurture their existing social connections (Folk et al., 2020). Doing so may be critical, salient, and memorable during the time of social distancing and quarantine, which for many led to the breakaway and loss of many interpersonal, in-person interactions, connections, and friendships.

Moore and March (2020) found that proactive coping behaviors were predicted by the frequency of non-face-to-face communications related to the frequency of initiating communications (i.e., telephone calls and messaging) and regular use of social media to sustain relationships. Reaching out during times of trauma to seek and give social support is well established and, during the 2020/2021 COVID-19 pandemic, the use of social media positively impacted social connectedness and well-being for those individuals who were proactive in using these technology tools and platforms regularly.

Lombardo et al. (2021) underscored the significance of social media in facilitating the growth of social capital to positively impact the growth, development, and efficacy of communities and organizations. Per our earlier discussion, social capital highlights the dynamics of collective action, which expands trust and collaboration among members who are interconnected as they exchange information rapidly among all individuals in the network. Sharing knowledge and information on social media that helps others make decisions or feel connected shows empathy and an understanding of what individuals might find valuable and important. This represents a positive strategy to build networks and share ideas and options to create clarity in the information saturated context prevalent in many organizations (Olson, 2014).

Nevertheless, it is worth noting that we need to exercise caution when we reference research published before and during COVID-19 pandemic. Many of the findings around social capital building, social connectedness, and social belonging to personal, community, and work networks may not as readily translate from the prepandemic times to the experience of individuals, employees, and communities during the pandemic. A few examples demonstrate this nicely. For example, it is important to remember at this stage that the COVID-19 pandemic represents a very unique situation. For example, pre-COVID-19 research suggests that face-to-face interactions had the strongest impact on building positive relationships and prosocial behaviors were muted through the use of social media (Majors et al., 2018). However, such research was conducted at a time where both options were available to individuals: having the choice to meet face-to-face or over social media suggests that choosing one option will readily decline the use of the other. However, the COVID-19 situations removed one of these choices for many individuals. As a result, what we know about social media prepandemic may not necessarily be predictive of how individuals use social media during the COVID-19 pandemic, or potentially, even in the long term.

What is more, prepandemic research suggested that individuals who were proactive in sharing information were also most likely to use the information posted by others and reciprocate by sharing more information in return (Kang et al., 2017). During COVID-19, we also saw a substantial increase in misinformation and a heavy focus on pandemic-related news (Venegas-Vera et al., 2020). As a result, many individuals often knowingly or unknowingly shared inaccurate information or worrisome trends (Islam et al., 2020), which actually increased the anxiety of many people who were using social media as their main source of information (Zhao & Zhou, 2020). As a result, how social media is used—as well as what is shared—will not by default necessarily increase the sense of social support but can also increase a sense of shared powerlessness. What is more, the vaccination safety issues often dominated social media news and further increased the sense of divisions among family, friends, neighbors, and coworkers. As a result, it is important to reflect on the conditions that promote social belonging and social support. As we have seen during the pandemic, the use of social media can have both positive and negative impacts on relationships if the use of this media leads to division, rather than a sense of mutual support and social capital.

## Professional relationships and social media

The following section focuses on the professional lives of individuals and the extent to which social media can help professionals access support networks, foster their own career development, and engage in professionally oriented social networking activities via social media. Here the emphasis is placed on the impact that social media can have, or the indirect effects of what social media afford, for the growth of employee's professional development and career. The first part focuses on many findings published pre-COVID 19, followed by a short critical reflection section given recent experiences, events, and new research.

Social media tools and social networking platforms have transformed the networking process for individuals in the 21st century to assist them in identifying new job opportunities and build relationships with others who share their expertise and industry knowledge. In the current section, we focus specifically on networking sites such as LinkedIn, as these sites support the connection and communication between users, aspects which also make these sites so attractive to career, business, and human resource (HR) professionals. Many HR professionals actively and increasingly recruit from these sites (Jeske & Holland, 2019), while these sites also provide ongoing networking and learning opportunities. The development and growth of LinkedIn, for example, shows that social networking platform enables individuals to curate professional identities. In addition, such networks facilitate networking and relationship building with individuals, groups, and organizations whom one would never have had the opportunity to meet in other contexts.

Social media and networks present job candidates and incumbents with the opportunity to network with current colleagues, but also potential employers (Jacobson, 2020). This means that these tools and networks now give individuals the opportunity to engage in personal branding and self-promotion (Jacobson, 2020). Furthermore, given the different niches that some of social networks are serving, more professionals opt to present different aspects of themselves online. Having a social media presence has shown to promote social capital and relationship building between employees (Cao et al., 2016; Tijunaitis et al., 2019). In addition, organizational practices related to career, learning, and knowledge management have increasingly absorbed social media and networks to support the flow of communication and provide a voice to employees and social groups. The importance of these developments for professional and career development, and general communication practice, is demonstrated next.

Research has demonstrated that social networking can generate multiple career benefits for social network users, including greater visibility to self-promote one's skillset and the opportunity to contact sponsors and mentors and, via these contacts, to be introduced to more opportunities (Davis et al., 2020; Jeske & Shultz, 2016). Furthermore, users of social networks report improved access to resources, new opportunities, and career outcomes through their professional network—within their own organizations and external organizations (Davis et al., 2020). As a result, numerous educational and career-related articles emphasize the importance of building digital skills, social media, and networking self-efficacy, for the employability and professional and career development of future graduates and professionals (e.g., Anders, 2018; Escoffery et al., 2018). These benefits are not a function of the number of contacts per se (Davis et al., 2020; Poncy et al., 2018).

Over the last few years, starting early 2020, many of the affordances of social media suddenly became more relevant as many workers saw a sudden shift to remote work. The pandemic generated great uncertainty and disruptions at work due to sudden workforce. This also created a desire for more—not necessarily less—communication, a more pronounced need to identify potential professional support groups and new or alternative career tracks. Social media and networking were instantly recognized as presenting essential means to facilitate relationship building, support knowledge management, and the steep learning curve that many organizations had to climb. Indeed, the COVID-19 pandemic accelerated online learning trends and remote working (see also Caligiuri et al., 2020), as millions of workers were sent to work from home—often with minimal notice, resources, or preparation. This often prompts immediate challenges for employees whose role requires more task interdependence and resources (Chong et al., 2020).

As a result, concepts such as virtual teamwork, virtual leadership, and new communication practices (see also Caligiuri et al., 2020; Kniffin et al., 2021)—including the use of new group chat, tools, and platforms to socially connect employees with one another—have become prominent concerns (e.g., Bolisani et al., 2020). The existing teleworking research, often conducted with minority and nontraditional work environments, has a critically important resource for many organizations (e.g., Chekwa, 2018; see Kniffin et al., 2021). These trends also led to a change in many relevant HR practices, to overcome the communication divide and generate new networking opportunities during employee hiring, onboarding, and team building. Social networking and media tools have played a pivotal role in addressing this communication divide. Furthermore, connecting these networks and tools further to knowledge and learning management systems represent ways in which communication can also feed into organizational knowledge and development. These connections can create invaluable knowledge and learning paths for new hires and talent keen to learn, develop, and grow in their new organization.

The pandemic has also demonstrated that the benefits of social media may at times be outweighed by the negatives of using social media as a channel of communication in workplace settings. Social media and networks have often been core components of the connected workplace, supporting communication and networking within the organization and across organizational boundaries. For example, communication tools have been essential for employee initiatives for years. However, even before the COVID-19 pandemic, research has highlighted the problem of employers potentially overwhelming their employees with a flood of information and expectations of constant connectivity, highlighting the dark side of technology (e.g., Bordi et al., 2018; Holland & Bardoel, 2016). The move to remote work, or for keyworkers, the separation of workstations and teams, often led employers to take to more online channels—including social media—to share information, to compensate for the lack of in-person communication. Not surprisingly, social media fatigue became an issue for many during the pandemic, as many workers were suddenly inundated with information via their personal and employer-based social media channel (Islam et al., 2020).

Another example similarly suggests that the use conditions influence the perceived benefits of social media for employees. Prepandemic research has shown that spending more time on a social network to interact with personal contacts is less likely to support career decision self-efficacy (Jeske & Shultz, 2019; Poncy et al., 2018). Yet, during the COVID-19 pandemic, interaction with personal contacts was not an option. As a result, many young professionals took to social media to connect with others to overcome sudden employment hurdles, such as the extensive decline in graduate jobs and internships. This also led to an enormous increase in the number of requests for many HR recruiters and professionals on a social media platform, which significantly increased their workload and led to demotivation for many struggling to cope with the number of requests. As a result, many recent joiners of social media might have found it more difficult than their predecessors to access the same degree of social support and role models in the last 2 years. Future researchers may wish to examine the long-term social media effects for different professional users and also query the effectiveness of social media use, as recent experiences suggest that social media use by employers and employees may foster conditions that promote constant connectivity, and potentially, over time, social media fatigue and disengagement.

## Recommendations to build positive relationships in personal and professional settings

In this final section, we offer several practical small-scale recommendations focused on building and nurturing networks that contribute to well-being for individuals, their communities, and organizational settings using social media, as well as other practical approaches. The recommendations can be implemented for personal and professional relationship building and maintenance.

### Intentional acts of kindness

The research of Epley and Schroeder (2014) reinforces the important link among intentional acts of support and the experience of well-being and quality of social relationships. Social media can be a tool by which users can share those experiences and reach a broad and often diverse set of potential recipients, from friends, to family, to neighbors, and fellow colleagues. Therefore, we recommend individuals take initiative to engage in actions that positively impact others (and yourself), for example, setting a goal to share five acts of kindness in one day (rather than spreading those acts of kindness over a week). The salience of sharing small acts of kindness in a short period of time (in one day) makes a stronger, sustained impact on well-being and happiness.

For example, posting an article that summarizes recent research on a key area with colleagues who are members of one of your LinkedIn groups to show you are thinking about them makes a difference. Likewise, taking a moment to comment and share a quick reply on social media or networks to a colleague who posted something you found valuable and how you used that information in your work helps to foster social connectedness at work. Be specific and genuine in your follow-up responses.

## Share pictures and memories on social media

Prepandemic research has shown that sharing a positive event can amplify the positive affect for those viewing the event and will thereby make it more memorable (Kurtz & Algoe, 2015). In addition, the shared event led to active positive responses by individuals who show more genuine concern and support for others as a result of experiencing the positive shared event (Gable & Reis, 2010). Savoring memories with others (to relive moments of emotional resonance) deepens relationships and reinforces positive feelings. Social media can play a critical role here—especially when it is often dominated by anxiety-provoking and misleading information as we saw during the COVID-19 pandemic (see also Islam et al., 2020; Venegas-Vera et al., 2020; Zhao & Zhou, 2020). Consciously making the effort to maintain social connections (Folk et al., 2020), taking the time to look through pictures you have taken and regularly share them with captions such as "Do you remember how hard we laughed when...?" and, for colleagues at work, "Remember this great conference we attended ... I learned so much and I am glad we are able to work on a project together to apply those skills. Thank you for being an amazing coworker." Savoring experiences that were meaningful allows you to relive the moments and nurture the relationships with others as well, thereby creating positive resonance (Fredrickson, 2018). Far too often we think about someone, but we do not take the time to share that with the person. Think about the number of times that you text, call, and message someone and the reply is, "Wow, I was just thinking about you." Be the first one to reach out and check in, do not wait for others to initiate.

## Create opportunities to share information, knowledge, and support

The need to initiate actions to support and expand relationship continues to grow. COVID-19 changed how we use social media platforms to share our stories, expertise, and authenticity (Brown & McDermott, 2021). As a result, recruiters and hiring managers have become more focused on searching social media for applicants looking for patterns that will demonstrate and reinforce the ability of individuals to add value to the organization and creative approaches that applicants have developed to position their talent, expertise, and skills to pivot and respond during the pandemic to show agility and resilience.

In addition, find and create opportunities to share knowledge and demonstrate your expertise through your social media and uploading documents into your organization's Knowledge Management System, intranet, or employee support groups (e.g., Jameel & Ahmad, 2020; Lee et al., 2021). Focus on patterns of information and practices that you believe will help others apply new knowledge and develop approaches or implement information that is relevant to them and helps them achieve their personal and professional goals. Target specific individuals in your social media contacts and groups whom you can help and support through sharing links and knowledge that they might not have accessed or to ensure that they have. Show that you are thinking about their success and that you are there to support and guide them with relevant, fact-based information, dispelling fake news and opinions that are not scientifically based. Showing that you are contributing to the knowledge base in your industry and your network demonstrates your personal commitment to expanding relationships and using your influence to help others become more successful in achieving their goals and outcomes.

## Engage in sharing through multiple platforms

Different communities "live" on different social media platforms. LinkedIn has been the primary platform used in organizational networking contexts (Osman, 2021). Find ways to reach out to use other social media platforms (e.g., Instagram, Clubhouse, Tumblr, and Slack) to engage a wide range of audiences to connect with your team, organization, and community. There are generational and subgroup differences, as well as individual preferences in social media platform use and engagement. Building a broad range of relationships using diverse platforms will expand your reach and positively impact your relationships. Think about the person and customize your approach to nurture those relationships in meaningful ways. Use more visuals (e.g., infographics) and sharing stories of positive relationships and teams who relied on each other's strengths to achieve important results and your willingness to think about their preferences and needs—which is the essence of building and maintaining strong relationships—by showing people that you see how they are unique.

### Be proactive and authentic to maintain social connections

One of the key insights for many social media users during the pandemic is that many "friends" were just connections or mere acquaintances—people that may not necessarily provide support. Being able to identify those you share a common philosophy with, a shared sense of purpose, or a shared identity can be a good way to identify those who provide support. Maintaining those relationships, however, requires engaging in mutual support behaviors. One way is to be proactive and authentic in your communication—an aspect that many marketing companies have already recognized as being critical to social media communication (Scott, 2020). For example, one option is to set up a system to regularly check in with others and share information, ideas, or just ask, "How are you" (see also Roy & Ayalon, 2021). During the COVID-19 pandemic, it became clear that messages sent asking "How are you" became an important way to show people they are seen and valued. Sustain that genuine and authentic concern that shows how you value the person individually and are aware of their unique situation and concerns. Being conscious about the importance of personalized connections to sustain relationships creates upward spirals and builds emotional resonance in relationships—those momentary shared experiences that make an impact and reinforce trusting relationships (Fredrickson, 2018).

Take the time every day to reach out to people. Count the number of times you take initiative to reach out every day and write that down in your gratitude journal. Tracking these social connections ensures that you stay intentional (just like the tracking of your workouts or calories consumed each day to keep it conscious), so you are making systematic investments in your relationships. Epley and Schroeder's (2014) research demonstrates how we underestimate how important taking initiative to interact with others contributes to positive interactions. Their research results highlight that even talking to strangers on a train leads to more positive feelings of connectedness rather than (the presumed) feelings of awkwardness or social anxiety. This positive impact of reaching out to make these social connections with acquaintances and strangers holds for both introverts and extraverts. Recognizing and appreciating these social connections through keeping a gratitude journal has a positive impact on your well-being and health.

# Conclusion

Social media platforms have proliferated in all domains of personal, public, and professional life. While some of us use certain networks with family and friends, other networks are used primarily for professional purposes and organizational interactions, and others yet again for hobbies and entertainment. Today, these tools and networks play a pivotal role in the way that people communicate with one another, connect with others, share knowledge, and promote their own profile to interested parties such as potential employers. In this chapter, we outlined the importance of social media and networks in relation to several aspects, including their role in today's relationship building in personal and work settings. Furthermore, as demonstrated, social media tools and sites play an important role in supporting networking and career development.

Today's online users cultivate different online identities, engage in different strategies to manage their online personas in order to balance their interests in privacy, visibility, and establishing their competitive presence, and support various personal strategies (Berkelaar, 2017). These developments have triggered a great deal of research and interest from academics and employers to identify their potential, but also the potential of social media within organizations (Poba-Nzaou et al., 2016). Particular areas of interest include the concept of digital social identity or multiple online identities, boundary management (e.g., McDonald & Thompson, 2016; van Zoonen et al., 2018), and new emergent HR practices (e.g., cybervetting of candidates during recruitment drives). However, new challenges, as well as opportunities, still exist to explore the optimal use of such options in personal and professional settings.

Despite the growing literature on the topic, numerous questions remain regarding the optimal integration of social media and social sites in existing learning, knowledge, and career management systems. At this stage, it is not entirely clear how such systems and potential system integrations—while desirable—will support the desire for relationship building as well as boundary management, visibility to different contacts, cultural differences, and privacy concern. The current chapter, and its focus on the development, nurturing, and expansion of personal and professional relationships through social media, therefore, represents the first foray and attempt to outline current insights to set the groundwork for the clarification of the existing challenges as well as unexplored opportunities.

## References

Algoe, S. B., Haidt, J., & Gable, S. L. (2008). Beyond reciprocity: Gratitude and relationships in everyday life. *Emotion (Washington, D.C.)*, *8*, 425−429. Available from https://doi.org/10.1037/1528-3542.8.3.425.

Anders, A. D. (2018). Networked learning with professionals boosts students' self-efficacy for social networking and professional development. *Computers & Education*, *127* (2018), 13−29. Available from https://doi.org/10.1016/j.compedu.2018.08.009.

Berkelaar, B. L. (2017). How implicit theories help differentiate approaches to online impression management: A preliminary typology. *New Media & Society*, *19*(12), 2039−2058. Available from https://doi.org/10.1177/1461444816654136.

Bolisani, E., Scarso, E., Ipsen, C., Kirchner, K., & Hansen, J. P. (2020). Working from home during COVID-19 pandemic: Lessons learned and issues. *Management & Marketing (Bucharest, Romania)*, *15*(1), 458−476. Available from https://doi.org/10.2478/mmcks-2020-0027.

Bordi, L., Okkonen, J., Mäkiniemi, J.-P., & Heikkilä-Tammi, K. (2018). Communication in the digital work environment: Implications for wellbeing at work. *Nordic Journal of Working Life Studies*, *8*(3), 29−48.

Brown, D., & McDermott, P. (2021). 5 Post-Pandemic rules for social media. Korn Ferry Insights. Available from https://www.kornferry.com/insights/articles

Buchanan, K., Aknin, L. B., Lotun, S., & Sandstrom, G. M. (2021). Brief exposure to social media during the COVID-19 pandemic: Doom-scrolling has negative emotional consequences, but kindness-scrolling does not. *PLoS One*, *16*(10). Available from https://doi.org/10.1371/journal.pone.0257728, *Article ID: e0257728*.

Caligiuri, P., De Cieri, H., Minbaeva, D., Verbeke, A., & Zimmermann, A. (2020). International HRM insights for navigating the COVID-19 pandemic: Implications for future research and practice. *Journal of International Business Studies*, *51*(5), 697−713.

Cao, X., Guo, X., Vogel, D., & Zhang, X. (2016). Exploring the influence of social media on employee work performance. *Internet Research*, *26*(2), 529−545. Available from https://doi.org/10.1108/intr-11-2014-0299.

Chancellor, J., Margolis, S., & Lyubomirsky, S. (2018). The propagation of everyday prosociality in the workplace. *The Journal of Positive Psychology*, *13*(3), 271−283.

Chekwa, C. (2018). Don't be left out - fostering networking opportunities to reduce workplace isolation among ethnic employees in remote settings. *Advances in Competitiveness Research; a Journal of Science and its Applications*, *26*(3/4), 217−235.

Chen, X., & Wei, S. (2020). The impact of social media use for communication and social exchange relationship on employee performance. *Journal of Knowledge Management*, *24*, 1289−1314. Available from https://doi.org/10.1108/JKM-04-2019-0167.

Chong, S., Huang, Y., & Chang, C. (2020). Supporting interdependent telework employees: A moderated-mediation model linking daily COVID-19 task setbacks to next-day work withdrawal. *Journal of Applied Psychology*, *105*(12), 1408−1422. Available from https://doi.org/10.1037/apl0000843.

Davis, J., Wolff, H., Forret, M. L., & Sullivan, S. E. (2020). Networking via LinkedIn: An examination of usage and career benefits. *Journal of Vocational Behavior, 118*, 1−15. Available from https://doi.org/10.1016/j.jvb.2020.103396, article 103396.

Deci, E. L., & Ryan, R. M. (2000). The "what" and "why" of goal pursuits: Human needs and the self-determination of behavior. *Psychological Inquiry, 11*, 227−268.

Epley, N., & Schroeder, J. (2014). Mistakenly seeking solitude. *Journal of Experimental Psychology: General, 143*(5), 1980−1999.

Escoffery, C., Kenzig, M., Hyden, C., & Hernandez, K. (2018). Capitalizing on social media for career development. *Health Promotion Practice, 19*(1), 11−15. Available from https://doi.org/10.1177/1524839917734522.

Folk, D., Okabe-Miyamoto, K., Dunn, E., & Lyubomirsky, S. (2020). Did social connection decline during the first wave of COVID-19?: The role of extraversion. *Collabra: Psychology, 6*(1), 37. Available from https://doi.org/10.1525/collabra.365.

Fredrickson, B. L. (2018). *Positivity: Groundbreaking research to release your inner optimist and thrive*. New York, NY: Harmony Books.

Gable, S.L., & Reis, H.T. (2010). Chapter 4 - Good News! Capitalizing on Positive Events in an Interpersonal Context. In B.-A. in E. S. Psychology (Ed.) (Vol. 42, pp. 195−257). Academic Press.

Grant, A. M., & Berry, J. W. (2011). The necessity of others is the mother of invention: Intrinsic and prosocial motivations, perspective taking, and creativity. *Academy of Management Journal, 54*, 73−96.

Grant, A. M., & Sonnentag, S. (2010). Doing good buffers against feeling bad: Prosocial impact compensates for negative task and self-evaluations. *Organizational Behavior and Human Decision Processes, 111*, 13−22.

Holland, P., & Bardoel, A. (2016). The impact of technology on work in the twenty-first century: Exploring the smart and dark side. *International Journal of Human Resource Management, 27*(21), 2579−2581. Available from https://doi.org/10.1080/09585192. 2016.1238126, https://www.youtube.com/watch?v = EimJNJXcta4.

Islam, A. K. M. N., Laato, S., Talukder, S., & Sutinen, E. (2020). Misinformation sharing and social media fatigue during COVID-19: An affordance and cognitive load perspective. *Technological Forecasting of Social Change, 2020*(159). Available from https://doi.org/10.1016/j.techfore.2020.120201, *Article ID: 120201*.

Jacobson, J. (2020). You are a brand: Social media managers' personal branding and "the future audience". *The Journal of Product & Brand Management, 29*(6), 715−727. Available from https://doi.org/10.1108/JPBM-03-2019-2299.

Jameel, A. S., & Ahmad, A. R. (2020). The role of information and communication technology on knowledge sharing among the academic staff during COVID-19 Pandemic. *Proceedings of the 2020 2nd Annual International Conference on Information and Sciences (AiCIS)*, 141−147. Available from https://doi.org/10.1109/AiCIS51645. 2020.00032.

Jeske, D., & Holland, P. (2019). Employer and employee vetting: Reputation management challenges. In P. Holland (Ed.), *Contemporary HRM issues in the 21st century* (pp. 149−158). Bingley, UK: Emerald Publishing.

Jeske, D., & Shultz, K. S. (2016). Using social media content for screening in recruitment and selection: Pros and cons. *Work, Employment & Society, 30*(3), 535−546. Available from https://doi.org/10.1177/0950017015613746.

Jeske, D., & Shultz, K. S. (2019). Social media screening and content effects: Implications for applicant reactions. *International Journal of Manpower, 40*(1), 73−86. Available from https://doi.org/10.1108/IJM-06-2017-0138.

Kang, Y. J., Lee, J. Y., & Kim, H. W. (2017). A psychological empowerment to online knowledge sharing. *Computers in Human Behavior, 74*, 175−187. Available from https://doi.org/10.1016/j.chb.2017.04.039.

Kniffin, K. M., Narayanan, J., & Anseel, F. (2021). COVID-19 and the workplace: Implications, issues, and insights for future research and action. *American Psychologist*. Available from https://doi.org/10.1037/amp0000716, ePub.

Koay, S. H., Ng, A. T., Tham, S. K., & Tan, C. S. (2020). Gratitude intervention on Instagram: An experimental study. *Psychological Studies*, 65(2), 168–173. Available from https://doi.org/10.1007/s12646-019-00547-6.

Kurtz, L. E., & Algoe, S. B. (2015). Putting laughter in context: Shared laughter as behavioral indicator of relationship well-being. *Personal Relationships*, 22(4), 573–590. Available from https://doi.org/10.1111/pere.12095.

Layous, K., Nelson, S. K., & Lyubomirsky, S. (2012). What is the optimal way to deliver a positive activity intervention? The case of writing about one's best possible selves. *Journal of Happiness Studies*. Available from https://doi.org/10.1007/s10902-012-9346-2, Advance online publication.

Lee, Y., Tao, W., Li, J. Y. Q., & Sun, R. (2021). Enhancing employees' knowledge sharing through diversity-oriented leadership and strategic internal communication during the COVID-19 outbreak. *Journal of Knowledge Management*, 25(6), 1526–1549. Available from https://doi.org/10.1108/JKM-06-2020-0483.

Liu, E. (2020). *Most Fortune 500 CEOs are on Social Media in 2020*. Available from https://influentialexecutive.com/.

Lombardo, G., Mordonini, M., & Tomaiuolo, M. (2021). Adoption of social media in sociotechnical systems: A survey. *Information*, 12, 132. Available from https://doi.org/10.3390/info12030132.

Ma, Y., Liang, C., Gu, D., Zhao, S., Yang, X., & Wang, X. (2021). How social media use affects improvement of older people's willingness to delay retirement during transfer from demographic bonus to health bonus: Causal relationship empirical study. *Journal of Medical Internet Research*, 23(2), e18264. Available from https://doi.org/10.2196/18264.

Majors, B. C., Nguyen, K. D. L., Lundberg, K. B., & Fredrickson, B. L. (2018). Well-being correlates of perceived positivity resonance: Evidence from trait and episode-level assessments. *Psychology Faculty Publications*, 48, 571–589, 69. Available from https://scholarship.richmond.edu/psychology-faculty-publications/69Management.

Mauss, I. B., Shallcross, A. J., Troy, A. S., John, O. P., Ferrer, E., Wilhelm, F. H., & Gross, J. J. (2011). Don't hide your happiness! Positive emotion dissociation, social connectedness, and psychological functioning. *Journal of Personality and Social Psychology*, 100, 738–748.

McDonald, P., & Thompson, P. (2016). Social media(tion) and the reshaping of public/private boundaries in employment relations. *International Journal of Management Reviews*, 18(1), 69–84. Available from https://doi.org/10.1111/ijmr.12061.

Moore, K. A., & March, E. (2020). Socially connected during COVID-19: Online social connections mediate the relationship between loneliness and positive coping Strategies. *Research Square*. Available from https://doi.org/10.21203/rs.3.rs-35835/v1.

Ng, T. W. H., & Feldman, D. (2011). Affective organizational commitment and citizenship behavior: Linear and non-linear moderating effects of organizational tenure. *Journal of Vocational Behavior*, 79, 528–537. Available from https://doi.org/10.1016/j.jvb.2011.03.006.

Olson, D.A. (2014). *Strengths-based leadership development: Two applications of a positive algorithm for growth and learning*. Paper presented at the Institute of Work Psychology, Biennial International Conference, Sheffield, United Kingdom.

Olson, D. A., Liu, J., & Shultz, K. S. (2012). Social media's influence on social support, efficacy, and life satisfaction. *Journal of Organizational Psychology*, 12, 133–144.

Osman, M. (2021, March 18). Mind-blowing LinkedIn statistics and facts. Kinsta blog. Available from https://kinsta.com/blog/linkedin-statistics/.

Poba-Nzaou, P., Lemieux, N., Beaupré, D., & Uwizeyemungu, S. (2016). Critical challenges associated with the adoption of social media: A Delphi of a panel of Canadian human resources managers. *Journal of Business Research, 69*(10), 4011−4019. Available from https://doi.org/10.1016/j.jbusres.2016.06.006.

Poncy, G., Kim, M., Ramos, K., & Lopez, F. G. (2018). Career planning confidence among facebook users: Contributions of adult attachment security and authenticity. *Journal of Career Assessment, 26*(4), 599−615. Available from https://doi.org/10.1177/1069072717723094.

Price, M., Legrand, A. C., Brier, Z. M., van Stolk-Cooke, K., Peck, K., Sheridan Dodds, P., Danforth, C. M., & Adams, Z. W. (2021). Doomscrolling during COVID-19: The negative association between daily social and traditional media consumption and mental health symptoms during the COVID-19 pandemic. *PsyArXiv PrePrints, ePpub*, 1−12. Available from https://doi.org/10.31234/osf.io/s2nfg.

Prinzing, M. M., Zhou, J., West, T. N., Nguyen, K. D. L., Wells, J. L., & Fredrickson, B. L. (2020). Staying 'in sync' with others during COVID-19: Perceived positivity resonance mediates cross-sectional and longitudinal links between trait resilience and mental health. *The Journal of Positive Psychology*. Available from https://doi.org/10.1080/17439760.2020.1858336.

Roy, S., & Ayalon, L. (2021). "Goodness and Kindness": Long-distance caregiving through volunteers during the COVID-19 Lockdown in India. *The Journals of Gerontology: Series B, 76*(7), e281−e289. Available from https://doi.org/10.1093/geronb/gbaa187.

Rudolph, C. W., Allan, B., Clark, M., Hertel, G., Hirschi, A., Kunze, F., Shockley, K., Shoss, M., Sonnentag, S., & Zacher, H. (2020). Pandemics: Implications for research and practice in industrial and organizational psychology. *Industrial and Organizational Psychology: Perspectives on Science and Practice, 13*(4). Available from https://www.siop.org/Portals/84/docs/Journal/13.4/focal2.PDF.

Ryan, T., Allen, K. A., Grey, D. L., & McInerney, D. M. (2017). How social are social media? A review of online social behaviour and connectedness. *Journal of Relationships Research, 8*(8), 1−8. Available from https://doi.org/10.1017/jrr.2017.13.

Scott, E. (2020). Why demonstrating authenticity on social media is important (& how we do it as Sendible). Available at: https://www.sendible.com/insights/authenticity-on-social-media (accessed 27 November 2021).

Tijunaitis, K., Jeske, D., & Shultz, K. (2019). Virtuality at work and social media use among dispersed workers: Promoting network ties, shared vision and trust. *Employee Relations, 41*(3), 358−373. Available from https://doi.org/10.1108/ER-03-2018-0093.

Tsang, J., & Martin, S. R. (2019). Four experiments on the relational dynamics and prosocial consequences of gratitude. *The Journal of Positive Psychology, 14*, 188−205. Available from https://doi.org/10.1080/17439760.2017.1388435.

Venegas-Vera, A. V., Colbert, G. B., & Lerma, E. V. (2020). Positive and negative impact of social media in the COVID-19 era. *Review of Cardiovascular Medicine, 21*(4), 561−564. Available from https://doi.org/10.31083/j.rcm.2020.04.195.

Wei, L., & Gao, F. (2017). Social media, social integration and subjective well-being among new urban migrants in China. *Telematics and Informatics, 34*(2017), 786−796. Available from https://doi.org/10.1016/j.tele.2016.05.017.

West, T. N., Nguyen, K. L., Zhou, J., Prinzing, M. M., Wells, T. L., & Fredrickson, B. L. (2021). How the affective quality of social connections may contribute to public health: Prosocial tendencies account for the links between positivity resonance and behaviors that reduce the spread of COVID-19. *Affective Science*. Available from https://doi.org/10.1007/s42761-021-00035-z.

Ytre-Arne, B., & Moe, H. (2021). Doomscrolling, monitoring and avoiding: News use in COVID-19 Pandemic Lockdown. *Journalism Studies*, 1−17. Available from https://doi.org/10.1080/1461670X.2021.1952475, in press.

Zhao, N., & Zhou, G. (2020). Social media use and mental health during the COVID-19 Pandemic: Moderator role of disaster stressor and mediator role of negative affect. *Applied Psychology: Health and Well-being, 12*(4), 1019–1038. Available from https://doi.org/10.1111/aphw.12226.

van Zoonen, W., Bartels, J., van Prooijen, A., & Schouten, A. P. (2018). Explaining online ambassadorship behaviors on Facebook and LinkedIn. *Computers in Human Behavior, 87* (October), 354–362. Available from https://doi.org/10.1016/j.chb.2018.05.031.

## Further reading

Berkelaar, B. L. (2014). Cybervetting, online information, and personnel selection: New transparency expectations and the emergence of a digital social contract. *Management Communication Quarterly, 28*(4), 479–506. Available from https://doi.org/10.1177/0893318914541966.

Gilbert, D. T., & Wilson, T. D. (2000). Miswanting: Some problems in the forecasting of future emotional states. In J. Forgas (Ed.), *Thinking and feeling: The role of affect in social cognition* (pp. 178–197). Cambridge: Cambridge University Press.

Hedenus, A., & Backman, C. (2017). Explaining the data double: Confessions and self-examinations in job recruitments. *Surveillance & Society, 15*(5), 640–654. Available from https://doi.org/10.24908/ss.v15i5.6380.

Hoek, J., O'Kane, P., & McCracken, M. (2016). Publishing personal information online. *Personnel Review, 45*(1), 67–83. Available from https://doi.org/10.1108/PR-05-2014-0099.

Holland, P., & Jeske, D. (2017). The changing role of social media at work: Implications for recruitment and selection. In T. Bondarouk, H. Ruel, & E. Parry (Eds.), *Electronic HRM in the Smart Era*. Bingley, UK: Emerald Publishing.

Holland, P., & Jeske, D. (2018). To cyber-vet or not to cyber-vet: An ethics question for HRM. In A. Malik (Ed.), *Strategic human resource management and employment relations: An international perspective*. Singapore: Springer.

Jacobson, J., & Gruzd, A. (2020). Cybervetting job applicants on social media: The new normal? *Ethics and Information Technology, 22*(3), 175–195. Available from https://doi.org/10.1007/s10676-020-09526-2.

Kahneman, D. (2011). *Thinking, fast and slow*. New York: NY: Farrar, Straus, & Giroux.

Levashina, J., Peck, J. A., & Ficht, L. (2017). Don't select until you check: Expected background checking practices. *Employee Responsibilities and Rights Journal, 29*(3), 127–148. Available from https://doi.org/10.1007/s10672-017-9294-4.

McCullough, M. E., Emmons, R. A., & Tsang, J. (2002). The grateful disposition: A conceptual and empirical topography. *Journal of Personality and Social Psychology, 82*, 112–127.

McDonald, P., Thompson, P., & O'Connor, P. (2016). Profiling employees online: Shifting public-private boundaries in organisational life. *Human Resource Management Journal, 26*(4), 541–556. Available from https://doi.org/10.1111/1748-8583.12121.

Moshin, M. (2021, February 16). 10 Facebook Statistics Every Marketer Should Know in 2021 [INFOGRAPHIC]. Oberlo blog. Available from https://www.oberlo.com/blog/facebook-statistics.

Polak, E. L., & McCullough, M. E. (2006). Is gratitude an alternative to materialism. *Journal of Happiness Studies, 7*, 343–360. Available from https://doi.org/10.1007/s10902-005-3649-5.

Santos, L. (2019). My Life is Awesome, So Why Can't I Enjoy It. Aspen Institute.

Teppers, E., Luyckx, K., Klimstra, T. A., & Goossens, L. (2014). Loneliness and Facebook motives in adolescence: A longitudinal inquiry into directionality of effect. *Journal of Adolescence, 37*, 691–699.

CHAPTER TEN

# The relationship between social media use and perceptions of online and offline loneliness during social distancing restrictions

**Jacqui Taylor[1] and Jeremy Lay[2]**
[1]Department of Psychology, Bournemouth University, Poole, Dorset, United Kingdom
[2]School of Psychology, Western Sydney University, Sydney, NSW, Australia

## Contents

*Handbook of Social Media Use Online Relationships, Security, Privacy, and Society, Volume 2*
DOI: https://doi.org/10.1016/B978-0-443-28804-3.00007-7
Copyright © 2024 Elsevier Inc. All rights reserved, including those for text and data mining,
AI training, and similar technologies.

## Introduction

With over 4.5 billion people in the world having access to internet services, it is no surprise that social media users now exceed 3.8 billion (Kemp, 2020). Social media is defined as any type of website or application that assists in socializing and networking among people that an individual may or may not know, allowing for the self-construction of these social networks (Pittman & Reich, 2016). The emergence of social media as a method of communication and socializing has created a new "world" that is accessible online. Miller et al. (2016) go so far as to say that there is no distinction between the online world and the offline world, instead that social media should be regarded as just another place where we live our lives. Recent research suggests that social media is beginning to replace face-to-face social interactions, especially for the younger generations (Halston et al., 2019). Therefore, it is becoming increasingly important to be aware of the impacts that social media can have on user's well-being.

One would expect that the availability of instant connectivity and the growth of social opportunities through social media would be associated with an increase in psychological well-being. However, despite the social opportunities afforded by social media, loneliness remains pervasive in our society. The European Commission's (2018) report on loneliness found that more than 75 million European adults meet with family or friends at most once a month, with around 30 million adults reporting frequent feelings of loneliness. In Australia, due to the social restrictions placed on citizens during the COVID-19 pandemic, loneliness was the most widely reported source of personal stress in April 2020 (Australian Bureau of Statistics, 2020). Loneliness is an area of particular importance when considering an individual's well-being, with current literature showing that loneliness increases the risk for low self-esteem (Vanhalst et al., 2013) and depression (Cacioppo et al., 2006; Heinrich & Gullone, 2006). Additionally, a wider range of health outcomes can be affected in later life, for example, poorer physical health, hypertension in old age (Momtaz et al., 2012), and impaired cognitive performance (Cacioppo et al., 2015). Understanding the impacts of loneliness, as well as its potential causes, is therefore an important area of research for social scientists.

Loneliness refers to a discrepancy between an individual's preferred and actual social relations (Peplau, 1982). Cacioppo et al. (2009) proposed that this discrepancy can lead to the negative experience of feeling alone or cause an individual to feel socially isolated even when among friends or family. This implies that loneliness does not directly correspond to being alone, nor does being physically alone lead to feeling lonely. Rather, it is the fulfillment or unfulfillment of preferred social relations that influences loneliness. Loneliness is therefore different from social isolation, despite the two phenomena sharing similarities and influencing each other. Cacioppo et al. (2015) emphasize that it is not necessarily the physical presence of significant others in one's social environment that diminishes feelings of loneliness. Instead, it is the individual's feelings of connectedness within their social environment that dictates their feelings of loneliness. With the introduction of social media, individuals now have the opportunity to establish and maintain social connections without the need for face-to-face relationships. It is therefore important to investigate how these online connections affect the perception of social relations, and whether this can alter the social discrepancy identified by Peplau (1982). This research reported in this chapter sought to explore the relationship between social media usage (SMU) and loneliness, in an effort to understand the effect of SMU on the individual's feelings and experience of loneliness. The theoretical background underlying the concepts of offline and online loneliness is discussed, along with a review of current literature on the relationship between loneliness and SMU.

Social presence theory (SPT) (Short et al., 1976) provides a framework to understand how communication is perceived by the individual through digital media. Social presence is defined as the "degree of salience of the other person in the interaction and the consequent salience of the interpersonal relationships" (Short et al., 1976, p. 65). SPT helps to explain the degree to which another person is perceived as "real" when involved in any form of mediated conversation. Short et al. (1976) suggested that the communication established through mediation is perceived as "real" to the extent that it is perceived as both immediate and intimate. Gunawardena (1995) applied SPT to the computer-mediated communication (CMC), which had become widely available and accessible in the 1990s and concluded that although computers may be lacking in social cues, they nevertheless provide an interactive and stimulating medium. Gunawardena suggested that this can be extended to a social context depending on whether CMC can provide or create a sense of community during virtual interactions. Social media has the capacity for immediacy, with "instant messaging" and "status updates" being regular characteristics of social media platforms, allowing individuals to share what is happening in their lives with little delay if desired. Intimacy is more subjective and thus would be perceived differently by each individual. Nevertheless, intimacy is an important feature of social connections and is a strong protective factor against loneliness (DiTommaso & Spinner, 1997). SPT therefore presents a sound and relevant theoretical perspective for understanding the impact of social media on loneliness through the perception of the individual.

There is much contention as to whether SMU is correlated with loneliness and if so whether this is a positive or negative correlation. Ye and Lin (2015) suggested that loneliness was positively correlated with a preference for online social interaction. Their self-report survey found that lonely and unhappy students were more likely to be engaged in online social interactions. Similarly, Savci and Aysan (2016) found SMU to be a strong predictor for loneliness, with self-reported loneliness increasing in individuals as SMU increased. An experimental study by Hunt et al. (2018) showed that individuals perceived decreased feelings of loneliness after limiting SMU. Participants were assigned to either limit SMU to a maximum of 10 minutes per day for 3 weeks, or to use social media as usual for 3 weeks, and reported their loneliness before and after this. The results showed that self-reported loneliness was significantly reduced in the limited use group compared to the control group, suggesting that a decrease in SMU can lead to a decrease in feelings of loneliness. Conversely, Pittman (2015) found that increased SMU was associated with lower scores of self-reported loneliness. This was found to be platform-dependent, with a greater reduction in loneliness scores found on Twitter and Instagram, compared to Facebook. Similarly, Pittman and Reich (2016) found that Instagram and other image-based platforms have a stronger effect on reducing loneliness, when compared to other social media platforms such as Facebook or Twitter. However, Deters and Mehl (2013) discovered that Facebook use may reduce feelings of loneliness, with the platform supporting and encouraging feelings of connectedness to friends on a daily basis. This reduction was seen to a greater extent when experimentally inducing an increase in status-updating activity with participants. This is contrary to Pittman and Reich's (2016) findings that this only occurs on image-based platforms. Şar et al. (2012) found that SMU was helpful for decreasing loneliness in the elderly, concluding that internet use has an important place in addressing loneliness in mature individuals. More recent research has also highlighted the benefits of technology-mediated interventions for older adults (Stuart et al., 2022). These findings suggest that social media can create and maintain social connection between users, which may be a contributing factor to the reduction of loneliness. However, the conflicting findings raise the question: Is SMU positively or negatively correlated with loneliness?

On the one hand, social media is replacing normal social relations in favor of those that are online (Halston et al., 2019), and this could prompt an individual to be aware of the social discrepancy due to them not engaging in regular face-to-face contact. By removing face-to-face contact, "real" social connection could disappear due to a potential perceived lack of intimacy from the absence of a real person, as described in SPT (Gunawardena, 1995). A meta-analysis by Masi et al. (2011) found that in order to reduce loneliness, intervention programs were most effective if they included increased opportunities for social contact (e.g., social recreation activities); enhanced social support skills; focused on social skills; and addressed maladaptive social cognition (through cognitive behavioral therapy). With the exception of addressing maladaptive cognition, all other effective interventions for reducing loneliness require face-to-face contact. This therefore supports the notion that SMU is positively correlated with loneliness (Savci & Aysan, 2016; Ye & Lin, 2015), as it detracts from face-to-face social contact. These findings imply that social media in its current form cannot fulfill the "realness" required for intimate contact (Gunawardena, 1995). On the other hand, Cacioppo et al. (2015) stated that loneliness is influenced by feelings of connectedness within a person's social environment. Social media can create a sense of belonging and connection without the need for face-to-face contact. Davis (2012) found that connection, particularly in young people, was experienced at a greater extent through social media, as it allowed individuals to feel connected "round-the-clock." Participants in this study reported that social media was helpful in providing opportunities to extend and broaden one's friendship group. This emphasizes the convenience of social media for creating and maintaining social connections, which could address the discrepancy that it fosters loneliness (Peplau, 1982). These findings suggest that intimacy may be found through the connections made over social media, therefore prompting these connections to be perceived as "real" for young people (Davis, 2012; Gunawardena, 1995). As this contradiction exists in current literature, it is important to consider reasons why this could occur.

Findings from Escobar-Viera et al. (2018) suggest that the way in which an individual participates and interacts with social media can influence their well-being. Using a scale created by Li (2016), participants were asked how much they engage in a number of behaviors on any social media site, and these behaviors were defined as being either passive or active. Passive use involves reading comments and discussions and watching videos and viewing pictures, while active use involves interacting with posts, such as adding likes and other reactions, sharing or commenting on posts, and starting new posts. A factor analysis revealed active and passive items to be distinct and robust variables, with the exception of the item "like/favorite/heart," which loaded equally on both variables. This scale item was therefore deleted from the analysis due to its ambiguity, despite being used in the original scale designed by Li (2016). This is important, as it ensured that the study was only performed using distinct and unique variables. Escobar-Viera et al. (2018) found a positive correlation between passive SMU and symptoms of depression and conversely a negative correlation between active SMU and symptoms of depression. While this study examines symptoms of depression, it remains very important as it provides a potential reason for the contradiction in literature regarding the relationship between loneliness and SMU. Its findings also support those of Deters and Mehl (2013), who found a reduction of loneliness achieved through active engagement on Facebook. Similarly, Burke et al. (2010) found that "directed" (more active) interaction was associated with greater feelings of bonding social capital and lower loneliness, while users who interacted more passively consumed greater levels of content reported less bonding social capital and increased loneliness.

Another reason for the contradiction found in the literature regarding loneliness and social media is proposed in a study performed by Martončik and Lokša (2016). They suggest that the online world is different and distinct to the offline world, contrary to the notion proposed by Miller et al. (2016), who argued that they are one and the same. Morahan-Martin and Schumacher (2003) proposed that the online world provides an opportunity for those who are lonely offline to feel more like themselves, stating that individuals online are more open and friendlier and experience a sense of connectedness that may not be obtained in their face-to-face relationships. This could address the question raised by SPT: How "real" is the online world? Martončik and Lokša (2016) argued that because of the existence of these two "worlds," there also exists two types of loneliness: online loneliness and offline loneliness. The authors state that the online world provides an ideal social space which can satisfy needs of belonging and connection that are not met in the offline world. To study this, they examined the online computer game World of Warcraft, which they describe as providing a rich social environment where new relationships and friendships originate. They also assert that these friendships often transcend into the online world, with individuals commonly becoming "in-person" friends with those who they initially met online. There is a stark similarity between the online gaming world described by Martončik and Lokša (2016) and the way that social media is used. It shows that many normal and personal interactions are slowly transitioning to becoming common in the online platform (Halston et al., 2019). Martončik and Lokša (2016) contacted participants who engaged in World of Warcraft and measured their self-reported loneliness through the UCLA Loneliness Scale (Russell et al., 1978). However, in order to capture loneliness online and offline, participants were administered the scale twice and were instructed to imagine that the questions related to either the real world or the online world. Their results revealed a significant difference between offline and online loneliness, suggesting that there is a distinct difference between the online and offline world and therefore rejecting the notion proposed by Miller et al. (2016). While this study examines online gaming and not social media, the similarities as described by the authors imply that social media and online gaming have comparable characteristics. This is particularly through the connectedness and sense of belonging that both platforms afford to their users. These findings suggest that the online world is "real" and therefore allows for intimate connection as proposed by SPT (Gunawardena, 1995). This study is therefore very important, as it provides a potential second explanation as to why the contradiction in literature between SMU and loneliness exists.

The social distancing restrictions response to reduce the COVID-19 virus presented a unique opportunity to examine these phenomena. The World Health Organisation (2020) announced on March 11, 2020 that they were categorizing COVID-19 as a pandemic. Social restrictions from COVID-19 have already had a significant impact on the well-being of individuals, with reports of loneliness being the most widely reported source of stress in April 2020 in Australia (Australian Bureau of Statistics, 2020). Due to the inability to physically interact with each other, the results of studying these phenomena at this specific time may be skewed as a result of internal validity being compromised by the situational context. This, however, presents a unique occasion to observe the effect of social isolation on both self-reported loneliness and also SMU. There were several articles regarding loneliness and COVID-19 at the time of the research (reviewed below). Further research has been undertaken since then, as the world struggles to deal with the after-effects following the relaxation of social restrictions, and the findings from these are included in the Discussion section.

Banerjee and Rai (2020) suggested that virtual connectedness afforded to us by our society dominated by technology has made us forget what physical proximity in relationships feel like. Similarly, Kushlev et al. (2017) suggested that while smartphone usage allows for problem solving to be performed more efficiently and obstacles to be overcome more easily, it removes the face-to-face aspect of these skills, leaving individuals feeling socially disconnected. They argue that while smartphone usage can actually increase and improve mood, the loss of social connection could potentially outweigh these benefits. This implies that social interaction through technology may decrease feelings of connection, suggesting that these interactions are not defined as "real" by the individual and therefore do not provide intimacy and connection, as shown by SPT (Gunawardena, 1995). However, a longitudinal study performed by Luchetti et al. (2020) examined self-reported loneliness over 3 consecutive months in the United States. Contrary to expectations, they found that loneliness levels did not increase over time, despite an increase in social restrictions over the 3-month period. Instead, participants reported an increase in perceived support from others, with authors suggesting that this is due to an increase in social connectedness that are maintained through means other than face-to-face. These findings are reinforced by a study performed by Ellis et al. (2020), who specifically examined psychological adjustment and stress among adolescents during the COVID-19 period. They found that both time with family and connecting virtually with friends were related to lower levels of loneliness during social restrictions. These findings directly refute those from Kushlev et al. (2017), instead proposing that connectedness through social media can have positive effects on loneliness. This unique time period provides a way to understand and examine SMU and loneliness in a way that was not previously possible. It is therefore important to explore the implications that the COVID-19 period has on the well-being of the individual.

## Research questions and hypotheses

This research examined why the existing research concerning SMU and loneliness shows contradictory results. By collecting quantitative and qualitative data, the study addressed two research questions:

1. What is the relationship between SMU and loneliness, and why does a review of the research reveal contradictory results?

2. How has SMU affected the individual's perception of loneliness during the COVID-19 period of social restrictions?

This study investigated whether SMU is positively or negatively correlated with loneliness. Loneliness was measured using the UCLA Loneliness Scale (Russell et al., 1978). In order to validate the Martončik and Lokša's (2016) study, the present study seeks to examine whether loneliness differs online to that experienced offline. Differences in how an individual uses social media was also examined, utilizing the passive and active SMU scale created by Li (2016). To validate Martončik and Lokša's (2016) study and to examine one possible reason for the discrepancy of the relationship between loneliness and SMU in the current literature, we hypothesized that:

Hypothesis 1: There will be a statistically significant difference between online and offline loneliness.

Furthermore, in an effort to examine the relationship between SMU and loneliness, taking into account the findings of Savci and Aysan (2016) and Hunt et al. (2018), we hypothesized that:

Hypothesis 2: There will be a statistically positive correlation between SMU and loneliness.

Additionally, it was suggested by Escobar-Viera et al. (2018) that the way in which one uses social media can predict the occurrence of depressive symptoms. Using the scale created by Li (2016) and to examine another possible reason for the discrepancy of the relationship between loneliness and SMU in current literature, we hypothesized that:

Hypothesis 3: Passive SMU will be statistically positively associated with loneliness.

Hypothesis 4: Active SMU will be statistically negatively associated with loneliness.

Finally, to examine the effect that SMU had on loneliness during COVID-19 social restrictions, an open-ended question was used to assess the difference in both loneliness experiences and SMU for individuals within that specific time period.

## Method

## Design

A concurrent nested design was employed in the current study to provide both quantitative and qualitative data for the analysis. This method provided a greater depth of information that may not have been yielded with a single method approach (Almalki, 2016). Regression analysis of quantitative data was used to determine the statistical relationship between two predictor variables social media use (SMU) measured in time (hours) and number of times checked and the dependent variable loneliness. Independent variables passive SMU and active SMU were measured by responses to seven questions created by Li (2016), which form two scales. The analysis of qualitative data from an open-ended survey question allowed for the exploration of participant experiences of SMU and loneliness during social restrictions due to COVID-19.

## Participants

157 participants between the ages of 17 and 50 were recruited through an Australian University research participation system (SONA). One participant was excluded due to partial completion of the survey. After data screening, the final sample consisted of 156 participants (30 Male, 125 Female, 1 other) ranging from ages 17 to 50 years ($M = 20.79$, $SD = 4.93$). Participants received course credit after the completion of the survey.

## Materials

All measures outlined in this section were administered to participants through an online survey using the Qualtrics Survey Software.

### Quantitative survey items

Social media use (SMU) was collected through two separate scales. The first was a 10-point self-report scale designed to measure the average number of times the participant checked social media in a day, and the second scale was an eight-point self-report scale designed to measure the average daily SMU in hours. Both of these scales did not discriminate based on which social media was checked or used.

The UCLA Loneliness Scale (Russell et al., 1978) measured self-reported loneliness. This scale includes 20 scale items, scored on a scale of 1 (never) to 4 (often). Sample items include "I lack companionship," "I am no longer close to anyone," and "I feel left out." This scale was administered twice to participants, measuring both online and offline loneliness. The scale displayed good internal consistency (Cronbach's $\alpha = 0.93$ for offline loneliness, and $= 0.95$ for online loneliness).

**Table 10.1** Results from a factor analysis of the passive and active SMU (social media usage) measure.

| Passive and active use item | Factor loading | |
| --- | --- | --- |
| | 1 | 2 |
| Factor 1: Active use | | |
| I post contents on my own social media page | **0.86** | 0.13 |
| I share contents on social media sites with my connections | **0.84** | 0.16 |
| I comment on others' posts on social media sites | **0.75** | 0.20 |
| I "like" or "love" posts on social media sites (clicking the like button) | **0.69** | 0.29 |
| Factor 2: Passive use | | |
| I read user comments/ratings/reviews on social media sites | 0.17 | **0.85** |
| I read online discussions on social media sites | 0.24 | **0.82** |
| I watch videos or pictures posted on social media sites | 0.18 | **0.79** |

*Note.* The extraction method was principle components analysis using varimax rotation. Factor loadings above 0.40 are in bold.

Passive and active SMU was assessed using Li's (2016) three passive and four active social media scale items. Passive items included "read discussions," "read comments/reviews," and "watch videos or view pictures." Active items included "like/favorite/heart," "sharing others' content," "comment on or respond to someone else's comment," and "post your own content." Participants were asked to respond on a seven-point scale ranging from "never" to "constantly/all the time." The passive and active SMU scales displayed adequate internal consistency (Cronbach's $\alpha = 0.80$, and $= 0.82$, respectively). Following the study performed by Escobar-Viera et al. (2018), a factor analysis using principle components analysis was performed to assess the factor structure of Li's (2016) scale. Results from the principal components analysis revealed all seven items matched their original variables and produced a two-factor solution explaining 68% of the total variance. Table 10.1 shows the factor loadings of each scale item. A composite score was created for each variable by taking the average score across each scale item.

### Qualitative survey item

An open-ended question was created to gather information from participants regarding the impact of COVID-19 on their SMU and loneliness. The question was "In what ways (if any) has social media increased/ decreased your loneliness in the period of COVID-19 restrictions?"

## Procedure

Ethics approval was granted by the University Human Research Ethics Committee. Participants were recruited through the University Research Participation System and were given access to the survey through a URL to the Qualtrics Online Survey Site and participants could access the survey through either mobile or computer. The survey took approximately 20 minutes, although no time limit was imposed, and a progression bar was displayed to indicate completion as a percentage. Participants were informed of the study purpose and summary, as well as outlining confidentiality, data storage, and researcher contact details. Data was collected from May 28, 2020 to June 8, 2020, which places the timing of this study just as social restrictions were beginning to be lifted in Australia (ABC, 2020).

After consent was given by participants, they began answering survey questions. Participants were asked three demographic questions, 20 UCLA Loneliness Scale questions, questions about their SMU (time used, number of checks, and passive and active SMU scale), the COVID-19 specific question, and finally another 20 UCLA Loneliness Scale questions. For the first UCLA Loneliness Scale, participants were instructed to answer questions with regard to their "face-to-face, real life (offline) relationships." For the second UCLA Loneliness Scale, participants were instructed to answer question with regard to their "social media, web-based (online) relationships." Participation in the survey was voluntary, and participants were made aware that they would be able to withdraw from the survey at any time with no consequences. Once all survey questions were completed, participants were rewarded with course credit.

## Results

### Quantitative analysis
#### Data screening and descriptive statistics
Data from 156 participants was screened to check the accuracy of the data file and to identify any missing values. No missing data was identified, and there were no univariate or multivariate outliers present in the dataset. Relevant assumptions for a dependent samples $t$-test, a bivariate correlation, and regression analyses were checked and met unless otherwise

stated. Alpha was set at 0.05 for all analyses by convention. Table 10.2 outlines descriptive statistics for each variable, where it can be seen that SMU variables (times accessed and hours) and passive SMU are significantly different from a normal distribution.

## Paired-samples *t*-test

A paired-samples *t*-test was performed to compare participants' loneliness in online and offline (real world) conditions. Significant differences were found for scores of loneliness in online ($M = 41.79$, $SD = 13.20$) and offline ($M = 43.26$, $SD = 11.94$) conditions, $t(155) = 3.53$, $P = .001$. The effect size for this analysis ($d = 0.28$) was found to have a small effect .

## Bivariate correlation

A bivariate correlation was performed to examine the relationship between active SMU, passive SMU, and both online and offline loneliness. The assumption of normality was not met for passive SMU, resulting in the use of nonparametric correlation analyses. Table 10.3 shows the bivariate correlations between each variable. Spearman's rho revealed no statistically significant relationships between loneliness and either passive or active SMU.

**Table 10.2** Descriptive statistics for each variable.

| Variable | n | M | SD | Minimum | Maximum |
|---|---|---|---|---|---|
| Offline loneliness score | 156 | 43.26 | 11.94 | 22 | 74 |
| Online loneliness score | 156 | 41.79 | 13.20 | 20 | 78 |
| Daily average access to social media | 156 | 7.60 | 2.67 | 1 | 10 |
| Daily average time (hours) of SMU | 156 | 4.22 | 1.88 | 1 | 8 |
| Passive SMU | 156 | 4.71 | 1.24 | 1.67 | 7.00 |
| Active SMU | 156 | 3.98 | 1.34 | 1.00 | 7.00 |

*Note.* SMU refers to social media use.

**Table 10.3** Bivariate correlations between loneliness and social media use (SMU) using Spearman's Rho.

| Variable | Passive SMU | Active SMU | Offline loneliness | Online loneliness |
|---|---|---|---|---|
| Passive SMU | – | | | |
| Active SMU | 0.43a | – | | |
| Offline loneliness | 0.09 | −0.08 | – | |
| Online loneliness | 0.04 | −0.19 | 0.91a | – |

[a] $P < .001$.

## Standard multiple regression

Due to the difference found between offline and online loneliness, two standard multiple regressions were performed. After relevant assumptions were met, a multiple regression was performed to examine the combined and individual relationships between offline loneliness as the criterion variable and the two predictor variables of SMU (time in hours) and SMU (number of times checked). Results in the regression displayed that the model of the two predictors did not significantly predict offline loneliness, $R = 0.07$, $R^2 = 0.01$, $R^2_{adjusted} = -0.01$, $F(2, 153) = 0.38$, $P = .686$. Number of times checked ($\beta = -0.01$, $t(153) = -0.15$, $P = .884$) and time hours ($\beta = 0.08$, $t(153) = 0.82$, $P = .414$) did not make significant contributions to the regression equation.

A second multiple regression was performed to examine the combined and individual relationships between online loneliness as the criterion and the same two predictors as shown above. Assumptions of normality of residuals were violated, so results should be interpreted with caution. Results in the regression displayed that the model of the two predictors did not significantly predict online loneliness $R = 0.049$, $R^2 = 0.00$, $R^2_{adjusted} = -0.01$, $F(2, 153) = 0.18$, $P = .832$. Times checked ($\beta = 0.05$, $t(153) = -0.57$, $P = .567$) and time hours ($\beta = -0.04$, $t(153) = -0.45$, $P = .653$) did not make significant contributions to the regression equation.

# Qualitative analysis

Responses were coded by an undergraduate student of a similar age to the majority of participants, who also used social media during the period of COVID-19 restrictions to keep in contact with family and friends. The open-ended question was analyzed using thematic analysis guided by Braun and Clarke's (2006) six phase outline, which followed a nonlinear process. This analysis used a semantic realist approach, which meant that themes were identified by only looking at what participants explicitly stated, and not going beyond what was said or written. Participants were assigned individual numbers (e.g., P1) in order to maintain anonymity.

Data from the analysis of the 156 responses led to the identification of three major themes present in the dataset reflecting how SMU impacted loneliness during COVID-19 social restrictions. These were labeled as "Using social media to maintain communication," "Social media and social comparison," and "Interpersonal connection through social media." The Coding Framework from the Thematic Analysis is presented in Table 10.4.

**Table 10.4** Coding framework for thematic analysis.

| Main theme | Subthemes | Description | Examples of codes |
|---|---|---|---|
| Using social media to maintain | communication | The usual method of | interactionIncrease of free time to communicate with others |
| The use of social media to maintain | communication despite being able to physically be with others | How I usually interact, more free time to chat, messaging/calling not a substitute | |
| Social media and social comparison | - | The effect of social media use on loneliness appeared to be mediated or moderated by social comparison | All in the same boat, missing out, social comparison, me too |
| Interpersonal connection through social media | - | Connection was identified as an important factor among participants. Some were able to experience connection through social media, while others were not | Connected, what it used to be like, miss face-to-face interaction, connection = support |

## Using social media to maintain communication

This theme explores the use of social media as a means to maintain communication despite being unable to physically see others due to COVID-19 social restrictions. Two subthemes were identified: "the usual method of interaction" and "increase of free time to communicate with others."

## The usual method of interaction

It was made evident by some participants that the social restrictions set in place due to COVID-19 did not increase feelings of loneliness, due to the ability to maintain communication as per usual through social media. P54 expressed: "[Loneliness has not increased] since my mates and I talk over social media apps." This is further voiced by P71 who stated: "... to be honest I can still communicate with those close to me." This reveals that social media is a common method of communication with friends and family amongst participants.

Some participants revealed a change in their usual behavior to mediate their feelings of loneliness. P144 stated that they: "Increased [SMU] to mediate loneliness and communicate with friends." This adaptation in order to decrease feelings of loneliness is further expressed by P16: "Due to COVID-19 restrictions, I am feeling significantly alone at home. However, to try and decrease my feelings of loneliness, I use social media to communicate with my friends since we cannot meet up in person." This shows that participants are able to change their usual method of interaction in order to maintain communication and mediate feelings of loneliness.

## Increase of free time to communicate with others

Several participants expressed that an increase in free time meant that they were able to communicate more easily with others. P149 stated: "Social media has decreased my loneliness during COVID-19. I am able to FaceTime and chat with my friends anytime." Furthermore, P126 shared that: "It was also an opportunity to talk to those I had neglected messaging in a while due to high work stress. Thus, the lack of work pressure due to COVID-19 allowed me to find the time to reach out." This emphasizes the positive benefits participants experienced due to an increase in free time, which they took advantage of to communicate with others that they may not be able to talk to regularly. This is exemplified through P153: "I believe that it has actually helped me stay in touch or connected to my peers, work, family members and the world, and without that connection I would have struggled within the pandemic."

## Social media and social comparison

This theme explores how social comparison caused by SMU affected levels of loneliness. Several participants revealed an increase of SMU due to COVID-19 social restrictions, which resulted in undesirable social comparison. P4 stated: "[Loneliness] has decreased by letting me a call a friend but increased because you can still compare your experience with others." This comparison is further seen through the experiences of P5:

*"Seeing people on social media platforms being motivating and productive when I am not further stimulates and increases loneliness and feelings of worthlessness. As other individuals on social media spend time with spouses or partners during this time, lacking that relationship also stimulates feelings of loneliness."*

While the increase of free time led to some individuals being more productive than usual or spending time with their partners, this created a challenge for others when they compared themselves to these individuals. However, some participants expressed that SMU led to a comparison of similar situations between them and their connections. P125 stated social media has: "Decreased loneliness because I don't see others out together without me." This is agreed upon by P31 who conveyed: "I don't feel lonely with everyone being in the same situation." This feeling of everyone being in a similar situation appears to decrease social comparison for some participants. P11 explains that their loneliness has: "Probably decreased as sometimes social media increases loneliness if friends are out and you are at home, whereas now nobody can go out." This further exemplifies that the usual comparative nature of SMU has reduced for some participants during the COVID-19 restrictions.

## Interpersonal connection through social media

Participants expressed differing experiences of connection achieved through social media. For some participants, social media acted as a medium to achieve interpersonal connection, resulting in a decrease in feelings of loneliness. P95 discovered an unexpected benefit to SMU: "It somehow helped decrease my loneliness as social media was my medium to stay connected with friends and family." Some participants found that this time period has helped become more connected to others through social media. P7 expressed:

> "More friends work from home and church services moved online that we use social media to contact with each other much more often than before. I feel I am connected with people even more than before as I studied along almost every day before the pandemic, sometimes I didn't talk with anyone over several days. Therefore, my loneliness is decreased, not only because of the social media, but also people's work pattern."

In contrast, there are many participants who express that real connection cannot be experienced through social media and miss face-to-face interactions. For these people, social restrictions posed a threat to their loneliness. P8 acknowledges: "Increased loneliness because I'm an extrovert who likes being with people and messaging/calling online doesn't do it for me." Interpersonal connection is also viewed as important to P80, who expressed: "I would say that it has increased my loneliness as I am no longer surrounded or active with my friends and hanging out."

There were also several participants who expressed a discrepancy between their expectations of social media and the reality of COVID-19 social restrictions. P64 stated: "I thought it helped me to stay connected but it was actually causing me significant distress and anxiety at the height of the pandemic and this made me feel isolated and alone." P150 echoed this feeling:

> "Though I communicate with my friends online using social media and I 'should' feel less lonely, it just makes me feel more lonely because it isn't the same communicating with someone online vs real life. So all in all, social media has increased my loneliness."

This displays a significant discrepancy between what some participants believe they should feel and what they actually feel, expressing that social media for them is not the same as communicating in real life.

## Discussion

This research aimed to investigate the relationship between SMU and loneliness and to explore the possible reasons as to why there are contradictory findings in previous research. The reasons for this contradiction explored in this study included examining whether there was a difference between online and offline loneliness, and whether passive SMU and active SMU altered self-reported loneliness. Data from this study was collected during the COVID-19 pandemic, with social restrictions in place (ABC, 2020). This study therefore also aimed to explore how SMU affected individual's perception of loneliness during these social restrictions through the collection of qualitative data. The quantitative component of this study revealed a significant difference between online and offline loneliness as predicted in hypothesis one. However, this study did not find any significant relationship between SMU and loneliness, contrary to hypothesis two. Furthermore, hypotheses three and four were not supported, with neither passive nor active SMU being significantly associated with loneliness.

The results display a lack of evidence regarding the relationship between SMU and loneliness, contrary to previous findings on both the positive and negative sides of literature (Pittman, 2015; Ye & Lin, 2015). This could be due to SMU being significantly different from normal due to COVID-19, therefore inviting further investigation on this relationship. While passive and active SMU were unable to explain the discrepancy in the literature, this study appears to validate Martončik and Lokša's (2016) findings, who originally displayed a significant difference between offline and online loneliness in participants of online computer gaming. This therefore reciprocates the original findings of this difference in the realm of SMU and by doing so rejecting the notion by Miller et al. (2016), who suggested that the online and offline world are one and the same. These findings indicate that participants' experience of the online world is real and separate from the offline world, suggesting that intimate connection can be achieved online. This reinforces Gunawardena's (1995) adaptation of SPT, referring to the degree of salience experienced by the individual in mediated conversations.

Despite the current study failing to confirm the direction of the relationship between SMU and loneliness, these findings provide one possible reason as to why there is a contradiction in previously reported findings. A difference between online and offline loneliness regarding SMU implies the need for online loneliness to be measured differently to offline loneliness. The UCLA Loneliness Scale remains the instrument of choice when measuring loneliness (Hartshorne, 1993). However, the results from this study could change the way that loneliness is approached and indicate a change needed in the way that online loneliness is measured exclusively. This is compounded by the fact that the UCLA Loneliness Scale was created prior to the existence of social media. Therefore, further investigation on the difference between online and offline loneliness is warranted, for example, the consideration of a new scale that better measures the characteristics of loneliness experienced online.

It is important to consider the unusual time period in which data was gathered. Banerjee and Rai (2020) and Kushlev et al. (2017) proposed that virtual relationships will decrease "real" feelings of connection as virtual interactions cannot provide intimacy. Instead, the current study suggests that SMU did not have such a negative impact for many participants during COVID-19 social restrictions, which is consistent with recent findings from Luchetti et al. (2020) and Ellis et al. (2020). Furthermore, the results from the online and offline loneliness surveys indicated that our sample displayed less self-reported loneliness than the Australian average in 2018 (Australian Psychological Society, 2018). Reasons as to why this would be the case are unknown. Therefore, further comparative investigation should be performed to examine the implications of these findings.

Results from a thematic analysis revealed that many participants utilize social media to communicate and interact with others, with COVID-19 affording more free time than usual to do so. It also revealed that the experience of social comparison is something that many participants experience when referring to SMU, which for some was exacerbated due to the social restrictions in place. Furthermore, findings from the thematic analysis indicated that SMU reduced loneliness if participants felt that SMU satisfied their desire for connection. These findings offer a unique understanding on the implications for SMU on the individual's well-being and give further context to the quantitative results.

Participant experiences indicate that SMU, for many, was the usual method of interaction and communication. This resulted in a decrease in loneliness. However, for participants who did not usually communicate through social media, it was evident that social media was not equivalent to face-to-face communication and connection. SPT in a computer-based context (Gunawardena, 1995) implies that individuals will perceive mediated conversation as "real" if it is both immediate and intimate. Having established that social media is immediate, the interest for this study's findings falls on whether it is perceived as intimate. Intimacy is an important feature of social connections and a protective factor against loneliness (DiTommaso & Spinner, 1997). Gunawardena (1995) suggested that computer-based interaction lacks social cues. This proposal could now potentially be invalid following the introduction of social media tools which afford greater social interaction, for example, emojis (Daniel & Camp, 2018). However, results from this study imply otherwise, as participants displayed contrasting views on whether SMU helped or hindered their loneliness. Interestingly, P8 alluded to extraversion being a factor as to why SMU did not alleviate feelings of loneliness, suggesting that online messaging or calling is not a substitute for face-to-face interactions, similar to findings from Masi et al. (2011). With similar ideas being echoed by several other participants, these findings suggest that an individual's extraversion could affect whether social media was perceived as intimate or not. This could explain why participants displayed contrasting experiences regarding the effect of SMU on their loneliness during the period of COVID-19 social restrictions. Thus, these results justify further examination on the relationship between loneliness and SMU, with the inclusion of extraversion as a moderator variable.

Furthermore, the qualitative results revealed that some participants experienced social comparison when engaging with SMU. This had subsequent effects on their perception of loneliness. Some participants indicated that feelings of loneliness changed due to social comparison through SMU, which was dependent on who they were comparing to. Responses indicated that upward comparison (Wood, 1989) appeared to result in an increase in loneliness, whereas downward comparison (Wills, 1981) appeared to result in a decrease in loneliness. It is interesting to note that this appears to add to the definition of loneliness proposed by Peplau (1982), who described loneliness as the discrepancy between one's preferred and actual social experience. The present findings suggest that this discrepancy can be influenced by the nature of one's social comparison to those around them. This appears to alter feelings of loneliness within the individual who engages in this comparison. An important characteristic of social media is the user's ability to select what they do and do not see, creating a feedback loop coined as a reinforcing spirals framework (Slater, 2007). This indicates that while users have the ability to change what they see, upward and downward social comparison can occur simultaneously on social media, depending on the user preferences. It is therefore feasible to imagine that in order to decrease loneliness, an individual could simply utilize downward comparison to those that they are connected with who are lonelier than them. Why users would subject themselves to upward comparison when it results in an increase of loneliness is unknown. Vogel et al. (2014) suggested that self-esteem may play a role in this relationship, therefore warranting further examination. It is assumed that the introduction of social media creates more opportunities for social comparison (Davis, 2012; Vanhalst et al., 2013), further highlighting the need, as emphasized above, for investigating online loneliness as an individual construct separate from offline loneliness. These findings also indicate that further investigation is warranted as to whether the relationship between SMU and loneliness is mediated or moderated by social comparison.

## Strengths and limitations

This study used a mixed methods approach, which allowed for a greater contextualization of gathered data within the unique time period. This provided a greater depth of information, which would not have been possible using a single method approach (Almalki, 2016). The use of an open-ended question made further exploration of quantitative data possible and provided further insight into how SMU affects feelings of loneliness. To our knowledge, this is the first study that examines the difference between online and offline loneliness regarding SMU. However, there are several limitations. Previous studies which displayed negative relationships between SMU and loneliness often used single-platform approaches (Deters & Mehl, 2013; Pittman & Reich, 2016; Pittman, 2015), whereas this study did not discriminate between social media platforms, potentially limiting the chance of finding a significant relationship. Furthermore, self-report measures may lead to an incorrect measure of participant experience due to social desirability bias (Van de Mortel, 2008). This is especially experienced when participants are required to estimate their SMU, which could potentially lead to reporting of inflated responses (Kobayashi & Boase, 2012).

Further research needs to understand the role of individual differences in shaping the perceptions and use of social media. The study was conducted within one country and research published since this study was conducted has indicated that there are likely to be cross-cultural differences in individual's responses to using social media during COVID-19. For example, Geirdal et al. (2021) compared people living in Norway, United States, United Kingdom, and Australia to explore associations between demographic, mental health, and psychosocial variables and use of social media. They found that in the four countries, between 50% and 74% of participants showed a high level of emotional distress. The Norwegian population reported significantly better mental health, quality of life and well-being, and lower levels of loneliness compared to the other countries. High and frequent use of social media during COVID-19 was associated with poorer mental and psychosocial health. Further cross-cultural research is needed, especially as countries have varied their regulations regarding relaxing COVID-19 restrictions. Similarly, our study was conducted with young students with a mean age of 21 years and social media is used differently by other age groups and likely to have different impacts. A recent study by Bonsaksen et al. (2021) examined the links between loneliness and social media use for people in different age groups during COVID-19 by employing a cross-sectional online survey. Multiple regression analyses examined associations between social media use and loneliness within separate age groups. Loneliness was higher among younger adults and also for those who used social media the most. While using more types of social media was associated with lower loneliness among the oldest participants, and higher loneliness among the youngest participants. For participants who were in the middle-aged category, using social media more frequently was associated with lower loneliness. Therefore, this study showed that associations between social media use and loneliness varied with age.

Many of the studies were conducted with small samples and over a short time span. Further research is needed to address these shortcomings. This is in line with Orben's (2020) assertion that high quality research is needed to identify potential moderating factors. She highlights that the quality of many of the studies in this area is not strong, for example, small negative correlations are often found, and it is not clear whether these correlations represent clear causal relationships or whether they are driven by other factors. In her review of systematic reviews of technology use, Orben (2020) noted that the direction of the link between digital technology use and well-being is still unclear and she stated, "effects have been found to exist in both directions and there has been little work done to rule out potential confounders" (p. 407). A promising way forward comes from Latikka et al. (2022), who conducted two longitudinal studies to investigate the role of social media use in loneliness and well-being before and during the COVID-19 pandemic in Finland. A regression analysis showed that perceived loneliness did not increase for this sample during the COVID-19 pandemic; in contrast, those more involved in social media groups experienced lower loneliness during the pandemic. The researchers also found that well-being became poorer during the pandemic mostly for lonely individuals. Latikka et al. concluded that perceived loneliness was a risk factor for ongoing negative mental health effects of the pandemic.

## Conclusion and recommendations

This study set out to examine the relationship between SMU and loneliness and also to explain why previous research identified conflicting findings regarding this relationship. While no relationship was found in this study, the results highlighted a difference between offline and online loneliness, suggesting the need for further investigation of online loneliness as an individual construct. These results may have been affected due to the current context of COVID-19 and social restrictions. However, COVID-19 also enabled us to explore how SMU impacted individuals' loneliness during this time period, when for some it was the only method of communication between friends and family. Some of the comments indicated that the relationship between SMU and loneliness may be influenced by personality and social comparison. Further research into the mediating or moderating effect of factors such as individual differences in personality and culture is required to extend our understanding of the relationship between SMU and well-being.

## References

ABC (2020, May 25). *The latest on which coronavirus lockdown restrictions will be eased in each state and territory across Australia this week.* ABC News. Retrieved August 21, 2020, Available from https://www.abc.net.au/news/2020-05-25/coronavirus-restrictions-eased-in-your-state-territory-this-week/12281004.

Almalki, S. (2016). Integrating quantitative and qualitative data in mixed methods research: Challenges and benefits. *Journal of Education and Learning, 5*(3), 288–296. Available from https://doi.org/10.5539/jel.v5n3p288.

Australian Bureau of Statistics (2020, April). *Household impacts of COVID-19 survey,* 29 Apr - 4 May 2020 (Publication No. 4940.0). Retrieved August 21, 2020, Available from https://www.abs.gov.au/ausstats/abs%40.nsf/mediareleasesbyCatalogue/DB259787916733E4CA25855B0003B21C?OpenDocument.

Australian Psychological Society (2018, November). *The Australian Loneliness Report. Australian Psychological Society.* Retrieved March 9, 2021, Available from https://psychweek.org.au/wp/wp-content/uploads/2018/11/Psychology-Week-2018-Australian-Loneliness-Report.pdf.

Banerjee, D., & Rai, M. (2020). Social isolation in Covid-19: The impact of loneliness. *International Journal of Social Psychiatry, 66*(6), 525–527. Available from https://doi.org/10.1177/0020764020922269.

Bonsaksen, T., Ruffolo, M., Leung, J., Price, D., Thygesen, H., Schoultz, M., & Geirdal, A. Ø. (2021). Loneliness and its association with social media use during the COVID-19 outbreak. *Social Media + Society, 7*(3)20563051211033821.

Braun, V., & Clarke, V. (2006). Using thematic analysis in psychology. *Qualitative Research in Psychology, 3*(2), 77–101. Available from https://doi.org/10.1191/1478088706qp063oa.

Burke, M., Marlow, C., & Lento, T. (2010, April). Social network activity and social well-being. In *Proceedings of the SIGCHI Conference on Human Factors in Computing Systems*, 3, 1909–1912. 10.1145/1753326.1753613.

Cacioppo, J. T., Fowler, J. H., & Christakis, N. A. (2009). Alone in the crowd: The structure and spread of loneliness in a large social network. *Journal of Personality and Social Psychology*, 97(6), 977. Available from https://doi.org/10.1037/a0016076.

Cacioppo, J. T., Hughes, M. E., Waite, L. J., Hawkley, L. C., & Thisted, R. A. (2006). Loneliness as a specific risk factor for depressive symptoms: Cross-sectional and longitudinal analyses. *Psychology and Aging*, 21(1), 140. Available from https://doi.org/10.1037/0882-7974.21.1.140.

Cacioppo, S., Grippo, A. J., London, S., Goossens, L., & Cacioppo, J. T. (2015). Loneliness: Clinical import and interventions. *Perspectives on Psychological Science*, 10(2), 238–249. Available from https://doi.org/10.1177/1745691615570616.

Daniel, T. A., & Camp, A. L. (2018). Emojis affect processing fluency on social media. *Psychology of Popular Media Culture*, 9(2). Available from https://doi.org/10.1037/ppm0000219.

Davis, K. (2012). Friendship 2.0: Adolescents' experiences of belonging and self-disclosure online. *Journal of Adolescence*, 35(6), 1527–1536. Available from https://doi.org/10.1016/j.adolescence.2012.02.013.

Deters, F. G., & Mehl, M. R. (2013). Does posting Facebook status updates increase or decrease loneliness? An online social networking experiment. *Social Psychological and Personality Science*, 4(5), 579–586. Available from https://doi.org/10.1177/1948550612469233.

DiTommaso, E., & Spinner, B. (1997). Social and emotional loneliness: A re-examination of Weiss' typology of loneliness. *Personality and Individual Differences*, 22(3), 417–427. Available from https://doi.org/10.1016/S0191-8869(96)00204-8.

Ellis, W. E., Dumas, T. M., & Forbes, L. M. (2020). Physically isolated but socially connected: Psychological adjustment and stress among adolescents during the initial COVID-19 crisis. *Canadian Journal of Behavioural Science*, 52(3), 177. Available from https://doi.org/10.1037/cbs0000215.

Escobar-Viera, C. G., Shensa, A., Bowman, N. D., Sidani, J. E., Knight, J., James, A. E., & Primack, B. A. (2018). Passive and active social media use and depressive symptoms among United States adults. *Cyberpsychology, Behavior, and Social Networking*, 21(7), 437–443. Available from https://doi.org/10.1089/cyber.2017.0668.

European Commission. (2018). *Loneliness – an unequally shared burden in Europe* (Publication No. JRC113146). Retrieved March 9, 2021, Available from https://ec.europa.eu/jrc/sites/jrcsh/files/fairness_pb2018_loneliness_jrc_i1.pdf.

Geirdal, A. Ø., Ruffolo, M., Leung, J., Thygesen, H., Price, D., Bonsaksen, T., & Schoultz, M. (2021). Mental health, quality of life, wellbeing, loneliness and use of social media in a time of social distancing during the COVID-19 outbreak. A cross-country comparative study. *Journal of Mental Health*, 30(2), 148–155. Available from https://www.tandfonline.com/doi/full/10.1080/09638237.2021.1875413.

Gunawardena, C. N. (1995). Social presence theory and implications for interaction and collaborative learning in computer conferences. *International Journal of Educational Telecommunications*, 1(2), 147–166.

Halston, A., Iwamoto, D., Junker, M., & Chun, H. (2019). Social media and loneliness. *International Journal of Psychological Studies*, 11(3), 27. Available from https://doi.org/10.5539/ijps.v11n3p27.

Hartshorne, T. S. (1993). Psychometric properties and confirmatory factor analysis of the UCLA Loneliness Scale. *Journal of Personality Assessment*, 61(1), 182–195. Available from https://doi.org/10.1207/s15327752jpa6101_14.

Heinrich, L. M., & Gullone, E. (2006). The clinical significance of loneliness: A literature review. *Clinical Psychology Review*, *26*(6), 695−718. Available from https://doi.org/10.1016/j.cpr.2006.04.002.

Hunt, M. G., Marx, R., Lipson, C., & Young, J. (2018). No more FOMO: Limiting social media decreases loneliness and depression. *Journal of Social and Clinical Psychology*, *37*(10), 751−768. Available from https://doi.org/10.1521/jscp.2018.37.10.751.

Kemp, S. (2020, January 30). *Digital 2020: 3.8 Billion people use social media*. We Are Social. Retrieved March 9, 2021, Available from https://wearesocial.com/blog/2020/01/digital-2020-3-8-billion-people-use-social-media

Kobayashi, T., & Boase, J. (2012). No such effect? The implications of measurement error in self-report measures of mobile communication use. *Communication Methods and Measures*, *6*(2), 126−143. Available from https://doi.org/10.1080/19312458.2012.679243.

Kushlev, K., Proulx, J. D., & Dunn, E. W. (2017). Digitally connected, socially disconnected: The effects of relying on technology rather than other people. *Computers in Human Behavior*, *76*, 68−74. Available from https://doi.org/10.1016/j.chb.2017.07.001.

Latikka, R., Koivula, A., Oksa, R., Savela, N., & Oksanen, A. (2022). Loneliness and psychological distress before and during the COVID-19 pandemic: Relationships with social media identity bubbles. *Social Science & Medicine*, *293*114674.

Li, Z. (2016). Psychological empowerment on social media: Who are the empowered users? *Public Relations Review*, *42*(1), 49−59. Available from https://doi.org/10.1016/j.pubrev.2015.09.001.

Luchetti, M., Lee, J. H., Aschwanden, D., Sesker, A., Strickhouser, J. E., Terracciano, A., & Sutin, A. R. (2020). The trajectory of loneliness in response to COVID-19. *American Psychologist*, *75*(7), 897. Available from https://doi.org/10.1037/amp0000690.

Martončik, M., & Lokša, J. (2016). Do World of Warcraft (MMORPG) players experience less loneliness and social anxiety in online world (virtual environment) than in real world (offline)? *Computers in Human Behavior*, *56*, 127−134. Available from https://doi.org/10.1016/j.chb.2015.11.035.

Masi, C. M., Chen, H. Y., Hawkley, L. C., & Cacioppo, J. T. (2011). A meta-analysis of interventions to reduce loneliness. *Personality and Social Psychology Review*, *15*(3), 219−266. Available from https://doi.org/10.1177/1088868310377394.

Miller, D., Sinanan, J., Wang, X., McDonald, T., Haynes, N., Costa, E., ... Nicolescu, R. (2016). *How the world changed social media*. London: UCL Press.

Momtaz, Y. A., Hamid, T. A., Yusoff, S., Ibrahim, R., Chai, S. T., Yahaya, N., & Abdullah, S. S. (2012). Loneliness as a risk factor for hypertension in later life. *Journal of Aging and Health*, *24*(4), 696−710. Available from https://doi.org/10.1177/0898264311431305.

Morahan-Martin, J., & Schumacher, P. (2003). Loneliness and social uses of the internet. *Computers in Human Behavior*, *19*(6), 659−671. Available from https://doi.org/10.1016/S0747-5632(03)00040-2.

Orben, A. (2020). Teenagers, screens and social media: A narrative review of reviews and key studies. *Social Psychiatry and Psychiatric Epidemiology*, *55*, 407−414. Available from https://doi.org/10.1007/s00127-019-01825-4.

Peplau, L. A. (1982). *Loneliness: A sourcebook of current theory, research, and therapy* (36). Chichester: John Wiley & Sons Inc.

Pittman, M. (2015). Creating, consuming, and connecting: Examining the relationship between social media engagement and loneliness. *The Journal of Social Media in Society*, *4*(1).

Pittman, M., & Reich, B. (2016). Social media and loneliness: Why an Instagram picture may be worth more than a thousand Twitter words. *Computers in Human Behavior*, *62*, 155−167. Available from https://doi.org/10.1016/j.chb.2016.03.084.

Russell, D., Peplau, L. A., & Ferguson, M. L. (1978). Developing a measure of loneliness. *Journal of Personality Assessment*, *42*(3), 290−294. Available from https://doi.org/ 10.1207/s15327752jpa4203_11.

Şar, A. H., Göktürk, G. Y., Tura, G., & Kazaz, N. (2012). Is the internet use an effective method to cope with elderly loneliness and decrease loneliness symptom? *Procedia-Social and Behavioral Sciences*, *55*, 1053−1059. Available from https://doi.org/10.1016/ j.sbspro.2012.09.597.

Savci, M., & Aysan, F. (2016). Relationship between impulsivity, social media usage and loneliness. *Educational Process: International Journal*, *5*(2), 106−115. Available from https://doi.org/10.12973/edupij.2016.52.2.

Short, J., Williams, E., & Christie, B. (1976). *The social psychology of telecommunications*. Chichester: John Wiley & Sons.

Slater, M. D. (2007). Reinforcing spirals: The mutual influence of media selectivity and media effects and their impact on individual behavior and social identity. *Communication Theory*, *17*(3), 281−303. Available from https://doi.org/10.1111/ j.1468-2885.2007.00296.x.

Stuart, A., Katz, D., Stevenson, C., Gooch, D., Harkin, L., Bennasar, M., ... Nuseibeh, B. (2022). Loneliness in older people and COVID-19: Applying the social identity approach to digital intervention design. *Computers in Human Behavior Reports*100179.

Van de Mortel, T. F. (2008). Faking it: Social desirability response bias in self-report research. *The Australian Journal of Advanced Nursing*, *25*(4), 40.

Vanhalst, J., Luyckx, K., Scholte, R. H., Engels, R. C., & Goossens, L. (2013). Low self-esteem as a risk factor for loneliness in adolescence: Perceived-but not actual-social acceptance as an underlying mechanism. *Journal of Abnormal Child Psychology*, *41*(7), 1067−1081. Available from https://doi.org/10.1007/s10802-013-9751-y.

Vogel, E. A., Rose, J. P., Roberts, L. R., & Eckles, K. (2014). Social comparison, social media, and self-esteem. *Psychology of Popular Media Culture*, *3*(4), 206. Available from https://doi.org/10.1037/ppm0000047.

Wills, T. A. (1981). Downward comparison principles in social psychology. *Psychological Bulletin*, *90*(2), 245. Available from https://doi.org/10.1037/0033-2909.90.2.245.

Wood, J. V. (1989). Theory and research concerning social comparisons of personal attributes. *Psychological Bulletin*, *106*(2), 231. Available from https://doi.org/10.1037/0033-2909.106.2.231.

World Health Organisation (2020, July 31). *Rolling updates on coronavirus disease (COVID-19)*. Retrieved August 21, 2020, Available from https://www.who.int/emergencies/diseases/ novel-coronavirus-2019/events-as-they-happen.

Ye, Y., & Lin, L. (2015). Examining relations between locus of control, loneliness, subjective well-being, and preference for online social interaction. *Psychological Reports*, *116* (1), 164−175. Available from https://doi.org/10.2466/07.09.PR0.116k14w3.

CHAPTER ELEVEN

# Dementia and digital selfhood: social networks and identity construction in the age of social media

**Catherine V. Talbot and Tommy Dunne**
Department of Psychology, Bournemouth University, Bournemouth, United Kingdom

## Contents

Dementia refers to a set of symptoms, produced by a number of different conditions in which there is progressive cognitive decline and functional impairments that impact daily life (McKhann et al., 2011). It is a terminal condition, and depending on the type and stage of dementia, symptoms can include memory loss, confusion, mood changes, hallucinations, language and communication problems, and difficulties with concentration and carrying out familiar tasks. Alzheimer's disease is the most common type of dementia, followed by vascular dementia, mixed dementia, dementia with Lewy bodies, and frontotemporal dementia (Prince et al., 2014). There are an estimated 54 million people living with dementia worldwide, with numbers set to rise to 130 million by 2025 (World Health Organization, 2020). Given the growing number of people being diagnosed with dementia, identifying cost-effective, far-reaching means of support is vital.

*Handbook of Social Media Use Online Relationships, Security, Privacy, and Society, Volume 2*
DOI: https://doi.org/10.1016/B978-0-443-28804-3.00014-4

## Dementia and identity

Until recently, there was debate about the extent to which the self persists or diminishes in people with dementia. People with dementia were previously thought to experience a loss or erosion of self (Cohen & Eisdorfer, 1986) and face a "living death" as the disease progressed (Woods, 1989). However, there is now a general consensus among researchers that the self is preserved to some degree throughout the course of the disease (Caddell & Clare, 2010). While there is evidence for a persistence of self, the diagnosis can have a strong impact on a person's sense of identity, affecting how they are treated by others and how they perceive themselves. For example, people with dementia have reported a reduction in meaningful social roles and diminishing power in social relationships following diagnosis (Ryan et al., 2009), identifying losses or changes in their identities as workers, partners, and parents (Greenwood & Smith, 2016; Griffin et al., 2016; Harris & Keady, 2009; Spreadbury & Kipps, 2019). They have also reported withdrawal from meaningful activities and social relationships, which are important sources of identity, self-worth, and wellbeing (Johannessen and Möller, 2011; Roach & Drummond, 2014). Consistent with this, a diagnosis of dementia has been associated with reduced self-worth and self-esteem (Roach & Drummond, 2014; Spreadbury & Kipps, 2019), as well as enhanced feelings of isolation, uncertainty, and frustration (Beard & Fox, 2008; Langdon et al., 2007).

These shifts in identity can also be accompanied by a "shrinking world" (Duggan et al., 2008). In interviews with people with mild to moderate dementia and their care partners, Duggan et al. (2008) found that people with dementia derive pleasure from being outdoors, but their symptoms limit the spaces in which they feel comfortable. The authors argue that the symptoms of dementia, such as memory loss, confusion, and disorientation, can lead people with dementia to experience a loss of confidence, anxiety, and a fear of getting lost, in turn shrinking their social worlds. According to Duggan et al. (2008), the consequence of this "shrinking world" is an overall decline in independence as certain spaces become inaccessible and traveling to local spaces requires the support of others.

The identities of people with dementia are also affected by the perceptions of others. Unfortunately, dementia continues to be associated with inaccurate stereotypes and those with the diagnosis face stigma. In a systematic review of dementia-related stigma research, Herrmann et al. (2018) found evidence of stigmatized attitudes among healthcare professionals, the general public, and in popular media, which often contained misleading and stigmatizing depictions of dementia. The influential work of Kitwood (1997) highlighted how the label of "dementia" restricts those with a diagnosis to a limited range of social roles through which all future behavior is interpreted. People with dementia are also thought to be vulnerable to "malignant positioning" by healthy others. Sabat (2001) theorized that malignant positioning occurs when others view the person with dementia solely in terms of their deficits—rather than their positive attributes—and fail to encourage their social abilities, thereby leading to depersonalized interactions. According to this theory, people with dementia are positioned as "patients" or "sufferers" by healthy others, which in turn causes them to withdraw from other meaningful social roles (Sabat & Harre, 1992; Sabat et al., 2011). Therefore people with dementia are disadvantaged by not only the disease, but also the actions and attitudes of others.

## Dementia and social media

The increasing number of people being diagnosed with dementia (World Health Organization, 2020) and recent push to diagnose people in the early stages of the disease (Department of Health, 2016) means that there is precedence to find innovative ways to support those with the diagnosis to "live well." For other groups of people, social media has been found to facilitate social connection and identity exploration and development (Talbot et al., 2022; Thomas et al., 2017). This could also be true for people with dementia, providing a valuable way of combatting some of the social challenges posed by the diagnosis. Moreover, older adults are becoming increasingly active on social media, with The PEW Research Centre reporting that social networking among those over the age of 65 increased from 13% in 2009 to 40% in 2018 (Smith & Anderson, 2018). While dementia is not necessarily a disease of old age, the risk of having dementia does increase with age (Baumgart et al., 2015), and it is therefore likely that people with dementia form part of this group of older adults using social media.

While there has been substantial research on the value of social media for carers and family members of people with dementia (Anderson et al., 2017; Danilovich et al., 2018; Gkotsis et al., 2020), relatively little attention has been paid to the use of social media by people with dementia. This may be due to the stereotypes associated with dementia and a general belief that people with dementia lack the willingness or ability to use digital technologies, such as social media. Despite this, emerging research shows that people with dementia are using a range of social media, including online forums (Johnson et al., 2019; Rodriquez, 2013), blogs (Kannaley et al., 2019), Facebook (Craig & Strivens, 2016), and Twitter (Talbot et al., 2020a, 2020b, Talbot et al., 2021). In this chapter, we aim to review and synthesize the scientific evidence on the use of social media by people with dementia.

## Method

For this scoping review, a literature search of PubMed, Web of Science, and Scopus was conducted up until 20th August 2022, using the following terms relating to dementia and social media: TS = ("Dementia" OR "Alzheimer*") AND TS = ("social media" OR "online forum" OR "Blog*"). Studies were included if they focused on people with dementia and their social media usage, and were written in English language. Studies were excluded if the full text was not accessible. Only empirical studies were included in this review (i.e., other literature reviews were not included). No limits were placed on the type or stage of dementia. Citations were transferred into excel and all duplicates removed. During Stage 1 screening, all titles and abstracts were screened for relevance by the first author. Following initial screening, each full paper was read by the first author and screened for relevance. Data were synthesized descriptively to map different aspects of the literature, with the second author (a person living with dementia) providing input on these findings.

In the following section, the second author provides an account of his experience of living with dementia and using social media, which guided our mapping of the evidence base.

## Positionality statement: Tommy's story

My name is Tommy Dunne, and I was diagnosed with early-onset dementia when I had just turned 58. I had never felt fear like it, I thought that my life was over and for all intents and purposes it was. I lost my job and my driving license, and we had to downsize the home that we had spent years getting exactly how we liked. Everything changed for the worst, most of my friends would never come to see me. In fact, some of them even crossed the road if they saw me. I had become invisible. When I was out with my wife, people would ask her "how's Tommy?," even though I was standing next to her. It still hurts that people do this. My world really began to shrink.

It is only when I discovered social media that my life started to improve. I discovered Twitter and found that it was a platform where I could start the healing process. It was beneficial to write down my thoughts and make sense of the senselessness that is dementia. The more I wrote down, the more I felt my confidence come back. I thought to myself "I am not going to let dementia take me without a fight." So, over the next few months I did more and more on Twitter, as it was nice to get my thoughts out without being interrupted. I had started to build up a following, and it was nice to see that my advice was helpful to other people with dementia and family carers. Social media has been a *lifeline* for me, and it has helped prevent social isolation and built up my sense of self-worth. The value of it in the care of people living with dementia should never be underestimated.

Tommy's experience speaks to the vast potential of social media for people with dementia. In the following section, we turn to the research evidence, providing a narrative review of the research evidence on the use of social media by people with dementia.

## Overview of included studies

Our search identified 505 published studies, of which 11 studies were eligible. Eight studies used online data, while the remaining three used interviews. The contextual focus of five studies was Twitter (Bartmess et al., 2022; Talbot et al., 2020a, 2020b; Talbot et al., 2021; Thomas, 2017). The remaining studies were related to online forums (Johnson et al., 2020; Rodriquez, 2013; Seifert et al., 2020) and blogs (Brooks & Savitch, 2022; Kannaley et al., 2019), and one focused on social media more generally (Talbot & Briggs, 2022) (Table 11.1).

**Table 11.1** Overview of included studies.

| Author(s) (years) | Data collection | Focus | Findings |
|---|---|---|---|
| Bartmess et al. (2022) | Online data | Twitter | People with dementia shared their experiences in response to COVID |
| Brooks and Savitch (2022) | Interviews | Blogs | Motivations for blogging were on three levels: the personal (as a journal and "a room of one's own"); community (as solidarity for other people with dementia, and as comfort for families and friends); and society (as an educational and campaigning tool) |
| Johnson et al. (2020) | Online data | Online forum | Forum posts by people with dementia began with a narrative of their own experiences, followed by either: (1) a positive outlook; (2) a statement declaring that they do not know what to do; or (3) a question |
| Kannaley et al. (2019) | Online data | Blogs | Bloggers wrote about the effects of Alzheimer's disease; seeing the positives; feeling out of control; advocacy and empowerment; coping mechanisms and compensatory strategies; and candid descriptions of dementia |
| Rodriquez (2013) | Online data | Online forum | Forum members shared stories, gave advice, offered encouragement, and commiserated about their symptoms in ways that generated a sense of solidarity |
| Seifert et al. (2020) | Online data | Online forum | People with Alzheimer's disease posted relatively rarely when compared with other groups. When they did post, they tended to seek information |
| Talbot and Briggs (2022) | Interviews | Social media (general) | Social media helped people with dementia cope with the stresses of the COVID-19 pandemic, by facilitating social connection, peer support, and advocacy work |
| Talbot et al. (2020a) | Online data | Twitter | Most account holders reported "living with" dementia, considered themselves dementia activists, or were affiliated with dementia organizations |

*(Continued)*

**Table 11.1** (Continued)

| Author(s) (years) | Data collection | Focus | Findings |
|---|---|---|---|
| Talbot et al. (2020b) | Online data | Twitter | Account holders used Twitter for representation, collective action, educating others, challenging stigma, providing support, and sharing lived experience |
| Talbot et al. (2021) | Interviews | Twitter | People with young-onset dementia used Twitter reestablish, redefine, communicate, and preserve their identities |
| Thomas (2017) | Online data | Twitter | Account holders used Twitter to develop and sustain social networks and describe their lived experiences in vivid detail |

## Communicating lived experience: narrative identity

Most studies described how people with dementia use social media to disclose lived experiences (Johnson et al., 2020; Kannaley et al., 2019), with one study finding that people with dementia used Twitter to share their experiences in response to the COVID-19 pandemic (Bartmess et al., 2022). These findings indicate that social media provides people with dementia with a means of constructing narrative—a core component of the self (Baldwin and The Bradford Dementia Group, 2008). In the context of dementia, researchers have theorized that narrative construction allows people with dementia to preserve, update, and define their identity following diagnosis (Hillman et al., 2018; Ryan et al., 2009). These narratives can be beneficial for people with dementia, as it provides them with an increased level of empowerment over the stories they wish to communicate (Ryan et al., 2009; Ryan, 2006). As Baldwin and The Bradford Dementia Group (2008) notes, narrative is an activity that requires both agency and opportunity—activities which people with dementia have traditionally been denied.

The freely accessible platforms of social media appear to provide an equitable pathway to narrative for people with dementia. Preliminary research supports this observation, with Kannaley et al. (2019) finding that people with Alzheimer's disease and related dementias communicated their experiences of living with the disease through blog writing. Bloggers wrote about the effects of dementia on them and their care partner; seeing the positives; feeling out of control; advocacy and empowerment; and coping mechanisms. Similar findings have been reported in research that focuses on Twitter, whereby people with dementia have used tweets to narrate lived experience, providing vivid insights into their condition (Bartmess et al., 2022; Talbot et al., 2020b; Thomas, 2017). These online narratives have been found to be beneficial for people with dementia, providing an activity which is both empowering and therapeutic (Brooks & Savitch, 2022; Talbot et al., 2021) and a means of "finding their voice again" (Thomas, 2017). Therefore, this preliminary research suggests that social media platforms may provide an important outlet for therapeutic self-expression and identity construction among people with dementia.

Social media also provides a space where lived experiences can be archived, which is particularly important for people with dementia, who can experience difficulties with memory. For example, in interviews with bloggers, Brooks and Savitch (2022) found several participants started their blogs partly to keep a record of activities. This is consistent with Thomas' (2017) ethnographic research, in which one person with dementia described first using social media to record their thoughts "before they became lost." Similarly, participants in Talbot et al.'s (2021) interview study posted about their experiences on social media so they could look back at them in future, to stimulate memories and engage in reminiscence. In the context of identity, social media appears to be providing a space where people with dementia can preserve aspects of their self. Since people with dementia are using social media in this way, platforms may be valuable tools for reminiscence work, whereby social media posts could be integrated into therapy to evoke memories and stimulate mental activity.

Social media appears to be providing a vehicle through which the narratives of people with dementia can be communicated and gain visibility. These narratives provide one way of challenging dominant discourses that frequently frame people with dementia as "sufferers" and reinforce harmful stereotypes, by amplifying the voices of those with lived experience and bringing their personal experiences to light (Ryan, 2006). This was highlighted by Thomas (2017), who found social media provides a space to challenge dominant narratives, with one user explaining that they used social media to demonstrate the contributions that people with dementia can still make to society despite their diagnosis. In an analysis of blogs, Kannaley et al. (2019) found people with dementia shared their stories to educate others and combat stereotypes and misconceptions about dementia. By using social media to influence dominant discourses and present dementia in a more positive way, account holders may be able to change how they are positioned by others (Sabat, 2001), thereby repositioning themselves as people who can *live* with the diagnosis and make meaningful contributions to society as active citizens. In turn, this could improve the everyday lives of people with dementia.

## Community membership and combatting the "shrinking world"

For people with other chronic health conditions, social media has provided access to communities of support (Berry et al., 2017; Mo & Coulson, 2008; Perkins et al., 2020). Similar results have been found for people with dementia, with research demonstrating that social media platforms have given rise to online communities of people with dementia (Talbot et al., 2020a, 2020b)—communities which are consistent with Wellman's (2001, p. 228) definition of "networks of interpersonal ties that provide sociability, support, information, a sense of belonging and social identity." These online communities were found to be particularly valuable during the COVID-19 pandemic, providing a means of connecting with peers and accessing support (Talbot & Briggs, 2022).

In research on online forums, Rodriquez (2013) found that people with early-onset Alzheimer's disease used illness narratives to connect with others and construct a sense of community. Specifically, forum members shared stories, gave advice, offered encouragement, and commiserated about their symptoms in ways that generated a sense of solidarity. On Twitter, researchers have found evidence of account holders tweeting messages of support to others with the diagnosis, which was interpreted as engendering a collective sense of identity (Talbot et al., 2020b). In a follow-up interview study, people with dementia reported that engaging with others with dementia on Twitter provided a meaningful way of reestablishing their sense of identity in the aftermath of diagnosis (Talbot et al., 2021). Thus, social media may provide a valuable source of post-diagnostic support for people with dementia, by providing access to others with the diagnosis and instilling a collective sense of identity at a time of perceived loss.

These findings are important, given the recent emphasis on nonmedical interventions that aim to help patients manage long-term conditions (Drinkwater et al., 2019). Advocates of the social identity approach to health (i.e., "the social cure") have identified the processes through which social identities and a sense of belonging are associated with health and wellbeing (Haslam et al., 2018). Social identities are thought to be key to addressing a lack of social group-based belonging (Cacioppo et al., 2015), providing a range of social and psychological resources that can help a person to deal with life's challenges, such as a sense of connection that engenders feelings of trust; a sense of meaning and purpose in life; and social support from other group members to cope with stresses (Haslam et al., 2005). This also appears true for groups of people with dementia on social media, as evidenced by research showing that people with dementia who use social media report a sense of collective identity and increased access to informational and social resources that help them to cope with the diagnosis (Talbot et al., 2021). Therefore, these online communities could be changing the experience of living with dementia, by combatting the loneliness and isolation that frequently accompanies the diagnosis (Spreadbury & Kipps, 2019) and providing opportunities to develop more positive identities with dementia.

Social media also provides unique opportunities for people with dementia to connect with others outside of their direct networks—something that would have been more difficult before the development of social media. For example, in qualitative interviews, people with young-onset dementia reported that Twitter opened "a new world" where they could connect with a range of people such as others with dementia, carers, researchers, clinicians, local NHS trusts, and organizations (Talbot et al., 2021). By facilitating social connections in this way, social media may provide a means of combatting the "shrinking world" effect (Duggan et al., 2008). This effect is not just limited to online spaces, but the offline worlds of people with dementia can also expand because of their online behaviors. For example, Talbot et al. (2021) found that Twitter acted as a "springboard" for meaningful offline activities and interactions, such as attending dementia group meetings, attending conferences, and getting involved in research. This suggests that the social worlds of people with dementia can potentially "expand" through their use of social media.

In this section, we have reviewed the literature on social media usage by people with dementia, highlighting that social media can facilitate social connection, self-expression, and a sense of identity and provide a means of combatting the "shrinking world" that often accompanies dementia. In the following section, we provide a consideration of the tensions and opportunities that may arise from this group's engagement with social media.

## Social media and dementia: tensions and opportunities

Despite the benefits of social media for people with dementia, research suggests that social media is not always an entirely positive experience for these individuals. For example, people with dementia have reported receiving negative comments online (Talbot et al., 2021) and researchers have found evidence of stigmatizing language associated with dementia on social media platforms (Oscar et al., 2017). Moreover, people with dementia have reported having their diagnoses publicly challenged by other account holders—who have been coined "dementia doubters"—due to not presenting in a *typical* manner (Talbot et al., 2021). These negative comments could negatively impact the wellbeing of people with dementia and their sense of identity.

It is unsurprising that people with dementia encounter stigma on social media platforms, given that it is pervasive offline (Herrmann et al., 2018). However, online stigma may be reduced through awareness and exposure to people living with dementia. For instance, the growing visibility of people with dementia online and associated influx of positive narratives may provide one way of combatting this stigma. Dementia organizations and charities could also play a role in reducing online stigma by developing social media campaigns that seek to raise awareness, challenge stereotypes, and educate people about dementia.

Another key issue is that many people with dementia may not have access to social media or possess the digital literacy skills required to use these platforms. This is supported by research showing that older adults have lower access to and usage of digital technologies when compared with younger adults (see Wu et al., 2015). People with mild to moderate dementia have also reported difficulties in knowing how to use digital technologies such as social media (Talbot & Briggs, 2022). To overcome this issue, training sessions and explanatory guides on how to use social media could be developed for people with dementia. However, it is important that any such resources are coproduced with people with dementia to ensure they are effective and meet the needs of those with the diagnosis. Similar training initiatives have been developed for older adults without cognitive impairments. For example, "CyberGuardians" is a citizen-centered cybersecurity initiative that aims to support older adults in becoming knowledgeable about cybersecurity practices and sharing best practices with their peers (Nicholson et al., 2021). A similar program could be coproduced with people with dementia, focusing on how to use social media safely and effectively. This may serve to promote the digital literacy and inclusion of people with dementia. In turn, this may improve their lived experiences by enhancing wellbeing, combating loneliness and isolation, and improving self-worth.

Another challenge concerns the symptoms and progressive nature of dementia, whereby symptoms can make it difficult to use social media and only those in the early stages of the disease may be represented on these platforms. For example, people with dementia have reported that creating social media posts requires considerable concentration and they have found the "pace" of some social media platforms difficult (Talbot et al., 2021). Similarly, in an online ethnography, Thomas (2017) found that after observing one account for some time, it became clear another person had taken over the account and was tweeting on behalf of the person with dementia, when the language suddenly changed to the third person. While there will come a time in the disease process when people with dementia are not able to use social media, it is important that they are supported in using it for as long as they want to, particularly as it appears to enhance social connectedness and provide important outlets for self-expression (Craig & Strivens, 2016; Talbot et al., 2021).

One way in which the digital inclusion of people with dementia can be promoted is through the design of social media platforms. In recent years, there has been growing pressure for offline spaces to be inclusive of people with dementia (Alzheimer's Society, 2013), and this should also apply to online spaces. However, human—computer interaction (HCI) research has traditionally focused on protecting or monitoring people with dementia (Astell, 2006; Kerssens et al., 2015), and technologies have typically been designed to be used by family members or carers, rather than the person with dementia (Joddrell & Astell, 2016; Smith & Mountain, 2012). This tendency within HCI research reflects traditional understandings of dementia that view them solely in terms of their deficits, rather than human beings who experience the world (Davis, 2004;

Gilmour & Brannelly, 2010). Despite this, there has been a recent movement within HCI research that champions the agency of people with dementia and takes a broader view that considers context, embodiment, sensorial experiences, and emotion (Lazar et al., 2017; Madjaroff & Mentis, 2017; Dixon & Lazar, 2020).

This is not to say that people with dementia are incapable of using social media, as research shows this is clearly not the case (Craig & Strivens, 2016; Thomas, 2017). Instead, social media has been designed in a "hyper-cognitive society," which places emphasis on cognitive abilities and a persistent bias against those with cognitive disabilities (Post, 2000). Therefore the current designs of social media may not be accessible for people with dementia and inadvertently contribute to their social inclusion. To overcome this issue, the designers and developers of social media could consider working with people with dementia to embed their voices throughout the design process and improve the accessibility of these platforms.

## Conclusion

In conclusion, there are active communities of people with dementia on social media. Social media appears to be valuable for these groups because it facilitates social connection, self-expression, and a sense of identity and provides a way of combatting the shrinking world that frequently accompanies dementia. However, there are some challenges, particularly concerning online stigma and issues with digital literacy and inclusion. In future, researchers could coproduce social media training for people with dementia and identify ways in which social media could be more accessible for this group.

## References

Alzheimer's Society (2013). *Building a dementia friendly community: A priority for everyone.* Retrieved from http://www.actonalz.org/sites/default/files/documents/Dementia_friendly_communities_full_report.pdf.

Anderson, J. G., Hundt, E., Dean, M., Keim-Malpass, J., & Lopez, R. P. (2017). "The church of online support": Examining the use of blogs among family caregivers of persons with dementia. *Journal of Family Nursing, 23*(1), 34–54. Available from https://doi.org/10.1177/1074840716681289.

Astell, A. J. (2006). Technology and personhood in dementia care. *Quality in Ageing: Policy, Practice and Research, 7*(1), 15–25. Available from https://doi.org/10.1108/14717794200600004.

Baldwin, C.The Bradford Dementia Group. (2008). Narrative(,) citizenship and dementia: The personal and the political. *Journal of Aging Studies, 22*(3), 222–228. Available from https://doi.org/10.1016/j.jaging.2007.04.002.

Bartmess, M., Talbot, C., O'Dwyer, S. T., Lopez, R. P., Rose, K. M., & Anderson, J. G. (2022). Using Twitter to understand perspectives and experiences of dementia and caregiving at the beginning of the COVID-19 pandemic. *Dementia, 21*(5), 1734–1752. Available from https://doi.org/10.1177/14713012221096982.

Baumgart, M., Snyder, H. M., Carrillo, M. C., Fazio, S., Kim, H., & Johns, H. (2015). Summary of the evidence on modifiable risk factors for cognitive decline and dementia: A population-based perspective. *Alzheimer's & Dementia, 11*(6), 718–726. Available from https://doi.org/10.1016/j.jalz.2015.05.016.

Beard, R. L., & Fox, P. J. (2008). Resisting social disenfranchisement: Negotiating collective identities and everyday life with memory loss. *Social Science & Medicine, 66*(7), 1509–1520. Available from https://doi.org/10.1016/j.socscimed.2007.12.024.

Berry, N., Lobban, F., Belousov, M., Emsley, R., Nenadic, G., & Bucci, S. (2017). WhyWeTweetMH: Understanding why people use Twitter to discuss mental health problems. *Journal of Medical Internet Research, 19*(4), e107. Available from https://doi.org/10.2196/jmir.6173.

Brooks, J., & Savitch, N. (2022). Blogging with dementia: Writing about lived experience of dementia in the public domain. *Dementia (Basel, Switzerland), 21*(8), 2402–2417. Available from https://doi.org/10.1177/14713012221112384.

Cacioppo, S., Grippo, A. J., London, S., Goossens, L., & Cacioppo, J. T. (2015). Loneliness: Clinical import and interventions. *Perspectives on Psychological Science, 10*(2), 238–249. Available from https://doi.org/10.1177/1745691615570616.

Caddell, L. S., & Clare, L. (2010). The impact of dementia on self and identity: A systematic review. *Clinical Psychology Review, 30*(1), 113–126. Available from https://doi.org/10.1016/j.cpr.2009.10.003.

Cohen, D., & Eisdorfer, C. (1986). *Alzheimer's disease: The loss of self.* New York, NY: W.W. Norton and Co.

Craig, D., & Strivens, E. (2016). Facing the times: A young onset dementia support group: Facebook™ style. *Australasian Journal on Ageing, 35*(1), 48–53. Available from https://doi.org/10.1111/ajag.12264.

Danilovich, M. K., Tsay, J., Al-Bahrani, R., Choudhary, A., & Agrawal, A. (2018). # Alzheimer's and dementia. *Topics in Geriatric Rehabilitation, 34*(1), 48–53. Available from https://doi.org/10.1097/TGR.0000000000000173.

Davis, D. H. (2004). Dementia: Sociological and philosophical constructions. *Social Science & Medicine, 58*(2), 369–378. Available from https://doi.org/10.1016/S0277-9536(03)00202-8.

Department of Health. (2016). *Prime Minister's challenge on dementia.* Retrieved from https://assets.publishing.service.gov.uk/government/uploads/system/uploads/attachment_data/file/414344/pm-dementia2020.pdf.

Dixon, E., & Lazar, A. (2020). Approach matters: Linking practitioner approaches to technology design for people with dementia. *Chi '20: Proceedings of the 2020 CHI Conference on Human Factors in Computing Systems. 1–15.* https://doi.org/10.1145/3313831.3376432.

Drinkwater, C., Wildman, J., & Moffatt, S. (2019). Social prescribing. *BMJ (Clinical Research ed.), 364.* Available from https://doi.org/10.1136/bmj.l1285.

Duggan, S., Blackman, T., Martyr, A., & Van Schaik, P. (2008). The impact of early dementia on outdoor life: A 'shrinking world'? *Dementia (Basel, Switzerland), 7*(2), 191–204. Available from https://doi.org/10.1177/1471301208090911.

Gilmour, J. A., & Brannelly, T. (2010). Representations of people with dementia – subaltern, person, citizen. *Nursing Inquiry, 17*(3), 240–247. Available from https://doi.org/10.1111/j.1440-1800.2009.00475.x.

Gkotsis, G., Mueller, C., Dobson, R. J., Hubbard, T. J., & Dutta, R. (2020). Mining social media data to study the consequences of dementia diagnosis on caregivers and relatives. *Dementia and Geriatric Cognitive Disorders*, *49*(3), 295−302. Available from https://doi.org/10.1159/000509123.

Greenwood, N., & Smith, R. (2016). The experiences of people with young-onset dementia: A meta-ethnographic review of the qualitative literature. *Maturitas*, *92*, 102−109. Available from https://doi.org/10.1016/j.maturitas.2016.07.019.

Griffin, J., Oyebode, J. R., & Allen, J. (2016). Living with a diagnosis of behavioural-variant frontotemporal dementia: The person's experience. *Dementia*, *15*(6), 1622−1642. Available from https://doi.org/10.1177/1471301214568164.

Harris, P. B., & Keady, J. (2009). Selfhood in younger onset dementia: Transitions and testimonies. *Aging & Mental Health*, *13*(3), 437−444. Available from https://doi.org/10.1080/13607860802534609.

Haslam, C., Jetten, J., Cruwys, T., Dingle, G. A., & Haslam, S. A. (2018). *The new psychology of health: Unlocking the social cure*. Routledge.

Haslam, S. A., O'Brien, A., Jetten, J., Vormedal, K., & Penna, S. (2005). Taking the strain: Social identity, social support, and the experience of stress. *British Journal of Social Psychology*, *44*(3). Available from https://doi.org/10.1348/014466605X37468.

Herrmann, L. K., Welter, E., Leverenz, J., Lerner, A. J., Udelson, N., Kanetsky, C., & Sajatovic, M. (2018). A systematic review of dementia-related stigma research: Can we move the stigma dial. *The American Journal of Geriatric Psychiatry*, *26*(3), 316−331. Available from https://doi.org/10.1016/j.jagp.2017.09.006.

Hillman, A., Jones, I.R., Quinn, C., M. Nelis, S., & Clare, L. (2018). Dualities of dementia illness narratives and their role in a narrative economy. *Sociology of Health & Illness*, *40*(5), 874−891. https://doi.org/10.1111/1467-9566.12729.

Joddrell, P., & Astell, A. J. (2016). Studies involving people with dementia and touchscreen technology: A literature review. *JMIR Rehabilitation and Assistive Technologies*, *3*(2), e10. Available from https://doi.org/10.2196/rehab.5788.

Johannessen, A., & Möller, A. (2011). Experiences of persons with early-onset dementia in everyday life: A qualitative study. *Dementia (Basel, Switzerland)*, *12*(4), 410−424. Available from https://doi.org/10.1177/1471301211430647.

Johnson, J., Black, R.W., Chen, Y., & Hayes, G.R. (2019). Older adults with dementia in an online forum: A preliminary analysis. *CSCW '19: Conference Companion Publication of the 2019 on Computer Supported Cooperative Work and Computing*, 231−235. https://doi.org/10.1145/3311957.3359477.

Johnson, J., Black, R.W., & Hayes, G.R. (2020). Roles in the discussion: An analysis of social support in an online forum for people with dementia. *Proceedings of the ACM on Human-Computer Interaction*, *4*(CSCW2), 1−30. https://doi.org/10.1145/3415198.

Kannaley, K., Mehta, S., Yelton, B., & Friedman, D. B. (2019). Thematic analysis of blog narratives written by people with Alzheimer's disease and other dementias and care partners. *Dementia (Basel, Switzerland)*, *18*(7-8), 3071−3090. Available from https://doi.org/10.1177/1471301218768162.

Kerssens, C., Kumar, R., Adams, A. E., Knott, C. C., Matalenas, L., Sanford, J. A., & Rogers, W. A. (2015). Personalized technology to support older adults with and without cognitive impairment living at home. *American Journal of Alzheimer's Disease & Other Dementias*, *30*(1), 85−97. Available from https://doi.org/10.1177/1533317514568338.

Kitwood, T. (1997). *Dementia reconsidered: The person comes first*. Milton: Open University Press.

Langdon, S. A., Eagle, A., & Warner, J. (2007). Making sense of dementia in the social world: A qualitative study. *Social Science & Medicine*, *64*(4), 989−1000. Available from https://doi.org/10.1016/j.socscimed.2006.10.029.

Lazar, A., Edasis, C., & Piper, A.M. (2017). A critical lens on dementia and design in HCI. *CHI '17: Proceedings of the 2017 CHI Conference on Human Factors in Computing Systems*, 2175–2188. https://doi.org/10.1145/3025453.3025522.

Madjaroff, G., & Mentis, H. (2017). Narratives of older adults with mild cognitive impairment and their caregivers. In *Proceedings of the 19th International ACM SIGACCESS Conference on Computers and Accessibility* (pp. 140–149). https://doi.org/10.1145/3132525.3132554.

McKhann, G. M., Knopman, D. S., Chertkow, H., Hyman, B. T., Jack, C. R., Jr, Kawas, C. H., & Mohs, R. C. (2011). The diagnosis of dementia due to Alzheimer's disease: Recommendations from the National Institute on Aging-Alzheimer's Association workgroups on diagnostic guidelines for Alzheimer's disease. *Alzheimer's & Dementia*, 7(3), 263–269. Available from https://doi.org/10.1016/j.jalz.2011.03.005.

Mo, P. K., & Coulson, N. S. (2008). Exploring the communication of social support within virtual communities: A content analysis of messages posted to an online HIV/AIDS support group. *Cyberpsychology & Behavior*, 11(3), 371–374. Available from https://doi.org/10.1089/cpb.2007.0118.

Nicholson, J., Morrison, B., Dixon, M., Holt, J., Coventry, L., & McGlasson, J. (2021). Training and embedding cybersecurity guardians in older communities, May*CHI '21: Proceedings of the 2021 CHI Conference on Human Factors in Computing Systems*, 86, 1–15. Available from https://doi.org/10.1145/3411764.3445078.

Oscar, N., Fox, P. A., Croucher, R., Wernick, R., Keune, J., & Hooker, K. (2017). Machine learning, sentiment analysis, and tweets: An examination of Alzheimer's disease stigma on Twitter. *Journals of Gerontology, Series B: Psychological Sciences & Social Sciences*, 72(5), 742–751. Available from https://doi.org/10.1093/geronb/gbx014.

Perkins, V., Coulson, N. S., & Davies, E. B. (2020). Using online support communities for Tourette Syndrome and Tic Disorders: Online survey of users' experiences. *Journal of Medical Internet Research*, 22(11), e18099. Available from https://doi.org/10.2196/18099.

Post, S. G. (2000). The concept of Alzheimer disease in a hypercognitive society. In J. C. Ballenger (Ed.), *Concepts of Alzheimer's disease: Biological, clinical and cultural perspectives*. Baltimore: The John Hopkins University Press.

Prince, M., Knapp, M., Guerchet, M., McCone, P., Prina, M., Comas-Herrera, A., Wittenberg, R., Adelaja, B., Hu, B., King, D., Rehill, A., Salimkumar, D. (2014). *Dementia UK second edition — overview*. Retrieved from http://eprints.lse.ac.uk/59437/1/Dementia_UK_Second_edition_-_Overview.pdf.

Roach, P., & Drummond, N. (2014). 'It's nice to have something to do': Early-onset dementia and maintaining purposeful activity. *Journal of Psychiatric and Mental Health Nursing*, 21(10), 889–895. Available from https://doi.org/10.1111/jpm.12154.

Rodriquez, J. (2013). Narrating dementia: Self and community in an online forum. *Qualitative Health Research*, 23(9), 1215–1227. Available from https://doi.org/10.1177/1049732313501725.

Ryan, E. B. (2006). Finding a new voice: Writing through health adversity. *Journal of Language and Social Psychology*, 25, 423–436. Available from https://doi.org/10.1177/0261927X06292768.

Ryan, E. B., Bannister, K. A., & Anas, A. P. (2009). The dementia narrative: Writing to reclaim social identity. *Journal of Aging Studies*, 23(3), 145–157. Available from https://doi.org/10.1016/j.jaging.2007.12.018.

Sabat, S. R. (2001). *The experience of Alzheimer's disease — Life through a tangled veil*. Oxford: Blackwell.

Sabat, S., & Harre, R. (1992). The construction and deconstruction of self in Alzheimer's disease. *Ageing and Society*, 12, 443–461. Available from https://doi.org/10.1017/S0144686X00005262.

Sabat, S. R., Johnson, A., Swarbrick, C., & Keady, J. (2011). The 'demented other 'or simply 'a person'? Extending the philosophical discourse of Naue and Kroll through the situated self. *Nursing Philosophy*, *12*(4), 282–292. Available from https://doi.org/10.1111/j.1466-769X.2011.00485.x.

Seifert, L. S., Kaelber, K., Flaherty, K., & Bowman, T. J. (2020). Experiences in Alzheimer's disease: What do stakeholders post on the internet? *Cyberpsychology Journal of Psychosocial Research on Cyberspace*, *14*(3). Available from https://doi.org/10.5817/CP2020-3-7.

Smith, A., & Anderson, M. (2018). *Social media use in 2018*. Pew Research Center. Retrieved from http://www.pewinternet.org/2018/03/01/socialmedia-use-in-2018/.

Smith, S. K., & Mountain, G. A. (2012). New forms of information and communication technology (ICT) and the potential to facilitate social and leisure activity for people living with dementia. *International Journal of Computers in Healthcare*, *1*(4), 332–345. Available from https://doi.org/10.1504/IJCIH.2012.051810.

Spreadbury, J. H., & Kipps, C. (2019). Measuring younger onset dementia: What the qualitative literature reveals about the 'lived experience' for patients and caregivers. *Dementia (Basel, Switzerland)*, *18*(2), 579–598. Available from https://doi.org/10.1177/1471301216684401.

Talbot, C. V., & Briggs, P. (2022). The use of digital technologies by people with mild-to-moderate dementia during the COVID-19 pandemic: A positive technology perspective. *Dementia (Basel, Switzerland)*, *21*(4), 1363–1380. Available from https://doi.org/10.1177/14713012221079477.

Talbot, C. V., O'Dwyer, S. T., Clare, L., & Heaton, J. (2021). The use of Twitter by people with young-onset dementia: A qualitative analysis of narratives and identity formation in the age of social media. *Dementia (Basel, Switzerland)*, *20*(7), 2542–2557. Available from https://doi.org/10.1177/14713012211002410.

Talbot, C., O'Dwyer, S., Clare, L., Heaton, J., & Anderson, J. (2020a). Identifying people with dementia on Twitter. *Dementia (Basel, Switzerland)*, *19*(4), 965–974. Available from https://doi.org/10.1177/1471301218792122.

Talbot, C. V., O'Dwyer, S., Clare, L., Heaton, J., & Anderson, J. (2020b). How people with dementia use Twitter: A qualitative analysis. *Computers in Human Behavior*, *102*, 112–119. Available from https://doi.org/10.1016/j.chb.2019.08.005.

Talbot, C. V., Talbot, A., Roe, D. J., & Briggs, P. (2022). The management of LGBTQ + identities on social media: A student perspective. *New Media & Society*, *24*(8), 1729–1750. Available from https://doi.org/10.1177/1461444820981009.

Thomas, B. (2017). Whose story is it anyway?: Following everyday accounts of living with dementia on social media. *Style*, *51*(3), 357–373. Available from https://doi.org/10.5325/style.51.3.0357.

Thomas, L., Briggs, P., Hart, A., & Kerrigan, F. (2017). Understanding social media and identity work in young people transitioning to university. *Computers in Human Behavior*, *76*, 541–553. Available from https://doi.org/10.1016/j.chb.2017.08.021.

Wellman, B. (2001). Physical place and cyberplace: The rise of personalized networking. *International Journal of Urban Regional Research*, *25*, 227–252. Available from https://doi.org/10.1111/1468-2427.00309.

Woods, R. T. (1989). *Alzheimer's disease: Coping with a living death*. London: Souvenir Press.

World Health Organization (2020). *Dementia*. Retrieved from https://www.who.int/news-room/fact-sheets/detail/dementia#:~:text = Worldwide%2C%20around%2050%20million%20people.dependency%20among%20older%20people%20worldwide.

Wu, Y.-H., Damnee, S., Kerherve, H., Ware, C., & Rigaud, A.-S. (2015). Bridging the digital divide in older adults: A study from an initiative to inform older adults about new technologies. *Clinical Interventions in Aging*, *10*, 193–201. Available from https://doi.org/10.2147/CIA.S72399.

CHAPTER TWELVE

# Why am I getting uncomfortable with others' life experiences? Neglected side effects of sharing through social media

## Inyoung Shin
Department of Computer Science, Yale University, New Haven, CT, United States

## Contents

## Introduction

Since the advent of social media, researchers have related the use of social media to deleterious mental health outcomes, such as stress,

*Handbook of Social Media Use Online Relationships, Security, Privacy, and Society, Volume 2*
DOI: https://doi.org/10.1016/B978-0-443-28804-3.00005-3

cognitive overload, and low self-esteem (Bevan et al., 2014; Chen & Lee, 2013; Kross et al., 2013). The underlying assumption of this line of research is that being tethered to mediated communication reduces the quantity and quality of social interactions; such deprivation increases psychological distress. However, a growing body of empirical research has shown that social media supplement communication with various social ties in person and online (Rainie & Wellman, 2012) and expand the paths for people to accrue social support (Lu & Hampton, 2017) and social capital (Ellison et al., 2007). Social media contribute to making one's personal networks stable and persistent (Hampton, 2016). In that sense, negative consequences of social media use may not result from low quality and quantity of interactions with others. With that in mind, why do many pundits blame social media use for increased anxiety, depression, and other emotional problems? Why do many people feel bad after using social media? This chapter argues that the psychological discomfort people feel while using social media is associated with social stress—stress stemming from social relationships (Turner et al., 1995).

One of the dominant activities on social media is sharing life experience (Choi & Toma, 2014). In other words, people continuously receive information about others' life experience by merely logging into social media and looking at their newsfeed. Such awareness can be paradoxical to one's well-being. By looking at the lives of others, people can perceive available resources and information embedded in their interpersonal environments (Coleman, 1988; Lin, 2002). They also indirectly learn how to handle their own lives by reflecting on the events experienced by others (Bandura & Walters, 1977). However, recognition of the needs and struggles of others often exerts a pressure to provide appropriate supports and tangible aids (Shumaker & Brownell, 1984). Even if one is not involved as a supporter, affective reactions, such as empathy, guilt, anger, or jealousy, can occur (Mittelmark, 1999).

This study is concerned with negative effects of social media on one's psychological well-being. There is no doubt that social media use entails positive effects, as well as negative ones, on one's well-being (Weinstein, 1989). However, compared to the positive effects of social media, the mechanisms of which have been well addressed in the literature, the reasons behind negative effects of social media remain unclear (Hampton, 2019). Focusing on the constant flows of information about life experience through social media, this study attempts to explain how and why Facebook users experience negative emotions while using the platform.

Drawing upon in-depth interviews with 25 Facebook users, this study identifies four specific types of psychological discomfort associated with disclosure of life events through Facebook: *sense of vulnerability, cost of caring, upward social comparison,* and *norm violations.* These negativities varied depending on the topics of life events and one's relationships with the people who experienced these events. These findings suggest implications about how to incorporate a wide range of research and claims regarding social media use and mental health.

## Background

### Life events and social sharing

The disclosure of life events is one of the most prevalent activities on social media (Saha et al., 2021). Life events generally include "normative transitions in life (e.g., first job and marriage), meaningful changes (e.g., birth of a child and moving in with a partner), and major individual experiences (e.g., death of a family member and unemployment)" (Specht et al., 2011, p. 863). Sharing life events is not a new phenomenon created by social media. People often shared their experiences of life events to satisfy their social and psychological needs, but their sharing was limited to a closed social circle composed of family or close friends (Kessler et al., 1985). Social media has increased the scope and speed of sharing life experience. Diverse social ties organized from different contexts such as home, schools, and other associations are integrated into one social media platform, resulting in what A. E. Marwick and Boyd (2010) called "context collapse." Further, the "broadcastability" of social media (Boyd et al., 2010) allow people to disclose their experience across social circles.

Due to higher visibility of disclosure through social media, some research suggests that people tend to showcase only their positive images and experiences (Bazarova & Choi, 2014; Utz, 2015). Indeed, desirable life events are more commonly shared than undesirable events on social media (Saha et al., 2021). Nevertheless, some social media users share undesirable personal experiences such as suffering from depression (Bazarova et al., 2017) and serious illnesses like cancer (Gage-Bouchard et al., 2018), the loss of a loved one (Marwick & Ellison, 2012), and relationship breakups (Haimson et al., 2018) to express negative emotions caused by those events. Such social sharing through social media also allows individual users to create "informed social networks" that potentially provide support to cope with the difficulties (Hartzler et al., 2011, p. 559). In general, people tend to pay more attention to and process bad news more thoroughly than good news (Baumeister et al., 2001). Thus, although not as frequent, Facebook posts revealing undesirable life events can be more salient and memorable. In addition, most social media platforms offer group chats or private messaging systems like Facebook Messenger, which may facilitate sharing life events that people are hesitant to do publicly (Choi & Toma, 2014).

## Network life events, social stress, and social media

From another perspective, the disclosure of life experience helps people become aware of what is happening in others' lives. Kessler et al. (1985) specifically define life events happening to others within one's personal network as "network life events." Communication is a key process for one's awareness of network life events. Such awareness of others is a foundational component of making and maintaining connections within personal networks. It represents a decrease of uncertainty about other people, playing a key role in initiating, maintaining, and enhancing intimacy with them (Berger, 1979). Despite its important social implication, awareness of life events in the lives of others remains an unstudied area, most likely because people were previously able to have subtle levels of awareness focusing on some members of certain social circles such as family and close friends. However, with the advancement of social media, awareness of network life events has evolved from subtle to pervasive (Hampton, 2016).

Pervasive awareness of network life events can have both positive and negative consequences to individual well-being. In general, positive experiences such as personal achievement and marriage induce positive emotions. The people around those who experience desirable life events tend to partake in joy with them (Cialdini et al., 1976) and become relieved from the pressure to provide appropriate supports (Kalra et al., 2008). On the other hand, those with pervasive awareness of undesirable life events may recognize more demands from their extensive networks, thus feeling burdened and spending actual resources such as time and money (Shumaker & Brownell, 1984). Even though they are not involved in the life events of others, the awareness itself can cause negative emotional reactions, such as feelings of loss of control, guilt, and jealousy (Mittelmark, 1999).

Multiple mental health outcomes of using social media, whether positive or negative, have been addressed in the existing literature, but many of them ignore the role of social influence in one's mental health (Hampton, 2019). In this context, this study argues that negative outcomes of social media are byproducts of pervasive awareness of network life events. To make this argument clear, this work first reviews relevant theories and research implying negative effects of awareness of network life events. Although their analytic focuses were not on social media, they provide many implications to discuss how people's self-disclosures through social media become sources of distress to those with whom they are connected.

## Emotion contagion

Individuals who experience undesirable life events often express their negative emotions caused by the events. Other people around these individuals consciously or unconsciously mimic such negative emotions (Hatfield et al., 1994). This suggests that people's emotional well-being can be affected by the presence of someone in negative mood. Recently, Kramer et al. (2014) found that emotion can be contagious through social media posts. It is possible that people feel distressed upon reading about the troubles and misfortunes of others through Facebook.

## Risk perception

Those who experience traumatic life events reveal a higher sense of risk and mistrust toward their social environment (Janoff-Bulman, 1989), but the real possibility of experiencing traumatic life events is extremely low. People are often exposed to such tragedy through mass media or social networks. Although not originally developed as a theory for risk perception, cultivation theory suggests that viewing television news of crime and violence leads people to overestimate the actual rate of crime and the possibility of being victimized (Gerbner & Gross, 1976). However, critics of cultivation theory argue that television has a relatively limited impact compared with personal experiences (Gross & Aday, 2006). Awareness of undesirable network life events, which are more relevant to one's real-life situations, may be more influential to people's risk perception than viewing TV news and stories. Many people share their misfortune on social media (Haimson et al., 2021). The awareness of such events may trigger feelings of vulnerability.

## Cost of caring

When aware of someone in need, individuals are often involved as supporters of that person. However, providing social support can be burdening. The provider actually needs to spend real time and money to help their network members (Shumaker & Brownell, 1984). The distressing impacts of providing social support are referred to as the "cost of caring" in the mental health literature (Kessler et al., 1985). It has been suggested that women are more likely to suffer from the cost of caring than men because of their caring positions in networks. Social media are now making others' life experiences more visible and salient across personal networks, which may intensify the cost of caring for both women and men (Hampton et al., 2016).

## Social comparison

According to Festinger (1954)'s original theory of social comparison, people typically make comparisons with those who are similar to them to obtain precise evaluation of themselves. However, there always exists those who are better off than oneself. Whether intended or not, upward social comparison—comparing oneself to those who are better off—can happen (Collins, 1996). Those who engage in upward comparison often feel miserable or deprived. As discussed, a growing body of research has argued that technological affordances of social media encourage people to broadcast positive experiences (Utz, 2015). As such, social media use can trigger jealousy and envy as a result of upward social comparison (Jang et al., 2016; Lin & Utz, 2015).

Altogether, awareness of network life events can put various psychological and social strains on individuals, depending on what life events are happening and to whom. Awareness of life events can lead people to recognize social pressures exerted by their personal networks. Some argue that self-disclosure through social media is of a different nature than face-to-face disclosure (see Ruppel et al., 2016 for details). In fact, technological affordances create unique norms and rules for social sharing (McLaughlin & Vitak, 2012). Social media users can see these norms and rules as new social strains. However, people disclose their experiences through social media for the same reasons that they do in person: to express their emotions, to present themselves, to recruit relevant resources and support, and to maintain relationships with others (Bazarova & Choi, 2014). The introduction of social media may complicate matters, but it does not fundamentally change the process through which awareness of network life events becomes a source of psychological discomfort.

Most empirical findings regarding the deleterious effects of social media are based on quantitative surveys or experiments (Fox & Moreland, 2015). Although they provide empirical evidence to support the actual occurrences of negative consequences of social media use, some questions still remain: how and why do people feel bad after using social media? As noted by Lindlof and Taylor (2017), a researcher can directly observe and inquire about these questions using a qualitative approach. To gain deeper insights into users' experiences, this study asked the following research questions and conducted in-depth interviews with 25 Facebook users to answer them.

RQ1: In what ways do social media contribute to people's awareness of network life events?

RQ2: What kinds of psychological discomfort do social media users feel when becoming aware of network life events through social media?

## Methods

To answer the proposed research questions, this study draws on empirical cases from 25 Facebook users who use Facebook as part of their daily lives. Facebook is the most popular social media platform and is used by approximately 70%−80% of adult Americans (Gramlich, 2019), making it the most salient source for network life events among social media platforms. Through in-depth interviews, this work was able to collect stories from each participant reflecting the process through which they were aware of network life events as well as their reactions to those events.

## Recruitment procedure

Interview participants were recruited using Amazon MTurk between June and September 2017. MTurk was selected as the sampling pool because it provides access to diverse populations of American internet users (Berinsky et al., 2012). Prior to the interviews, prospective participants took an online screening survey including questionnaires regarding basic demographics, frequency of Facebook use, awareness of network life events, and personal experience of life events. To ask about their recent awareness of network life events and personal experience of life events, the traditional approach of using a checklist (Turner & Wheaton, 1995) was adopted; prospective participants were shown a list of 25 life events and asked to indicate whether themselves, their family, their friends, and/ or their acquaintances had experienced any of the listed events within the past six months (see Table 12.1 for details).

Upon review of the responses from the completed screening survey, eligible participants were identified for interviews. Participants were selected based on maximum variation sampling strategy (Lindlof & Taylor, 2017) focused on age and gender, known to be the main sociodemographic factors affecting people's awareness of network life events (Turner et al., 1995).

## Semistructured in-depth interviews

All participants were interviewed one on one by phone or online video at a mutually agreed-upon time. Table 12.2 presents the list of 25 participants with their demographic characteristics. All pseudonyms were randomly chosen from among the most common names in the United States.

Interview questions were semistructured based on reviews of the responses on the screening survey. Participants were specifically asked about network life events that they indicated in the screening survey. For example, if a participant indicated knowing someone who experienced a listed event in the online survey, they were asked how they learned about and reacted to this event. Depending on participants' responses, prestructured questions were occasionally modified. All interviews were audio-recorded and later transcribed verbatim. The transcripts were imported into Nvivo 12.0, for analysis.

## Analysis of interviews

To analyze the interview data, a thematic analysis was used based on a combination of inductive and deductive approaches. Each network

**Table 12.1** Number of network life events and personal experiences reported by participants.

| Desirability | List of major life events |
|---|---|
| Undesirable | Argument with spouse |
| | Financial trouble |
| | Credit difficulties |
| | Broken romantic relationships or divorce |
| | Serious illness, injury, and hospitalization |
| | Loss of loved ones |
| | Loss of pet |
| | Damage or loss of property |
| | Mental illness |
| | Out of work over 1 month |
| | Serious argument with neighbors |
| | Trouble with boss or coworkers |
| | Trouble with in-laws |
| | Married without parental approval |
| | Unwanted pregnancy[a] |
| | Violating the law |
| Desirable | Engagement |
| | Financial improvement |
| | Having a child |
| | Marriage |
| | Movement to a better neighborhood |
| | New job |
| | Wanted pregnancy |
| | Religious changes[a] |
| | Retirement |
| | Start a significant relationship |
| | Personal achievement or success at work |

[a]These network life events were not included in the screening survey, but participants additionally reported them during interviews.

life event reported by participants was considered as one thematic unit. 25 participants provided their experiences related to 49 major life events happening to themselves and 214 network life events experienced by their network members (see Table 12.1). However, Facebook use was not involved in all thematic units. To narrow down the boundary of analysis, only 122 thematic units, all of which involved the use of Facebook, were employed. For the initial phase, open coding was done across the thematic units. Types of life events (e.g., desirable, undesirable, traumatic, and shocking); the relationship with the person who experienced the

**Table 12.2** List of interview participants.

| Participants | Age | Gender | Race | Location | Monthly visits on Facebook |
|---|---|---|---|---|---|
| James | 28 | Male | Hispanic | Texas | Several times a day |
| Emily | 39 | Female | White | Kansas | Several times a day |
| Hannah | 41 | Female | White | Arizona | Several times a day |
| Samantha | 56 | Female | White | North Carolina | Several times a day |
| John | 42 | Male | White | South Carolina | Once a day |
| Sarah | 57 | Female | White | New York | Once a day |
| Grace | 33 | Female | White | Washington | Several times a day |
| Robert | 41 | Male | White | North Carolina | Less often |
| Michael | 25 | Male | White | Michigan | Several times a day |
| Anna | 42 | Female | White | Ohio | Several times a day |
| William | 25 | Male | White | Texas | Several times a day |
| Ashely | 28 | Male | Asian | New Jersey | Several times a day |
| David | 32 | Male | White | California | Several times a day |
| Lauren | 26 | Female | White | California | Once a day |
| Lisa | 33 | Female | White | Pennsylvania | Several times a day |
| Julia | 34 | Female | Black | Virginia | 3–5 days a week |
| Kaitlyn | 45 | Female | White | Illinois | Once a day |
| Rachel | 29 | Female | White | Nebraska | Several times a day |
| Richard | 39 | Male | Asian | California | Several times a day |
| Daniel | 42 | Male | White | New Jersey | Several times a day |
| Paul | 43 | Male | White | New York | Several times a day |
| Mark | 38 | Male | Mixed | Michigan | Several times a day |
| Brian | 31 | Male | Native American | Pennsylvania | Several times a day |
| Jennifer | 52 | Female | White | Hawaii | Several times a day |
| Matthew | 25 | Male | White | Michigan | 3–5 days a week |

events (immediate family, extended relatives, best friends, coworkers, etc.); ways of using Facebook (visiting personal pages, looking at the News Feed, sending and/or receiving private messages, etc.); and feelings, attitudes, and reactions toward network life events (stressed, upset, embarrassed, etc.) were coded without any limitations. Based on the constant comparison method (Corbin & Strauss, 2008), the initial codes were merged/renamed and later integrated into broader core themes.

## Findings

## How Facebook contributes to awareness of network life events

Almost all participants shared a similar perception of Facebook: it is the easiest way to communicate with a huge audience at one time. Although Ashely, one participant, did not frequently post on Facebook, she did admit that "instead of calling, it's better just to post on Facebook so that everyone will know." In most cases, participants were able to learn about the life events of various social ties by habitually visiting their Facebook News Feed. Facebook provides an aggregated awareness of others and their lives, as reflected by one participant, Richard, who remarked, "Most of my friends are on Facebook, so I just go on Facebook and find out what's going on with other people."

Consistent with previous studies suggesting that there is a bias toward positive self-disclosures on Facebook (Choi & Toma, 2014; Utz, 2015), participants learned about a greater number of desirable network life events through Facebook. However, as Daniel said, "People's lives are much more out in the open than they used to be because of social media." Participants did occasionally encounter information about undesirable life events through Facebook News Feed. Richard also added, "Now you see more and more people sharing things about the negative things in their lives."

Consistent with what media multiplexity theory (Haythornthwaite, 2005) predicts, among family and close friends (i.e., strong ties), Facebook was not the only communication channel for awareness. Participants often saw Facebook posts regarding life events happening to family members, but most of them acquired the same information in advance through other private communication modes such as phone calls and texting. For example, Jennifer saw a Facebook post about her niece's engagement on her News Feed, but she was already made aware of this news from a text message received in advance. She did not think that post was especially tailored for her. "It was just kind of an easy way to tell everybody besides family." On the other hand, participants learned about acquaintances, also known as weak ties, while browsing Facebook News Feed. As Richard explained, "If social media didn't exist, then we would hear less of acquaintances' news because we wouldn't hear it from phone calls, texts, or things like that."

In addition to connecting through Facebook News Feed, some participants actively used Facebook Messenger to exchange their life experiences. Facebook Messenger was likely used in a similar way as mobile texting—participants used it to convey their major life events to their family and close friends. However, one participant, Hannah, shared a unique experience associated with Facebook Messenger. She had recently received Facebook messages from an unexpected person: her ex-husband's wife, who wanted to ask advice about her marriage with Hannah's ex-husband. Hannah said, "Her contacting me is just weird in the first place, because we are not friends on Facebook."

Overall, analysis of in-depth interviews with 25 Facebook users shows how Facebook contributes to developing people's pervasive awareness of network life events more than other communication channels. Facebook News Feed and Messenger enable people to become aware of the life events of social ties, especially weak ties. If not for Facebook, there would be no way to be aware of the life events happening to acquaintances. However, Hannah added, regarding Facebook messages from her ex-husband's wife, "It is not something that I look for, but she keeps on messaging me." Her remarks implicate the negative aspects of extensive connections: increased probability of encountering unfavored others and/or information.

## Negativities of awareness of network life events through Facebook

In general, participants expressed sympathy when realizing someone's misfortune, whereas they reported positive emotions, such as vicarious joy and comfort, toward desirable events of others. These findings were consistent with the studies on emotional contagion through Facebook (Kramer et al., 2014). Table 12.3 presents details of the participants' reactions to network life events.

However, most reactions toward network life events were simple, like "I feel bad for them" or "I am happy for them." Participants shared memorable stories when specific network life events happened to certain people. I categorized these reactions into four different themes. Some of them are deeply related to people's usage practices of Facebook rather

**Table 12.3** Key themes on reactions to network life events.

| Area | Common theme; description | Subcategories |
|---|---|---|
| Negative reactions | Cost of caring | Helping is emotionally draining |
| | | Helping is burdening |
| | | Hard to see someone having difficulties |
| | Sense of vulnerability | Life is out of control |
| | | Life is meaningless |
| | | Life is insecure |
| | Dirty laundry | Embarrassed by private issues |
| | | Judging others' posting activities |
| | | Overloaded by private information |
| | | Entertained by seeing private stuff |
| | Upward social comparison | Feel jealousy and envy |
| | | Life is not fair to me |
| | Media selection among family | Facebook is not an appropriate way to communicate about family events |
| | General sympathy: displaying general negative reactions to negative NLE[a] | |
| No impact | Indifference[a] | I am used to being exposed to undesirable NLE |
| | | I am not close to the person who experienced NLE |
| Positive reactions | Navigation[a] | NLE teaches how to handle my situation |
| | General positive emotions: displaying general positive reactions to positive NLE[a] | |

NLE, Network life event.
[a]These themes were not reported in this chapter, as they did not align with the overall research goal.

than awareness of network life events itself. The details of the findings are as follows:

## Sense of vulnerability

The first negative aspect of Facebook use was related to an awareness of traumatic network life events, such as a sudden death of a loved one or a serious illness. The uncontrollable and unpredictable nature of such events lead people to think "it could happen to anyone" and, in turn, see themselves and others as weak and vulnerable. For example, while browsing her Facebook News Feed, Sarah found that one of her friends was diagnosed with breast cancer. Even though she was not directly involved with her friend's situation, she said that "it was scary in general." She described her concern as follows: "When you learn that someone you know has cancer, it goes through your mind that, 'it could happen to anyone, me or someone I know, someone I love.'" David shared his similar experience when he learned of the unexpected death of his aunt's husband while browsing his Facebook News Feed:

It's a very shocking story because he never drank, smoked, or did anything unhealthy from what I know. So, it just makes me think, why? ... Even if you think you have control, you don't have control (David, 32, California).

The negative influence of awareness of traumatic network life events would be stronger if the victims of such events were closer to an individual (Gross & Aday, 2006). However, Jennifer reported the feeling of vulnerability after reading a Facebook post made by one of her elderly acquaintances, Carol, who had recently lost her husband. Jennifer did not personally contact Carol afterward because they were not "close enough to call." Nevertheless, Jennifer described her feelings as follows:

I worry a lot if I get a late-night phone call kind of thing. I think, "Oh, something happened to my dad," stuff like that (Jennifer, 33, Pennsylvania).

As discussed, Facebook provided an awareness of network life events for an extensive range of social ties. The finding about a sense of vulnerability indicates that Facebook exposes people to information about traumatic life events happening within their personal networks, leading them to realize possible risks that exist in their own lives.

## Cost of caring

Another negative aspect of Facebook use was associated with the cost of caring (Kessler et al., 1985), demonstrating social strains derived from the provision of social support. When participants became aware of undesirable life events happening to their family and close friends, they were often involved as supporters who provided appropriate aid, whether they wanted to or not. However, the provision of social support was not always pleasurable. Many participants directly or indirectly referred to how helping their network members was challenging.

Participants first described that they paid an emotional toll by simply listening to someone's problem. One participant, Michael, recently received Facebook messages from a close friend, who wanted to vent his frustrations after having an argument with neighbors. However, from Michael's perspective, listening itself was emotionally draining. Knowing his friend's distress influenced his mood as well: "...Talking to him, it just sucks. Pardon my language, but I really felt annoyed for him about the whole situation."

Another participant, Julia, mentioned that she often felt emotional stress while using Facebook because she kept being informed about others' troubles: "I'm okay to learn about their lives and events as long as I don't have a lot going on in my life, but if I have too much going on in my life, I can't handle their life." She reduced the frequency of visiting Facebook because "I'm not comfortable seeing some stuff on Facebook. I don't really like that."

The emotional cost of caring also occurred when participants perceived their limitations as supporters, triggering negative emotions such as helplessness, guilt, and frustration. Kaitlyn's comment below describes how distressing it was to be an incompetent supporter:

Recently, her [my friend's] 3-month-old died. I first found out this news through Facebook. I tried to reach out and call her often but it's really hard because I don't know what to say and how to help her. (...) So, it's been very stressful, and I'm not sure what my role as a friend is (Kaitlyn, 45, Illinois).

If family were going through undesirable events, strains associated with cost of caring became more intensified. Family often demanded actual material goods and financial aid as well as emotional support. In those cases, Facebook was a secondary source of life event awareness. Family members usually contacted participants multiple times using a variety of technologies. For example, Rachel's sister had financial problems. Rachel learned this because "it's been an accumulation of times she's told me that she's struggling, on the phone, texts, Facebook message, or in person." She was annoyed by her sister but said, "I have to help her, because she's my family."

Almost all cases related to the cost of caring stemmed from helping strong ties who experienced undesirable life events. Facebook was somehow involved in those cases, but it is difficult to argue that the cost of caring is created or intensified by disclosure through Facebook. Although Facebook may have been the first place where participants learned about their family's or friends' difficulties, it was unlikely to serve as the primary communication channel between them. Even if Facebook did not exist, participants would be able to be aware of network life events, resulting in a cost of caring.

## Upward social comparison

In addition to undesirable and traumatic network life events, desirable network life events can cause unpleasant emotions, such as envy and jealousy, as described in upward social comparison (Collins, 1996). However, not all participants reported such severe discomfort. Only a couple of participants expressed strong negative feelings toward a certain desirable network life event because they also "really desired" to experience the same event. For instance, Emily recently heard the news that her cousin had a child. She said, "To be honest, I was a little bit jealous because my husband and I, we've struggled to have a child, and this is her fourth kid and she got pregnant even on birth control."

Another participant, Kaitlyn, was currently supporting her family because her husband had recently closed his business. Her former coworker, who had recently retired, kept posting pictures to Facebook of trips she went on, inducing jealousy in Kaitlyn. "I'd love to do that stuff, so it's really depressing to think I have to work in my 60 s." In addition, Kaitlyn showed a similar reaction when receiving mobile texts from a friend about her husband's job offer:

I bet her husband got a job that paid $250,000 a year. I kind of wish my husband was bringing in a lot of money too. (...) I think my husband works harder than anybody and has nothing to show for it. So, it's really disheartening. Positive people feel, "If you work hard, you'll get ahead." However, that's not how it's been for us (Kaitlyn, 45, Illinois).

Kaitlyn's stories show that personal situations are a main cause of feeling jealousy and envy. Although Facebook makes it easier to become aware of others' positive life events, people suffer from jealousy when they are longing for the same events.

## Negative experiences resulting from norm and expectancy violations

Although sharing one's life experience with others is one of people's basic social needs, people do not indiscriminately disclose their personal experiences. Depending on the nature of groups and the relational dynamic with others, people have different norms and expectations toward sharing life experience and regulate their disclosure accordingly (Burgoon, 1993).

Disclosure through Facebook is not an exception. Combined with the technological affordance of Facebook, there are unique norms and expectations in terms of sharing life events through Facebook (McLaughlin & Vitak, 2012). Some negative experiences participants reported were related to observing violations of such norms and expectations. Two different themes emerged in terms of norm and expectancy violation, as explained below.

### Exposure to dirty laundry

Many participants described Facebook News Feed as a place where "announceable" content should be shared. In that sense, they considered sharing negative and personal disclosures through Facebook—that is, personal problems or disputes—as an inappropriate behavior. One participant described such disclosure of negative and private life events using the metaphor of *dirty laundry*.

There's an old saying: "Don't air your dirty laundry in public." I'm surprised that so many people are completely okay with putting things like that out there [on Facebook]. I think some things should just be kept private and handled definitely outside a public arena (Grace, 33, Washington).

When people were exposed to posts reflecting dirty laundry, they felt embarrassed and irritated. For example, Richard had a "casual acquaintance" who frequently posted about her work on Facebook. These posts often made him uncomfortable because they violated the norms associated with dirty laundry. "I feel like it's her way of venting and just letting her thoughts and feelings out, but as a reader, it's a little too much for me because sometimes you don't need to share how you feel about certain people and especially about work."

Annoyance caused by a single exposure to dirty laundry was mild, but Grace's comment below shows that accumulated exposure can lead people to have a negative attitude toward using Facebook and judge other users who actively post to Facebook.

Those posts [reflecting dirty laundry] that I see on Facebook make me sick and there's been a couple of times where friends have posted... I can't see that. It shows an absolute lack of maturity.

### Media selection among family

As explored, family and close friends can gain an awareness of life events through a wide range of communication technologies, including phone calls and Facebook. However, if participants heard news about strong ties, especially family, merely through their Facebook News Feed, they expressed strong disappointment and felt hurt and ignored. For example, Anna learned of her stepson's engagement only through her Facebook News Feed; neither she nor her husband received any private contact from her son. "We kind of felt that we deserved an actual phone call before something like that was posted in public, but we were disappointed that we were not considered important enough to receive a phone call beforehand." Anna saw her son's way of informing them as a sign of disrespect, because he violated the norm of media selection among family members. Anna's episode suggests individuals tend to view traditional interpersonal channels (i.e., phone calls or face-to-face conversations) as signs of relational commitment. If their family shared their major life events through Facebook updates, people would feel that they are treated with less consideration, as Anna did.

## Discussion

The purpose of this study was to unravel the reasons why people experience emotional discomfort while using social media. Although a large body of research on this topic has been conducted, a rich analysis of social media users' experiences was lacking (Fox & Moreland, 2015). In this context, this study focused on the disclosure of life events, one of the dominant activities on social media, and posited that Facebook use makes people uncomfortable because it exposes users to unfavorable others and information. Drawing upon in-depth interviews with Facebook users, this study found that using Facebook—especially by habitually browsing the News Feed—leads people to become aware of life events in the lives of all types of social ties. Such heightened awareness often accompanies negative emotional experiences associated with a sense of vulnerability, the cost of caring, upward social comparison, and/or norm violation, depending on which life events are happening and to whom. These findings indicate that social media can perpetuate or intensify relational pressures and norms by making people informed about their social networks.

The findings of this study can be discussed in the light of several theoretical concepts and frameworks. First, the findings related to a sense of vulnerability contribute to risk communication research by demonstrating the role of network information in the formation of one's risk-related perceptions. Inspired by cultivation theory suggesting the relationship between television viewing and fear of victimization, the focus of risk communication research has been on the effects of TV viewing or exposure to mass-produced campaign messages (So, 2012). However, as Gross and Aday (2006) put it, "People's levels of fear should be based more on the reality of where they live than what they see on television" (p. 412). This study's findings suggest that tragic life events happening within personal networks can influence people's risk perceptions, and social media play a key role in distributing such network information. However, these findings do not suggest that social media have uniformly powerful effects. Unlike television, which consistently depicts the social world as a mean and risky place (Gerbner & Gross, 1976), social media spread news about triumphs happening within social networks as well as tragedies. Although not described in detail, this study also found that desirable network life events conveyed through Facebook provide vicarious joy and comfort to individuals. Future research focusing on the comparison between the effects of desirable and undesirable information would provide a better understanding of the role of social media in one's risk perception.

Second, the findings about "dirty laundry" extend expectation violation theory (Burgoon, 1993) into the social media context. In this study, participants share a similar rule for disclosure through Facebook: Facebook status updates should deal with key personal information, such as marriage, the birth of a child, and the loss of loved ones. Those who encounter Facebook posts violating such norms (e.g., posts about an argument with a romantic partner or troubles at work) feel annoyed and irritated. Aggregated exposure to dirty laundry can lead people to form a negative attitude toward the use of social media in general. However, it is difficult to conclude that self-disclosure through Facebook is detrimental to one's well-being and social relationships. As other studies have pointed out (Lu & Hampton, 2017; Zhang, 2017), Facebook status updating is one of the most efficient ways to mitigate the effects of stressful life events and recruit needed resources and therefore can be beneficial in those stressful situations. Fox and Moreland (2015) found that Facebook users tend to think their own negative disclosures on Facebook are prompted by external circumstances (e.g., needing information or advice), whereas they blame others' negative disclosures on careless and immature behaviors. Thus, while some people may feel annoyed by the disclosure of negative, private events through Facebook, understanding and avoiding the fundamental attribution error existing in people's judgment of others' Facebook use may preserve the overall social benefits of Facebook usage.

The findings of this study also suggest that strong ties, especially family, have the highest potential to become a source of stress. Participants reported intensive distress when they became aware of and helped their immediate family in need. Combined with constant contact through multiple communication technologies (including Facebook), life events occurring to family members exert more pressure on individuals. Further, people expect their family to strictly follow normative media selection. If individuals heard news about life events of their family only through Facebook, they expressed strong hurt and disappointment. These findings corroborate the idea that family is based on "normative obligation, structural connectedness, and genetic forces" (Wellman & Wortley, 1990, p. 581). It is often thought that social media lure people away from families and destroy family structures. However, the findings imply that the bonds and obligations shared within families are still thriving in the era of social media. Discomfort associated with the cost of caring or norm violation is probably a side effect of strong connectedness among family.

This work reduces concerns that social media causes "new" mental health problems associated with social media use. As social media inflate the joys of others rather than their distress, some scholars argue that social media increase the possibility of experiencing negative emotions such as jealousy and envy (Jang et al., 2016). However, the findings show that people do not always respond negatively to positive events in the lives of others. They feel envy and jealousy only when they become unexpectedly aware of life events that they desire to experience themselves. Even though emotional pain occurs after upward social comparison, these negative emotions likely turn into other positive emotions. As Tesser (1988) pointed out, upward social comparison often evokes one's inspiration to improve. In the long term, upward social comparison becomes a driving force for better quality of life. Another line of research on social media and mental health addresses the issue regarding FOMO, which indicates people's compulsive concerns about missing an opportunity for social integration (Przybylski et al., 2013). Along with this argument, this study found that people habitually browsed their Facebook News Feed to stay updated on others' experiences and remain connected with them. However, at the same time, individuals sometimes felt overloaded with too much information about others. These findings are consistent with the relational dialectical theory (Baxter, 2011), which suggests a tension between one's desire for integration with others and the need for separation from others. Social media users may find it more difficult to keep decent distances from others rather than to miss out on information.

Like other studies, this work has several limitations. First, it utilized in-depth qualitative interviews to gain a granular understanding of conditions in which people feel bad after using Facebook. Indeed, this study was able to gather participants' personal stories revealing negative experiences associated with everyday use of Facebook, which may not be captured by content analysis and quantitative survey methods. Nevertheless, participants in this study did not represent the U.S. population, and thus the findings of this study do not provide a comprehensive understanding of all users' experiences. Future research employing a quantitative approach with a nationally representative sample may supplement the findings of this study. Second, the findings of this study do not provide conclusive evidence suggesting that negative effects outweigh positive ones. The goal of this study was focused on the negative effects of social media use, which could underrate its positive effects. In fact, a few participants did report positive experiences related to network life events and Facebook, but they were beyond the scope of this work and thus were not discussed in detail. Further, this study focused on the short-term awareness of network life events occurring within the previous six months. However, as suggested by cultivation theory, the long-term, cumulative exposure to media messages may change people's beliefs and perceptions of reality beyond emotional states. Future research focusing on the long-term relationship between social media, awareness of network life events, and psychological well-being would offer insightful and conclusive suggestions on the role of social media in mental health.

Despite the limitations, the findings of this study organized and clarified a wide range of mechanisms that explain the negative relationship between social media use and psychological well-being from the perspective of social stress. Altogether, the findings present a challenge to those who directly relate social media use to negative psychological outcomes. Although a heightened awareness of network life events can cause negative side effects, it also provides opportunities to capitalize on potential resources embedded in social networks such as social support (Lu & Hampton, 2017), social capital (Hampton et al., 2011), and access to job-related or professional knowledge (Leonardi, 2015). These social goods may outweigh the negative side effects of disclosing life events on

Facebook. Public discourse should focus on how to develop social skills dealing with social stress rather than restricting social media use.

# References

Bandura, A., & Walters, R. H. (1977). Social learning theory. Englewood cliffs, NJ: Prentice Hall.

Baumeister, R. F., Bratslavsky, E., Finkenauer, C., & Vohs, K. D. (2001). Bad is stronger than good. *Review of General Psychology, 5*(4), 323−370.

Baxter, L. A. (2011). *Voicing relationships*. Thousand Oaks, CA: Sage.

Bazarova, N. N., & Choi, Y. H. (2014). Self-disclosure in social media: Extending the functional approach to disclosure motivations and characteristics on social network sites. *Journal of Communication, 64*(4), 635−657.

Bazarova, N. N., Choi, Y. H., Whitlock, J., Cosley, D., & Sosik, V. (2017). Psychological distress and emotional expression on Facebook. *Cyberpsychology, Behavior, and Social Networking, 20*(3), 157−163.

Berger, C. R. (1979). *Beyond initial interaction: Uncertainty, understanding, and the development of interpersonal relationships. Language and Social Psychology* (pp. 122−144). Oxford, UK: Blackwell.

Berinsky, A. J., Huber, G. A., & Lenz, G. S. (2012). Evaluating online labor markets for experimental research: Amazon.com's mechanical turk. *Political Analysis, 20*(3), 351−368.

Bevan, J. L., Gomez, R., & Sparks, L. (2014). Disclosures about important life events on Facebook: Relationships with stress and quality of life. *Computers in Human Behavior, 39*, 246−253.

Boyd, D., Golder, S., & Lotan, G. (2010). Tweet, tweet, retweet: Conversational aspects of retweeting on twitter. *In 2010 43rd Hawaii international conference on system sciences* (p. 1-1p). IEEE.

Burgoon, J. K. (1993). Interpersonal expectations, expectancy violations, and emotional communication. *Journal of Language and Social Psychology, 12*(1−2), 30−48.

Chen, W., & Lee, K.-H. (2013). Sharing, liking, commenting, and distressed? The pathway between Facebook interaction and psychological distress. *Cyberpsychology, Behavior, and Social Networking, 16*(10), 728−734.

Choi, M., & Toma, C. L. (2014). Social sharing through interpersonal media: Patterns and effects on emotional well-being. *Computers in Human Behavior, 36*, 530−541.

Cialdini, R. B., Borden, R. J., Thorne, A., Walker, M. R., Freeman, S., & Sloan, L. R. (1976). Basking in reflected glory: Three (football) field studies. *Journal of Personality and Social Psychology, 34*(3), 366.

Coleman, J. S. (1988). Social capital in the creation of human capital. *American journal of sociology, 94*, S95−S120.

Collins, R. L. (1996). For better or worse: The impact of upward social comparison on self-evaluations. *Psychological Bulletin, 119*(1), 51.

Corbin, J., & Strauss, A. (2008). *Basics of qualitative research: Techniques and procedures for developing grounded theory* (3rd ed). Sage.

Ellison, N. B., Steinfield, C., & Lampe, C. (2007). The benefits of Facebook "friends": Social capital and college students' use of online social network sites. *Journal of Computer-Mediated Communication, 12*(4), 1143−1168.

Festinger, L. (1954). A theory of social comparison processes. *Human Relations, 7*(2), 117−140.

Fox, J., & Moreland, J. J. (2015). The dark side of social networking sites: An exploration of the relational and psychological stressors associated with Facebook use and affordances. *Computers in Human Behavior, 45*, 168−176.

Gage-Bouchard, E. A., LaValley, S., Warunek, M., Beaupin, L. K., & Mollica, M. (2018). Is cancer information exchanged on social media scientifically accurate? *Journal of cancer Education, 33*(6), 1328–1332.

Gerbner, G., & Gross, L. (1976). Living with television: The violence profile. *Journal of Communication, 26*(2), 172–194.

Gramlich, J. (2019). *10 facts about Americans and Facebook.* Retrieved from https://www.pewresearch.org/fact-tank/2019/05/16/facts-about-americans-and-facebook/.

Gross, K., & Aday, S. (2006). The scary world in your living room and neighborhood: Using local broadcast news, neighborhood crime rates, and personal experience to test agenda setting and cultivation. *Journal of Communication, 53*(3), 411–426.

Haimson, O. L., Andalibi, N., De Choudhury, M., & Hayes, G. R. (2018). Relationship breakup disclosures and media ideologies on Facebook. *New Media & Society, 20*(5), 1931–1952.

Haimson, O. L., Carter, A. J., Corvite, S., Wheeler, B., Wang, L., Liu, T., & Lige, A. (2021). The major life events taxonomy: Social readjustment, social media information sharing, and online network separation during times of life transition. *Journal of the Association for Information Science and Technology, 72*(7), 933–947.

Hampton, K. N. (2016). Persistent and pervasive community: New communication technologies and the future of community. *American Behavioral Scientist, 60*(1), 101–124.

Hampton, K. N. (2019). Social Media and Change in Psychological Distress Over Time: The Role of Social Causation. *Journal of Computer-Mediated Communication, 24*(5), 205–222.

Hampton, K. N., Lee, C. J., & Her, E. J. (2011). How new media afford network diversity: Direct and mediated access to social capital through participation in local social settings. *New Media & Society, 13*(7), 1031–1049.

Hampton, K. N., Lu, W., & Shin, I. (2016). Digital media and stress: Cost of Caring 2.0. *Information, Communication & Society, 19*(9), 1267–1286.

Hartzler, A., Skeels, M. M., Mukai, M., Powell, C., Klasnja, P., & Pratt, W. (2011). *Sharing is caring, but not error free: transparency of granular controls for sharing personal health information in social networks.* Paper presented at the AMIA Annual Symposium Proceedings.

Hatfield, E., Hatfield, C., Cacioppo, J. T., Rapson, R. L., Manstead, A., & Oatley, K. (1994). *Emotional contagion.* Cambridge University Press.

Haythornthwaite, C. (2005). Social networks and internet connectivity effects. *Information, Community & Society, 8*(2), 125–147.

Jang, K., Park, N., & Song, H. (2016). Social comparison on Facebook: Its antecedents and psychological outcomes. *Computers in Human Behavior, 62*, 147–154.

Janoff-Bulman, R. (1989). Assumptive worlds and the stress of traumatic events: Applications of the schema construct. *Social Cognition, 7*(2), 113–136.

Kalra, H., Kamath, P., Trivedi, J. K., & Janca, A. (2008). Caregiver burden in anxiety disorders. *Current Opinion in Psychiatry, 21*(1), 70–73.

Kessler, R. C., McLeod, J. D., & Wethington, E. (1985). *The costs of caring: A perspective on the relationship between sex and psychological distress. Social support: Theory, research and applications* (pp. 491–506). Springer.

Kramer, A. D., Guillory, J. E., & Hancock, J. T. (2014). Experimental evidence of massive-scale emotional contagion through social networks. *Proceedings of the National Academy of Sciences, 111*(24), 8788–8790.

Kross, E., Verduyn, P., Demiralp, E., Park, J., Lee, D. S., Lin, N., & Ybarra, O. (2013). Facebook use predicts declines in subjective well-being in young adults. *PLoS One, 8*(8), e69841.

Leonardi, P. M. (2015). Ambient awareness and knowledge acquisition: Using social media to learn "Who Knows What" and "Who Knows Whom. *MIS Quarterly, 39*(4), 747−762.

Lindlof, T. R., & Taylor, B. C. (2017). *Qualitative communication research methods.* Sage Publications.

Lin, N. (2002). Social capital: A theory of social structure and action. New York: Cambridge university press.

Lin, R., & Utz, S. (2015). The emotional responses of browsing Facebook: Happiness, envy, and the role of tie strength. *Computers in Human Behavior, 52,* 29−38.

Lu, W., & Hampton, K. N. (2017). Beyond the power of networks: Differentiating network structure from social media affordances for perceived social support. *New Media & Society, 19*(6), 861−879.

Marwick, A. E., & boyd, d. (2010). I Tweet honestly, I Tweet passionately: Twitter users, context collapse, and the imagined audience. *New Media & Society, 13*(1), 114−133.

Marwick, A., & Ellison, N. B. (2012). "There isn't Wifi in heaven!" Negotiating visibility on Facebook memorial pages. *Journal of Broadcasting & Electronic Media, 56*(3), 378−400.

McLaughlin, C., & Vitak, J. (2012). Norm evolution and violation on Facebook. *New Media & Society, 14*(2), 299−315.

Mittelmark, M. (1999). *Health promotion at the communitywide level: Lessons from diverse perspectives.* Sage Publications.

Przybylski, A. K., Murayama, K., DeHaan, C. R., & Gladwell, V. (2013). Motivational, emotional, and behavioral correlates of fear of missing out. *Computers in Human Behavior, 29*(4), 1841−1848.

Rainie, L., & Wellman, B. (2012). *Networked: The new social operating system.* Cambridge, MA: MIT Press.

Ruppel, E. K., Gross, C., Stoll, A., Peck, B. S., Allen, M., & Kim, S.-Y. (2016). Reflecting on connecting: Meta-analysis of differences between computer-mediated and face-to-face self-disclosure. *Journal of Computer-Mediated Communication, 22*(1), 18−34.

Saha, K., Seybolt, J., Mattingly, S. M., Aledavood, T., Konjeti, C., Martinez, G. J., & De Choudhury, M. (2021). *What life events are disclosed on social media, how, when, and by whom.* Paper presented at the Proc. CHI.

Shumaker, S. A., & Brownell, A. (1984). Toward a theory of social support: Closing conceptual gaps. *Journal of Social Issues, 40*(4), 11−36.

So, J. (2012). Uses, gratifications, and beyond: Toward a model of motivated media exposure and its effects on risk perception. *Communication Theory, 22*(2), 116−137.

Specht, J., Egloff, B., & Schmukle, S. C. (2011). Stability and change of personality across the life course: The impact of age and major life events on mean-level and rank-order stability of the Big Five. *Journal of Personality and Social Psychology, 101*(4), 862−882.

Tesser, A. (1988). *Toward a self-evaluation maintenance model of social behavior. Advances in experimental social psychology* (Vol. 21, pp. 181−227). Elsevier.

Turner, R. J., & Wheaton, B. (1995). *Checklist measurement of stressful life events. Measuring stress: A guide for health and social scientists* (pp. 29−58). Oxford University Press.

Turner, R. J., Wheaton, B., & Lloyd, D. (1995). The epidemiology of social stress. *American Sociological Review, 60*(1), 104−125.

Utz, S. (2015). The function of self-disclosure on social network sites: Not only intimate, but also positive and entertaining self-disclosures increase the feeling of connection. *Computers in Human Behavior, 45,* 1−10.

Weinstein, N. D. (1989). Optimistic biases about personal risks. *Science, 246*(4935), 1232−1233.

Wellman, B., & Wortley, S. (1990). Different strokes from different folks: Community ties and social support. *American Journal of Sociology, 96*(3), 558–588.

Zhang, R. (2017). The stress-buffering effect of self-disclosure on Facebook: An examination of stressful life events, social support, and mental health among college students. *Computers in Human Behavior, 75,* 527–537.

# CHAPTER THIRTEEN

# Exploring the attitudes of young people toward catfish impersonating and feigning illness on social media

**Jacqui Taylor[1], Andy Pulman[2] and Olivia Tickle[3]**

[1]Faculty of Science and Technology, Bournemouth University, Poole, United Kingdom
[2]Faculty of Health and Social Sciences, Bournemouth University, Bournemouth, BH, United Kingdom
[3]HM Prison & Probation Service, United Kingdom

## Contents

## Introduction

There are many positive benefits of social media, such as enhanced self-expression, online mental and physical health support groups, and enhanced socializing capabilities. However, there are also a number of negative aspects including trolling, bullying, online deception, and negative mental health impacts (Taylor-Jackson & Moustafa, 2021). Often it is the case that the social media companies are unable to provide effective policing and control of users to avoid or reduce these negative impacts (Antoci et al., 2019; Duggan, 2017), resulting in the closure of some user accounts to avoid online harassment or identity theft. An interesting aspect of negative online behavior concerns whether people are more inclined to lie online compared to face to face and whether online and offline trust beliefs are distinct (Lankton & McKnight, 2011). This introduction will review research addressing online deception and catfishing more widely, before focusing on deception related to fake illnesses, notably Munchausen's syndrome (MS), factitious disorder (FD), and Munchausen by Internet.

## Online deception

Anderson et al. (2019) explored the motivations and the psychological characteristics associated with those who undertake cyberdeception. They conducted a systematic review and a thematic analysis, which identified six "motivational" themes: acquiring attention and sympathy; a response to negative childhood experiences; presenting your "true" self; to cause intentional harm and to pursue personal enjoyment; to exploit materially; and deception as a stress-reliever in response to life strain. However, they identified only one "individual" theme, and this was termed perpetrator personality. They concluded that because of this lack of findings relating to individual differences, future research could determine if psychological differences are of value; the alternative is the view that cyberdeception may be better understood through consideration of the motivational factors.

Successful online communities are based on interpersonal trust and the connections users feel toward their online friends, to the extent that they join multiple social networking sites (SNSs). With active participation on these platforms, users have the responsibility to make an assessment on the authenticity of an online profile before it is accepted (Kim & Ahmad, 2013), and unless information from a profile suggests to the contrary, online relationships rely on trusting and accepting this profile. Threats to interpersonal trust occur when an inaccurate identity is used or identity theft occurs, and when this is discovered, it can diminish the integrity of an online environment and lead to community fallouts (Lawlor & Kirakowski, 2017).

Tsikerdekis and Zeadally (2014) suggested two motivations for identity deception: (1) definition and exploration of the self and (2) deceiving others using personas deliberately crafted to be unrepresentative of the true self. Identity deception for the use of expression and exploration purposes is viewed as logical and benign (Shpigelman & Gill, 2014). However, identity deception that originates with stolen photos and information alongside false relationships is viewed more negatively due to undesirable and malicious outcomes. One type of identity deception is *catfishing*, the act of luring others into online relationships using false identities (Lovelock, 2017). This can occur using a variety of SNSs including Facebook, Twitter, and Instagram by using private messaging features. Facebook alone was once predicted to have 83 million fake profiles (Fire et al., 2014). The motivations to engage in catfishing are difficult to identify, given that attitudes of perpetrators and victims are not well-researched. Nonetheless, Lovelock (2017) examined the responses of catfishes that were caught and outed on the MTV show "Catfish." Culprits showed remorse and immediately disclosed depression and low self-esteem challenges that lead them to crave a new identity. However, Wieland (2015) found that a desire to engage in an online relationship was a common theme. Therefore self-esteem issues and depression may persist until relationships are realized. Furthermore, catfishes are likely to move onto new profiles and audiences, as due to the unregulated nature of the Internet, there are few physical judicial consequences for this type of behavior.

## Munchausen's syndrome, factitious disorder, and Munchausen by Internet

MS is an FD, by which those affected deliberately fake psychological trauma or illness. Individuals work to create the symptoms of disease by fabricating symptoms or appearing to show self-inflicted injury (Koufagued et al., 2015). The end goal of MS is to gain attention, sympathy, and control from peers and healthcare professionals (Feldman, 2000). Detection of MS is not uncommon (Amlani et al., 2016); however, 59% opted to induce injury rather than fabricate it (Yates & Feldman, 2016). As such, individual cases of inflicted injury are eligible for surgery before an FD diagnosis, whereby treatment can exceed £157,000 prior to the reveal (Yates & Feldman, 2016). MS as an FD has descended from hypochondria or malingering, in that a person has an underlying mental condition. The individual can be categorized as consciously seeking attention for external incentives (Young et al., 2016) as a malingerer, or as responding to health worries that escalate to fears of clinical illness with hypochondriasis (Surawy et al., 2015). Historically, external incentives to malingering have included financial benefits or escaping work or employment (Sendín Bande & García-Alba, 2008). Therefore establishing the absence of exterior motives eliminates malingering to diagnose FD.

Munchausen by Internet (MBI) is the online equivalent of MS. MBI individuals use social media platforms to pose as a sick person for sympathy (Feldman, 2000), and it can severely diminish trust in online communities. Detection is less common than offline MS, as new audiences can be reached in a few clicks and culprits can create many profiles in different communities, which is not possible offline (Xiao et al., 2015). Assuming that mental disorders exist for those who commit online deception can be problematic due to not having existing records of all cases and the elusiveness of FD sufferers (Lawlor & Kirakowski, 2014). Research on MBI and the impact on beliefs and dynamics of online communities remain scarce. A recent study by Greyson and Costello (2021) introduced a new related term "sympathy sockpuppets," to refer to people who joined online communities using a so-called "sockpuppet" account with the sole motivation to gain sympathy; a key factor previously identified by Anderson et al. (2019). Greyson and Costello (2021) recommends that research is needed to not only understand the motivations of "sympathy sockpuppets" but also the impacts on individuals and communities.

Unlike malingering, MBI is physically inflicted with physical symptoms (Glenton, 2003), therefore tests and psychological assessment can weaken false allegations. However, without a confession to malingering and MBI, healthcare cannot be certain as to whether it was deliberate and conscious. In these cases, a doctor will make a statement that symptoms are not truly indicative of the illness in question, with no further action (Vanderploeg & Curtiss, 2001). Culprits are allowed to move onto new doctors to restart the process and some were shown to revisit the same hospital after a long period of time (Pessina et al., 2013). Hypochondriasis is distinct from MS, in that it originates with genuine health worries and anxiety (Bailer et al., 2016). The ubiquity of freely available medical images and text on the

Internet have served to exacerbate a hypochondriac's ability to convince themselves of suffering from a condition or disease. Hypochondria sufferers have split traits of the disorder between excessive avoidance of seeking medical help and actively seeking help, which rules out an initial objective to attention seek (Doherty-Torstrick et al., 2016). However, similar to MS, patients return for medical care despite reassurance of their claims (Van Den Heuvel et al., 2014). It is clear that there are overlaps between MS, malingering, and hypochondria.

Research has shown that young adolescents are reluctant to seek help and advice regarding their own health (Yap et al., 2013). Considerably less research has explored adolescent attitudes toward others' mental health in terms of authenticity when disclosing illness online. Teng et al. (2017) interviewed 16 adolescents aged between 12 and 16 years, and their findings suggested that young people's attitudes toward mental health had become desensitized. This included the finding that adolescents were confident that others who disclosed mental illness were "looking for attention." They felt that the term "mental illness" was overused, and they were skeptical about mental illness in their own family, doubting whether their claims were true or not. Also, they did not overly sympathize with others who were mentally ill because they thought they preferred to be treated as normal. It is not a straightforward process to encourage young people to acknowledge mental health (O'Connor et al., 2014), with a complex interplay between adolescents' personality, perceived benefits of seeking help, and negative attitudes toward healthcare.

The extent that adolescents and young adults felt reluctant to seek support or discuss their mental health issues with peers or anonymous communities was highlighted in recent research by Yeo (2021). Yeo analyzed over 100 accounts written on a Facebook "secrets" group by students in Hong Kong. The accounts recalled suicidal thoughts and self-harm behaviors, and Yeo identified that students felt able to tell their stories and disclose details online because they would not be discredited or mischaracterized. Yeo proposes that the culture of depicting one's life as being happy on SNSs prevented many from telling such negative stories and refers to it as a communication gap and an interpersonal communication breakdown. In his conclusion, Yeo calls on mental health promotion campaigns to highlight the problem with a culture highlighting just messages of positivity. If adolescents are already wary of revealing mental health issues due to stigma or revealing negative experiences in a culture of positivity, then finding out that they have been deceived by someone revealing a false mental health issue is likely to be even more distressing. This needs research to identify if this might be the case.

Corry and Leavey (2017) found that adolescents distrusted GPs and they were perceived as strangers, uncaring and impersonal. Clement et al. (2015) suggested that these negative attitudes might arise from disclosure concerns. This could explain why when students see others disclose mental illness it is treated as a societal taboo and this reaction can lead to assumptions of attention seeking. It is rarely considered that negative self-impressions online by others may be a cry for help and signify clinical symptoms of a real mental disorder (Rosen et al., 2013). Rather than confrontations, encouraging students to ask their peers how they cope with stress and other problems may be more useful. This is a good way forward as some find it easier to discuss their stressors rather than their deceptions (Martin & Schroeder, 2015).

## Rationale for research

What is known about MBI is dependent on a series of case studies initially highlighted by Feldman (2000), while catfishing is often discussed within the media based on observational or anecdotal accounts. Research is needed to add a new perspective, by exploring how young people understand online deception and particularly MBI and catfishing. This was addressed by conducting a mixed methods approach. A pilot study collected qualitative data using interviews to identify areas and questions to explore in detail. The main study then used the pilot study themes to develop a quantitative survey containing mainly closed and some open-ended questions. The aim of the research was to explore student attitudes to online deception, catfish impersonating, and feigning illness online.

 **Method**

## Participants

The two studies received separate ethical approval and took place in subsequent years. For the pilot study, 15 undergraduate students (14 female and 1 male) aged 18—49 years took part in semistructured interviews. Participants were recruited from a university research participation system and Facebook. The following year, first- and second-year psychology students from one University were invited to take part in an online survey. 198 students aged between 18 and 35 years participated in the survey. Both samples received course credits for their participation.

## Materials

### Development of survey questions from the pilot study

The pilot study collected participants' perceptions of identity deception using face-to-face semistructured interviews. Two case studies, one of MBI and one of catfishing, were described to ensure a basic understanding of each topic. The data collected provided empirical accounts of participants' own online behavior and their attitudes toward MBI and catfishing. Grounded theory (Glaser & Strauss, 2017) was used to analyze the qualitative data. Core categories emerged to form a comprehensive model that addressed how adolescents perceived authentic and nonauthentic sufferers of illness and deception in online dating. Participants felt that MBI culprits contaminated online communities and were almost impossible to detect. A common theme was "self-perceived vigilance," where participants thought that they would have been more vigilant in an online health support community. Another theme was "empathy to understand," where participants were keen to understand why someone would commit online deceptions and they offered reasons why they may do this. However, many comments highlighted how participants became less trusting and tolerant toward others that did not adhere to social rules and norms for online behavior. A final theme was "no going back," where participants felt that experiencing an incidence of catfishing or MBI would destroy their trust in future online communities. Many participants felt worried by the potential collateral damage that MBI culprits caused and felt that the therapeutic benefits of the internet for support became useless.

### Final survey questions

In the pilot, it was clear that some participants were initially unaware of the example case studies used or they had an incomplete recollection; therefore it was decided to use these two case studies again at the start of the main study as a focus to help stimulate participant perceptions. The 19-item questionnaire consisted of both open and closed questions. The questions drew upon the three themes identified from the pilot study data. Relating to the "self-perceived vigilance" theme, questions were included that asked participants how vigilant they were to online deception. For example, "Do you think you are vigilant about whom you speak to online and who speaks to you?" and "Have you ever chatted to others online you have not met before? Roughly how many?" Relating to the "empathy to understand" theme, questions were developed to ask participants why they thought people committed MBI and catfishing. For example, questions included "Some people say lying about illness online is deliberate and strategic, do you agree with this and why/why not?," and "How social would you assume a catfish is offline compared to when they are online?" Relating to the "no going back" theme, questions were developed to ask participants whether observing an incidence of online identity deception would make them less trusting and tolerant toward those who did not adhere to social rules and norms for online behavior. In addition, other questions captured the extent that participants had committed different types of online deception and how aware they were of MBI and catfishing behaviors. Also, questions explored the participant's views about the legal status of online deception, for example, they were asked, "Do you think that social network providers have a duty to tighten up their own procedures regarding catfishing or MBI, or should this fall to an individual country to legislate?" and "Is there a case for considering the sadistic misuse of health-related forums or catfishing as a form of cybercrime, rather than as an everyday negative risk of using the Internet?"

## Procedure

After reading an information sheet and agreeing to informed consent, a link to the online survey (using the Qualtrics software) was provided. Due to the sensitive nature of discussion, participants were reminded that if they were upset by this topic, they could contact Victim Support or the Student Counselling Service using the links provided. Also, at the start and during the survey participants were reminded of their right to withdraw or "pass" questions.

## Results

Responses in five areas were analyzed: (1) vigilance; (2) personal experiences of deception; (3) awareness; (4) perceived motivations for deception, and (5) legal views. Where open questions were asked, content analysis was conducted by two independent reviewers with themes being identified and coded separately and then agreed between the reviewers.

## Vigilance

Participants were asked, "Do you think you are vigilant about whom you speak to online and who speaks to you?" This was an open-ended answer, so responses were categorized, and this produced four responses, as shown in Table 13.1. As might be expected for this sample demographic, vigilance was perceived as high regarding who participants interacted with online (88%).

Table 13.2 shows the number of participants answering the question, "Have you ever chatted to others online you have not met before?" The median and modal number of unknown others that participants chatted to was less than 10. However, five participants had chatted to over 100 unknown people online.

## Personal experiences of deception

The responses to three questions asking about personal experiences are displayed in Table 13.3; this shows that 32.5% had lied to a family member online and 52.5% had lied to a friend online; however, only 14.1% had moved on to creating a fake profile online.

**Table 13.1** Responses to item, "Do you think you are vigilant about whom you speak to online and who speaks to you?"

| Response | Number of respondents |
|---|---|
| Yes | 176 (88%) |
| Somewhat | 11 (5.5%) |
| Not really | 3 (1.5%) |
| No | 8 (4%) |
| Declined | 2 (1%) |

**Table 13.2** Responses to item, "Have you ever chatted to others online you have not met before? Roughly how many?"

| Response | Number of respondents |
|---|---|
| Declined to answer | 2 |
| None | 42 |
| Less than 10 | 66 |
| 10–40 | 61 |
| 41–100 | 24 |
| 101–200 | 4 |
| Over 200 | 1 |

**Table 13.3** Responses to questions asking about personal experiences of online deception.

| Response | "Have you ever lied to a family member online?" | "Have you ever lied to a friend online?" | "Have you ever created a fake profile online?" |
|---|---|---|---|
| No | 135 (67.5%) | 95 (47.5%) | 171 (85.9%) |
| Yes | 65 (32.5%) | 105 (52.5%) | 28 (14.1%) |

**Table 13.4** Responses to two items related to participant's awareness of online deception through personal networks.

| Response | "Have you ever heard of MBI incidences? Was this through the news, family, or a friend?" | "Have you ever heard of incidences of catfishing? Was this through the news, family, or a friend?" |
|---|---|---|
| No/unsure | 124 (62%) | 87 (43.5%) |
| Family | 2 (1%) | 3 (1.5%) |
| Yes, through a friend | 2 (1%) | 15 (7.5%) |
| Yes, through a colleague (at work/school) | 10 (5%) | 3 (1.5%) |
| Yes, through news (social media and TV) | 50 (25%) | 60 (30%) |
| Yes (uncategorized) | 1 (1.5%) | 15 (7.5%) |
| Declined to answer | 9 (4.5%) | 17 (8.5%) |

Where participants answered yes to these questions, they were asked if they would have behaved the same way if they were talking to others over the phone or in person and why their behavior was different (if it was). The sample was split, with 53 participants responding that they would behave differently (and 31 provided detailed justifications) and 44 participants responding that they would not have behaved differently (with 29 providing detailed justifications). The majority of these justifications related to the nonverbal properties of phone and face-to-face interactions, focusing on the ease of deceiving others online due to the limited nonverbal cues.

## Awareness of deception

Table 13.4 shows that 33.5% of participants were aware of MBI, and most of these were via news sources (25%), 7% indicated a personal experience (family/friends/colleagues), and 1.5% were not categorized. Of the sample, 48% of participants were aware of catfishing behaviors via either news sources (30%) or personal experience (family 1.5%, friends 7.5%, and colleagues 1.5%).

To explore emotions, participants were asked, "How would you feel if someone on your social media admitted to lying about cancer online?" Open-ended responses were categorized using Key Word Analysis and 48 individual terms were expressed. The most frequent feelings expressed were naturally negative, with the top nine words as follows: disgusted (n = 64), angry (n = 62), annoyed (n = 19), disappointed (n = 11), upset (n = 10), horrified (n = 9), confused (n = 7), shocked (n = 6), and betrayed (n = 5). However, it was interesting to observe some supportive terms being expressed: empathetic (n = 1), sorry (n = 2), understanding (n = 2), concerned (n = 1), and care (n = 1).

## Perceived motivations for deception

To gage participant's perceptions regarding the motivations of online deceivers, two questions were asked. As can be seen in Table 13.5, the majority agreed that online deception was deliberate or strategic and further comments made gave extra insight. Although the numbers were small, three participants related this to attention seeking, five related it to loneliness or low self-esteem, while two attributed it to revenge or jealousy. Interestingly, none of the responses referred to entertainment as a

Table 13.5 Responses to items, "Some people say that this type of lying online is deliberate and strategic, do you agree with this?" and "If you do agree, what do you think motivates this online deception?"

| Response | Number of respondents |
|---|---|
| No/unsure | 15 (7.5%) |
| Yes—uncategorized | 143 (71.5%) |
| Sometimes | 9 (4.5%) |
| Yes—deliberate | 8 (4%) |
| Yes—strategic | 13 (6.5%) |
| Yes—attention | 3 (1.5%) |
| Yes—revenge | 1 (0.5%) |
| Yes—self-esteem | 1 (0.5%) |
| Yes—escape/lonely | 4 (2%) |
| Yes—reaction | 1 (0.5%) |
| Yes—jealous | 1 (0.5%) |
| Declined to answer | 1 (0.5%) |

**Table 13.6** Responses to item, "How social would you assume a catfish is offline compared to when they are online?"

| Response | Number of respondents |
| --- | --- |
| Average | 4 (2%) |
| Less sociable offline | 104 (52%) |
| Antisocial offline | 66 (33%) |
| More outgoing offline | 3 (1.5%) |
| More sociable online | 10 (5%) |
| No relation to sociability | 6 (3%) |
| Other | 4 (2%) |
| Declined to answer | 3 (1.5%) |

**Table 13.7** Responses to item, "Do you think that social network providers have a duty to tighten up their own procedures regarding catfishing or MBI (Munchausen by Internet), or should this fall to individual country legislation?"

| Response | Number of respondents |
| --- | --- |
| No/unsure | 11 (5.5%) |
| Yes—uncategorized | 57 (28.5%) |
| Yes—social networks | 74 (37%) |
| Yes—country | 12 (6%) |
| Both | 31 (15.5%) |
| Individual | 9 (4.5%) |
| Declined to answer | 6 (3%) |

motivation. As can be seen in Table 13.6, 86% of participants perceived catfishes to be either less social or antisocial offline, compared to when they are online.

## Legal views

As illustrated in Table 13.7, participants felt that the duty of care regarding legislation rested more with the social media providers (37%) than at a national level (6%), with slightly more requiring both to take more action (15.5%) and a few feeling that the onus was on the individual to realize that this was a risk of using these tools (4.5%).

Respondents tended to view positively the categorization of misuse of health-related forums and/or catfishing as cybercrimes (see Table 13.8). Only a small percentage indicated that there should be different levels of categorization dependent on the severity of the incident (9.5%) and a minor number viewing it as a risk of using the Internet (3%).

**Table 13.8** Responses to item, "Is there a case for considering the sadistic misuse of health-related forums or catfishing as a form of cybercrime, rather than as an everyday negative risk of using the Internet?"

| Response | Number of respondents |
|---|---|
| No/unsure | 20 (10%) |
| Yes—uncategorized | 98 (49%) |
| Cybercrime | 26 (13%) |
| Catfish cybercrime | 5 (2.5%) |
| MBI cybercrime | 3 (1.5%) |
| Different levels according to severity | 19 (9.5%) |
| Everyday risk | 3 (1.5%) |
| Declined to answer | 26 (13%) |

## Discussion

The findings across the five areas of interest will now be discussed in relation to previous research. In the final section, we discuss our future research, which addresses some of the questions raised and which is designed to avoid some of the methodological limitations highlighted in our study.

### Vigilance and digital awareness

The majority of participants in this study had communicated, with varying frequencies, with people that they did not know. One way of taking a proactive approach to protecting people from being deceived online is to focus on ensuring that more users of social media tools are educated on the potential pitfalls and ethics of using social media and in particular the checking of identities to other sources. For members of a community self-help group or dating community, this might include initially highlighting to members upon induction that they should be aware of the possibility of this type of incident occurring, rather than communicating and using social media tools and applications without awareness. This could then extend to be included as one part of wider digital awareness sessions introduced for different demographic groups (school children, older people, health professionals and online health communities, etc.). This would assist community members in having a greater awareness of the risks and benefits of sharing information in online environments.

## Experiences and awareness of Munchausen by Internet and catfishing

Although online users may be at risk of misleading information and trolling, research into online healthcare support shows significant benefits of online support communities (Lal & Adair, 2014). In this study, the number of personal experiences highlight more instances of MBI than would have been expected in such a small pool of participants (only 3.5% less than for catfishing), which means that the problem might be greater than what was thought at first. Enhanced self-regulation continues to be the most positive action to reduce group risk, and it is still advisable for health support groups to identify a gatekeeper (Pulman & Taylor, 2012). In terms of moving forward once a case has been identified, one recommendation suggested by Morrell and Tilley (2012) is for certain groups of victims to come together to raise awareness. We would have expected catfishing to be higher than for MBI behaviors, as this has a higher profile within global media, with the MTV program "Catfish" (Lovelock, 2017) being mentioned frequently as a source of information. Again, from a small pool of participants the percentage of personal experiences show that this issue is more common than might have been expected across a small sample of students.

## Motivations for deception

A higher number of participants than expected had lied online. One would expect participants to feel less inclined to lie to their family (32.5%) than friends (52.5%), but these numbers seem to be on the large side. One reason for this can be found in Suler's (2004) article, which points to two areas where the inherent design of the Internet makes deception easier. The first area is synchronicity, which encourages a dynamic approach to identity presentation, allowing for rapid alterations between styles and identities. The second area is the lack of feedback and the anonymity or unfamiliarity of the audience reducing concern for other's views. This might suggest that the ability to get away with lying to a friend and/or a family member and the lack of consequences if this behavior was discovered or not could encourage further instances or more complex examples. This requires further investigation. This might also be highlighting a similar trend to that shown with criminal behavior, where a number of people may commit minor infractions but a percentage then move on to more serious infractions as time passes. Social media is not and historically has not been designed with issues of security and authentication as a priority. Anderson's (2007) web 2.0 technology definition reflects an enhanced generation of web-based communities and services seeking to altruistically facilitate creativity, collaboration, and sharing between people. Unfortunately, these goals conflict with basic human nature and mechanisms of policing and ensuring author authenticity, with most providers tending to be reactive to issues in this area rather than including it into the initial software developed. In 2018, Ramalingam & Chinnaiah (2018) concluded that despite numerous existing schemes, there is still no systematic solution for fake profile detection in SNSs that can provide efficient, fast and reliable recognition of user information. Thus fake profiles can be easily created without repercussions, which might encourage and embolden users to go further than they might in a face-to-face situation. This situation is gradually changing with the incorporation of artificial intelligence in face recognition; however, there is still some way to go for this to become common place.

## Legal aspects and legislation

Ahmad et al. (2014) suggested that online users lacked knowledge of privacy settings, cyber laws, and awareness, which resulted in overconfidence in using social media. Although online users' privacy settings do not always align with deception concerns (Hallam & Zanella, 2017), our research highlighted how online users were less trusting and tolerant toward others that did not adhere to social rules and norms. As more cases are reported and global awareness grows (Gunn & Goldstein, 2017; Lawlor & Kirakowski, 2017), it seems that over time opinions are hardening in this age group regarding how these incidents should be treated. The onus on tightening up procedures is seen as resting at the feet of the social media providers, although they have so far been lax at actually taking positive action to date. The sheer numbers of users of social media make policing this effectively a virtually impossible job, but suggestions for making changes to processes might be able to mitigate some instances. One participant noted that dating apps like Bumble (2018) have a feature that confirms identity by asking you to take a photo of yourself in a certain pose and then the provider can check if the user is the same person as the photographs on their profile. Instigating this on other sites might be more difficult if the user base runs into the millions (such as on Twitter and Facebook). It is fair to say that the Internet is a place equivalent to the wild west in terms of what could and could not be done, in terms of action toward trolling and flaming as an acceptable risk of using the internet, which has taken a long time to start to change from an acceptable risk of using the Internet. This might be seen in relation to other cultural phenomena such as the #metoo campaign to help demonstrate the widespread prevalence of sexual assault and harassment, especially in the workplace where people have had enough and a tipping point has been reached (Wexler et al., 2018). At the very least, SNSs should continue to add enhanced "report fraud" links and look at the possibility of including image checkers. Nationally, governments have started to address the legalities of online behaviors, for example, in the United Kingdom, a wide-ranging consultation took place around the "Online Harms" white paper (Wright & Javid, 2019). However, for many organizations, charities, and individuals, the recommendations contained in this white paper do not go far enough.

## Strengths, limitations, and further research

A strength of this study was the use of mixed methods, where qualitative data was initially collected and analyzed and on which the survey questions were then based. The self-report survey was easy to complete for participants and resulted in an understanding of student's views on a variety of topics related to these two types of online deception. However, this study was exploratory and is based on descriptive analysis. Future research needs to start with predicted hypotheses and to use inferential statistics to test these. Also, another limitation is that the self-report nature of this data may be unreliable due to participant's inaccurate memory or their reluctance to disclose. What is needed is a more naturalistic way to observe both incidences of online deception as well as an indication of motivation for and reactions to it. Further research is planned to use an observational method to analyze the discussions and perceptions held on Twitter regarding online deception. This new study has three aims: to identify the motivations and attitudes of deceivers; to identify the awareness of twitter users of catfishing and MBI; and to identify the emotions expressed by victims. An online data extraction tool will be used to collect tweets, and an automated linguistic analysis tool will be used to determine patterns and trends within the tweets (Pennebaker et al., 2015). The search terms to extract the tweets will come from the findings from the study reported in this chapter. The outcome of this further research could provide guidance on detection and managing the impacts of online deception.

## Conclusion

The findings from this study reaffirmed the review from Pulman and Taylor (2012) that the negative effects of MBI and catfishing require continued research focus. Incidences of impersonation and feigning illness online continue to increase (as evidenced by this study) and are probably underreported globally. Although there is some action currently being taken by social media providers or government organizations, so far this is a voluntary code of practice, therefore this behavior will still occur due to the lack of any consequences. Therefore we must continue to look at other ways of raising awareness and increasing online safety by understanding the motivations and attitudes of deceivers and educating users through digital awareness and how to better support the victims. Additionally, we recommend that social media providers add enhanced "report fraud" links and include image checkers. As highlighted in the Introduction, Greyson and Costello (2021) recommend that the motivations of those who engage in forms of online deception such as catfishing and MBI are not well understood. Research is needed to not only understand the motivations of perpetrators but also to identify the impacts on individuals and communities. Our further research will address this gap in research.

## References

Ahmad, A., Afnan, A., S., A., Hanan, B. A., & Maha, S. A. (2014). Social networks' benefits, privacy, and identity theft: KSA Case study. *International Journal of Advanced Computer Science and Applications, 5*(12), 129−143. Available from https://doi.org/10.14569/IJACSA.2014.051218.

Amlani, A., Grewal, G. S., & Feldman, M. D. (2016). Malingering by proxy: A literature review and current perspectives. *Journal of Forensic Sciences, 61*(1), 171−176. Available from https://doi.org/10.1111/1556-4029.12977.

Anderson, A., Bryce, J., Ireland, C. A., & Ireland, J. L. (2019). A preliminary review of cyber-detection factors: Offering from a systematic review. *Salus: An International Journal of Law Enforcement and Public Safety, 7*(1), 88−107.

Anderson, P. (2007). *What is web 2.0? Ideas, technologies and implications for education. Technology and standards watch*. Bristol: JISC Retrieved on 11/3/21. Available from https://www.webarchive.org.uk/wayback/archive/20130607115252, http://www.jisc.ac.uk/whatwedo/services/techwatch/reports/horizonscanning/hs0701.aspx.

Antoci, A., Bonelli, L., Paglieri, F., Reggiani, T., & Sabatini, F. (2019). Civility and trust in social media. *Journal of Economic Behavior & Organization, 160*, 83−99.

Bailer, J., Kerstner, T., Witthöft, M., Diener, C., Mier, D., Rist, F., & Witthöft, M. (2016). Health anxiety and hypochondriasis in the light of DSM-5. *Anxiety, Stress & Coping, 29*(2), 219−239.

Bumble. (2018). , October 29*Bumble homepage*. Available from https://bumble.com/.

Clement, S., Schauman, O., Graham, T., Maggioni, F., Evans-Lacko, S., Bezborodovs, N., & Thornicroft, G. (2015). What is the impact of mental health-related stigma on help-seeking? A systematic review of quantitative and qualitative studies. *Psychological Medicine*, *45*(1), 11–27. Available from https://doi.org/10.1017/S0033291714000129.

Corry, D. S., & Leavey, G. (2017). Adolescent trust and primary care: Help-seeking for emotional and psychological difficulties. *Journal of Adolescence*, *45*, 1–8. Available from https://doi.org/10.1016/j.adolescence.2016.11.003.

Doherty-Torstrick, E. R., Walton, K. E., Barsky, A. J., & Fallon, B. A. (2016). Avoidance in hypochondriasis. *Journal of Psychosomatic Research*, *89*, 46–52. Available from https://doi.org/10.1016/j.jpsychores.2016.07.010.

Duggan, M. (2017). *Online harassment 2017*. Technical report, Pew Research Center.

Feldman, M. D. (2000). Munchausen by Internet: Detecting factitious illness and crisis on the Internet. *Southern Medical Journal*, *93*(7), 669–672.

Fire, M., Kagan, D., Elyashar, A., & Elovici, Y. (2014). Friend or foe? Fake profile identification in online social networks. *Social Network Analysis & Mining*, *4*(1), 1–23. Available from https://doi.org/10.1007/s13278-014-0194-4.

Glaser, B. G., & Strauss, A. L. (2017). *The discovery of grounded theory*. London: Routledge.

Glenton, C. (2003). Chronic back pain sufferers—striving for the sick role. *Social Science & Medicine*, *57*(11), 2243–2252.

Greyson, D., & Costello, K. L. (2021). Emotional strip-mining": Sympathy sockpuppets in online communities. *New Media & Society*, published online September, 2021. Available from https://doi.org/10.1177/14614448211040521.

Gunn, J. F., & Goldstein, S. E. (2017). Bullying and suicidal behavior during adolescence: A developmental perspective. *Adolescent Research Review*, *2*(2), 77–97.

Hallam, C., & Zanella, G. (2017). Full length article: Online self-disclosure: The privacy paradox explained as a temporally discounted balance between concerns and rewards. *Computers in Human Behavior*, *68*, 217–227. Available from https://doi.org/10.1016/j.chb.2016.11.033.

Kim, Y. A., & Ahmad, M. A. (2013). Trust, distrust and lack of confidence of users in online social media-sharing communities. *Knowledge-Based Systems*, *37*, 438–450. Available from https://doi.org/10.1016/j.knosys.2012.09.002.

Koufagued, K., Chafry, B., Benyass, Y., Abissegue, Y., Benchebba, D., Bouabid, S., & Belkacem, C. (2015). Munchausen syndrome revealed by subcutaneous limb emphysema: A case report. *Journal of Medical Case Reports*, *9*, 172. Available from https://doi.org/10.1186/s13256-015-0649-x.

Lal, S., & Adair, C. E. (2014). E-mental health: A rapid review of the literature. *Psychiatric Services*, *65*(1), 24. Available from https://doi.org/10.1176/appi.ps.201300009.

Lankton, N. K., & McKnight, D. H. (2011). What does it mean to trust Facebook?: Examining technology and interpersonal trust beliefs. *ACM SiGMiS Database*, *42*(2), 32–54.

Lawlor, A., & Kirakowski, J. (2014). When the lie is the truth: Grounded theory analysis of an online support group for factitious disorder. *Psychiatry Research*, *218*(1–2), 209–218. Available from https://doi.org/10.1016/j.psychres.2014.03.034.

Lawlor, A., & Kirakowski, J. (2017). Claiming someone else's pain: A grounded theory analysis of online community participants experiences of Munchausen by Internet. *Computers in Human Behavior*, *74*, 101–111.

Lovelock, M. (2017). Catching a catfish. *Television & New Media*, *18*(3), 203–217. Available from https://doi.org/10.1177/1527476416662709.

Martin, P. K., & Schroeder, R. W. (2015). Challenges in assessing and managing malingering, factitious disorder, and related somatic disorders. *Psychiatric Times*, *32*(10), 1–4.

Morrell, B., & Tilley, D. S. (2012). The role of non-perpetrating fathers in Munchausen syndrome by proxy: A review of the literature. *Journal of Pediatric Nursing*, *27*(4), 328–335. Available from https://doi.org/10.1016/j.pedn.2011.03.008.

O'Connor, P. J., Martin, B., Weeks, C. S., & Ong, L. (2014). Factors that influence young people's mental health help-seeking behaviour: A study based on the Health Belief Model. *Journal of Advanced Nursing, 70*(11), 2577−2587. Available from https://doi.org/10.1111/jan.12423.

Pennebaker, J. W., Boyd, R. L., Jordan, K., & Blackburn, K. (2015). *The development and psychometric properties of LIWC2015.* Austin, TX: University of Texas at Austin.

Pessina, A. C., Bisogni, V., Fassina, A., & Rossi, G. P. (2013). Munchausen syndrome: A novel cause of drug-resistant hypertension. *Journal of Hypertension, 31*(7), 1473−1476. Available from https://doi.org/10.1097/HJH.0b013e328360e9ae.

Pulman, A., & Taylor, J. (2012). Munchausen by internet: Current research and future directions. *Journal of Medical Internet Research, 14*(4), e115. Available from https://doi.org/10.2196/jmir.2011.

Ramalingam, D., & Chinnaiah, V. (2018). Fake profile detection techniques in large-scale online social networks: A comprehensive review. *Computers & Electrical Engineering, 65,* 165−177.

Rosen, Ll, Whaling, K., Rab, S., Carrier, L., & Cheever, N. (2013). Is Facebook creating "iDisorders"? The link between clinical symptoms of psychiatric disorders and technology use, attitudes and anxiety. *Computers in Human Behavior, 29*(3), 1243−1254. Available from https://doi.org/10.1016/j.chb.2012.11.012.

Sendín Bande, C., & García-Alba, C. (2008). Munchausen syndrome by proxy: A dilemma for diagnosis. *Rorschachiana, 29*(2), 183−200. Available from https://doi.org/10.1027/1192-5604.29.2.183.

Shpigelman, C., & Gill, C. J. (2014). Facebook use by persons with disabilities. *Journal of Computer-Mediated Communication, 19*(3), 610−624. Available from https://doi.org/10.1111/jcc4.12059.

Suler, J. (2004). The online disinhibition effect: The impact of the internet, multimedia and virtual reality on behavior and society. *Cyberpsychology & Behavior, 7*(3), 321−326.

Surawy, C., McManus, F., Muse, K., & Williams, J. G. (2015). Mindfulness-based cognitive therapy (MBCT) for health anxiety (hypochondriasis): Rationale, implementation and case illustration. *Mindfulness, 6*(2), 382−392. Available from https://doi.org/10.1007/s12671-013-0271-1.

Taylor-Jackson, J., & Moustafa, A. A. (2021). The relationships between social media use and factors relating to depression. *The Nature of Depression,* 171−182. Available from https://doi.org/10.1016/B978-0-12-817676-4.00010-9.

Teng, E., Crabb, S., Winefield, H., & Venning, A. (2017). Crying wolf? Australian adolescents' perceptions of the ambiguity of visible indicators of mental health and authenticity of mental illness. *Qualitative Research in Psychology, 14*(2), 171−199.

Tsikerdekis, M., & Zeadally, S. (2014). Online deception in social media. *Communications of the ACM, 57*(9), 72−80. Available from https://doi.org/10.1145/2629612.

Van Den Heuvel, O. A., Veale, D., & Stein, D. J. (2014). Hypochondriasis: Considerations for ICD-11. *Revista Brasileira De Psiquiatria, 36,* 21−27. Available from https://doi.org/10.1590/1516-4446-2013-1218.

Vanderploeg, R., & Curtiss, G. (2001). Malingering assessment: Evaluation of validity of performance. *NeuroRehabilitation, 16*(4), 245−251.

Wexler, L., Robbennolt, J.K., & Murphy, C. (2018). *# MeToo, Time's Up, and Theories of Justice.* University of Illinois College of Law Legal Studies Research Paper, No. 18-14, p.45-46. University of Illinois. Retrieved from https://heinonline.org/HOL/P?h = hein.journals/unilllr2019&i = 50 (accessed12.09.22).

Wieland, D. M. (2015). Psychiatric-mental health nurses' exposure to clients with problematic internet experiences: A mixed-methods pilot study. *Journal of Psychosocial Nursing and Mental Health Services, 53*(10), 31−40. Available from https://doi.org/10.3928/02793695-20150923-02.

Wright, J., & Javid, S. (2019). *Online harms white paper.* HM Government. Retrieved from https://assets.publishing.service.gov.uk/governROment/uploads/system/uploads/attachment_data/file/973939/Online_Harms_White_Paper_V2.pdf (accessed15.06.22).

Xiao, C., Freeman, D. M., & Hwa, T. (2015). *Detecting clusters of fake accounts in online social networks. Proceedings of the 8th ACM Workshop on Artificial Intelligence and Security* (pp. 91−101). ACM.

Yap, M. H., Reavley, N., & Jorm, A. F. (2013). Where would young people seek help for mental disorders and what stops them? Findings from an Australian national survey. *Journal of Affective Disorders, 147*(1-3), 255−261. Available from https://doi.org/10.1016/j.jad.2012.11.014.

Yates, G. P., & Feldman, M. D. (2016). Factitious disorder: A systematic review of 455 cases in the professional literature. *General Hospital Psychiatry, 41*, 20−28. Available from https://doi.org/10.1016/j.genhosppsych.2016.05.002.

Yeo, T. E. D. (2021). "Do you know how much I suffer?": How young people negotiate the tellability of their mental health disruption in anonymous distress narratives on social media. *Health Communication, 36*, 1606−1615.

Young, S., Jacobson, R., Einzig, S., Gray, K., & Gudjonsson, G. H. (2016). Can we recognise malingerers? The association between malingering, personality traits and clinical impression among complainants in civil compensation cases. *Personality and Individual Differences, 98*, 235−238. Available from https://doi.org/10.1016/j.paid.2016.04.052.

CHAPTER FOURTEEN

# Pornography, social media, and sexuality

**Mark McCormack[1] and Liam Wignall[2]**
[1]University of Roehampton, London, United Kingdom
[2]University of Brighton, Sussex, United Kingdom

## Contents

## Introduction

The internet has transformed the consumption of pornography (McNair, 2012), challenging legal regulation, the potential profits of most porn producers, and how porn is engaged with across society. There is renewed social concern about damaging consumption, risk to young people, and "porn addiction" (Ley et al., 2014), while also recognition of democratization of desire and educating sexual minorities where school curricula remain severely lacking (see Astle et al., 2021). This has spurred a new research paradigm in pornography, including a subdiscipline of "porn studies" and a journal of the same name (Attwood & Smith, 2014). This approach moves beyond "pro" and "anti" positions of pornography and simultaneously challenges a dominant approach in much psychology and sexology that examines for the harms of pornography—known as the "negative effects paradigm."

Much of ongoing research focuses on internet pornography, generally consumed via specific websites—either of the production company, or

*Handbook of Social Media Use Online Relationships, Security, Privacy, and Society, Volume 2*
DOI: https://doi.org/10.1016/B978-0-443-28804-3.00011-9

through general sites such as Pornhub.com. Furthermore, shifts in technology and the availability of high-quality low-cost video recording capabilities have resulted in new websites such as OnlyFans and JustForFans, which enable porn actors to create adult content and charge consumers to access their content (e.g., Pezzutto, 2019; Ryan, 2019). These platforms have the potential to provide more control for porn actors over their content, with porn actors also using social media platforms, such as X (formely Twitter) and Instagram, to advertise their adult content and build a follower base (McKee, 2018). This also facilitates an interactive approach to pornography and the opportunity for consumers to engage with performers in new ways, such as commenting on performers' content and the ability to offer donations for more personalized content, although they are also the target of advocacy work by right-wing commentators and political groups seeking to further regulate pornography (see Turner, 2020 for journalistic account of this issue).

Less attention has been paid to internet pornography on social media platforms, such as Facebook, Instagram, and Twitter, compared to general pornography websites. At the time of writing, on many platforms (e.g., Facebook, Instagram, YouTube, and Pinterest), pornographic content is banned, while others (e.g., Twitter) allow it subject to restrictions and content warnings. Guidelines for pornography on social media lack consistency and clarity, with questions about what counts as pornography, how it is policed, and whether transnational companies can navigate national laws. Furthermore, legal regulation often focuses on pornography sites while not recognizing evidence that pornography is shared primarily through sites such as Facebook or messaging apps like WhatsApp or Telegram, despite its attempts to ban it (McKee & Lumby, 2022).

In exploring how pornography is present on social media, this chapter argues the need to move beyond the negative effects paradigm, considering what conceptual frameworks could be applied to pornography to help understand its presence on social media. Leisure frameworks are applied to pornography, which recognize pornography as a form of entertainment, reflecting sociocultural attitudes toward sex, and acknowledge the utility of pornography as a tool for exploring individual sexuality. We draw on an example of how social media was adopted by a sexual minority community and the impact that had, alongside the increase in porn actors using such sites to sell their products.

We then turn to critically consider several concerns that have been raised about pornography on social media, focusing on the availability of porn to young people, the normalization of violence, and concerns about criminality and criminalization. Evaluating these claims, we also consider counterconcerns, such as censorship and sex education, hurting sexual minority communities and the potential for deviance amplification. This includes recognition that young people's concerns about pornography are often different from adults' concerns.

## Paradigms of negative effect and leisure in porn research

A core strand of research on pornography has come from sexological and psychological perspectives and investigates how consumption of pornography negatively affects people's sex lives or body image, as well as their attitudes toward sex and women (e.g., Antevska & Gavey, 2015; Brown & L'Engle, 2009). This approach holds that pornography transmits a sexual script that consumers of pornography adopt and apply to their own behavior (Wright, 2013) and, more broadly, that these scripts damage society through a "cultural harm" because sexual violence is normalized and thus more readily perpetrated (e.g., Vera-Gray et al., 2021). We have called this approach a "negative effects paradigm" because of the focus on the damaging impact of porn alongside the historic dominance this approach has maintained (see McCormack & Wignall, 2017).

The negative effects paradigm has faced empirical, theoretical, and methodological critiques (see McCormack & Wignall, 2017; Ruddock, 2015). Systematic reviews of literature in peer-reviewed academic journals tend to find limited evidence in support of pornography having damaging effects (e.g., Litsou et al., 2021; Mellor & Duff, 2019; Owens et al., 2012). Furthermore, longitudinal research supports the argument that negative traits such as aggressiveness are only correlated with pornography consumption rather than causing it (Dawson et al., 2019). Substantial evidence shows that people tend to perceive negative effects of watching pornography when it goes against their moral beliefs rather than any inherent damaging effect—theorized as "moral incongruence" (Grubbs & Perry, 2019; Štulhofer et al., 2022).

A core methodological critique of the negative effects paradigm is that it fails to demonstrate causality of harm, only showing correlation. While many negative outcomes are associated with porn use, there is only limited evidence of a causal impact (Ley et al., 2014). Studies which show causality have only occurred in laboratory conditions that do not reflect the conditions in which people consume porn, such as not being able to select the type of porn to watch or being allowed to masturbate. Research on pornography effects tends to use self-reported time viewing pornography as an objective measure, despite considerable evidence that such reports are unreliable (Parry et al., 2021)—meaning that findings that show increased porn viewing time results in worse behaviors are also unreliable. The findings of causality likely reflect the context of consumption rather than the content of the pornography.

Negative effects are often theorized by social learning theory or sexual script theory, with both being used in simplistic ways that position the consumer as a passive viewer who uncritically mimics the behaviors or adopts the scripts they see in the pornography (Dymock, 2018). This approach fails to account for consumers' motivations for viewing porn and how people engage in scripts in diverse and multifaceted ways (Wiederman, 2015). Despite trends in research on pornography shifting away from this approach, as we discuss in the next section, it is still a core strand that influences research, media, and policymaking in the area.

One recent high-profile example of research in the negative effects paradigm used computer-led data mining to document the frequency of violence in online video pornography accessed via major "tube" sites, such as Pornhub.com, by analyzing the titles of these videos (Vera-Gray et al., 2021). The study contends that sexual scripts in pornography contain sexual violence that can have damaging effects. The authors claim that they are not arguing for a "causal relationship...[but] a nuanced model where social meanings flow into and out of the media world...to augment, attune, and/or alter our understandings and experiences of the social world" (Vera-Gray et al., 2021, p. 1244). However, this argument merely shifts the moment of cause and effect from a *falsifiable* model where the consumer is changed by watching the porn to an ambiguous model where broader culture or society is impacted or harmed through "normalization" of attitudes and behaviors—where falsifiability is rendered impossible. The question of how normalization occurs other than through a cause-and-effect process is not addressed, with "cultural harm" being seen as self-evident (see Dymock [2018] and Palmer [2018] for nuanced critiques of cultural harm as a concept).

Vera-Gray et al. (2021)'s research was presented as breaking new methodological ground in the study of the effects of pornography, yet it contained significant methodological problems. The most fundamental of these was the classification of sexual violence through the video title text without viewing any content to determine whether the titles were accurate, or whether the pornography contained sexual violence. This is despite much content on tube sites being pirated and/or uploaded by bots with little accuracy in terms used to describe them. Surprisingly, while the authors recognize that corroborating content with video names would have been methodologically rigorous, they cite Pornhub.com guidance about how to label content as evidence that such content is correctly labeled (Vera-Gray et al., 2021, p. 1248)—essentially "terms and conditions" that are most likely not adhered to by bots and users who upload pirated material, in contravention of these guidelines.

Another significant issue was how the study classified titles as sexual violence. Words such as "expose," "money," "spanked," and "plowed" and nonblood family relation (such as "stepbrother") counted as violence, unless other text in the title "clearly identified the material as BDSM" (p. 1248) (e.g., when titles included terms like "BDSM" or "slave" [p. 1251]). This means that it is possible for one title to be coded as containing sexual violence while a different title with identical text and the addition of "BDSM" would not be considered sexual violence. The authors argue that this approach may "lead to claims about both overcounting and undercounting the extent of violence in our sample" (Vera-Gray et al., 2021, p. 1249), concerned that sexual violence may not have been included because of "overlaps between BDSM pornographic content and content depicting aggression and assault" (p. 1251). Situating the issue as one of claims and counterclaims is novel, but the issue is not one of external claims about the findings but an intrinsic flaw in the study design: specifically, the decision not to view any content. The divergent claims come from a lack of confidence in the classification system, undermining the validity and reliability of the statistics.

The use of the word "claims" by the authors is notable, given that it is a key term in the social problems literature (e.g., Best, 1990; Schneider, 1985). Here, significant concern is raised that defining terms in overly broad ways may increase the likelihood of false positives and bolster numbers related to a social problem (Best, 1990; Rubin, 2011). This is an issue that was present in the recent study. The study found that 12% of videos on the homepages of these sites included some form of "sexual violence," yet terms that were classed as sexual violence were broad. "Pound" and "rough" were by far the most common forms of activity classed as sexual violence, with 830 and 703 instances, respectively; with "punish" having 445 instances and the fourth most common being "drill" on 342. Words much more commonly associated with violence, such as "rape" and "assault," occurred far less. The word "rape" occurred in just one video, with "assault" occurring in four—thus constituting less than 0.001% of videos. Despite this, the central claim presented in the abstract of the article is that "We found that one in eight titles [12.5%] ... describe sexual activity that constitutes sexual violence." Unsurprisingly, much of the media reporting also emphasized the 12% statistic while using the rare worst-case terms like "rape" and "assault" as their examples of sexual violence. As Joel Best has argued, "the combination of big numbers, broad definitions, and horrible examples make...claims compelling" (Rubin, 2011, p. 78).

These issues occur despite a new paradigm of research on pornography emerging that challenges such assumptions and approaches and offers a more diverse way of understanding pornography in society. The past 15 years have seen a diversification in research on pornography with new theoretical approaches from broader disciplinary perspectives. Cultural studies have led the critique, showing that while pornography is a form of media, it is currently treated notably differently from other media such as films, television shows, and books (Attwood, 2011). The cultural studies critique has thus been to theorize pornography as a form of entertainment (McKee, 2012), as a leisure activity, and as an industry that has broader social and community aspects (Jackson et al., 2020). The point is not to be "pro" or "anti" pornography but to approach the topic with attentiveness to the range of potential outcomes of pornography, and the broad social and cultural context in which pornography is produced, consumed, and regulated (Smith & Attwood, 2014).

This approach can open new areas of research and consider the pornography in a more nuanced and less effects-based perspective. This has helped show the diverse reasons people consume porn—not just for sexual satisfaction, but out of boredom, to explore sexual identity and unfamiliar sexual practices, as a form of sex education, among other reasons (Mulholland, 2013; Smith et al., 2015; Wignall, 2020). Similarly, it can help understand the gender attitudes and social dynamics of porn "superfans" at porn exhibitions, including how consent is negotiated in these contexts (Jackson et al., 2019, 2020). In this way, the study of pornography not just as an act of consumption but also as a form of culture helps understand the complexity of porn and how it is situated within broader forms of gender and sexual reproduction (Comella, 2014).

While theories of leisure are gaining credence within psychology and sexology, and while porn studies is an interdisciplinary body of scholarship, there is a preponderance of research within arts and humanities, particularly cultural studies, which might partly explain why research within psychology and sexology has not always engaged with the critiques it has put forward. In the following sections, we draw liberally on this new paradigm and make connections between this body of research and how it can be applied for psychological perspectives on pornography, sexuality, and social media. Before doing that in detail, we consider social media in the context of sexuality.

## Social media and sexuality

One of the most common forms of social media is social networking sites (SNSs). These were initially created for keeping people connected to each other creating online networks (Boyd & Ellison, 2007). However, the functions of SNSs have become so diverse that they are now almost embedded in our lives (Rozgonjuk et al., 2020), serving multiple functions, including acting as primary tools of communication with linked messaging services (Waechter et al., 2010); a form of entertainment keeping people on the platform through different types of media (Nardello, 2017); and as an extension of one's work life through helping to create online work networks (including for academics; Mohammadi et al., 2018). While it may have been accurate initially to distinguish SNSs, like Facebook, from social media platforms, like YouTube, the difference between the two formats has lessened as both have adopted aspects of each other (McMahon, 2019). Therefore, we use the term social media and SNS somewhat interchangeably in this chapter.

SNSs were originally created to connect people to others' social networks, effectively linking people to friends of friends. However, there were also examples of SNS created with a focus on sexuality; specifically connecting sexual minorities. These sites mirrored the components of bigger SNS, but the target audiences were sexual minorities (Mowlabocus, 2010; Wignall, 2022). For some sexual minorities, these sites have been integral in helping form online connections, particularly when in-person connections were lacking (e.g., Cassidy, 2016; Gudelunas, 2012; Shield, 2017; Wignall, 2017). Despite technological advances and the increased functionality of SNS targeted at sexual minorities, their primary purpose remains the same—connecting users and facilitating communication.

SNSs aimed at gay and bisexual men have often been framed as being purely or primarily about facilitating sexual encounters. Sites such as Gaydar in the United Kingdom and Adam4Adam in the United States emerged in the early 2000s, and while they are often framed as websites and then aps for "hook-ups," they were also used by individuals to chat with others online and form friendships (Mowlabocus, 2010). Yet, even with this multifaceted usage, the sites remained quite sexualized and users would often post sexually explicit content, both publicly and privately, including blog and forum posts, pictures, and videos. For this reason, we refer to these and other similar sites as *sociosexual* networking sites (SSNS) (see Wignall, 2022). While earlier iterations of these sites were predominantly accessible from a computer, contemporary examples are primarily featured on mobile apps (e.g., Jaspal, 2017 ).

The notion of SSNS can apply to even the most well-known SNS, including Twitter. This is possible if one views users of SNS as active adopters of technology, who can adapt technology for their own use, rather than passively use it as the designers intended. In his discussion of Pup Twitter, Wignall (2017) showed how kinky individuals who identify as "pups" (see Wignall, McCormack, et al., 2022) used Twitter in sexual and social ways most likely distinct from how it was originally intended. On Pup Twitter, individuals will create Twitter profiles based on their pup persona and engage in online discussions with others, provide information about their pup/general lives, and share content. Some of this content features sexually explicit material, including pictures and videos. This type of content is allowed, according to Twitter's guidelines, providing it does not feature in a profile picture or a Twitter profile header. While Pup Twitter has social aspects in how it is used (e.g., to explore a pup identity, interact with other pups, and feel part of an online community), the sexual materials and sexual aspects of pup play support the notion that Twitter is an SSNS for these individuals.

Messaging apps, such as WhatsApp and Telegram, have also been used regularly for sexual purposes. Their use of end-to-end encryption and the ability to register anonymously has made them particularly popular for sexual purposes, both positively, between consenting adults, and also in more problematic ways. The internet and social media have been shown to bring couples together when they are apart (McCormack & Ogilvie, 2020), yet they can also be sites of nonconsensual sharing of images and a way to harass or target individuals, most often women. These are serious issues we return to later in this chapter.

## Moral panics at the intersection of social media and pornography

New technologies have long been a cause of social concern about public order and moral rectitude. With the mass production of books suddenly possible in the late 1800s because of the printing press, social elites feared that books would threaten public morality because the public would be able to read revolutionary ideas that ran contrary to the orthodoxy of the time (Furedi, 2016). More recently, TV shows that include graphic sex or violence were seen as liable to promote sexual or innercity violence, while so-called "Video Nasties" in the 1980s were the source of a moral panic about violence among young people (Barker & Petley, 1997). Moral panic around these Video Nasties resulted in censorship of these materials, at least in part through a combination of how they were shown and, suddenly, available to anyone including children through the then-new technology of VHS videotapes (Barker, 2020). This history should serve as a warning to think carefully and critically about claims made regarding harm as they pertain to internet pornography, particularly when sexuality or protecting "childhood innocence" is involved.

Sexuality is also often a site for social concerns about changes in society more broadly (Rubin, 1984). In his book *Threatened Children*, Best (1990) argued that the intersection of sexuality, social change, and young people was particularly salient for social concern that could often lead to moral panics. Analyzing the rhetorical tools that advocate use when making claims about social problems related to young people, he showed that these were often aimed at raising public anxiety—with frightening statistics used to try and mobilize public opinion to make social policy change but in ways that were often ineffective at best or distracting from more significant problems particularly related to poverty.

The use of concern about pornography to distract from other social issues was exemplified in Florida in 2018. Following a high school mass shooting where 17 people were murdered, the Florida House of Representatives was set to vote on a ban on assault weapons and large-capacity magazines that hold many bullets. However, the Republican-controlled House refused to consider the ban and on the same day instead passed Bill HR157, which declared pornography to be a "public health crisis," diverting attention from their refusal to put in place legislation to reduce the number of gun deaths. This effort has continued in the United States, with legislators in 16 states declaring that pornography constitutes a public health crisis. This has also seen legislation in the United States that has sought to ban websites that are seen to enable prostitution (an illegal activity in most of the United States), as evidenced by the closure of the website Backpage as a result of FOSTA-SESTA law in the United States, which increased risk and harm for sex workers (Blunt & Wolf, 2020; Tripp, 2019).

## Problems of social media and sexuality

One of the key recent concerns related to sexuality and social media is the availability of pornography to young people, not least that young people will view pornography before they are "ready" and will also be sent it without their knowledge or consent (Lim et al., 2017). Another concern for parents is that digital technologies have made it far easier for young people to access pornography against their parents' wishes, or without their parents knowing. Internet pornography also marks a shift from notions of "magazines under the bed" to a huge range of pornographic videos that appear to be more explicit than in the past. There are widespread concerns that viewing pornography at a young age will harm the viewer, although there is little evidence for long-lasting damage particularly if the young person sought the porn rather than being sent it non-consensually (Owens et al., 2012).

Governments and educators are right in seeking to address concerns although the measures investigated have not always been successful. One core approach, particularly in the United Kingdom context, has been to try and introduce age verification to access internet pornography. However, this has been remarkably difficult to implement for several reasons. The first reason is that the technology currently does not work, or at least has unintended consequences. For example, when age verification checks are implemented, often in schools or on an ad hoc basis, they do not merely block pornography but also a range of websites that offer important services, education, and support to young people—including sexual health information, LGBT sites, and abortion services. Second, there are concerns that age verification would result in a "blackmailer's charter," as it would require a database of people who have paid to watch pornography, which could be of significant interest to hackers. Third, there is evidence that young people who seek out pornography can do so even against their parents' wishes and strategies (Mulholland, 2013). The concern with age verification then is that it would be both counterproductive and ineffective.

An additional issue is that the focus of age verification is misplaced, as there is evidence that much of the harms around pornography are not through such sites but via social media. This is because pornography watched on these sites tends to be sought out by the user, whereas evidence of harm is when the sharing or viewing of pornography or other sexually explicit material is not consensual. It is on social media where the material is often sent without the receiver's consent. As such, age verification could limit to some extent people who wanted to watch pornography but not the nonconsensual sharing of images via social media.

To argue against age verification for pornography and to trouble the negative effects paradigm is not to suggest that the intersections of social media and sexuality are without issue but rather to contend that the frame of problems related to pornography mischaracterize the issue and divert attention from social problems that need particular attention. One key example here is women's experiences of receiving unwanted dick pics through social media (Amundsen, 2020). Recent research shows that this is a significant issue among school students as well, with teenage girls regularly being sent unwanted dick pics on social media platforms that constitute a form of image-based sexual harassment (Ringrose et al., 2021). There is a clear need for intervention here, but age verification checks would not resolve the issue.

Social media and camera phones have meant that sexual violence can be perpetrated digitally and created by individuals, and these collections of practices have been conceptualized as "image-based sexual abuse" (McGlynn & Rackley, 2017). This important intervention highlights that social media can be the medium for a range of harmful practices oriented around the nonconsensual sharing of sexual images. Colloquially known as "revenge porn," this is where nude images that had been taken normally consensually between partners are then shared nonconsensually by one partner following a breakup or as a form of coercive control. McGlynn and Rackley (2017) critique this colloquial term for skewing the debate away from a broader set of images that do not have to be private sexual images and "fails to focus on the harms of these practices" (p. 536). The issue with these images is not that they are pornographic, but they are shared either without consent or to harass an individual.

The nonconsensual sharing and unsolicited sending of nude images on social media also reveals troubling norms of sexuality more generally. While sexting can be an appropriate and enjoyable activity between consenting individuals where norms of consent, mutuality, and respect prevail (e.g., Roberts & Ravn, 2020; Setty, 2022), sexist practices exist where sexual double standards and coercion mirror issues around sexual consent in broader society (Ringrose et al., 2013). Sexting practices among young people more generally are also a source of concern, often framed as being inherently risky or harmful (Albury, 2017). This points to the need for interventions that are not based around technological solutions or legal prohibition but through methods that address the social, cultural, and psychological causes of the issues (Roberts et al., 2021).

## Sex education and a balanced approach to considering social media and pornography

Across many aspects of "deviant" leisure and freedoms related to sexuality, prohibition is seen to fail. The criminalization of drugs has been a costly failure, and criminalizing abortions does not lower rates of abortion. Rather, rates of abortion decrease when abortion is legal and accompanied by the availability of free contraception, sexual health services, and sex education (Finer & Fine, 2013). The criminalization of sex work increases risk for sex workers (Graham, 2017). Across these areas, criminalization and prohibition fail in their intended outcomes. There are calls across these areas for "harm reduction," most explicitly in drugs policy but similar arguments can be seen in other areas. Calls for decriminalization usually occur alongside plans for support and education. It is notable that the current legislative push related to pornography is away from education and harm reduction and toward criminalization.

Such laws tend to have unintended consequences. For example, while we doubt the accuracy of the statistical claims from the Vera-Gray et al. (2021) study of the content of pornography on widely used porntube sites, if their findings are accurate, it would mean that many users of pornography—including those who visit such sites by accident or only occasionally to watch the most vanilla of porn—would leave themselves open to criminal sanctions for "possession" of extreme pornography, given the law in this area. As Dymock (2018) argues, the legal environment shifts focus away from damaging practices that exist in the porn industry to an arena where the law can exert authority. This is connected to David's (2017) argument about the criminalization of sharing in an internet age, where nation states have focused on regulating the consumer rather than the manufacturer or (criminal) distributor because it is the most practicable way of doing so.

While not discounting criminal justice interventions entirely, there is a clearer role for formal education to address these issues. This needs to avoid abstinence-only forms of education that are seen as ineffective and moralistic (Jørgensen et al., 2018). Setty (2019), for example, highlights that given cultural norms in education and society, "what is required is opportunities for young people to critically engage with youth cultural processes and their roles and responsibilities as the audience" (p. 309). This would include shifting from individuals' practices within sexting to considering ethics, rights, responsibilities, and social justice, as they pertain to issues of gender and sexuality more broadly. This is part of a broader call for collaborative approach to sex education that rejects a didactic teacher-student pedagogy with a focus instead of peer learning that is youth focused and aimed at building knowledge and understanding (De Ridder, 2018).

Smith et al. (2019) call for a shift in focus to thinking about young people's "digital intimacies." Young people's concerns about sex will be different from the concerns of adults (Albury, 2017), and education needs to shift from abstinence and prevention to enabling ethical decision making, which means that young people have the capacity to consent and reject engaging in these practices. Smith et al. (2019) also argue that these forms of education should include guidance on how to challenge problematic social norms and ensure that sex education is inclusive and comprehensive and incorporates digital literacy.

However, action that is solely focused on calls for better sex education about pornography has limited value for two reasons. First, academics suggest challenging of homophobia and heteronormativity in schools should occur outside of sex education and include cross-curricular activities as well as groups to support sexual minority peers (Bain & Podmore, 2020; Cumming-Potvin & Martino, 2018). This suggests that sex education as it is taught in schools offers limited ability to challenge problematic norms related to sexuality and speaks to a seeming unwillingness of governments across many years to substantively reform sex education (McCormack, 2015). This is likely because discussing sex education for young people still attracts significant media attention and social concern, bordering on moral panic—not least because of how such issues bring are an arena used to pit religious freedom against same-sex relationships (Vanderbeck & Johnson, 2015). Calls for sex education to deal with the issues around sexting, social media, and pornography seem likely to have marginal impact in this context. This has parallels with calls for age verification to stop young people accessing pornography. Both are attempts to develop a specific, demarcated intervention to deal with problems that are societal and require interventions across different arenas. While sex education changes at least engage with education and collaborative learning, compared to age verification checks which purely try and suppress the problem, both have an underlying assumption that such issues can be bracketed off from the broader structures and dynamics of society.

For researchers interested in questions of social media, sexuality, and pornography, we suggest that what is most important is to recognize the complexity and *contextuality* of these issues. Adopting a leisure approach to pornography is to recognize that it is consumed for a range of reasons and that it is a form of media like film and television; yet it also recognizes that people can experience harm through the intersection of pornography and sexuality. This can be via watching pornography or, we think more frequently, it can be via image-based sexual harassment and abuse shared via messaging services and SNSs. What we consider to be most important for future research is to recognize that pornography is not the *cause* of these problems and harms but reflects broader social dynamics of gender and sexuality. We are skeptical of interventions that focus on technological solutions to "problems" of pornography and instead call for greater attention to the *intersections* of pornography, sexuality, social media, technology, and harm. Research that investigates these in culturally and socially sensitive ways, while also recognizing the pleasure they can bring in other contexts, will likely be the most able to address the social harms related to sexuality, pornography, and social media.

# References

Albury, K. (2017). Just because it's public doesn't mean it's any of your business: Adults' and children's sexual rights in digitally mediated spaces. *New Media & Society, 19*(5), 713–725.

Amundsen, R. (2020). "A male dominance kind of vibe": Approaching unsolicited dick pics as sexism. *New Media & Society, 23*(6), 1465–1480.

Antevska, A., & Gavey, N. (2015). Out of sight and out of mind. *Men and Masculinities, 18* (5), 605–629.

Astle, S., McAllister, P., Emanuels, S., Rogers, J., Toews, M., & Yazedjian, A. (2021). College students' suggestions for improving sex education in schools beyond 'blah blah blah condoms and STDs'. *Sex Education, 21*(1), 91–105.

Attwood, F. (2011). After the paradigm shift: Contemporary pornography research. *Sociological Compass, 5*(1), 13–22.

Attwood, F., & Smith, C. (2014). Porn Studies: An introduction. *Porn Studies, 1*(1–2), 1–6.

Bain, A. L., & Podmore, J. A. (2020). Challenging heteronormativity in suburban high schools through "surplus visibility": Gay-straight alliances in the Vancouver city-region. *Gender. Place & Culture, 27*(9), 1223–1246.

Barker, M. (2020). The UK 'Video Nasties' campaign revisited: Panics, claims-making, risks, and politics. In L. Tsaliki, & D. Chronaki (Eds.), *Discourses of anxiety over childhood and youth across cultures* (pp. 29–50). New York, NY: Springer.

Barker, M., & Petley, J. (1997). *Ill effects: The media/violence debate.* London: Routledge.

Best, J. (1990). *Threatened children.* Chicago, IL: University of Chicago Press.

Blunt, D., & Wolf, A. (2020). Erased: The impact of FOSTA-SESTA and the removal of Backpage on sex workers. *Anti-trafficking Review* (14), 117–121.

Boyd, D. M., & Ellison, N. B. (2007). Social network sites: Definition, history, and scholarship. *Journal of Computer-Mediated Communication, 13*(1), 210–230.

Brown, J., & L'Engle, K. (2009). X-rated sexual attitudes and behaviors associated with US early adolescents' exposure to sexually explicit media. *Communication Research, 36* (1), 129–151.

Cassidy, E. (2016). Social networking sites and participatory reluctance: A case study of Gaydar, user resistance and interface rejection. *New Media & Society, 18*(11), 2613–2628.

Comella, L. (2014). Studying porn cultures. *Porn Studies, 1*(1–2), 64–70.

Cumming-Potvin, W. M., & Martino, W. (2018). Countering heteronormativity and cis-normativity in Australian schools: Examining English teachers' reflections on gender and sexual diversity in the classroom. *Teaching and Teacher Education, 74*, 35–48.

David, M. (2017). *Sharing: Crime against capitalism.* Cambridge: Polity.

Dawson, K., Tafro, A., & Štulhofer, A. (2019). Adolescent sexual aggressiveness and pornography use: A longitudinal assessment. *Aggressive Behavior, 45*(6), 587–597.

De Ridder, S. (2018). Sexting as sexual stigma: The paradox of sexual self-representation in digital youth cultures. *European Journal of Cultural Studies, 22*(5–6), 563–578.

Dymock, A. (2018). A doubling of the offence? 'Extreme' pornography and cultural harm. In A. Boukli, & J. Kotze (Eds.), *Zemiology* (pp. 165–182). Basingstoke: Palgrave Macmillan.

Finer, J., & Fine, J. (2013). Abortion law around the world. *American Journal of Public Health, 103*(4), 585–589.

Furedi, F. (2016). Moral panic and reading: Early elite anxieties about the media effect. *Cultural Sociology, 10*(4), 523–537.

Graham, L. (2017). Governing sex work through crime: Creating the context for violence and exploitation. *Journal of Criminal Law, 81*(3), 201–216.

Grubbs, J., & Perry, S. (2019). Moral incongruence and pornography use: A critical review and integration. *The Journal of Sex Research*, *56*(1), 29–37.

Gudelunas, D. (2012). There's an app for that: The uses and gratifications of online social networks for gay men. *Sexuality & Culture*, *16*(4), 347–365.

Jackson, C. A., Baldwin, A., Brents, B. G., & Maginn, P. J. (2019). EXPOsing men's gender role attitudes as porn superfans. *Sociological Forum*, *34*(2), 483–500.

Jackson, C. A., Maginn, P. J., Baldwin, A., & Brents, B. G. (2020). Consent and sexualized leisure in Sin City: Observations from a US pornography expo in Las Vegas. *Leisure Sciences*, *42*(3–4), 393–410.

Jaspal, R. (2017). Gay men's construction and management of identity on Grindr. *Sexuality & Culture*, *21*(1), 187–204.

Jørgensen, C. R., Weckesser, A., Turner, J., & Wade, A. (2018). Young people's views on sexting education and support needs: Findings and recommendations from a UK-based study. *Sex Education*, *19*(1), 25–40.

Ley, D., Prause, N., & Finn, P. (2014). The emperor has no clothes: A review of the 'pornography addiction' model. *Current Sexual Health Reports*, *6*(2), 94–105.

Lim, M. S., Agius, P. A., Carrotte, E. R., Vella, A. M., & Hellard, M. E. (2017). Young Australians' use of pornography and associations with sexual risk behaviours. *Australian and New Zealand Journal of Public Health*, *41*(4), 438–443.

Litsou, K., Byron, P., McKee, A., & Ingham, R. (2021). Learning from pornography: Results of a mixed methods systematic review. *Sex Education*, *21*(2), 236–252.

McCormack, M. (2015). *Young people's attitudes toward and discussion of safe sex and condom use*. Durham: Durham University.

McCormack, M., & Ogilvie, M. F. (2020). Keeping couples together when apart, and driving them apart when together: Exploring the impact of smartphones on relationships in the UK. In A. Abela, S. Vella, & S. Piscopo (Eds.), *Couple relationships in a global context* (pp. 245–259). New York, NY: Springer.

McCormack, M., & Wignall, L. (2017). Enjoyment, exploration and education: Understanding the consumption of pornography among young men with non-exclusive sexual orientations. *Sociology*, *51*(5), 975–991.

McGlynn, C., & Rackley, E. (2017). Image-based sexual abuse. *Oxford Journal of Legal Studies*, *37*(3), 534–561.

McKee, A. (2012). Pornography as entertainment. *Continuum: Journal of Media & Cultural Studies*, *26*(4), 541–552.

McKee, A. (2018). Porn consumers as fans. In P. Booth (Ed.), *A companion to media fandom and fan studies* (pp. 509–520). New York, NY: John Wiley & Sons.

McKee, A., & Lumby, C. (2022). Pornhub, child sexual abuse materials and anti-pornography campaigning. *Porn Studies*, *9*(4), 464–476.

McMahon, C. (2019). *The psychology of social media*. London: Routledge.

McNair, B. (2012). *Porno? Chic!: How pornography changed the world and made it a better place*. London: Routledge.

Mellor, E., & Duff, S. (2019). The use of pornography and the relationship between pornography exposure and sexual offending in males: A systematic review. *Aggression and Violent Behavior*, *46*, 116–126.

Mohammadi, E., Thelwall, M., Kwasny, M., & Holmes, K. L. (2018). Academic information on Twitter: A user survey. *PLoS One*, *13*(5)e0197265.

Mowlabocus, S. (2010). *Gaydar culture*. London: Routledge.

Mulholland, M. (2013). *Young people and pornography*. Basingstoke: Palgrave.

Nardello, E. (2017). Best practices for producing stories on Instagram. *Journal of Digital & Social Media Marketing*, *5*(4), 332–340.

Owens, E. W., Behun, R. J., Manning, J. C., & Reid, R. C. (2012). The impact of internet pornography on adolescents: A review of the research. *Sexual Addiction & Compulsivity*, *19*(1−2), 99−122.

Palmer, T. (2018). Rape pornography, cultural harm and criminalisation. *Northern Ireland Legal Quarterly*, *69*(1), 37−58.

Parry, D. A., Davidson, B. I., Sewall, C. J., Fisher, J. T., Mieczkowski, H., & Quintana, D. S. (2021). A systematic review and meta-analysis of discrepancies between logged and self-reported digital media use. *Nature Human Behaviour*, *5*, 1535−1547.

Pezzutto, S. (2019). From porn performer to porntropreneur: Online entrepreneurship, social media branding, and selfhood in contemporary trans pornography. *About Gender: International Journal of Gender Studies*, *8*(16), 30−60.

Ringrose, J., Harvey, L., Gill, R., & Livingstone, S. (2013). Teen girls, sexual double standards and 'sexting': Gendered value in digital image exchange. *Feminist Theory*, *14*(3), 305−323.

Ringrose, J., Regehr, K., & Whitehead, S. (2021). Teen girls' experiences negotiating the ubiquitous dick pic: Sexual double standards and the normalization of image based sexual harassment. *Sex Roles*, *85*, 558−576.

Roberts, S., & Ravn, S. (2020). Towards a sociological understanding of sexting as a social practice: A case study of university undergraduate men. *Sociology*, *54*(2), 258−274.

Roberts, S., Ravn, S., Maloney, M., & Ralph, B. (2021). Navigating the tensions of normative masculinity: Homosocial dynamics in Australian young men's discussions of sexting practices. *Cultural Sociology*, *15*(1), 22−43.

Rozgonjuk, D., Sindermann, C., Elhai, J. D., & Montag, C. (2020). Fear of missing out (FoMO) and social media's impact on daily-life and productivity at work: Do WhatsApp, Facebook, Instagram, and Snapchat use disorders mediate that association? *Addictive Behaviors*, *110*106487.

Rubin, G. (1984). Thinking sex: Towards a political economy of 'sex'. In C. Vance (Ed.), *Pleasure and danger* (pp. 267−319). Boston, MA: Routledge & Kegan Paul.

Rubin, G. (2011). The trouble with trafficking. In G. Rubin (Ed.), *Deviations* (pp. 66−86). Durham, NC: Duke University Press.

Ruddock, A. (2015). Pornography and effects studies. In L. Comella, & S. Tarrant (Eds.), *New views on pornography* (pp. 287−306). London: Praeger.

Ryan, P. (2019). *Male sex work in the digital age*. London: Palgrave Macmillan.

Schneider, J. W. (1985). Social problems theory. *Annual Review of Sociology*, *11*, 209−229.

Setty, E. (2019). A rights-based approach to youth sexting: Challenging risk, shame, and the denial of rights to bodily and sexual expression within youth digital sexual culture. *International Journal of Bullying Prevention*, *1*, 298−311.

Setty, E. (2022). 'Frexting': Exploring homosociality among girls who share intimate images. *Journal of Youth Studies*, *25*(5), 667−682.

Shield, A. (2017). New in town: Gay immigrants and geosocial dating apps. In A. Dhoest, L. Szulc, & B. Eeckhout (Eds.), *LGBTQs, media and culture in Europe* (pp. 244−261). London: Routledge.

Smith, C., & Attwood, F. (2014). Anti/pro/critical porn studies. *Porn Studies*, *1*(1−2), 7−23.

Smith, C., Attwood, F., & Scott, R. (2019). *Young people and digital intimacies*. Sunderland: University of Sunderland.

Smith, C., Barker, M., & Attwood, F. (2015). Why do people watch porn? In L. Comella, & S. Tarrant (Eds.), *New views on pornography* (pp. 307−322). London: Praeger.

Štulhofer, A., Wiessner, C., Koletić, G., Pietras, L., & Briken, P. (2022). Religiosity, perceived effects of pornography use on personal sex life, and moral incongruence: Insights from the German health and sexuality survey (GeSiD). *The Journal of Sex Research*, *59*(6), 720−730.

Tripp, H. (2019). All sex workers deserve protection: How FOSTA/SESTA overlooks consensual sex workers in an attempt to protect sex trafficking victims. *Penn State Law Review, 124*(1), 219–246.

Turner, G. (2020). *Why is liberal paper The Guardian publishing 'porn is human trafficking' propaganda?* XBiz, Available online: https://www.xbiz.com/news/251170/why-is-liberal-paper-the-guardian-publishing-porn-is-human-trafficking-propaganda (accessed on 13 June 2022).

Vanderbeck, R. M., & Johnson, P. (2015). Homosexuality, religion and the contested legal framework governing sex education in England. *Journal of Social Welfare and Family Law, 37*(2), 161–179.

Vera-Gray, F., McGlynn, C., Kureshi, I., & Butterby, K. (2021). Sexual violence as a sexual script in mainstream online pornography. *The British Journal of Criminology, 61*(5), 1243–1260.

Waechter, N., Subrahmanyam, K., Reich, S. M., & Espinoza, G. (2010). Youth connecting online: From chat rooms to social networking sites. In D. Riha, & A. Maj (Eds.), *Emerging practices in cyberculture and social networking* (pp. 149–178). London: Brill.

Wiederman, M. (2015). Sexual script theory. In J. DeLameter, & R. Plante (Eds.), *Handbook of the sociology of sexualities* (pp. 7–22). New York, NY: Springer.

Wignall, L. (2017). The sexual use of a social networking site: The case of pup twitter. *Sociological Research Online, 22*(3), 21–37.

Wignall, L. (2020). Beyond safe, sane, and consensual: Navigating risk and consent online for kinky gay and bisexual men. *Journal of Positive Sexuality, 6*(2), 66–74.

Wignall, L. (2022). *Kinky in the digital age: Gay men's subcultures and social identities.* New York, NY: Oxford University Press.

Wignall, L., McCormack, M., Cook, T., & Jaspal, R. (2022). Findings from a community survey of individuals who engage in pup play. *Archives of Sexual Behavior, online first, 51*(7), 3637–3646.

Wright, P. (2013). U.S. Males and pornography, 1973-2010: Consumption, predictors, correlates. *The Journal of Sex Research, 50*(1), 60–71. Available from https://doi.org/10.1080/00224499.2011.628132.

# Index

Note: Page numbers followed by "*t*" refer to tables.